TIGERS IN COMBAT

Volume III

Wolfgang Schneider
Frank Köhler

Translated by Derik Hammond

Helion & Company

Helion & Company Limited
26 Willow Road
Solihull
West Midlands
B91 1UE
England
Tel. 0121 705 3393
Fax 0121 711 4075
Email: info@helion.co.uk
Website: www.helion.co.uk
Twitter: @helionbooks
Visit our blog http://blog.helion.co.uk/

Published by Helion & Company 2016
Designed and typeset by Mach 3 Solutions Ltd (www.mach3solutions.co.uk)
Cover designed by Paul Hewitt, Battlefield Design (www.battlefield-design.co.uk)
Printed by Gutenberg Press Limited, Tarxien, Malta

Text © Verlag Wolfgang Schneider 2013. English edition translated by Derik Hammond 2016
All images © Verlag Wolfgang Schneider unless otherwise noted.

Originally published in German in 2013 by Verlag Wolfgang Schneider as *Tiger im Kampf* Band III.

ISBN 978-1-910777-97-8

British Library Cataloguing-in-Publication Data.
A catalogue record for this book is available from the British Library.

For details of other military history titles published by Helion & Company Limited contact the above address, or visit our website: http://www.helion.co.uk.

We always welcome receiving book proposals from prospective authors.

Contents

Foreword

Dear Reader,

You now hold Volume III of the series *Tigers in Combat* in your hands and this completes the documentation of the combat and deployment of the Tiger battle tank (types E and B). This work focuses on all aspects of the operation and tactical-technical handling of the tank. In doing so bridges the gap between the descriptions of the tank formations in the first two volumes and the technical documentation by Walter Spielberger and Thomas Jentz who made such an immense contribution to the documentation of German armoured vehicles of the Second World War.

I am very pleased to have worked with Herr Frank Köhler, my co-author, who with great expertise and meticulous care created substantial sections of this volume. I have also included a long article from the (unpublished) memoirs of Herr *Dipl.-Ing.* Robert Pertuss as well as part of his interesting portfolio of photographs about the production and testing of the Tiger tank. Such content might not satisfy the main tenor of this work, namely the Tiger as an armoured fighting vehicle, but it does contain many interesting details that I would not have liked to have denied the reader. My special thanks are also due to Herr Ludwig Teichmann and to the leader of the German liaison command at the training facility at Senne, *Oberstleutnant* Wolfgang Mann, who made significant contributions to the creation of Chapter 2.

As is customary, the work of other authors has not been plagiarized nor have 'sources' found in popular literature been used. Without exception this work is based on primary sources for all regulations, official information notices, reports and the many descriptions of actual experiences of former soldiers of all service grades. Where quotations occur, typing errors have been corrected; otherwise the then current orthographic rules have been adhered to. They have also been printed in blue type to make it easier for the reader to identify them. No attempt has been made to save space by abbreviating available reports which have been reproduced to their full extent. Unless otherwise indicated, the line drawings are reproduced by the kind courtesy of the Japanese magazine *PANZER*. Photographs designated 'BA' (*Bundesarchiv Koblenz*) are consistently sourced from *Bestand 101I* (collection 101I). The photographs of the interior of the Tiger were taken at museums.

Of the almost 5,000 images that had not yet been used in my previous books, we selected the most relevant and always named, where possible, not only the units they refer to but also the date and place they were taken. Even if in the meantime the ownership rights had expired, the name of the photographer – if known – or the original owner of the rights has been specified. These pictures are intended to occupy the foreground in this work, that is to say they are presented with captions that are relevant and which largely avoid repeating the accompanying narrative. Presenting already well-known photographs is also inevitable. However, I have used ones of the best quality and where possible provided the most accurate explanation of their contents. Unfortunately the few available images of regulations were of mediocre quality but, because they were indispensable, they were nevertheless used and for this we beg the reader's understanding.

This book should put the reader in the position of being able to gauge the comprehensive training content communicated to the Tiger crews before they were in the position to use the vehicle appropriately and successfully in all situations. The aims of the training were the complete mastery of all of the vehicle's controls and the application of tactically correct procedures and principles that were in accord with the situation – even though exhausted, under immediate threat and while operating in demanding environmental conditions. The description of the tactical framework focusses on the particular characteristics of the weapons system. General tactical principles are covered in my book *Panzer Tactics* and are not unnecessarily repeated in this volume. Sections with technical descriptions are included only insofar as they are necessary for the understanding of operational matters.

Hence considerable space is taken up by descriptions of the training organization including, among other things, the *Panzerersatz- und Ausbildungsabteilung 500* and the *Tiger-Lehrgänge* as well as by the consideration of logistics and repair and maintenance procedures. Sections about the structure and composition of troop units, the internal allocation of tasks – including during periods between deployments – and about the use of the Tiger as a means of propaganda complete the subject matter.

Finally, I would like to offer my sincere thanks to my loyal readers whose interest has made the realization of this book project possible. It was their interest that gave me the strength to launch into a self-publishing venture because no publishing house in Germany was prepared to offer this standard of production at an affordable price.

Uelzen, October 2013

1 The Establishment and Structure of the Tiger Units

It was clear long before the start of production of the armoured fighting vehicle known as the 'Tiger' that it would never be produced in very great quantities. The widespread equipping of whole regiments or even the majority of units in the Panzer regiments was precluded from the outset. Two possibilities arose: either they would be divided across the armoured units or they would form special detachments that would be deployed at the focal points of combat. The latter of these two variants was chosen and this was without doubt the correct choice. The former of these possibilities would have been tactically absurd and would also have created insoluble logistical problems.

In total, 24 formations were formed in the *Wehrmacht* and *Waffen SS* and two units that were destroyed in Tunisia were reformed (see table). The fact that in the first formations the *Panzerkampfwagen III* was also put to use was simply a matter of necessity because insufficient Tigers had been delivered. It is only mentioned in passing that later, proposals were frequently submitted to allocate medium tanks to the Tiger units (for example for reconnaissance and security tasks). Also, frequent demands were made to integrate the Tigers in company strength into regular *Panzerregimente* (Panzer regiments). Rightly so, such proposals were rejected.

The structure of the unit as a whole, as well as individual companies, had at first to adjust to that of existing units during the course of 1943 (see *Kriegsstärkenachweise*/ *K.St.N.*/ table of organization and equipment) but from March 1943, the Panzer companies achieved their ultimate form of 14 vehicles, a *Stab* (staff) and a *Stabskompanie* (headquarters company) from June 1943 (with three Tigers in each *'Gruppe Führer'*/ battalion command group). The Panzer supply and workshop companies (and also the headquarters companies) were modified step by step in light of the experiences gained during deployment. The numerous peculiarities that occurred during the first year of their deployment do not readily lend themselves to review. The differing organizational structures of individual units are described in Volumes I and II.

First of all, the role of individual (sub-) units of the Tiger formations will be examined briefly.

The tasks of a *Panzerkompanie* are almost self-explanatory. It is one of the several manoeuvrable elements in the hands of a unit commander and is able to carry out independent tactical combat tasks. The division of the companies in battle (for example by deployment in platoons) was necessary, and practical, only for the fulfilment of specific tactical missions. Such missions might be for providing security either when stationary or on the march

(for example at the spearhead of a unit) or for monitoring the flanks or taking up blocking positions. When subordinated to a larger unit (division or corps) the coherent deployment of the unit (as a company in reserve if circumstances required it) offered the greatest penetrating power and was therefore at its most promising. If the unit was issued independent tactical tasks (for example the execution of a probing attack or a counterattack with limited aims) the deployment of specific companies was left to the unit commander though this was always in close cooperation with the different weapons of supporting forces on the ground or in the air. Details of this are explained in the chapter entitled 'Tactics.'

A heavy tank company, in accordance with the *K.St.N.*, consisted of three *Panzerzüge* (Panzer platoons) each with four Tiger tanks and a *'Gruppe Führer.'* According to the *K.St.N.*, each of the three Panzer platoons was led by an officer with the rank of either *Leutnant* (lieutenant) or *Oberleutnant* (first lieutenant). However in practice, an experienced *Oberfeldwebel* (warrant officer/senior sergeant) sometimes fulfilled this task. Deputies, and leaders of the second 'half-platoons' were *Feldwebel* (sergeants) while the remaining tank commanders were *Unteroffiziere* (NCOs non-commissioned officers).

'Gruppe Führer' had a compliment of two Tiger armoured fighting vehicles, a medium sized off-road vehicle (this was later increased to two light off-road vehicles) and four (later reduced to two) motor cycles. Also, on the Eastern Front, *Ketten-kräder* (half-track motorcycles) were sometimes used. One of the two *Kradmelder* (motorcycle despatch riders) stayed predominantly with the headquarters company as a courier of the Panzer company. The wheeled car 'belonged' to the *Hauptfeld-webel* (who was at the same time the *Kompaniefeldwebel*) and his clerk. In the absence of a second vehicle, the *Waffenmeister* (armourer), who was also an NCO, and the *Geräteunteroffizier* (equipment NCO) were unable to move independently and this presented a serious problem which also affected the transport of the crew's luggage that could not be stowed inside their tank. The second tank functioned as a replacement vehicle for the *Kompanieführer* (company commander) who was usually a *Hauptmann* (captain) if his own vehicle suffered a breakdown; or it could be deployed for the operation of a third radio base. This is examined in more detail in the section dealing with the means of command (*Führungsmittel*) in the chapter entitled 'Tactics'. The provision of such equipment indicates that in every task – over and above its own combat missions – each company was dependent on external support.

The Establishment Dates for the Tiger Units

Date	Unit	Remarks
16.02.1942	*s.Pz.Komp. 501*	from 10.05.42 *1./s.Pz.Abt. 501*
16.02.1942	*s.Pz.Komp. 502*	from 10.05.42 *2./s.Pz.Abt. 501*
05.05.1942	*s.Pz.Abt. 503*	from 21.12.44 renamed *s.Pz.Abt. FHH*
10.05.1942	*s.Pz.Abt. 501*	*3. Komp.* established 06.03.43
25.05.1942	*s.Pz.Abt. 502*	*2. Komp.* on 10.02.43 to *s.Pz.Abt. 503* *2.* and *3. Komp.* established 01.04.43 05.01.45 renamed *s.Pz.Abt. 511*
13.11.1942	*s.Pz.Komp. LSSAH*	used as *13./SS-Pz.Rgt. 1* disbanded 01.03.44, to *s.SS-Pz.Abt. 101*
15.11.1942	*s.Pz.Komp. SS-DR*	used as *8./SS-Pz.Rgt. 2* disbanded 14.04.44, to *s.SS-Pz.Abt. 102*
15.11.1942	*s.Pz.Komp. SS-T*	used as *4./-*, from August 1943 as *13./SS-Pz.Rgt. 3*
24.12.1942	*s.SS-Pz.Abt.*	not established
13.01.1943	*13./Pz.Rgt. "GD"*	until 01.07.43 then *III./Pz.Rgt. "GD"*
18.01.1943	*s.Pz.Abt. 504*	*3. Komp.* established 20.03.43
18.02.1943	*s.Pz.Abt. 505*	*3. Komp.* established 03.04.43
08.05.1943	*s.Pz.Abt. 506*	
01.07.1943	*III./Pz.Rgt. "GD"*	with *3./s.Pz.Abt. 501* and *-/504*
19.07.1943	*s.SS-Pz.Abt. 101*	on 22.09.44 renamed *s.SS-Pz.Abt. 501*
19.07.1943	*s.SS-Pz.Abt. 102*	on 22.09.44 renamed *s.SS-Pz.Abt. 502*
26.07.1943	*s.Pz.Komp. Meyer*	on 03.03.44 merged with *s.Pz.Abt. 508*
09.09.1943	*s.Pz.Abt. 501*	re-established on 27.11.44 renamed *s.Pz.Abt. 424*
09.09.1943	*s.Pz.Abt. 509*	
23.09.1943	*s.Pz.Abt. 507*	
25.09.1943	*s.Pz.Abt. 508*	
01.11.1943	*s.SS-Pz.Abt. 103*	on 14.11.44 renamed *s.SS-Pz.Abt. 503*
18.11.1943	*s.Pz.Abt. 504*	re-established
03.11.1944	*Pz.Komp. (FkL) 316*	
06.06.1944	*s.Pz.Abt. 510*	
01.07.1944	*s.Pz.Komp. Hummel*	18.12.44–16.02.45 with *s.Pz.Abt. 506*
19.08.1944	*s.Pz.Abt. (FkL) 301*	previously equipped with *Sturmgesch. III*

K.St.N.	Date of issue	Designation	No. of tanks
1107	01.11.1941	*Stab Panzer-Abteilung*	
1107	01.04.1943	*Stab Panzer-Abteilung*	
1107b*(fG)*	01.06.1944	*Stab* and *Stabskomp. S. Pz.Abt.*	3 Tiger
1107*(fG)*Ausf. D	01.11.1944	*Stab* and *Stabskomp. S. Pz.Abt.*	3 Tiger
1150b	25.04.1942	*Stabskompanie*	
1150d	15.08.1942	*Stabskomp. S. Pz.Abt. Tiger*	2 Tiger, 6 Pz III
1150e	05.03.1943	*Stabskomp. s. Pz.Abt. Tiger*	2 Tiger, 6 Pz III
1150e	01.11.1943	*Stabskomp. s. Pz.Abt. Tiger*	3 Tiger
1151b*(fG)*	01.06.1944	*Vers.Komp. S. Pz.Abt. Tiger*	
1151b*(fG)*	01.11.1944	*Vers.Komp. S. Pz.Abt. Tiger*	
1176d	15.08.1942	*s. Panzerkompanie d*	9 Tiger, 10 Pz III
1776d	15.12.1942	*s. Panzerkompanie d*	
1176e	05.03.1943	*s. Panzerkompanie e*	14 Tiger
1176e	01.11.1943	*s. Panzerkompanie e*	14 Tiger
1176*(fG)*	01.06.1944	*s. Pz.Komp. Tiger*	14 Tiger
1176*(fG)*	01.11.1944	*s. Pz.Komp. Tiger*	14 Tiger
1187b	25.04.1942	*Panzer-Werkstatt-Kompanie*	
1187b*(fG)*	01.07.1944	*Panzer-Werkstatt-Kompanie*	
1187b*(fG)*	01.11.1944	*Panzer-Werkstatt-Kompanie*	

fG = *freie Gliederung*

Kriegsstärkenachweisungen (K.St.N.) for Tiger Units (without radio-control equipment)

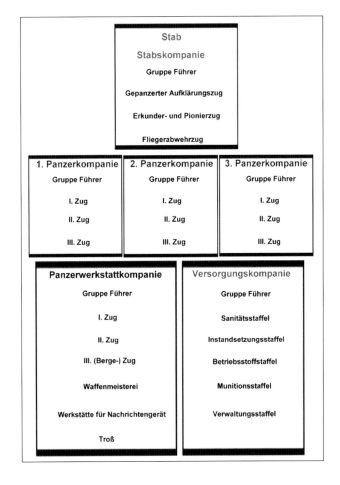

Overall structure of heavy armoured units from 1 June 1944

1. Panzerkopanie

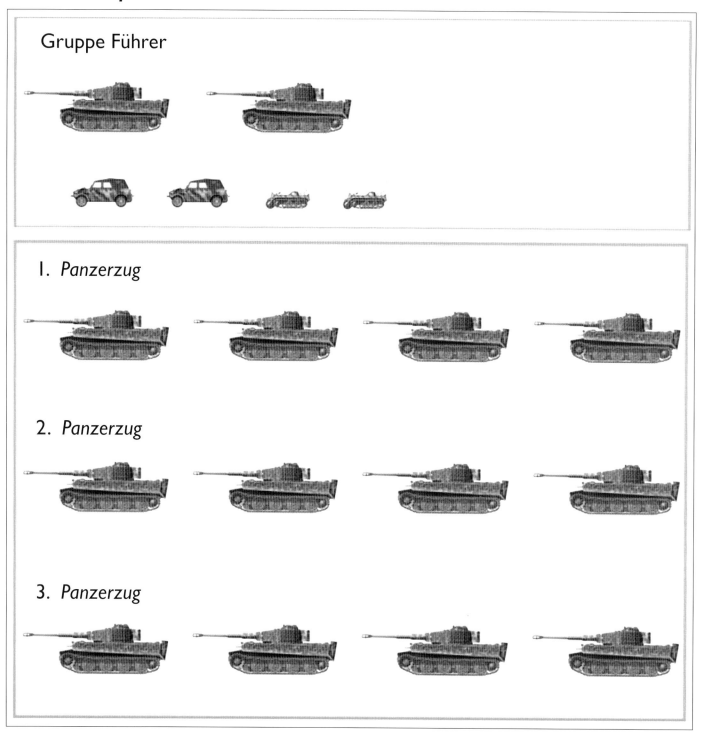

The structure of the *2.* and *3. Kompanie* was completely identical with regards to target strength and personnel allocation with the command group (*Gruppe Führer*) and three tank platoons (*Panzerzüge*). Details and the allocation of hand weapons are given in the following tables. The personnel of a *Panzerkompanie* consisted of four officers, 46 non-commissioned officers and 38 crews.

The *K.St.N.* – tables were provided by Piet Duits

K.St.N. 1176 (fG)   **Stand 1.6.44**

schwere Panzerkompanie "Tiger" (freie Gliederung)	Kopfzahl				Waffen				Fahrzeuge					
	Offiziere	Beamte	Unteroffiziere	Mannschaften	Gewehre, Karabiner (Sturmgewehr)	Pistolen (Masch. Pist.)	s MG (le MG) [Panzerbüchsen]	besp. (unbesp.) Geschütze und Werfer	besp. (unbesp.) Fahrzeuge und Wasserfahrzg.	Krad (Krad mit Seitenwagen) [Kettenkrad]	Personenkraftwagen (Lastkraftwagen)	Zugkw. (Volkettenschlepper) [Gleisketten-Lkw]	gp. Volk. Kfz. (gp. Halbk. Kfz) [gp. Räderkfz]	Fahrräder (Anhänger) [Eisenbahnfahrzeuge]
	A	B	C	D	E	F	G	H	I	J	K	L	M	N
a) Gruppe Führer														
K, Kompanieführer (zugl. Kommandant)	1					1								
O, Hauptfeldwebel			1			(1)								
O, Waffenunteroffizier (Wffm)			1			1								
G, Gerätunteroffizier			1		1									
G, Kommandant			1			1								
G, Richtschütze			2											
G, Kraftwagenfahrer für gp.Kw.			2			2								
G, Funker			1			1								
M, Ladeschütze				2		2								
M, Funker				1		1								
M, Melder				1	1									
M, Kradmelder (auf Kettenkraftrad SdKfz 2)				2	2					[2]				
M, Kraftwagenfahrer für Pkw (1 zugl. Schreiber)				2	2									
leichte Pkw gl., (4-sitzig)											2			
"Tiger I" Ausf. E (8,8cm KwK 36 L/56) (SdKfz 181) 1)						(2)	(4)	(2)					2	
Summe zu a) Gruppe Führer	1		9	8	6	9 (3)	(4)	(2)		[2]	2		2	
b) 1. Zug														
Z, Zugführer (zugl. Kommandant)	1					1								
G, Kommandant (1 zugl. stellv. Zugführer)			3			3								
G, Richtschütze			3											
G, Sprechfunker			1			1								
G, Kraftwagenfahrer für gp.Kw.			4			4								
M, Richtschütze				1										
M, Sprechfunker				3		3								
M, Ladeschütze				4		4								
"Tiger I" Ausf. E (8,8cm KwK 36 L/56) (SdKfz 181) 1)						(4)	(8)	(4)					4	
Summe zu b) 1. Zug	1		11	8		16 (4)	(8)	(4)					4	
c) 2. Zug (wie 1.)	1		11	8		16 (4)	(8)	(4)					4	
d) 3. Zug (wie 1.)	1		11	8		16 (4)	(8)	(4)					4	

K.St.N. 1176 (fG)　　　　　　　　　　　　　　　　　　　**Stand 1.6.44**

	A	B	C	D	E	F	G	H	I	J	K	L	M	N
e) <u>Wechselbesatzung</u>　　2														
G, Kommandant			2			2								
G, Kraftwagenfahrer für gp.Kw.			2			2								
M, Richtschütze				2		2								
M, Sprechfunker				2		2								
M, Ladeschütze				2		2								
Summe zu e) Wechselbesatzung			4	6		10								
<u>Zusammenstellung</u>														
a) Gruppe Führer	1		9	8	6	9 (3)	(4)	(2)		[2]	2		2	
b) 1. Zug	1		11	8		16 (4)	(8)	(4)					4	
c) 2. Zug	1		11	8		16 (4)	(8)	(4)					4	
d) 3. Zug	1		11	8		16 (4)	(8)	(4)					4	
e) Wechselbesatzung			4	6		10								
Gesamtstärke	4		46	38	6	67 (15)	(28)	(14)		[2]	2		14	

Remarks:

a)　8 men allocated as *Hi.Kr.Trg.* [*Hilfskrankenträger*/auxiliary stretcher bearers]

b)　At *Stellengruppen G* [soldiers at pay grade 'G'] there are 3 *Oberfeldwebel* and 12 *Feldwebel* posts (of these 4 are drivers for the group cars; each platoon and *Kompanietrupp* = 1)

c)　One *Unteroffizier* assigned to gas protection duties

d)　*Richtschützen* [gunners] trained to use the on-board submachine pistols

e)　*Kettenkraftrad (Sd.Kfz. 2)* [*Sonderkraftfahrzeug* 2/half-track motor cycle] only the Eastern Front.

1)　Including *Panzerkampfwagen* Tiger II *Ausf. B* (8.8 cm KwK 43 L/71). [This was also known informally as the Königstiger.]

2)　The *Wechselbesatzung* [replacement crew] travel with the *Versorg. Komp.* and are to be at the disposal of the fuel and munitions detachment.

The personnel of a Tiger company were a reasonable bunch. The photograph, taken at the end of January 1943 at the troop training ground Neuhammer in the Saganer Heide, shows a company under the leadership of *Hauptmann* Wallroth that was destined for the *Pz.Gren.Div. 'Großdeutschland'*.

The *Stabskompanie*

Until 1 June 1944 the **Stab** (staff) and the **Stabskompanie** (headqurters company) were distinct elements of the unit structure. Besides the unit commander, the *Stab* of a heavy *Panzerabteilung* consisted of the *Adjutant* (aide-de-camp), *Ordonnanzoffizier* (an orderly officer who also acted as the *Nachrichtenoffizier*/signals intelligence officer), *Verpflegungsoffizier* (food logistics officer/a position that was left unfilled and later removed), a *Führer der Trosse* (officer in charge of supply column – a post that was dropped on 1 November 1943), a *Waffenoffizier* (weapons officer), two doctors (this was implemented but later reduced to one), three *Unteroffiziere* and ten other ranks (later reduced to eight). It was only the Tiger units that had an *'Offizier der Kraft.Parktr.'* (motor pool officer), an engineer who led and organized the procedures carried out by the repair and maintenance staff and who – in fulfilment of his main task – remained [with these units] almost without exception. The vehicle allocation consisted of two motorcycles and three light or medium off-road passenger vehicles. The commander and his two subordinate officers generally remained with *Gruppe Führer* at the headqurters company. This ultimately led to the merging of the two organizational elements.

The task of the **Stabskompanie** was to ensure the command of the unit at all times and, in addition, to fulfil the task of providing support during combat. For the latter task, it had an organic *Aufklärungszug* (armoured reconnaissance platoon) made up of seven *Sd.Kfz. 250s* (*Sonderkraftfahrzeuge 250s*/ light armoured half-track vehicles which were later replaced with *Sd.Kfz. 251s*), an *Erkundungszug* (scout platoon) and *Pionierzug* (engineer platoon) as well as a *Fliegerabwehrzug* (anti-aircraft platoon) with three 2cm *Vierlinge* (four-barrelled anti-aircraft cannons) each of which was mounted on an *MTW Halbkette* (*Mannschaftstransportwagen* / half-tracked personnel carrier). Each company also had a *Maultier* special-purpose half-tracked vehicle which was used for munitions transport but these were in part replaced by *Flakpanzer IVs* armed with *Vierlinge*. These sub-units were retained in the new *K.St.N.* from 1 June 1944 in the so-called *'freie Gliederung' (fG)* (open TOE).

The four detachments of the scout unit each had a (half-tracked) motorcycle and a light off-road vehicle which were only suitable for road scouting and mopping up operations while the reconnaissance platoon was quite capable of undertaking combat reconnaissance missions. The three engineer detachments each had a truck for transporting their equipment and an *Sd.Kfz. 251/7*. They were capable only of carrying out more minor tasks such as engineer reconnaissance and the clearing and laying of individual minefields or barriers. In combat they required the support of other forces belonging to the engineers.

In the first formations, a signals intelligence platoon was listed. From these the bulk of the crews of the three tanks of the battalion command group were drawn which in each case had a second radio operator (loaders along with regular radio operators had the rank of non-commissioned officers). In addition there was a 2-ton radio communications truck equipped with a medium wave transceiver. For previously mentioned reasons the designation *'Nachrichtenzug'* was dropped on 1 June 1944.

It is particularly striking that the headquarters company did not have a sub-unit for the establishment of its own command post. Command posts fulfilled a routine role in terms of command and control, maintained contact with the superior command posts on a tactical level and would have substantially reduced the burden on a unit commander who found himself leading a combat situation from his own armoured fighting vehicle. The Tiger units therefore had to make do with what they had. Accordingly one or two of the *'Führer'* unit tanks (with the exception of the radio station) were used for this purpose, often relying on buildings for protection from the weather while working. To some extent, other vehicles equipped with radio were also appropriated – for example, those of the reconnaissance platoon.

The remaining sub-units:

- vehicle repair team
- combat transport unit (with medical unit)
- administration and supplies staff
- provisioning unit
- baggage transport detachment

were, according to *K.St.N. 1107b (fG)*, attached to the *Versorgungskompanie* (supply company) to allow the *Stabskompanie* to concentrate on its core tasks. This also made sense because to a large extent they already worked operationally with the *Versorgungskompanie*.

In fact, the number of personnel at non-commissioned officer and troops of 'other ranks' level – and also the number of vehicles – was considerably reduced by the adoption of the structure of 1 June 1944; from 60 and 257 respectively to 37 and 130 respectively.

Stab and Stabskompanie

Stab

Stabskompanie

Gruppe Führer

Gepanzerter Aufklärungszug

I. *Gruppe*   2. *Gruppe*   3. *Gruppe*

Stabskompanie

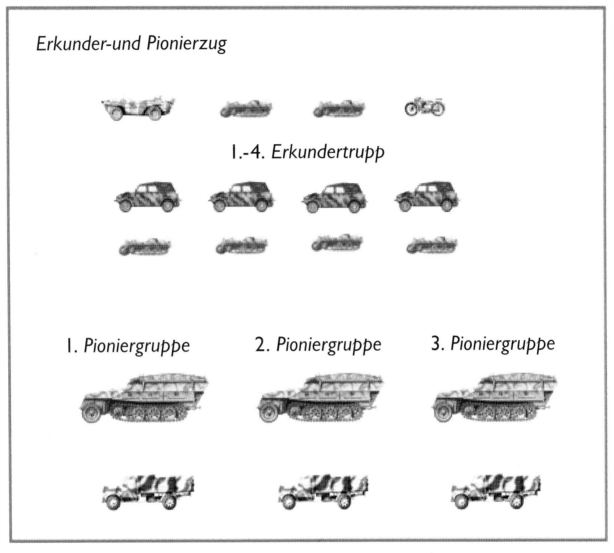

Erkunder-und Pionierzug

1.-4. Erkundertrupp

1. Pioniergruppe   2. Pioniergruppe   3. Pioniergruppe

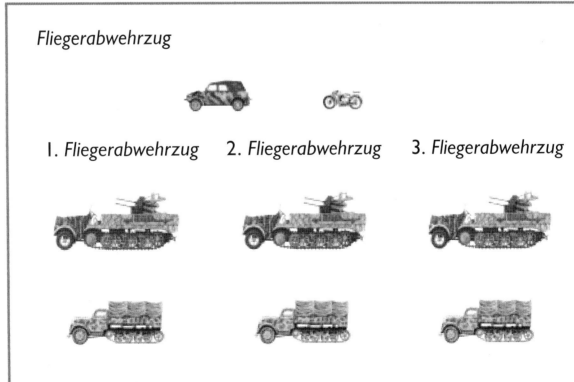

Fliegerabwehrzug

1. Fliegerabwehrzug   2. Fliegerabwehrzug   3. Fliegerabwehrzug

K.St.N. 1107b (fG)   **Stand 1.6.44**

Stab und Stabskompanie einer schweren Panzerabteilung "Tiger" (freie Gliederung)	Kopfzahl				Waffen				Fahrzeuge					
	Offiziere	Beamte	Unteroffiziere	Mannschaften	Gewehre, Karabiner (Sturmgewehr)	Pistolen (Masch. Pist.)	s MG (le MG) [Panzerbüchsen]	besp. (unbesp.) Geschütze und Werfer	besp. (unbesp.) Fahrzeuge und Wasserfahrzg.	Krad (Krad mit Seitenwagen) [Kettenkrad]	Personenkraftwagen (Lastkraftwagen)	Zugkw. (Volkettenschlepper) [Gleisketten-Lkw]	gp. Volk. Kfz. (gp. Halbk. Kfz) [gp. Räderkfz]	Fahrräder (Anhänger) [Eisenbahnfahrzeuge]
	A	B	C	D	E	F	G	H	I	J	K	L	M	N
A) <u>Stab</u>														
B, Abteilungskommandeur	1					1								
K, Adjutant	1					(1)								
Z, Ordonnanzoffizier	1					1								
K, Sanitätsoffizier, Abteilungsarzt	1					1								
K, Abteilungskraftfahroffizier, Leiter der Instandsetzungsdienste	1					1								
Z, Offizier für Sondergerät 1)	1					1								
G, Gefechtsschreiber			1			1								
G, Führer der Melder und Kfz. (zugl. Schreiber)			1			1								
O, Sanitätsunteroffizier			1			1								
M, Kraftwagenfahrer für Pkw (1 zugl. als Hi.Kr.Trg.)				4	4									
M, Kraftradfahrer (auf Kettenkraftrad SdKfz 2)				2	2					[2]				
M, Melder				2	2									
leichtes Maschinengewehr							(1)							
leichte Pkw, gl., (4-sitzig)											2			
mittlerer Pkw, gl.											1			
mittlerer Pkw											1			
Summe zu A) Stab	6		3	8	10	6 (1)	(1)			[2]	4			
B) <u>Stabskompanie</u>														
a) <u>Gruppe Führer</u>														
K, Kompanieführer (zugl. Nachrichtenoffizier) 2)	1					1								
O, Hauptfeldwebel			1			1								
O, Funkmeister			1			1								
G, Fernsprecher und Funker z.b.V. (auf le Krad. 350ccm)			1		1					1				
G, Gerätunteroffizier			1		1									
G, Kommandant			1			1								
G, Richtschütze			2											
G, Funker im gp.Kw.			2			2								
G, Kraftwagenfahrer im gp.Kw.			3			3								
G, Sanitätsunteroffizier (zugl. Sprechfunker im Kr.Pz.Wg.)			1			1								
M, Schreiber (zugl. Melder)				1	1									
M, Funker im gp.Kw.				1	1									
M, Ladeschütze (zugl. Sprechfunker)				3	3									
M, Krankenträger (zugl. 2. Kw.Fahr. für Zgkw)				1	1									
M, Kraftwagenfahrer (1 für Pkw, 1 für Lkw, 1 für Zgkw)				3	2									
leichter Pkw, gl., (4-sitzig)											1			

K.St.N. 1107b (fG)   **Stand 1.6.44**

	A	B	C	D	E	F	G	H	I	J	K	L	M	N
Lkw 2t, offen, gl. 3)											(1)			
mittlerer Krankenpanzerwagen (SdKfz 251/8)						(1)							(1)	
Panz.Bef.Wg. "Tiger" Ausf. E (8,8cm KwK 36 L/56) 4)						(3)	(6)	(3)					3	
Summe zu a) Gruppe Führer	1		14	9	6	15 (4)	(6)	(3)		1	1 (1)		3 (1)	
b) gepanzerter Aufklärungszug														
Z, Zugführer	1					1								
G, Zugtruppführer (zugl. stellv. Zugführer)			1			(1)								
M, Funker (zugl. MG-Schütze)				2	1	1	(1)							
M, Kraftwagenfahrer für Zgkw				1										
mittlerer Beobachtungspanzerwagen (SdKfz 251/5)						(1)	(1)						(1)	
1.-3. Gruppe														
G, Gruppenführer (zugl. Sprechfunker)			3			(3)								
G, stellv. Gruppenführer (zugl. Sprechfunker)			3			(3)								
M, MG-Schütze (2 zugl. Funker)				24	12	12	(6)							
M, Kraftwagenfahrer für Zgkw				6										
mittlere Schützenpanzerwagen (SdKfz 251/1)						(3)	(3)						(3)	
mittlere Beobachtungspanzerwagen (SdKfz 251/5)						(3)	(3)						(3)	
Summe zu b) gepanzerter Aufklärungszug	1		7	33	13	14(14)	(4)						(7)	
c) Erkunder- und Pionierzug														
Z, Zugführer	1					1								
G, z.b.V. (auf Kettenkrad.)			1	1										
M, Kradmelder (auf Kettenraftrad SdKfz 2)				2	2					[2]				
M, Melder (auf le Krad. 350ccm)				1	1					1				
M, MG-Schütze				1		1	(1)							
M, Kraftwagenfahrer für Pkw				1	1									
leichter Pkw, gl., schwf.											1			
1.-4. Erkundertrupp														
G, Truppführer (zugl. MG-Führer)			4			(4)								
M, MG-Schütze (im Kettenkrad.)				4		4	(4)							
M, Melder (zugl. 2. Kw.Fahr., auf Pkw oder Kettenkrad.)				4	4									
M, Kradmelder (auf Kettenkraftrad SdKfz 2)				4	4					[4]				
M, Kraftwagenfahrer für Pkw				4	4									
leichte Pkw, gl., (4-sitzig)											4			
1.-3. Pioniergruppe														
G, Gruppenführer			3			(6)								
M, für Pionierdienst (1 zugl. Sprechfunker)				6	6									
M, für Pionierdienst (1 zugl. 2. Kw.Fahr. für Lkw, 1 für Zgkw)				6	6									
M, MG-Schütze				6		6	(3)							
M, Kraftwagenfahrer (1 für Lkw, 1 für Zgkw)				6	3									
Lkw 3t, offen, gl., für Pionierbehelfsgerät 5)											(3)			
mittlere Pionierpanzerwagen (SdKfz 251/7)						(3)	(3)						(3)	
Summe zu c) Erkunder- und Pionierzug	1		8	45	3	12 (10)	(11)			1 [6]	5 (3)		(3)	
d) Fliegerabwehrzug														
O, Zugführer			1			(1)								
G, für Luftspäh- und Warndienst (zugl. stellv. Zugführer)			1		1									
M, Melder (auf le. Krad. 350ccm)				1	1					1				
M, Kraftwagenfahrer für Pkw				1	1									
leichter Pkw, gl., (4-sitzig)											1			

K.St.N. 1107b (fG)   **Stand 1.6.44**

	A	B	C	D	E	F	G	H	I	J	K	L	M	N
1.-3. Fliegerabwehrtrupp														
G, Geschützführer			3			(1)								
M, Schütze				18	9	9								
M, Mun.Schütze (1 zugl. Flugmelder, 1 zugl. 2. Kw.Fahr. für Lkw)				6	6									
M, Entfernungsmesser				3		3								
M, Kraftwagenfahrer (1 für Lkw, 1 für Zgkw)				6	6									
Gleisketten-Lkw 2t (SdKfz 3) für Munition 6)												[3]		
mittlere Zgkw 8t, als Sfl. (2cm Flakvierling 38/1) (SdKfz 7/1)								(3)				3		
Summe zu d) Fliegerabwehrzug			5	35	24	12 (4)		(3)		1	1	3 [3]		
Zusammenstellung:														
A) Stab	6		3	8	10	6 (1)	(1)			[2]	4			
B) Stabskompanie														
a) Gruppe Führer	1		14	9	6	15 (4)	(6)	(3)		1	1 (1)		3 (1)	
b) gepanzerter Aufklärungszug	1		7	33	13	14 (14)	(4)						(7)	
c) Erkunder- und Pionierzug	1		8	45	3	12 (10)	(11)			1 [6]	5 (3)		(3)	
d) Fliegerabwehrzug			5	35	24	12 (4)		(3)		1	1	3 [3]		
Gesamtstärke	9		37	130	85	59 (33)	(32)	(6)		3 [8]	11 (4)	3 [3]	3 (11)	

Remarks:

a)   10 men to be allocated to *Hi.Kr.Trg.* (auxiliary stretcher bearers) duties.

b)   At pay grade 'G' (excluding those on specialists' career paths) there are 3 *Oberfeldwebel* and 7 *Feldwebel* posts (of these one is the driver for the car 'belonging' to *Gruppe Führer*).

c)   One officer is to be temporarily responsible for the instruction of gas protection measures.

d)   One *Unteroffizier* is to be assigned as gas protection officer.

e)   The *Richtschützen* (gunners) and *Kraftwagenfahrer* (drivers) for the platoon cars were instructed in the use of the on-board machine pistols in the command Tiger and the *Schützenpanzerwagen* (armoured personnel carriers).

1)   Only relevant if there was a *F.K.L.Kp.* (*Funklenkpanzer Kompanie*/radio controlled tank coy) in the battalion.

2)   Also a gunner in the commander's tank.

3)   Equipped with signals apparatus for *le. Feldkabeltrupp 6 (mot)*.

4)   Of which two were equipped with Fu 8 SE 30 radios, one with a Fu 5 SE 10 radio (SdKfz 267) and one with Fu 7 SE 20 (*SdKfz 268*). Command Tiger (8.8cm *KwK 43 L/71*) taken into account.

5)   Including tracked, open-backed 2-ton truck (*SdKfz 3*).

6)   Tracked truck only relevant for deployment on Eastern Front (top speed 16 km/hr on a long run).

The personnel of the *Stabskompanie* consisted of three officers, 34 non-commissioned officers and 122 other ranks, while that of the *Stab* consisted of six officers, three non-commissioned officers and eight men of other ranks. A disadvantage of this structure was that the *Kompaniefführer's* (company leader's) main duty was that of an intelligence officer. This meant that the unit frequently had to make do with the *Ordonnanzoffizier* acting as the company leader.

The tanks belonging to the command group, as well as the command tank, were equipped with a second transceiver and are easily recognisable by their 'star' antennae. The picture shows the lead panzer of the *13./Pz.Rgt. GD* on 7 March 1943 near Perekop (Dietrich)

The command vehicles of the unit and company commanders were at first of many varied types (Ford, Hanomag and so on) but were later mainly *VW Kübel*. This picture shows a *Kfz. 15 Horch* (with radio) belonging to the chief of the *3./s.Pz.Abt. 503 (Hauptmann* Lange) in Charkow on 5 June 1943. The vehicles of chiefs and commanders carried command insignia on metal pennants; the insignia were on a black background and had a pink border. (Wunderlich)

The commander of the *13./ Pz.Rgt. GD* had a particularly exotic vehicle made by the Steyr factory. In this picture *Hauptmann* Wallroth can be seen at the steering wheel. On the left-hand mudguard is the prominent *Stahlhelm-Symbol* (steel helmet symbol) of the *Großdeutschland Division*.

From autumn 1943 the *VW Schwimmkübel* (an amphibious car) was delivered in increasing numbers. This picture shows an example with officers of the *s.Pz.Abt.504* in one of these popular vehicles which were capable of crossing small stretches of water.

The standard transport truck was the three-tonner and usually Ford or Opel. Here the *Geräteunteroffizier* (weapons and equipment NCO) of the *3./s. Pz.Abt. 508* is with his crew members as they are about to enjoy a meal break in the country in October 1943. This picture was taken in the vicinity of Fresnay, France. (Heimberger)

In this picture, taken in August 1943, a *Kfz. 17* belonging to *s.Pz. Abt. 502* is being used as the unit's radio post. It is equipped with both SW and MW transceivers.

Until they were equipped with the *Sd.Kfz. 251/1*, the armoured reconnaissance platoons had to make do with the Sd.Kfz. 250. The picture shows the *Sd.Kfz. 251/1* belonging to *Unteroffizier* Fischer of *s.Pz.Abt.502*. (Fischer)

From the middle of 1944 the unit's doctor had an Sd.Kfz.251 at his disposal. This image shows the vehicle belonging to *s.Pz.Abt. 503* at the beginning of August 1944, during the retreat from the River Seine.

The flak *Vierling* of the anti-aircraft platoon of the *Stabskompanie* could be mounted on an *Sd.Kfz. 7/1* but could also, if required, be demounted which enabled much better possibilities for its camouflage. This picture shows the vehicle under the command of *Unteroffizier* Fürlinger of *s.Pz.Abt. 508*. (Fürlinger)

Motorcycles were of fundamental importance to every company (with or without side-cars). They were used for carrying out scouting tasks and vital for the passing on of reports. This picture shows *Gefreiter* (private) Reichwein of *s.Pz.Abt.503* with his Zündapp in May 1943. Standing behind the motorcycle is a *Hilfswilliger* (*Hiwi*/voluntary helper). (Rubbel)

The *Kompaniefeldwebel* (company sergeant major), or as he was called in soldiers' parlance '*Spieß*', is easily identified by the distinctive '*Kolbenringe*' ('piston rings') on the cuffs of his coat. This picture shows *Hauptfeldwebel* Otto Hänsel of *s.Pz. Abt. 503* in January 1944. (Rubbel)

Panzerwerkstattkompanie

Basically, the *Panzerwerkstattkompanie* (Panzer workshop company) at its core consisted of – not including the obligatory *Gruppe Führer* – two workshop platoons and a third platoon responsible for the recovery of armoured vehicles; the *3. (Berge-) zug*.

The two workshop platoons were identically structured and well-manned with tank-engine mechanics (three *Unteroffiziere* and seven soldiers of other ranks), tank-gearbox technicians (three *Unteroffiziere* and eight soldiers of other ranks) and automobile mechanics (two *Unteroffiziere* and five other soldiers). Additional tank workshop staff included an electro-mechanical engineer, two arc welders, a turner/grinder, smith, plumber, upholsterer, wheelwright, painter as well as an *Unteroffizier* who also carried out the administration tasks relating to spare parts. These men, in part, also filled in as drivers along with the ten regular drivers.

The vehicular equipment was extensive and consisted of: nine *Lkw* 4.5t (four-and-a half-ton trucks); four medium weight *Lkws* (I-IV) allocated to each of the platoons; one *Lkw* 4.5t with a 3-ton crane; an *Sd.Kfz. 9/1* with a 6-ton capacity swivel crane; and a bus with between 16 and 30 seats. In addition, there were four trailers for, amongst other items, the *schwere Maschinensatz A* (arc welding apparatus) and for the repair-tent equipment. The *Zugführer* (platoon leader) was also a *Werkmeister* (foreman).

The crucially important **Bergezug** (vehicle recovery platoon) was equipped with four, then later six, *Sd.Kfz. 9* (s.Zg.Kw. 18t) and an *Lkw* 4.5t with a 3-ton capacity crane and an *Sd.Kfz. 9/1* with a 6-ton crane. After the start of delivery of the *Sd.Kfz. 179* armoured recovery vehicles, a

target of five of these powerful *Bergepantherwagen* 'Panthers' was set for each Tiger unit. The actual provision of *Bergpanthers* (see table) was lower. The leader of the platoon was an officer of the *Kraftfahrparktruppen* (motor pool troops). At his side stood five *Unteroffiziere* as tank supervisors and a total of altogether 26 drivers some of whom were also supervisors.

In addition there were **armourers** with two 4.5t *Lkws* that served as the armourer's workshops and an equipment truck as well as a light four-seater passenger vehicle. The personnel were made up of an armoury *Feldwebel* (sergeant), a tank electrical engineer and three drivers.

Another mainstay was the **signals-equipment workshop** which was led by a senior radio operator and a signals-equipment technician (an *Unteroffizier*) and three other engineers. There were also three drivers (for an *Lkw* 2t which supplied equipment for tanks, a covered *Lkw* 3t that was configured as a signals equipment repair shop and a covered *Lkw*. 3t that served as battery charging vehicle.

The supply detachment (*Troß*) transported equipment and fuel (using three *Lkw* 4,5ts) for two field kitchens (*Lkw* 2ts each with a provisions and a military chef officer) and two light passenger vehicles served the transport requirements of the company's sergeant, accounting officer and *Schirrmeister* (a non-commissioned officer in charge of a motor vehicle unit). The supply detachment also had an anti-aircraft capability with two machine guns mounted on tripods.

Total strength of the company in the *fG* provisions, excluding the three officers and officials, consisted of 35 *Unteroffiziere* and 148 men of other ranks.

The picture taken early in 1943 shows an 'officer of the *Kraftfahrparktruppen*' on duty; in this case *Hauptmann* Fest of *s.Pz.Abt.503*. These officers were in general technically skilled engineers. They were responsible for overall coordination of repair work in the unit, including the management and procurement of spare parts. (Rubbel)

Panzerwerkstattkompanie

Gruppe Führer

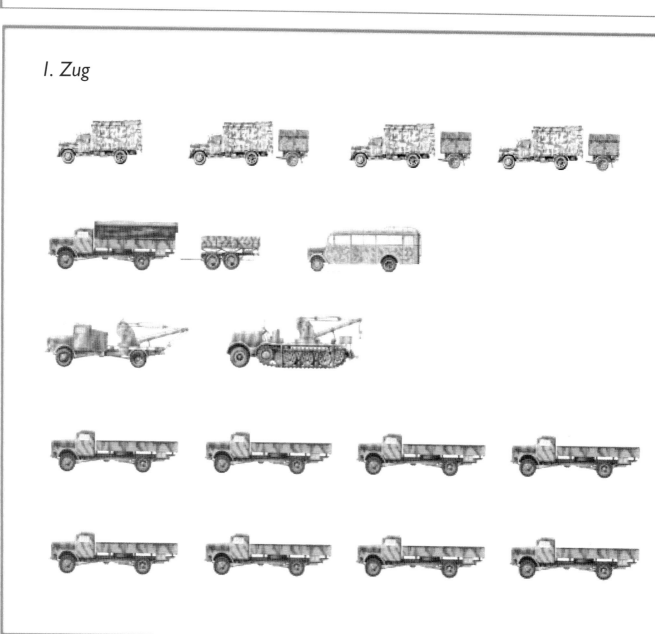

1. Zug

2. Zug

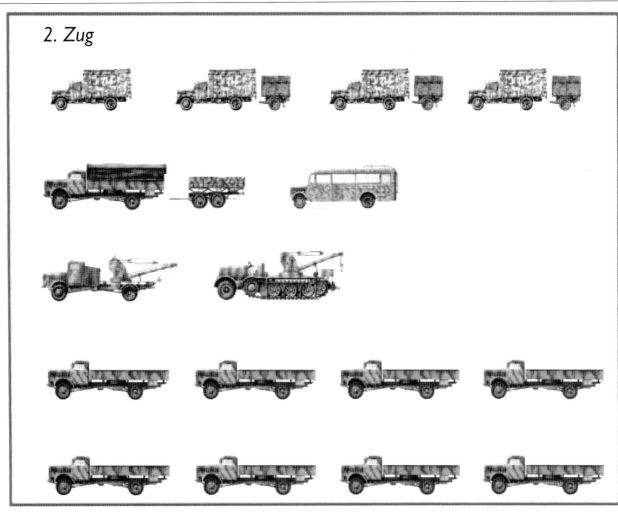

3. (Berge-) Zug

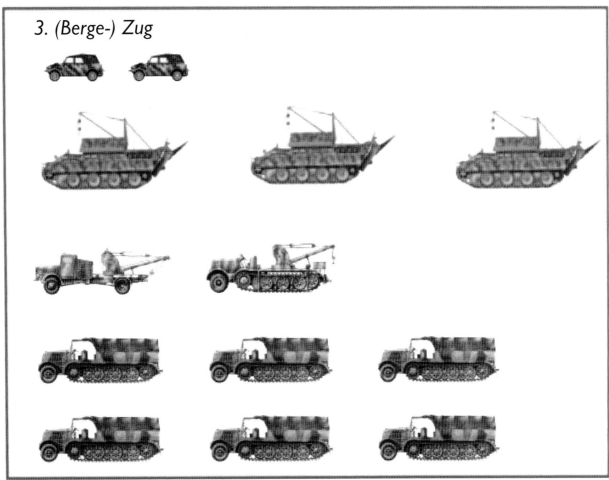

Waffenmeisterei

Werkstätte für Nachrichtengerät

Troß

Fliegerabwehrtrupp

K.St.N. 1187b   **Stand 1.7.44**

Panzerwerkstattkompanie einer schweren Panzerabteilung	Kopfzahl				Waffen				Fahrzeuge					
	Offiziere	Beamte	Unteroffiziere	Mannschaften	Gewehre, Karabiner (Sturmgewehr)	Pistolen (Masch. Pist.)	s MG (le MG) [Panzerbüchsen]	besp. (unbesp.) Geschütze und Werfer	besp. (unbesp.) Fahrzeuge und Wasserfahrzg.	Krad (Krad mit Seitenwagen) [Kettenkrad]	Personenkraftwagen (Lastkraftwagen)	Zugkw. (Volkettenschlepper) [Gleisketten-Lkw]	gp. Volk. Kfz. (gp. Halbk. Kfz) [gp. Räderkfz]	Fahrräder (Anhänger) [Eisenbahnfahrzeuge]
	A	B	C	D	E	F	G	H	I	J	K	L	M	N
a) <u>Gruppe Führer</u>														
K, Kompanieführer, Offizier der Kraftfahrparktruppen	1					1								
Z, Hilfsoffizier, Offizier der Kraftfahrparktruppen	1					1								
G, Ersatzteilverwaltung- und Nachschubunteroffizier			1		1									
M, Kradmelder (auf le Krad. 350ccm)				1	1					1				
M, für Ersatzteilverwaltung und Nachschub				1	1									
M, Schreiber (zugl. Zeichner)				1	1									
M, Kraftwagenfahrer (2 für Pkw, 1 für Lkw)				3	3									
M, 2. Kraftwagenfahrer für Lkw (zugl. Schreiber)				1	1									
leichte Pkw, gl., (4-sitzig)											2			
Lkw 4,5t, offen, für Ersatzteil- und Gerätnachschub											(1)			
Summe zu a) Gruppe Führer	2		1	7	8	2				1	2 (1)			
b) <u>1. Zug</u>														
Z, Werkmeister, Beamter des mittl. techn. Dienstes (K), Zugführer		1				1								
G, Vorhandwerker, Panzermotorenschlosser			3		3									
G, Vorhandwerker, Panzergetriebeschlosser			3		3									
G, Vorhandwerker, Kraftwagenschlosser			2		2									
G, Ersatzteilverwalter (zugl. 2. Kw.Fahr. für Lkw)			1		1									
M, für Ersatzteillager (zugl. 2. Kw.Fahr.)				1	1									
M, Kraftwagenfahrer (9 für Lkw, 1 für Zgkw)				10	10									
M, Panzermotorenschlosser				7	7									
M, Panzergetriebeschlosser)				8	8									
M, Kraftwagenschlosser)				5	5									
M, Panzerelektromechaniker) 6 zugl. Kw.Fahr.				1	1									
M, Panzerelektroschweißer) für Lkw, 4 zugl.				2	2									
M, Dreher und Schleifer) 2. Kw.Fahr. für Lkw				1	1									
M, Schmied) 1 für Zgkw				1	1									
M, Klempner)				1	1									
M, Sattler (K)				1	1									
M, Stellmacher				1	1									
M, Maler				1	1									
M, Werkstattschreiber				1	1									
leichte Maschinengewehre							(2)							
Lkw 4,5t, offen, für Gepäck											(1)			
Lkw 4,5t, offen, für Ersatzteile, Austauschaggregate und Sd. Werkzeuge											(8)			

K.St.N. 1187b   **Stand 1.7.44**

	A	B	C	D	E	F	G	H	I	J	K	L	M	N
Kraftwagen I für mittl. Kfz.-I.-Zug, mit Ausstattung nach D 623/14a											(1)			
Kraftwagen II für mittl. Kfz.-I.-Zug, mit Ausstattung nach D 623/14b											(1)			
Kraftwagen III für mittl. Kfz.-I.-Zug, mit Ausstattung nach D 623/14c											(1)			
Kraftwagen IV für mittl. Kfz.-I.-Zug, mit Ausstattung nach D 623/14d											(1)			
Lkw 4,5t, als Drehkrankraftwagen (Hebekraft 3t) (Kfz. 100)											(1)			
schwerer Zgkw 18t, als Drehkrankraftwagen (Hebekraft 6t) (SdKfz 9/1)												1		
Lkw 3t, geschlossen, als Kraftomnibus (16-30 Sitzen)											(1)			
Anhänger für mittl. Kfz.-I.-Zug. mit Ausstattung nach D 623/14e														(1)
schwerer Maschinensatz A als Anhänger (1 achs) fahrbar														(1)
Maschinensatz (Lichtbogenschweißaggregat) als Anhänger (1 achs) fahrbar														(1)
Anhänger (mehrachs), offen, (o), 3t, für Zeltverlastung														(1)
Summe zu b) 1. Zug		1	9	41	50	1	(2)				(15)	1		(4)
c) 2. Zug (wie 1.)		1	9	41	50	1	(2)				(15)	1		(4)
d) 3. (Berge-) Zug														
Z, Zugführer, Offizier der Kraftfahrparktruppen	1					1								
G, stellv. Führer (zugl. Panzerwart)			1			1								
G, für Abschleppdienst (zugl. Panzerwart)			4		4									
M, Kraftwagenfahrer (2 für Pkw, 1 für Lkw, 7 für Zgkw, 3 für gp.Kw.)				13	3									
M, 2. Kraftwagenfahrer (1 für Lkw, 5 für Zgkw, 3 für gp.Kw.)				9	9									
M, für Abschleppdienst (zugl. Panzerwart)				4	4									
leichte Pkw, gl., (4-sitzig)											2			
Lkw 4,5t, als Drehkrankraftwagen (Hebekraft 3t) (Kfz. 100)											(1)			
schwerer Zgkw 18t, als Drehkrankraftwagen (Hebekraft 6t) (SdKfz 9/1)						(1)						1		
schwere Zgkw 18t (SdKfz 9)						(6)						6		
Bergepanzerwagen "Panther" (SdKfz 179)						(3)							3	
Summe zu d) 3. Zug (Bergezug)	1		5	26	20	2 (10)					2 (1)	7	3	
e) Waffenmeisterei														
Z, Waffenmeister, Führer		1				1								
O, Waffenunteroffizier (Wffm)		1				1								
M, Waffenmeistergehilfe) 2 zugl. Kw. Beifahrer				4	4									
M, Panzerelektromechaniker)				2	2									
M, Kraftwagenfahrer (2 für Pkw, 2 für Lkw)				3	3									
leichter Pkw, gl., (4-sitzig)											1			
Lkw 4,5t, offen, als Panz. Wffm. Werkst. Kw.											(1)			
Lkw 4,5t, offen, als Panz. Wffm. Ger. Kw.											(1)			
Summe zu e) Waffenmeisterei		1	1	9	9	2					1 (2)			
f) Werkstätte für Nachrichtengerät														
O, Funkmeister, Werkstättenführer			1			1								
G, Nachrichtenmechaniker			1		1									
M, Nachrichtenmechaniker (zugl. 2. Kw.Fahr. für Lkw)				3	3									
M, Kraftwagenfahrer für Lkw				3	3									
Lkw 2t, offen, gl., für Panzerfunkgerätvorrat											(1)			
Lkw 3t, geschlossen, gl., als Nachrichtenwerkstattkw.											(1)			
Lkw 3t, geschlossen, gl., als Sammlerkw.											(1)			
Anhänger für Sammlerladegerät D (Sd.Ah. 23)														(1)
Summe zu f) Werkstätte für Nachrichtengerät			2	6	7	1					(3)			(1)
g) Troß														
O, Hauptfeldwebel			1			1								
O, Schirrmeister (K)			1			(1)								

K.St.N. 1187b **Stand 1.7.44**

	A	B	C	D	E	F	G	H	I	J	K	L	M	N
G, Gerätunteroffizier, Troßführer			1		1									
G, Verpflegungsunteroffizier (zugl. 2. Kw.Fahr. für Lkw)			1		1									
G, Rechnungsführer			1		1									
G, Feldkochunteroffizier			1		1									
G, Sanitätsunteroffizier			1			1								
M, Funker (1 zugl. Kw.Fahr. für Lkw)				2	2									
M, Schreiber (zugl. 2. Kw.Fahr. für Lkw)				1	1									
M, Kraftwagenfahrer (2 für Pkw, 1 zugl. Schreiber, 5 für Lkw)				7	7									
M, 2. Kraftwagenfahrer für Lkw (zugl. für Betriebsstoffausgabe)				1	1									
M, Feldkoch (1 zugl. 2. Kw.Fahr. für Lkw)				3	3									
M, Schuhmacher (zugl. 2. Kw.Fahr. für Lkw)				1	1									
M, Schneider				1	1									
leichte Pkw, gl., (4-sitzig)											2			
Lkw 2t, geschlossen, gl, für gr. Feldkochherd											(2)			
Lkw 4,5t, offen, für Verpflegung, Gepäck und Mannschaftstransport											(1)			
Lkw 4,5t, offen, für Betriebsstoff											(1)			
Lkw 4,5t, offen, für Betriebsstofftransport											(1)			
Fliegerabwehrtrupp														
G, Truppführer (zugl. MG-Führer)			1			1								
M, MG-Schütze				1		1								
M, Kraftwagenfahrer für Pkw				1	1									
mittlerer Pkw, als Truppenluftschützkraftwagen (Kfz. 4)							(2)				1			
Summe zu g) Troß			8	18	21	4 (1)	(2)				3 (5)			
Zusammenstellung														
a) Gruppe Führer	2		1	7	8	2				1	2 (1)			
b) 1. Zug		1	9	41	50	1	(2)				(15)	1		(4)
c) 2. Zug		1	9	41	50	1	(2)				(15)	1		(4)
d) 3. Zug (Bergezug)	1		5	26	20	2 (10)					2 (1)	7	3	
e) Waffenmeisterei		1	1	9	9	2					1 (2)			
f) Werkstatt für Nachrichtengerät			2	6	7	1					(3)			(1)
g) Troß			8	18	21	4 (1)	(2)				3 (5)			
Gesamtstärke	3	3	35	148	165	13 (11)	(6)			1	8 (42)	9	3	(7)

Remarks:

a) 10 men allocated as *Hi.Kr.Trg.* [*Hilfskrankenträger*/auxiliary stretcher bearers.].

b) At *Stellengruppen* G [soldiers at pay grade 'G'] there are 6 *Feldwebel* posts.

c) One *Unteroffizier* to be assigned to gas protection duties.

d) Drivers of the gp.Kw. and *ZgKw* will use the on-board sub-machine pistols in the *Bergepanther* and s. *ZgKw*. 18t.

e) Out of the 148 'M' ranks up to 18 can be covered by *Hilfswilligen*, according to unit commander's choice.

In the *Lkws* converted into covered workshops, work could be carried out under protection against the weather. On the left hand side of the picture the electrical generator for supplying power to the arc-welding apparatus can be seen.

The *Strabo (Straßenbockkran/* transportable gantry crane) was a distinctive piece of equipment. Early examples had a capacity of 15 tons while later models could lift 16 t. This picture shows a tank turret being lifted at the workshop area of *s.Pz.Abt. 506* in January 1944, in Vinnytsia (Ukraine). In the foreground on the left is a two-stroke diesel Lanz tractor.

Trucks were not sufficient for the transport of personnel so every company also had a bus – these easily became bogged down when travelling off-road! This picture shows the bus belonging to *s.Pz.Abt.508* after being loading onto a train on 4 February 1944. (Schlamm)

The 6 ton crane mounted on an *Sd.Kfz. 9/1* was a versatile piece of equipment, for example for the removal and fitting of engines. The picture shows one of the two units belonging to *s.Pz.Abt. 508* on 23 July 1944 in Casciano. (Schlumberger)

The 'work horse' of the *Bergezüge* was the legendary 18-ton *Zg.Kw.* 'Famo', (prime mover truck). The picture shows it in action on 29 February 1944 with the *s.Pz.Abt.508*. (BA 311-904-3a)

The *Bergepanther* was significantly more efficient. The example in the picture (taken around the end of March 1945 in Hungary) belonged to *Pz.Rgt. 3 'Totenkopf'*.

Supply of *Bergepanthers* to units equipped with Tigers and *s.Pz.Jg.Abt. 512*

s.Pz.Abt.	Allocated		Number
504		14.04.1944	1
508		12.04.1944	1
SS 101		20.04.1944	1
III./GD		22.04.1944	2
SS T		30.04.1944	2
505		18.05.1944	1
SS LAH	26.05.1944	14.06.1944	2
SS DR	26.05.1944	05.06.1944	2
503	13.06.1944	15.06.1944	2
SS 102	13.06.1944	29.07.1944	2
510	05.07.1944	06.07.1977	2
501	07.07.1944	10.07.1944	2
507	14.08.1944	19.08.1944	2
505	10.08.1944	17.08.1944	2
506	09.09.1944	12.09.1944	2
503	09.09.1944	20.09.1944	2
GD	13.09.1944	19.09.1944	2
507	13.09.1944	19.09.1944	1
502	13.09.1944	17.09.1944	2
504	13.09.1944	16.09.1944	1
508	13.09.1944	16.09.1944	1
SS T	13.09.1944	04.10.1944	2
509	27.09.1944	29.09.1944	2
SS LAH	10.10.1944	14.10.1944	2
SS 501	15.10.1944	17.10.1944	2
301 (FkL)	16.10.1944	20.10.1944	2
503	28.10.1944	01.11.1944	2
SS T	28.10.1944	15.11.1944	2
SS DR	04.11.1944	06.11.1944	2
506	08.11.1944	10.11.1944	1
508	14.11.1944	18.11.1944	1
GD	07.12.1944	13.12.1944	2
509	03.01.1945	05.01.1945	1
502	03.01.1945	12.01.1945	2
SS 502	11.01.1945	15.01.1945	2
SS 502	19.02.1945	20.02.1945	2
FHH	04.03.1945	11.03.1945	2
507	04.03.1945	09.03.1945	2
506	10.03.1945	12.03.1945	1
512	11.03.1945	13.03.1945	4

From the middle of 1944 the detachments designated as the *'I-Trupps'* (later *'I-Gruppen'*) nominally belonged to the *Versorgungskompanie* but were led in practice by the *Werkstattkompanie*. This picture, taken in June 1943, shows one from *s.Pz.Abt. 505.*

Above is a picture of a *lei.Zg.Kw.* (*leichte Zugkraftwagen*/ prime mover vehicle). The picture below shows an *Lkw* belonging *s.Pz. Abt. 505* in January 1944.

Versorgungskompanie

The *Versorgungskompanie*, according to *K.St.N. 1151b (fG)*, took on all the tasks of the unit regarding logistics support except for those fulfilled by the *Panzerwerkstattkompanie*.

Except for the usual *'Gruppe Führer'*, the company had at its command
- a medical sub-unit (*Sanitätsstaffel*)
- repair services (*Instandsetzungsdienste*)
- a refuelling detachment (*Betriebsstoffstaffel*)
- a munitions detachment (*Munitionsstaffel*)
- an administration team (*Verwaltungsstaffel*).

These detachments fulfilled their tasks more or less autonomously but in combat they were dispersed between the front and rear services to facilitate their management and organization and enable them to react flexibly to changes in the operational situation.

The **Sanitätsstaffel** was too small. Its personnel consisted of a so-called *Hilfsarzt* (assistant doctor) and two medical orderlies (each with the rank of NCO) who also drove the *Kfz. 31* ambulance. A second *Kfz. 31* transported medical and gas-attack protection equipment by means of which provisional first-aid posts could be set up, whenever possible, in buildings. The retrieval of the wounded was left to the sub-units and crews – the so-called *Hilfskrankenträger* of which there were eight in each tank company. These personnel received additional training in the stabilization and the management of wounded soldiers. Transport of the wounded to cover or to the first-aid post was to some extent problematic and it was often necessary to use tanks for this purpose. The personnel at the first-aid post could then only make the wounded fit for transport – mostly in empty supply trucks or transport provided by the field hospital organization – to the field hospitals.

The **Instandsetzungsdienste** consisted of a repair and maintenance squad built around 27 mechanics (six of whom were NCOs) and a tank electrician. The unit's self-sufficiency in practical skills was further enhanced by the provision of a blacksmith (who was also a welder) and a *Klempner* (pipe-fitter). An officer of the *Kraftfahrparktruppen* acted as the squad leader. A special feature was the provision of a uniformed official – the so-called *Werkmeister* – who had been intensively trained by the Tiger manufacturing company.

Three repair and maintenance groups, each under the leadership of a *Schirrmeister* (sergeant-technician), were assigned to their respective *Panzerkompanien*. The *'I-Gruppe'* (*Instandsetzung Gruppe*) each consisted of four *Panzerwarte* (tank mechanics) who were NCOs, one of whom was the leader of the group, a *Schweißer* (welder), a *Panzerelektriker* (tank electrician), a *Panzerfunkwart* (tank radio-technician) and two assistants to the *Waffenmeister* (armourer). Together with three regular drivers, four other *Panzerwarte* acted as drivers of the passenger vehicles and trucks. The trucks were essentially the *Lkw* 3 ts (open-backed, off-road vehicles used for the transport of workshop equipment), *Lkw* 4.5 ts (these were also open-backed, off-road vehicles and were used to transport spare parts) and the two light Zgkw.1 t *Sd.Kfz. 10*s (prime movers). The *Schirrmeister* and group leader used a four-seater, off-road passenger vehicle as their means of transport. The *Schirrmeister* was not committed to remain in any particular location since his primary role was to assess the extent of damage or the amount of repair work required. The main task of the repair groups was to carry out routine maintenance tasks in conjunction with the tank crew and to repair instances of less serious damage. Heavily damaged vehicles were, as a matter of course, handed over to the *Panzerwerkstatt-Kompanie*.

In addition to these groups, the *Bergegruppe* (vehicle recovery group) which – due to the lack of heavy recovery equipment – served only as a towing unit or was attached to the recovery platoon of the *Panzerwerkstattkompanie*.

Also, the *Instandsetzungsdienste* had another 'group for carrying out weapons and signals apparatus repairs' each with two *Waffenmeister*, a *Funkmeister* (chief radio operator with the rank of *Unteroffizier*), four assistant armourers (*Waffenmeistergehilfen*), a *Panzerfunkwart* and a communications equipment engineer (*Nachrichtenmechaniker*). The vehicle allocation consisted of three open, off-road *Lkw* 3 ts used for transporting weapons and radio communications equipment.

The *'I-Dienste'* (*Instandsetzungsdienste*) were completed by an *Ersatzteilgruppe* (spares group) which consisted of two *Unteroffiziere* and six other soldiers together with five open-backed, off-road *Lkw* 4.5 ts for the transport and supply of spare parts. The **Betriebsstoffstaffel** and the **Munitionsstaffel** were responsible for delivery of consumable items. These detachments each consisted of three *Unteroffiziere* and 20 and 16 drivers with 19 and 15 open-backed transport *Lkws* respectively. The leader of the *Munitionsstaffel* was also a trained *Feuerwerker* (explosives expert) who also dealt with unexploded ordnance and mines. During large military operations, goods that were consumed in quantity were supplied directly by the transport companies of major military units.

The following detachments belonged to the **Verwaltungsstaffel**: *Gruppe Verwaltung* (an administration detachment with a purser and accounting officer; *Gruppe Verpflegung* (catering detachment) with four *Lkws* of either three or four tons); the *Feldküchengruppe* (field-kitchen detachment) with a two cooks (one of whom held the rank of *Unteroffizier*) and a total of five *Lkw* 3 ts and, finally, a *Wirtschaftsgruppe* to which belonged two chief accountants (with the rank of *Unteroffizier*), a *Bekleidungsunteroffizier* (an NCO who dealt with matters relating to clothing), and three each of *Schneider* (tailors) and *Schuhmacher* (shoe makers). Transport for the *Wirtschafts-gruppe* consisted of a total of four open-backed *Lkw* 4.5 ts for the transport of equipment and luggage. Moreover it was also possible – and widely practiced – for *Gruppe Verpflegung* to purchase foodstuffs (such as cattle, eggs, poultry, potatoes and grain) from the surrounding countryside even in occupied areas. Food supplies were also supplemented by hunting and fishing the indigenous wildlife. Contrary to descriptions perpetrated in 'modern' history, it was strictly forbidden for soldiers to plunder the local area!

According to *K.St.N. 1151B (fG)* of 1 June 1944, the *Versorgungskompanie* had a total strength of five officers, two officials, 55 *Unteroffiziere*, and 188 men of other ranks.

Versorgungskompanie

Gruppe Führer

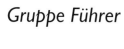 

Sanitätsstaffel

Verwaltungsstaffel

Gruppe Verwaltung

Gruppe Verpflegung

Feldküchengruppe

Wirschaftsgruppe

Instandsetzungsstaffel

1.–3. Kfz.Instandsetzungsgruppe

Bergegruppe

Ersatzteilgruppe

Gruppe für Waffen- und Nachrichtengerät-Instandsetzung

Betriebsstoffstaffel

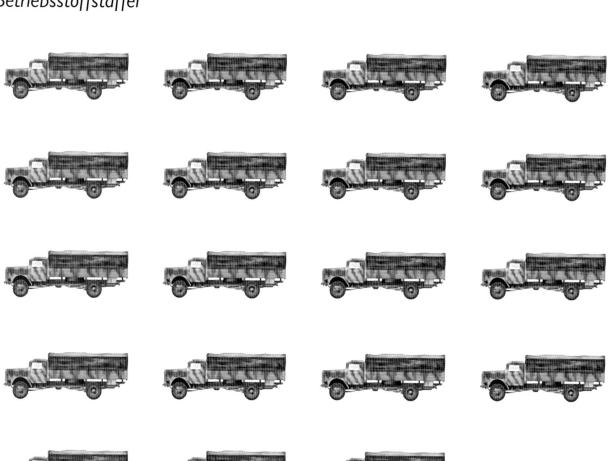

Munitionsstoffstaffel

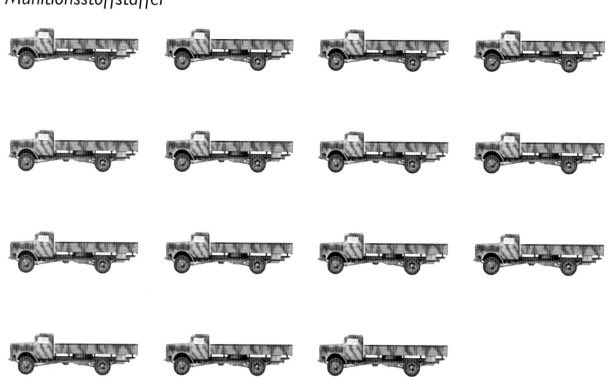

K.St.N. 1151b (fG) — **Stand 1.6.44**

Versorgungskompanie (fG) einer schweren Panzerabteilung "Tiger"	Offiziere	Beamte	Unteroffiziere	Mannschaften	Gewehre, Karabiner (Sturmgewehr)	Pistolen (Masch. Pist.)	s MG (le MG) [Panzerbüchsen]	besp. (unbesp.) Geschütze und Werfer	besp. (unbesp.) Fahrzeuge und Wasserfahrzg.	Krad (Krad mit Seitenwagen) [Kettenkrad]	Personenkraftwagen (Lastkraftwagen)	Zugkw. (Volkkettenschlepper) [Gleisketten-Lkw]	gp. Volk. Kfz. (gp. Halbk. Kfz) [gp. Räderkfz]	Fahrräder (Anhänger) [Eisenbahnfahrzeuge]
	A	B	C	D	E	F	G	H	I	J	K	L	M	N
a) Gruppe Führer														
B, Kompanieführer	1					1								
K, Offizier (W)	1					1								
Z, Ordonnanzoffizier 1)	1					(1)								
O, Hauptfeldwebel			1			1								
O, Abteilungsschreiber			1			1								
O, Schirrmeister (K) (im Pkw)			1			(1)								
G, Gerätunteroffizier			1		1									
G, Wechselbesatzung (Funker, zugl. im Fernsprechdienst ausgebildet)			2			2								
M, Schreiber				4	4									
M, Wechselbesatzung (Funker, zugl. im Fernsprechdienst ausgebildet)				2		2								
M, Wechselbesatzung (Kw.Fahr. f. gp.Kw., zugl. 2. Kw.Fahr. für Lkw)				1		1								
M, Funker				1	1									
M, Kradmelder (1 zugl. Schreiber) (auf le Krad 350ccm)				2	2					2				
M, Kraftwagenfahrer (3 für Pkw, 3 für Lkw) (1 zugl. Funker)				6	6									
leichte Pkw, gl., (4-sitzig)											3			
Lkw 2t, geschlossen, gl. 2)											(1)			
Lkw 3t, offen, gl., für Mannschaftstransport und Fernsprechgerät 3)											(1)			
Lkw 3t, offen, gl., für Geschäftszimmer (Stbs.Kp., Vers.Kp., 1.-3. Kp.)											(1)			
Summe zu a) Gruppe Führer	3		6	16	14	8 (3)				2	3 (3)			
b) Sanitätsstaffel														
Z, Hilfarzt, Führer	1					1								
G, Sanitätsunteroffizier (1 zugl. stellv. Staffelführer)			2			2								
M, Krankenträger (zugl. Kw.Fahr. für Pkw)				1		1								
M, Krankenträger (zugl. 2. Kw.Fahr. für Lkw)				2		2								
M, Kraftwagenfahrer für Lkw				2	2									
leichter Pkw, gl., (4-sitzig)											1			
Lkw 2t, geschlossen, gl., als Krankenkraftwagen (Kfz. 31)											(1)			
Lkw 3t, offen, gl, für Sanitäts- und Gasschutzgerät											(1)			
Summe zu b) Sanitätsstaffel	1		2	5	2	6					1 (2)			
c) Instandsetzungsstaffel														
K, Offizier der Kraftfahrparktruppen, Staffelführer 4)	1					(1)								
Z, Werkmeister (K) (zugl. stellv. Staffelführer)		1				1								
G, Vorhandwerker, Panzermotorenschlosser			2		2									

K.St.N. 1151b (fG)   **Stand 1.6.44**

	A	B	C	D	E	F	G	H	I	J	K	L	M	N
G, Vorhandwerker, Panzergetriebeschlosser			2		2									
G, Vorhandwerker, Panzerschlosser			2		2									
M, Kraftwagenfahrer für Pkw (zugl. Schreiber)				1	1									
M, Kraftwagenfahrer (3 für Lkw, 1 für Zgkw) (zugl. Kw.Schlosser)				4	4									
M, Panzermotorenschlosser)				6	6									
M, Panzergetriebeschlosser) 1 zugl. Kw.Fahr. für Pkw, 2 für Lkw				6	6									
M, Panzerschlosser) 1 für Zgkw. 5 zugl. 2. Kw.Fahr. für				5	5									
M, Panzerelektriker) Lkw, 1 für Zgkw				1	1									
M, Schmied (zugl. Schweißer)				1	1									
M, Klempner				1	1									
leichte Pkw, gl., (4-sitzig)											2			
Lkw 3t, offen, gl., für Werkstattgerät, mit Ausstatt. für Kfz.-I-Gruppe											(1)			
Werkstattkraftwagen. für Kfz.-I-Staffel oder le. Kfz.-I-Zug											(1)			
Lkw 3t, geschlossen, gl., als Gerätkw. für Kfz.-I-Staffel											(1)			
Lkw 3t, geschlossen, gl., als Werkstattmaschinenkw. für Kfz.-I-Staffel											(1)			
Lkw 4,5t, als Drehkrankraftwagen (Habekraft 3t) (Kfz. 100)											(1)			
leichter Zgkw 1t (SdKfz 10)												1		
schwerer Zgkw 18t, als Drehkrankraftwagen (Hebekraft 6t) (SdKfz 9/1)												1		
schwerer Maschinensatz A als Anhänger (1 achs), fahrbar														(1)
1.-3. Kfz. Instandsetzungsgruppe														
O, Schirrmeister (K)			3		3									
G, Panzerwarte (3 zugl. Gruppenführer)			12			(12)								
G, Panzerfunkwart			3			(3)								
M, Panzerwart (6 zugl. Kw. Fahr. für Pkw, 3 für Lkw)				12	12									
M, Panzerwart, Schweißer				3	3									
M, Panzerwart, Panzerelektriker				3	3									
M, Waffenmeistergehilfe				6	6									
M, Panzerfunkwart				3	3									
M, Kraftwagenfahrer (1 für Lkw, 2 für Zgkw)				9	9									
leichte Pkw, gl., (4-sitzig)											6			
Lkw 3t, offen, gl., für Werkstattgerät, mit Ausstatt. für Kfz.-I-Gruppe											(3)			
Lkw 4,5t, offen, gl., für Ersatzteile											(3)			
leichte Zgkw 1t (SdKfz 10)												6		
Bergegruppe														
G, für Abschleppdienst (1 zugl. Gruppenführer)			2			(2)								
M, Pz.Wart (1 zugl. Kw.Fahr. für Pkw, 2 zugl. 2. Kw.Fahr. für gp.Kw.)				4	1	3								
M, Kraftwagenfahrer für gp.Kw.				2		2								
leichter Pkw, gl., (4-sitzig)												1		
Bergepanzerwagen "Panther" (SdKfz 179)													2	
Ersatzteilgruppe														
G, für Ersatzteilnachschub			1			(1)								
G, für Ersatzteilverwaltung			1		1									
M, Kraftwagenfahrer für Lkw				5	5									
M, 2. Kraftwagenfahrer für Lkw (zugl. Schreiber)				1	1									
Lkw 4,5t, offen, gl., für Ersatzteilnachschub											(2)			
Lkw 4,5t, offen, gl., für Ersatzteilverlastung											(3)			
Gruppe für Waffen- und Nachrichtengerät-Instandsetzung														
O, Waffenunteroffizier (Wffm)			2			2								
O, Funkmeister			1			1								
M, Waffenmeistergehilfe (2 zugl. Kw.Fahr. für Lkw)				4	4									

K.St.N. 1151b (fG) | | | | | | | | | | | | | **Stand 1.6.44**

	A	B	C	D	E	F	G	H	I	J	K	L	M	N
M, Panzerfunkwart (zugl. Kw.Fahr. für Lkw)				1	1									
M, Nachrichtenmechaniker				1	1									
Lkw 3t, offen, gl., für Waffen- und Nachrichtengerät											(3)			
Summe zu c) Instandsetzungsdienste	1	1	31	103	105	12 (19)					9 (19)	8	2	(1)
d) Betriebsstoffstaffel														
G, für Betriebsstoff (1 zugl. Staffelführer) (2 zugl. MG-Führer)			3			2 (1)	(2)							
M, für Betriebsstoff (zugl. 2. Kw.Fahr für Lkw und Schreiber) 5)				1	1									
M, Kraftwagenfahrer für Lkw				19	19									
Lkw 4,5t, gl., für Betriebsstoff											(19)			
Summe zu d) Betriebsstoffstaffel			3	20	20	2 (1)	(2)				(19)			
e) Munitionsstaffel														
O, Feuerwerker (zugl. Staffelführer)			1			(1)								
G, für Munition (1 zugl. MG-Führer)			2		1	1	(1)							
M, für Munition (zugl. 2. Kw.Fahr. für Lkw und Schreiber) 5)				1	1									
M, Kraftwagenfahrer für Lkw				15	15									
Lkw 4,5t, offen, gl., für Munition											(15)			
Summe zu e) Munitionsstaffel			3	16	17	1 (1)	(1)				(15)			
f) Verwaltungsstaffel														
Gruppe Verwaltung														
Z, Zahlmeister, Beamter des gehob. Verw. Dienstes (zugl. Staffelführer)		1				1								
G, Rechnungsführer			1		1									
M, Kraftwagenfahrer für Pkw				1	1									
leichter Pkw, gl., (4-sitzig)											1			
Gruppe Verpflegung														
G, für Verpflegung, Gruppenführer (zugl. 2. Kw.Fahr. für Lkw)			1		1									
M, für Verpflegung (zugl. 2. Kw.Fahr. für Lkw) (2 zugl. MG-Schützen)				3	3		(1)							
M, Kraftwagenfahrer für Lkw				4	4									
Lkw 3t, offen, gl., für Verpflegung											(3)			
Lkw 4,5t, offen, für Verpflegung und Marketenderei											(1)			
Feldküchengruppe														
G, Feldkochunteroffizier (zugl. 2. Kw.Fahr. für Lkw)			5		5									
M, Feldkoch				5	5									
M, Kraftwagenfahrer für Lkw				5	5									
Lkw 3t, offen, gl., für gr. Feldkochherd											(5)			
Wirschaftsgruppe														
G, Rechnungsführer (zugl. Kw. Beifahrer) (1 zugl. Gruppenführer)			2		2									
G, für Bekleidung (zugl. für Handwerker)			1		1									
M, Schuhmacher (zugl. 2. Kw.Fahr. für Lkw)				3	3									
M, Schneider (zugl. 2. Kw.Fahr. für Lkw)				3	3									
Kraftwagenfahrer für Lkw				4	4									
Lkw 4,5t, offen für Gerät und Gepäck											(4)			
Summe zu f) Verwaltungsstaffel	1		10	28	38	1	(1)				1 (13)			

K.St.N. 1151b (fG)   **Stand 1.6.44**

Zusammenstellung	A	B	C	D	E	F	G	H	I	J	K	L	M	N
a) Gruppe Führer	3		6	16	14	8 (3)				2	3 (3)			
b) Sanitätsstaffel	1		2	5	2	6					1 (2)			
c) Instandsetzungsdienste	1	1	31	103	105	12 (19)					9 (19)	8	2	(1)
d) Betriebsstoffstaffel			3	20	20	2 (1)	(2)				(19)			
e) Munitionsstaffel			3	16	17	1 (1)	(1)				(15)			
f) Verwaltungsstaffel	1		10	28	38	1	(1)				1 (13)			
Gesamtstärke	5	2	55	188	196	30 (24)	(4)			2	14 (71)	8	2	(1)

Remarks:

a)   12 men to be designated as *Hi.Kr.Trg*.

b)   At pay grade 'G' there are 9 *Feldwebel* posts (excluding those undergoing a specialist career path).

c)   In specified areas, of the 188 'M' grade posts, 13 are to be filled by volunteers.

1)   At this point in time the post is to be filled by an *Unteroffizier* (pay grade 'O').

2)   Equipped with one set Fu 8 SE 30 (30 W transceiver).

3)   Equipped with signals apparatus for *le. FeldKab. Tr. 3 (mot)*.

4)   This post could also be filled by an official with a higher technical-service grade ('K').

5)   The remaining drivers can also be taken from the company's reserve crews.

In everyday service, because of the war situation and the number of wounded, the personnel strength clearly fell short of the numbers stated in the *K.St.N.* of 1 November 1944 and the subsequent *K.St.N.* amendments which on the whole were considered as merely target strengths. A proportion of the manpower (approximately a tenth) could be made up from *Hilfswilligen* (auxiliary volunteers), prisoners of war who had switched sides and volunteers recruited by army units. However, this did not apply to Panzer companies.

Overall, the strength of the military units (excluding *Hilfswillige*) developed as follows:

Date	Total	Officers/Officials	NCOs	Other ranks
1 Nov 1943	1,097	35	274	698
1 June 1944	967	32	260	675
1 Nov 1944	878	33	265	580

An evaluation of the available monthly reports of the units indicates that the actual service strengths were in part substantially lower (mostly due to the losses).

It must also be pointed out once more that the provisions, particularly of armoured fighting vehicles, were somewhat different. This was partly due to the longer time required to supply individual units and was the result of the late delivery of replacement vehicles for accrued losses. These were to a large extent new vehicles but could however be ones that had been repaired back in Germany, or refurbished by the larger repair and maintenance workshops of the *Heeresgruppen* (army groups). The descriptions of the equipment status were taken with permission from the two excellent books by Thomas L. Jentz (with graphics by Hilary L. Doyle): *Germany's Tiger Tanks – D.W. to Tiger I* and *VK.45.02 to Tiger II*.

An *Lkw* belonging to the *Munitionsstaffel* (displaying the 'M' identification mark). The snow chains on the wheels were also useful in muddy conditions. The co-driver has painted the pet name of his sweetheart on the passenger door. (Wunderlich)

The *Versorgungsstaffeln* (supply detachments) were always on the go – day and night and whatever the weather conditions – leaving little time for taking souvenir photos… (Wunderlich)

The units deployed to the Eastern Front sometimes were allocated *Maultier-Lkws* which were more capable off-road vehicles than the standard issue *Lkws*. (BA 279-0949-13)

'*Ohne Mampf kein Kampf!*' (no fighting without chow). The field kitchens were an important element of the *Versorgungskompanie*. These were box trucks with cookers on trailers. This picture, taken in June 1943, shows one that belongs to *s.Pz.Abt. 503*.

Gruppe Führer of the *Versorgungskompanie* had a *Lkw* box truck fitted out as an office; in this picture we see the vehicle belonging to *s.Pz.Abt. 503* in summer 1943. The wheels are covered to protect the tyres from the strong sunshine. (Rubbel)

The kitchen was always at the centre of attention. This picture, taken at the end of August 1943 in France, shows a requisitioned vehicle allocated to *s.Pz.Abt. 503* – a practice that occurred frequently. (Wunderlich)

The rearward elements (in this picture we see the *I-Gruppe* of *1./s.Pz. Abt. 505* during September 1943) changed location independently of the combat units in separate march groups.

A single *VW Kübel* of *s.Pz.Abt. 501* with a transport frame for stretchers at the station in Sidi Asim shows the rather modest motor vehicle resources of the medical unit. (BA 657-1039-18A)

The command groups of all companies each had an off-road *Lkw* 3t that served as office accommodation. This picture, taken on 25 June 1944, shows a loaded *Lkw* of a *Panzerkompanie* en route to Maciejow.

The first Tiger units had a mixed compliment of armoured vehicles which included the *Pz.Kpfw. III*. In this picture, taken in Trapani on 1 December 1942, a vehicle belonging to the *2./s.Pz.Abt. 501* carries supplementary jerry cans in preparation for transport to Africa.

After the phasing out of the *Pz.Kpfw. III*, *s.Pz.Abt.505* converted a dozen of these vehicles by removing their turrets and deploying them as supply vehicles. The picture shows one of these vehicles with a roof fashioned from wire netting as a means of protection against hand grenades and a Russian *Panzerbüchse* (anti-tank rifle) used for close-quarter protection.

The so-called *Funklenk-truppenteile* [units with radio-controlled vehicles packed with explosives] were a speciality…here we see a *B IV* belonging to *3./s.Pz.Abt. 508*. (Hirlinger)

Allocation of Responsibilities inside the Units

Descriptions of operations carried out by the Tiger units focus purely on engagements with the enemy. They are captivating and interesting and demonstrate the danger, commitment and the life of the crews in areas near the front line. However, many authors do not take the trouble to throw any light on the time before and after such operations. In purely quantitative terms, such times were clearly longer than the time spent in actual operations. They were filled in part with similarly strenuous phases of preparation and follow-up and – though it is not often mentioned – with days for the recuperation of bodies and souls. The opportunity therefore presents itself – supported by the use of numerous photographs – to offer a glimpse of this side of the life of the Panzer crews.

As already mentioned, the follow-up periods without active deployment lasted for more or less lengthy periods – when there were no operations – during which the focus was on the repair of technical or combat-related damage, the resupply of ammunition and fuel, care of the injured and wounded, operations-related preparations (such as the cleaning of weapons) and the documentation of combat experiences. The latter of these included the preparation of reports and messages, the completion of the war diary of the unit and the entry of remarks in the soldiers' Soldbücher (identification and pay books that also contained remarks about the owners' decorations etc.), reconnoitring and selecting (new) accommodation and the regulation of rations. Furthermore, there was always a whole series of tasks that had to be postponed because of combat activities such as the care and routine maintenance of weapons, vehicles and equipment (including the careful assessment of wear and damage), cleaning of equipment and washing clothes and the like. Because there was always a continual influx of replacement personnel, they had to be instructed or trained to perform their intended function; new leaders had to become acquainted with their units or sub-units; camouflage measures in the assembly areas had to be inspected daily (and rectified if necessary) and routine reports completed. These periods of 'peace and quiet' were therefore not necessarily spent in idleness. Each unit also had to make its own security arrangements by posting sentries, organizing patrols and monitoring the skies for enemy aircraft. Consequently, about a quarter of the personnel were permanently engaged in such activities.

Usually, the transition from the preparation phase – for planned operations or potential deployment for which the unit had to be held in a state of readiness – was seamless. Leaders and sub-unit leaders sometimes had to drive over long distances on reconnaissance to build contact with neighbouring units or supporting forces, make arrangements of various kinds and issue plans and orders. Actual 'leisure' periods were mostly rather short and never predictable. As a general rule, personal hygiene, reading and writing letters to be delivered by the Feldpost (German forces postal service), or making use of one or the other of the support facilities, could only be carried out under the pressure of time. With only hours between missions and operations remaining the crews were often simply completely exhausted and tried to rest and to draw new courage. The permanent physical, and above all psychological, stress can hardly be imagined by outsiders to this world. Accordingly, the many ignorant reinterpretations of history and the clever statements made by moralists of the old and new '68-er' [a German student movement] generations, who underestimate the personal sacrifices and hardships prevailing at the time, permanently dwell on the subject of misconduct and 'blame' – all in light of the 'knowledge' of today…

All of this was endured within a circle of Kameraden on whom one could rely and within units led by superiors who at all levels were enthusiastic and had a sense of responsibility. In the Panzer companies there was an important division of tasks between the Kompaniechef and the Hauptfeldwebel or 'Spieß' as he was referred to in the parlance of the troops. The Kompaniechef was completely responsible for – and completely exhausted by – his leadership duties during the fighting, preparations and follow up activities. The Spieß, together with his Geräteunteroffizier and driver (who was at the same time the company's clerk), maintained the essentially important connection with the unit's support elements with regard to general supply and catering. The organization of tactically relevant supplies (for example bulk consumable goods) as well as measures for undertaking repairs were part of the tactical operational planning and was usually undertaken by the Kompaniechef himself or regulated by him from the outset by the issue of tactical orders.

Because of the ever-present threat from the enemy during continuous combat, it was only occasionally possible for the Spieß to directly provide food. If such were the case, he organized the delivery and distribution of ration packages as well as drinking water for the water bottles of the crews. With this, the crews could fend for themselves for a few days. In addition, the Spieß arranged for the receipt and distribution of official letters and letters delivered by Feldpost and maintained contact with the logistics elements of the Versorgungskompanie which stored and transported additional equipment and replacement clothing. In the execution of this work, which could be very time consuming if the units were scattered during deployment, he was supported by the crew members of knocked-out tanks or by the replacement crews (if available).

These tasks were considerably more complex at the staff, workshop and supply company level. In the latter, transport columns – loaded with essential supplies of every kind for delivery (and on their return journey with the wounded, the dead, empty containers and damaged equipment) – were continuously on the road. When stationary, the repair and maintenance columns were used as field kitchens and for administrative purposes. They also served as wound dressing stations manned by doctors and medics – if they were not directly involved in combat, that is to say close to the front to provide first aid during the evacuation of the wounded. Parts of the repair and maintenance units were deployed alongside the combat troops in order to assess damage and to restore mobility to broken-down vehicles. The recovery platoons usually took on 'a hell of a job' if the combat troops were granted some rest. Their task was not only to recover vehicles that had been left behind but also to provide immediate support for the repair and maintenance work (see photos). Because the forces involved in operational support were dispersed to different locations, the tasks of leading, relocating and keeping them supplied were particularly complex.

The reconnaissance sections were usually in the vicinity of the battalion's command while the anti-aircraft platoons were deployed depending on the focal point of combat. During times when the enemy enjoyed superiority in the air, they were mostly deployed for the protection of important logistics facilities. The fighting troops rarely saw them.

The following picture section illustrates examples of the lifestyle of the crews before and after combat as well as tasks just mentioned.

The time between missions was chiefly filled with making preparations for the next one. Here, a member of *s.Pz.Abt. 503* is busy cleaning weapons and equipment during the summer of 1943.

This picture shows *Unteroffizier* Jaeckel with a copy of *'Front und Heimat'* (a newspaper for soldiers) in August 1944 in Mailly…it does not seem to offer uplifting reading. (Wunderlich)

The orderly room was the social centre of the soldiers' quarters. In this picture we see the '*Spieß*', *Hauptfeldwebel* Haas of the *1./s. Pz.Abt. 502* on 29 July 1944, near Daugavpils. It is interesting to note that the old mammoth symbol was still in use at this point. (Lötsch)

This building which provided accommodation in Sillamä was clearly representative of the area and had a front yard. The picture was taken in April 1944. (Carius)

In the colder times of the year, the units were particularly anxious to find substantial buildings for their accommodation. This photo shows the *1./s.Pz.Abt. 501* on 12 December 1943 in Vitebsk. (Zorn)

After spending days inside the cramped conditions of a tank, the lack of personal hygiene was a problem…and one that the men always longed to remedy. This picture shows soldiers of *s.Pz.Abt. 501* at Djebel Solbia on 18 January 1943. (Hartmann)

This picture shows tank number 314 of the *3./s.Pz.Abt. 502*. It was stationed at Lake Beloye Ozero, near to Gatchina during September 1943. The crew members are preparing themselves for a refreshing swim. There is time too for cleaning shoes, shaving and cleaning equipment. (BA 4309 461-216-37)

Regulation haircuts were still in order! Here, *Obergefreiter* Angerhöfer, of *s.Pz.Abt. 502*, is at work on the 2 August 1943.

Cleaning clothes was a problem that had to be mastered, as was keeping them reasonably safe from pests.

For such purposes all tanks carried a bucket, or even a complete bath, in the hope that they were not cut to shreds by machine-gun fire.

Often there were only sufficient vessels available for a '*Katzenwäsche*' (cat's lick/a quick wash) as we see in this picture of *Stabstiger* '002' of *s.Pz.Abt. 502*. The picture was taken in open countryside in the summer of 1944.

The second most important thing (after rest) was food. Here, *Oberleutnant* Knauth of *s.Pz.Abt. 505* stirs warm soup as he sits with his crew. In front of him are two packets of the not particularly well-loved hard biscuits that made up part of the 'iron rations.'

Rations were usually collected at a dispensing post – in this case in the supply area of *Pz.Gren.Div. 'GD'* at the beginning of 1943 – and prepared at a field kitchen. (BA 748-0090-28A)

To enrich the menu, food was also bought from the local population by the members of the administrative authorities who in this case belonged to *s.Pz.Abt.501*. The picture was taken in Djedeida on 25 November 1942. (Hartmann)

The crews themselves were not shy about improving their choice of food. The picture above, taken in April 1944, shows the fruits of angling by members of *s.Pz.Abt. 506*. To the right, members of *3./s.Pz.Abt.503* prepare for a feast of meat in the Don-Steppe in March 1943.

Now and then there were alcoholic drinks. Here a crew led by *Unteroffizier* Mausberg (*s.Pz.Abt. 505*) polishes off a bottle of brandy together. The picture was taken near Vitebsk in December 1943.

If in Italy…the crew belonging to *s.Pz.Abt.504* appreciate a small glass of wine on 1 July 1944 in Ortona. (Hirlinger)

And if there was still time for leisure, the crews knew how to keep themselves busy. In the picture on the left, two crew members belonging to *s.Pz.Abt. 508* play a board game while the picture below shows a favourite card game (Skat) in progress. (Heimberger)

Piano concerts did not always take place indoors as this picture – taken in September 1943 – of men belonging to *s.Pz.Abt. 505* demonstrates. (Neubauer)

Opportunities for socializing were all too rare. In these images showing men of *s.Pz.Abt. 503*, the *Spieß'* is holding a meeting to music (right) while (below) they drink brandy and smoke cigars. (Wunderlich)

A feast for the most successful gunner in the unit, *Unteroffizier* Knispel, (in the background third from the left). (Müller-Nobiling)

Sports training is on offer the following morning!

And if boredom ever did set in then it was maybe time for an equipment inspection as shown in this picture, taken in September, of a crew belonging to *2./s.Pz.Abt. 503.*

But formality did not suffer in the field of combat… here, a report is presented in the proper manner by a member of *s.Pz. Abt. 505*, in January 1944. (Krönke)

There were roll calls too, such as this one at Charkow with the *SS-Pz.Rgt. 2* on the occasion of Hitler's birthday in 1943, when promotions and decorations were presented.

But there were also celebrations. Here May Day, a public holiday since 1933, is celebrated by *s.Pz.Abt. 505*, in Beverloo. On the tank are ethnic German-Belgian women in traditional dress. (BA 199-1444-30)

Then there were special events such as the award of the Knight's Cross. This picture shows *Leutnant* Bölter of *s.Pz.Abt. 502* on 16 April 1944 after the award of this prestigious decoration. (Loke)

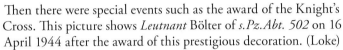

The award of the Iron Cross Second Class was a rather more mundane event. The picture on the left shows *Obergefreiter* Schneider of *s.Pz.Abt. 503* after receiving his EK-2 decoration. Above we see *Oberscharf.* Soretz being congratulated for his destruction of the 2,000th tank by the *'Das Reich'* Division. (BA 94-57-18)

And here...a *Ferntrauung* [a wedding conducted by proxy over a long distance while the bride was at a local church back home] on Christmas Day in Manouba. The ceremony is conducted by the *Kommandeur* of *s.Pz.Abt. 501*, *Major* Lueder. (Lueder)

An unfortunate but everyday event at the front line: a sad moment for *Leutnant* von Rosen (*s.Pz.Abt. 503*) at the graveside of a comrade. *Leutnant* von Rosen was himself wounded in the air attack near Emieville that killed his comrade on 18 July1944.

The funeral of *Oberleutnant* Kurt Stein of *s.Pz.Abt. 508* on 15 September 1944, in Imola. The address is conducted by a field chaplain. (Hirlinger)

Comradeship!
The photograph albums of former soldiers are full of pictures of this sort – group photographs of Panzer platoons. The picture on the right shows *Leutnant* Rambow of *s.Pz.Abt. 503* in August 1944. Below is *Leutnant* Herwig, *s.Pz.Abt. 508*. (Wunderlich and Heimberger resp.)

Of course this applied to all other units too…the picture to the right, for example, shows soldiers belonging to the *Munitionsgruppe* of *s.Pz.Abt. 503* in May 1943, in Charkow.

Here soldiers belonging to the first platoon of *1./s.Pz.Abt. 501* (*Leutnant* Vermehren) pose for a photograph taken on 13 January 1943, before the launch of *Unternehmen 'Eilbote'* (Operation Express). Behind the group stands Tiger '131.' (Hartmann)

It was strictly prohibited to keep animals as mascots; however this rule was often violated. The picture on the left, taken in July 1944, shows Gotthold Wunderlich as he feeds a tawny owl that 'flew up to him'. Note the self-made, fashionable wooden clogs. (Wunderlich)

This crew belonging to *1./s.Pz.Abt. 502* came across a dog near Tossno in September 1943. (BA 455-20-13)

Hauptmann Scherf (*3./s.Pz.Abt.503*) keeps an eye on a fellow traveller on his *Kettenkrad* (half-tracked motor cycle) in August 1944. (Wunderlich)

Even though the 'modern historical narrative' would like us to believe otherwise, it was not customary to plunder the possessions of the local population; or even to kill them! The picture on the right shows at Tiger belonging to *s.Pz.Abt. 501* in El Jem. (BA 420-2033-20). Below is a *lei. Zg.Kw.* belonging to *s.Pz.Abt. 509* with two additional 'crew members.'

In the picture above, taken in February 1944, a local inhabitant ignores the presence of a tank belonging to *s.Pz.Abt. 502*. (BA 458-79-18)

Unteroffizier Wiegand of *s.Pz.Abt. 503* marks his 'home' with the pennant on the right-hand side of the picture. (Rubbel)

Soldiers belonging to *s.Pz.Abt. 501* visit the Roman amphitheatre at El Jem on 18 March 1943.

Culture was also taken care of, but sometimes not really recognized by the crews! The picture on the right shows a tank belonging to *s.Pz. Abt. 508* as it passes by Piazza de Angelis, Rome, on 14 February 1944. (BA 310-880-33)

The newly formed *3./s.Pz.Abt 503* marches towards the Allies' bridgeheads at the Seine on 21 August 1944. Here they have just passed under the Arc de Triomphe, Paris, as they make their way along the Champs Elysees. (Wunderlich)

Early Experiences with the Tiger

It has already been mentioned that the repair and maintenance personnel (and occasionally tank drivers) received practical training at the Henschel factory in Kassel. For this reason, the following section has been incorporated. Furthermore, the author was allowed to use a series of hitherto largely unpublished of photographs from the estate of Herr Robert Pertuss, a professional engineer who had attained the qualification of *Diplom-Ingenieur* (Master's Degree in Engineering).

I am also pleased to have been able to include personal, and until now unpublished, records written by Herr Pertuss during the early years of the Tiger because they offer an insight into the atmosphere at the time and reveal some interesting details over and above those relating to purely technical aspects:

The history of the Tiger begins in the old Henschel factory in Holländischer Platz, Kassel. There, next to the locomotive assembly area, *'Abteilung C'* (Section C) was housed in which gun and tank assembly was pooled under the leadership of *Betriebsdirektor* (plant manager) Hannover. The engineering section, led by Herr Ader, was to be found in the old administration building.

Abteilung C did not function particularly well, its output amounted to just 20 Panzer IIIs per month instead of the required 60 units; a fact that caused great concern in the *Heereswaffenamt* (Army Weapons Office) and the *Ministerium für Rüstung und Munition* (Ministry for Armaments and Munitions). One day, not surprisingly, the Henschel factory received a visit by a large investigatory commission under the leadership of General Philips and, notably, *'eisernen* Roland' (iron Roland) who was also the director general of the Deutschen Edelstahlwerke (stainless steel works). In Henschel GmbH's new administrative building, the discussions turned very stormy, particularly, as it was revealed, because the workforce of 2,000 – intended for *Abteilung C* – had in reality 'disappeared' into the locomotive construction part of the business. Nevertheless, Oskar R. Henschel invited the gentlemen of the commission to his house in order to pour oil on the troubled waters but was unable to silence accusations of culpability. Finally, as a precautionary measure, he appointed Herr von Heyking as a commissioner to oversee the production of the Tiger and believed that by doing this he had found a solution to the problem. That, however, was not the case.

The Minister of Armaments and War Production, Albert Speer, was convinced that the culprits were at the top level of management and sought to replace Oskar R. Henschel with Herr Dr. Stieler von Heydekampf, the chief of the Opel truck factory in Brandenburg/Havel. Henschel had to give up his post as the chief executive in Kassel and withdraw to Henschel's corporate administration offices in Berlin thus leaving his chair in the boardroom vacant for Dr. von Heydekampf.

In the few weeks that went by in the meantime, the first prototype of the Panzer VI was completed in the development facility during the tenure of Herr von Heyking and this was presented at the *Führer's* headquarters at the same time as the Porsche version of the Tiger tank. It was not a success. Porsche's men felt they had won the day as was evident by their singing in the evening.

However, Herr von Heyking's scheming had compromised his position in Kassel, and particularly with the two authorities in Berlin, and was thus presented with the opportunity of serving his Führer in a grey uniform by Herrn von Heydekampf. With this his interest in the Tiger project was came to an end.

At that time I was the director of car production at the Henschel Mittelfeld works [the Henschel factory in Kassel]. Herr von Heydekampf discussed with me the conditions that would have to be met, if – as was expected – Henschel was to be commissioned for the manufacture [of the Tiger]. Porsche's diesel-electric drive system might prove to be a failure and was therefore not chosen. Construction by Henschel largely depended on the experience gained with the WUG 6, the expertise of *Oberbaurat* Röver [chief advisor in the *OKH*] and *Ministerialrat* Kniekamp [a senior civil servant]. There was therefore reason to believe that the Henschel version would be selected.

Professor Porsche was – as always – so confident of himself and his connections with Hitler that he also thought he could get by without having to make contact with professional specialists.

The result of this misconception became obvious in Berka.

On a test drive on the Autobahn to Eisenach [on 29 October 1942] Porsche stepped on the accelerator and disappeared at full speed over the horizon. I was sitting on the Henschel Tiger and was strongly advised by Herr Kniekamp, who described how the Autobahn was the worst thing for the tracks, that only by driving slowly would we have the chance to keep up. We – and I still had no experience in this area – therefore drove slowly and were sweating with anxiety as we were left behind by all the other participants at the meeting as they drove towards the Porsche [tank] in a sizeable pack of cars. Herr von Heydekampf, when he lost sight of us, stayed behind and vigorously urged me to show that we could at least keep up. I wondered if Heydekampf and I were thinking the same thing: we wanted to win but as car makers neither of us understood anything about tracked vehicles so Kniekamp was probably correct. Anyway, I continued to drive slowly. Heydekampf was furious and drove on ahead to the Porsche vehicle.

Therefore alone, abandoned by everyone except Kniekamp, we drove through the area until the Wartburg was visible on the horizon. In front of us a column of smoke was recognizable. As we drove over a hill – which until then had obscured our view – there, suddenly, burning on the Autobahn and surrounded by a good 50 cars with officers and various other participants in the show, stood the Porsche vehicle. From his car, Kniekamp looked at me and grinned. We were given room to pass and continued to drive back alone on the opposite lane with spectators following on behind. On the last few kilometres before the exit [from the Autobahn] Kniekamp, winking and laughing, called for full speed ahead and we selected eighth gear and showed what we too were capable of.

The following day we had some trouble in open countryside. Heavy rain had fallen on the muddy soil and showed us where the limits of the specific ground pressure [exerted by the tank's tracks] of approximately 1kg / cm² lay. But the audience were experienced tank-men and just laughed. They were at home on such ground.

In the afternoon (31 October), a final discussion, led by *Oberst* Thomale, took place. Herr Professor Porsche was no longer present. His son took the floor and explained the advantages of his father's design in detail. Then, finally, Herr Dr. von Heydekampf was asked to offer his opinion of the Henschel design. However he pointed to me. Therefore, regarding Tomale's request, I had no other choice but to say – without preparation – that the vehicle could be built, driven, and likewise shoot and that at the moment no one knew what it would cost. And that was all I knew. Nevertheless it seemed to be enough because everyone laughed and I sat down again. To all intents and purposes that was the end of the inquiry.

While we were still sitting at the tables, *Oberst* Thomale was in a neighbouring room taking a telephone call to which he had been summoned by von Heydekampf. The latter returned from this with a bright red face and told me then that he had just spoken with Hitler and that the decision had been made in our favour.

The same night we went back to Kassel with General Philips, *Ministerialrat* Kniekamp and Herr Saur who, as Minister Speer's representative, began the task of getting the production underway. I called *Oberingenieur* (chief engineer) Sawatski and the leader of the preparatory work and said that they should immediately start thinking about everything that was necessary to begin the production of the series; the floor space required, the number of workers, machine tools, accommodation for the additional personnel and their social and medical support, post, and washing and sanitary needs too.

On the very same night we arrived in Kassel, a decisive conference began in which we addressed these questions. The meeting ended when the announcement of the *Führerbefehl* (a directive from Hitler) to deliver 12 tanks by August of the same year and more at a later time yet to be agreed upon. I was urged to give my opinion regarding the *Führerbefehl*. I said that everything humanly possible would be done and that in particular it was important to also obtain the necessary help. At this point in time, the development work was complete and the production of the series began. The factory was awarded the 'Silver Flag' as a model war company and, as far vehicle construction was concerned, Herr von Heydekampf became one of the 12 'wise men from the east' as one Speer's closest advisors and I myself remained his friend until his death on 25 January 1983.

On 26 May 1941, Hitler instructed Porsche and its competitor Henschel each to complete the construction of six heavy armoured fighting vehicles by summer 1942. In developmental terms this was a very tight time schedule, particularly since important design details were made in the intervening period. For example, the calibre of the main gun was changed from 7.5cm to 8.8cm. From the end of 1942, the number produced could then be gradually increased. (Pertuss)

It is generally well known that neither the *Wehrmacht* – that is to say the *Panzertruppe* (armour branch) – nor the *Heereswaffenamt*, had themselves explicitly raised the issue of the development or even the production of a heavily armoured tank. On the contrary, the prevailing opinion at the time was that it would be more advantageous to deploy highly mobile tanks to carry out wide-ranging movements in order to be able to engage the enemy in its flanks and rear areas. Furthermore, tank technology was still in its infancy and this was particularly true for their propulsion units and weaponry. Quite simply, there were no propulsion units with the power capable driving vehicles beyond of a weight of 30 tons. As far as guns were concerned, the calibre of the *Pak* (anti-tank) weapons (at 3.7 cm and 5 cm) was greater than those of the first tanks. In other words the installation of large-calibre tank guns was also still at an early stage of development. In terms of protection a similar situation prevailed. The tanks at that time – which weighed 20 tons or just over – had comparatively light armour and this was considered to be sufficient even into the first years of the war. This view changed after the evaluation of the heavy French tanks and particularly so after the appearance of the Soviet T-34. These tanks had, for that time, a remarkably well-rounded fighting capacity with strong, sloping front armour and a relatively large cannon of 76 mm calibre. From an account (The Development of the Vehicles Tiger E and B) written on 6 February 1945 by Herr Ader (Henschel's chief design engineer for the later Tigers) it is evident that although the initial 'construction tasks' were indeed awarded to Henschel (and other companies) in 1937, they were by no means provided with a definite time limit to deliver experimental vehicles for appraisal. Only the '*Großtraktor*' (the 'large tractor') and '*Neubaufahrzeug*' ('new construction vehicle') designs pointed in this direction. ['*Großtraktor*' and '*Neubaufahrzeug*' were the cover names for early proto-type models of heavy tank designs that were forbidden by the Treaty of Versailles.] However these still involved models well below 25 tons and stemmed from the tactically erroneous concept of developing heavily armed vehicles specially for accompanying infantry. Also, with these vehicles, moderate manoeuvrability was acceptable. They can therefore – in contradiction to claims presented in non-academic literature – by no means be considered as the precursors to the Tiger. These vehicles were also subject to scrutiny in Kazan through the German-Russian cooperation agreement and led to, among other things, the Soviet T-28 (medium) and T-34 (heavy) tank series. Furthermore, it should be added that the findings of the large-scale test exercises in Munster/Bergen during 1935, demanded that the focus should be on medium-weight armoured fighting vehicles.

Also, the 'breakthrough vehicles' ordered at the start of 1937 were nothing more than further derivatives of the *Pz.Kpfw. IV*. Originally, it was the tactical and technical requirements of the *VK. 30.01* (the Henschel and Porsche variant) that were the stepping stone to the *VK 36.01 (H)* and the *VK 45.01 (H)* and *(P)*. [In these designations, *VK* (*Voll Ketten*) indicates a fully tracked vehicle while the first two numerals indicate the weight in tons and the second pair of numerals the prototype version. The letter in brackets defines the manufacturer, for example '*(P)*' indicates that the vehicle was produced by the Porsche factory.]

With the beginning of *Operation Barbarossa* German tanks (Panzer II-IV), which employed superior tactics, encountered better armed and better protected enemy tanks in the form of the Soviet T-34 and KV-1 and 2 and it was suddenly clear to the German side that action had to be taken. This did not happen because previous measures had been completely misguided but because the nature of the threat had significantly changed – a situation that is entirely normal in war. The *OKW* (*Oberkom-mando der Wehrmacht*/Supreme Command of the Armed Forces) of course reproached the intelligence services for having conspicuously failed to highlight this important aspect of the equipping of the Red Army in good time.

Such was the background against which this brutal pressure of time to produce something out of almost nothing suddenly appeared. And what was created within a few months – despite all the shortages and justified criticism – in the form of the *Pz.Kpfw.* Tiger, was not only without precedence but also outstanding.

Building the thick-walled hull was the easiest problem to solve. Furthermore, the experiences gained during the development of large-calibre naval and anti-aircraft guns were able to be transferred without delay. The greatest challenges lay mostly in the areas of engine and transmission technology and the development of the running gear, suspension and braking system. Despite its controllable elements, the construction work on the gun turret (which included the installation of the drive mechanism, aiming devices, mounting brackets, armaments and storage area) simply took time. The fact that barely half a year passed between the issue of a formal order to build the tank (*Wa A*) by the *OKH* (*Oberkommando des Heeres*/ Supreme High Command of the German Army), which was received by Henschel on 21 October 1941, and the demonstration of the first vehicle is, by today's standards, simply incredible. This is especially so because the order – in the section relating to 'technical requirements' – was anything but descriptive and omitted a whole series of data – a problem that was left for Henschel to overcome. Nowadays, if the procurement of a major weapons system was conducted in such an amateurish manner, those responsible would find themselves in prison for the misappropriation of funds not to mention the circumvention of statutory legal requirements. This was also the reason why a *Führerbefehl* was obtained.

Insightful descriptions, given on 6 February 1945, can be found in Herr Erwin Aders' dossier:

(...) The heavy VK 36.01 – for which no battle-worthy turret had yet been developed – was still not at the trial stage.

Even so, important assembly teams were borrowed for the project which began at a discussion at the *Heereswaffenamt* when a verbal order was placed on 1 July 1941. With this, the basis of the design of the Tiger E – known at the time as the VK 45.01 – was set down: steering mechanism, final drive, running gear, tracks and driving pinions.

Three weeks after the start of the design work, the steel mills were informed of the programme for the production of the armoured sheet metal for the tanks' hulls; after two months, on 1 September 1941, they had the workshop drawings for the most important armour plates in their hands.

The task was made more difficult to an extraordinary extent by special demands for which solutions first had to be found; the ability to pass through stretches of water up to 4.5m deep was stipulated; the tracks were to be protected against shellfire by an armoured apron that could be lifted or lowered when driving on even ground.

After the initial development of the complete design of the vehicle, the total weight and the position of the centre of gravity was determined and it was obvious that the full rubber rings – which incidentally were still under development – that were planned for fitting onto the running wheels were not up to the task of bearing the continuous load of the expected 58 tons. It was therefore necessary to increase the number of rubber rings on each (suspension) wheel from two to three and for this too a design solution had to be found.

At around the middle of the year 1941, the number of vehicles to be constructed in the first series was still set at 60 and the building material for 100 procured (the H&S factory pressed for this because of the small scale of the order). In the course of a few months the requirement for vehicles quickly grew into the hundreds. Although there was only one vehicle in existence that had been test-driven, all the construction material, all the means of production for a series-run of eventually 1,300 pieces and additional replacement parts, were ordered. For the Tiger E, the following components to be engineered from scratch:

- watertight engine compartment cover
- an exhaust pipe cooling system that also cooled the transmission
- a turret drive link from the main drive-shaft train
- a fuel system which included four containers, two of which were set up for submersion to a depth of 4.5 metres
- a demountable air-intake pipe for use when submerged
- an arrangement of shock absorbers and stops for the front and rear wheel cranks
- storage for 92 rounds of 8.8cm shells (this had to be redesigned because of the provision of faulty documentation)
- supports for accessories and equipment inside and out

- radios with antennae assembly (later, a special version was produced for the command vehicle)
- additional dust filters for desert use
- close-combat, anti-personnel mines on the roof
- oil-operated lifting and lowering installation with control device and high-pressure oil-pump for the armoured side-aprons
- bilge pump installation for use when submerged
- additional gear for the ventilation system (after the production of the 250th vehicle because conformity with the Panther engine was required).

Components were also ordered from other companies:

- engine (Maybach-Motorenbau)
- transmission OG 40 12 16 (Maybach-Motorenbau)
- tracks (Ritscher-Moorburg)
- brakes (Südd. Argus Werke)
- armoured turret and gun (Friedrich Krupp)
- machine gun bezel (Daimler Benz AG)
- driver's vision slide (Alkett-Berlin)
- rubber-sprung steel wheels (Deutsche Eisen-Werke)

With the existing designers and draughtsmen, whose numbers were supplemented by the transfer of personnel from the locomotive and car-building departments of H & S and by the appointment of conscripted personnel, the work could be speeded up so that the first operationally ready production vehicles could be presented and demonstrated at the headquarters on 20 April 1942. The efforts made by the construction material procurement staff and the workshops, by the pattern shop to the machining department – and to acknowledge the personal sacrifices of the engineers and workers – would provide material for a small book. The last days and nights before loading the vehicles were spent in constant work during which the fitters, foremen and engineers hardly got a night's rest. This achievement – and the cooperation between design engineers, procurement and production personnel – is unique and difficult to repeat or surpass. It need hardly be mentioned that with the rushed nature of the design work, economical production techniques did not come into consideration. If – so to speak 'at the drop of a hat' – the production of a series was achieved after relatively unimportant interruptions for modifications, then this can be attributed to the prudent cooperation of the participating authorities. (...) For uninterrupted mass production, an in-depth revision of the manufacturing processes – lasting 24 to 30 months – would have been necessary.

The foregoing descriptions are, in part, published in *Tiger I* by T. Jentz but until now have not been available in German. In his memoirs, Aders impressively describes the frantic action on Hitler's birthday (20 April). Aders' recollections are to be found in a volume about the Tiger tank by Spielberger – published by the Motorbuch-Verlag in 1977 – and therefore do not need to be repeated here.

The Difficult Start to Production

The renovation of production facilities and the peripheral infrastructure required a considerable effort because Henschel und Sohn in Kassel was an armaments company already working at full capacity and this is vividly described by Herr Pertuss in his memoirs:

Because the start of production required the creation of space, the construction of tanks was transferred from Holländischen Platz to Werk Mittelfeld where, particularly in *Halle 3*, there were a sufficient number of cranes with the required lifting capacity on hand. First of all, locomotive construction had to be cleared from *Halle 3* without disrupting their production (which also had a high degree of priority). At Mittelfeld, the plant necessary for the construction of cars was already in place and, more importantly, an excellent, skilled workforce was available. Truck production had to give way and was therefore transferred to the Saurer factory in Vienna which was owned and led by its proprietor and director, Gaston Radio de Radiis. However this measure was not welcomed by the army which favoured Henschel above Saurer trucks.

Organization Todt [a civil and military engineering group] built a town of barracks within just eight days in the vicinity of Wilhelmsthal where we then found our running-in area. Within three weeks 3,000 men arrived. At first these were Germans who were mostly barbers, bakers, confectioners, commercial travellers and the like. There were also skilled metal-workers who were understandably 'overjoyed' to be torn away from their activities, professions and families. Before they landed up with us they had already sprouted substantial beards. However,

in the course of time we had to let them go, particularly because of the '*Heldenklau*' ['snatching of heroes'] which transferred men to the *Wehrmacht* because the war still was not nearing its conclusion. They were continuously replaced by foreigners – Ukrainians, Poles, Yugoslavians, Dutch, and later '*Imis*' – so that we eventually had a universal European workforce which was made all the more colourful by French and Russian prisoners of war although these were not permitted to get involved with armaments.*

The establishment of *Halle 3* took place at breakneck speed. An assembly line was built to enable the work to be conducted in a continuous cycle. Around 1,000 machine tools were installed about 10% of which were newly developed: for example, the centring-machine for the blanks of the chain tensioner cranks, a four-spindle horizontal boring machine for the suspension arms of the running gear and much more including the turning lathe with which the turret bearing on the hull could be accurately machined.

It would be going too far to report here in detail the technical achievements of the department led by Post, the engineer.

From today's perspective, it seems almost impossible to recall what was achieved during the extremely short start-up time: clearing a production area; not restricting the output to single units; establishing a new production line; acquiring a workforce, instructing them, teaching them; procuring the necessary construction materials and parts in good time; purchasing and installing machine tools – though some of these had been confiscated. We built a hut in *Halle 3* where we set up our provisional office, on site.

Henschel und Sohn was originally a foundry that had been established in 1810. It developed into a large locomotive construction company in Kassel and consisted of three core factories or *Werke*. *Werk 3* was conveniently located on the railway line and, in the 1930s, five additional construction halls were added to it (see below).

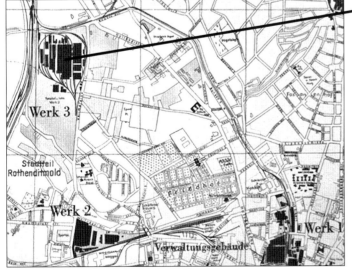

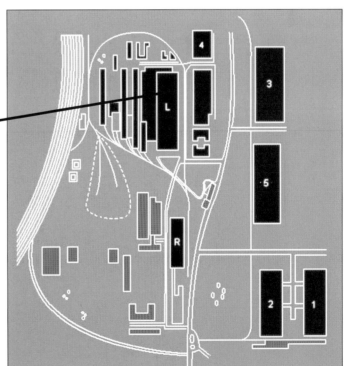

Note: '*Zwangsarbeiter*' (forced labourers) were used in the Henschel factories and these should not be confused with the '*Fremdarbeitern*' (foreign workers) who were hired in the German occupied zones. '*Imis*' were ethnic German refugees from areas near the front and therefore from endangered areas.

Even today it seems inconceivable that one could make do with just 20 hours sleep each month but then we had to adhere to the requested delivery dates. Our legs were so swollen [with standing for long periods] that 'walking' was possible only with difficulty. We were taken home but hardly had the strength to be able to get out of the bath tub and at last fall into bed. That time was the actually the greatest physical effort of my life.

When, on the day of the deadline, Herr Saur and his crew – under the leadership of Herr von Heydekampf – appeared in *Halle 3* and saw the number of vehicles standing there in accordance with the *Führerbefehl*, he was so ecstatic that he grabbed the telephone right there and then and made a *Staatsgespräch* to Rastenburg – a call that took precedence over all other calls on the line – to report the success. I was as good as finished but unfortunately the Tigers were not. They still had to be run-in then tested and officially accepted. It then took some time before they were loaded for delivery.

Herr Köhler was the production engineer for the running-in department of car manufacturing. Logically, after the transfer of car manufacturing to Vienna, the responsibility for running-in the tanks fell to him. The vehicles, without turrets but with cast iron rings of the same weight, were driven in open countryside and on streets. That was necessary because one was often forced to remedy errors after the running-in procedure and this saved removing the turret. The run-in vehicle then reached its final stage of construction when the turret, together with the main gun and machine gun, was installed. The fitting out was completed and the vehicle – washed when it returned from the factory site – received its camouflage. The vehicles' acceptance by the army was under the control of *Hauptmann* Günter – known as the 'tea merchant' in the firm – who then then stamped 'dkr' on the hull as a visible sign of acceptance.

The drawings received by the workshop were never finally revised so that not a single measurement in them agreed; in fact it had even been forgotten to draw complete parts. This situation arose as a result of a lack of time. I wouldn't like to say today how many components had to be repeatedly recrafted until they finally fitted and functioned properly at the beginning of production. I only remember that, later, we faced the same catastrophic situation when we were supposed to build the Königstiger as well as the Panther, which had been developed by MAN [*Maschinenfabrik Augsburg-Nürnberg AG*].

There was nothing we could do but have the necessary corrections to the drawings made by our foremen and use these documents to the end. The official drawings from the design office remained uncorrected, and wrong, until the last of the series was produced. They were seized in this condition by the US armed forces.

Halle 3 (top right) was already equipped with crane installations that had been used in the construction of locomotives. These were used to heave the tank hulls onto the assembly line. A proving ground was prepared in Wilhelmsthal. The pictures (centre and bottom) respectively show a tank chassis on a 40° slope and the workers' accommodation with a queue for food which is not overseen by a guard; evidently these are not forced labour. (Pertuss)

Tiger production itself took place in several phases (so-called 'Takte'), which corresponded logically with the manufacture of parts or fitting out as close as possible to the *Taktstraße* (production line) itself. Most of the components, for example the hull and certain assemblies such as the engine, were delivered in a pre-finished state and were then completed or prepared for installation.

In *Takt 1* (the first stage of the assembly line) the hull casings that had been delivered (with predrilled holes) were hoisted from the wagons and manoeuvred for attachment to a six-spindled drilling machine.

In neighbouring *Takt 2*, the lateral running gear openings (for the torsion bars and retaining bolts) were precision machined.

In *Takt 3*, a total of three four-spindle drilling stands were available for precision drilling the final drive and bogie wheel spindle apertures.

A drilling stand in *Takt 4* precision machined the turret turning assembly opening as well as the floor opening. Then the housings were laid one after the other onto the manoeuvering frame where parts and components were mounted in the hull housing in three processing operations.

Next, in *Takt 5*, the gear shaft, turret rotation gear, slip-ring assembly, steering assembly and gearbox were fitted together with the ball-mount for the machine gun. Following this the ammunition containers, chain tensioner,

some of the [storage] tanks, ventilation fans and coolers were installed. At the same time linkage rods, brackets and the tank's wiring system were installed.

In *Takt 6*, after applying paint to the sides of the hull, the engine was mounted and all the components of the running gear, brake assemblies and the remaining [storage] tanks installed.

Takt 7 was the part of *Halle 3* where the vehicle was filled with oil, fluids and fuel and the functional testing of the automotive parts was carried out before test-driving the vehicle according to a standard schedule. Part of this schedule was to simulate the weight of the turret by mounting iron rings to the turret slewing ring. This had the advantage that any deficiencies that were detected could then easily be solved [because of easy access to the interior of the hull].

Back once more in *Halle 3*, in *Takt 8*, the hull was fitted with a previously fully equipped turret and its switching-circuitry connections made.

In *Takt 9*, the exterior paint, and sometimes also Zimmerit, was applied. [Zimmerit was a coating designed to prevent the attachment of magnetic mines to the hull of the tank.]

Finally, in *Takt 10*, the vehicle was formally accepted by the *Waffenamt* and loaded onto rail trucks together with ancillary equipment (tools and such like).

Some of the machinery (such as the milling machines in this photograph) had been dismantled in tank factories in France and moved to Kassel. The picture also demonstrates that women also worked in the Henschel factories. (Pertuss, on the following pages photos are also courtesy of Pertuss.)

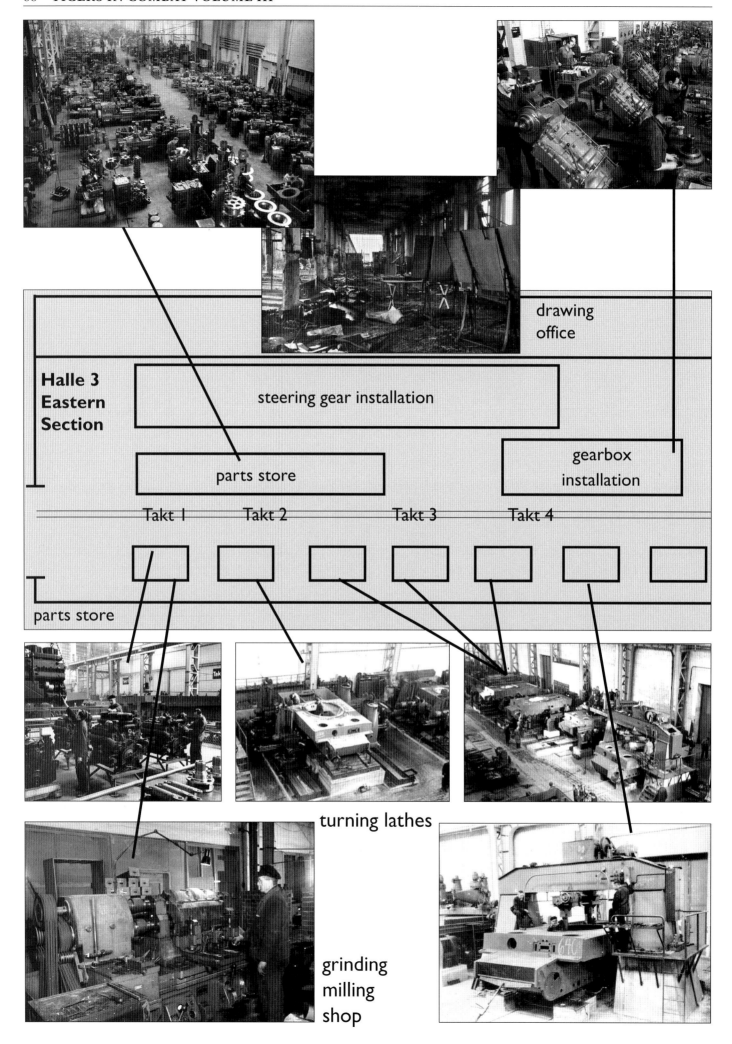

**Halle 3
Eastern
Section**

drawing
office

steering gear installation

parts store

gearbox
installation

Takt 1   Takt 2   Takt 3   Takt 4

parts store

turning lathes

grinding
milling
shop

management

| gear-box inspec-tion | test stands | mechanical department | | test drive >>> |

	Takt 5	Takt 6	Takt 7

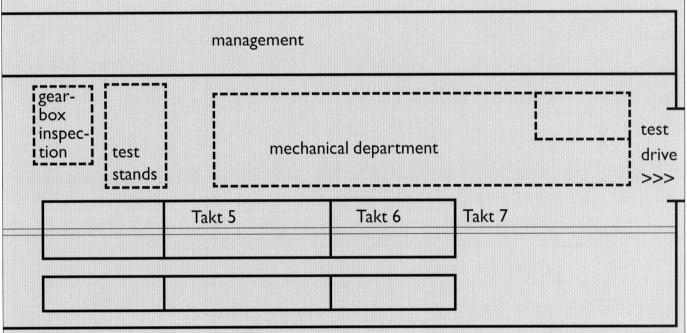

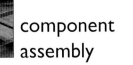

component parts
assembly store

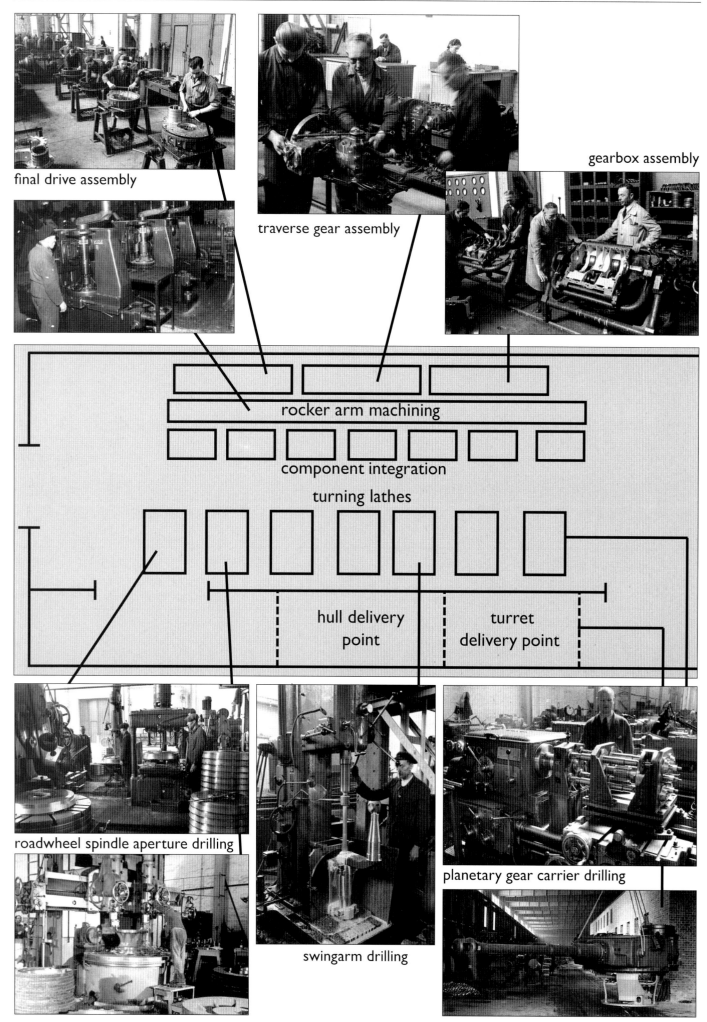

final drive assembly

traverse gear assembly

gearbox assembly

rocker arm machining

component integration

turning lathes

hull delivery
point

turret
delivery point

roadwheel spindle aperture drilling

swingarm drilling

planetary gear carrier drilling

drive sprocket milling

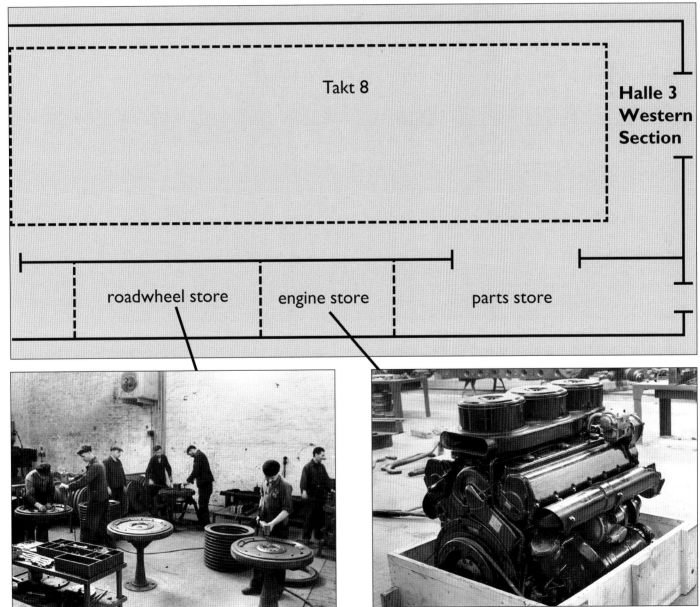

Takt 8

Halle 3 Western Section

roadwheel store | engine store | parts store

During the production of the series a high degree of flexibility was required by the engineers and works management staff because hundreds of technical changes and version details and modifications arising from user experience and the demands of the troop units had to be taken into consideration. The following are a few examples taken from Pertuss' account:

During production we frequently had to react rapidly to the experiences and wishes of the troop units. One day, Herr Kniekamp turned up in Kassel and reported that the Russians were using limpet mines; during close quarters combat they attached them to the sides or back of the vehicles. The limpet mines were extremely dangerous to the tanks and to render them ineffective the tank walls were to be coated with a compound, applied as thickly as possible, and ridged too. By this means the magnets that held the explosive would not have sufficient loading capacity to stick to the tank. In the afternoon, our purchasing department succeeded – in a telephone call to IG-Farben – in settling on a material that was physically suitable, in stock and available at short notice. Not only did it have to be quick drying, it also had to dry stone-hard. After just two days we had received the first barrels of Nitro-Spachtel [a filler paste] on the premises. With a comb-spreader we made ourselves from thin metal, the first trial was made with great success. After just three hours the substance had hardened and could take the camouflage paint. On the first day after the receipt of the delivery, the tanks coming off the production line had been provided with this protective layer.

After the collapse [of Germany] I was particularly amused by the interest shown in this substance by the English military – they were like the devil after a soul. They used every means possible to suss out what sort of substance it was.

Another example that comes to mind is the introduction of steel bands in place of the rubber tyres on the tank wheels. The troops – and we ourselves – had established that tyres made of rubber running inside the tanks' tracks quickly frayed. For example, when the vehicle turned on the spot or on sand, gravel or stones or, in winter, on compressed snow, the free-play in the tracks became too small and the tension in the tracks therefore too high. The result was that the tyres wore out more quickly.

One day Herr Krömer – the official in charge of the Tiger at the Ministry of Munitions – happily reported that the Russians were, in terms of materials, finished. They had run out of rubber. Their T-34s were already running on steel while we could still use rubber on steel. He then went on to say that one of these T-34s had been captured entirely intact and was therefore available for inspection. This tank could also be tested because it was capable of being driven. I made use of this offer and discovered that he was correct – steel did indeed run on steel. But why? I immediately had one of the track bogie wheels removed and saw that the steel ring on it had a T-shaped cross-section with grooves on both sides of the vertical faces in which rubber rings were installed,

the front surfaces of which were fixed to the two wheel discs…but why? We began to drive. After about a week, we discovered that the track lasted twice as long as rubber on steel. I was not clear why this should be. A repeat of the test yielded the same result. It therefore seemed worthwhile to simply copy this design. In two or three weeks, our purchasing department succeeded in having similarly profiled bogie-wheel components milled. With this, one of the Tiger's most serious teething problems had been eliminated.

Our relationship with the Berlin authorities and also with *Heereswaffenamt* and *Ministerium Speer* [Speer was at this point in time the minister for armaments and munitions] was polite and correct all the time. However, there were individual events that surprized us. For example, one day Cösitz in Saxony was bombed and our supplier of chrome leather was out of action. Chrome leather was specified for the seats in the Tiger. Our purchasing office was unable to find a second supplier and enquiries made to the *Ministerium* were unsuccessful. At first I did not consider this to be a tragedy; Henschel still had at its disposal a large stock imitation leather of peacetime quality from the time we made cars and, as experience had already shown that it certainly lasted well when used in trucks, I took it that in the absence of anything else, it would have to suffice. However, our army acceptance inspector told me point blank, '*Njet!*' Phone calls to *In. 6* [*Inspection des Kraftfahrwesens*/motor vehicle inspection office] were without success. No one in the *Heereswaffenamt* dared make a decision. The question as to whether we should end Tiger production because we were now unable to obtain chrome leather and the crews could not be reasonably expected to sit on imitation leather – although we knew the Russians sat on ammunition boxes in their T-34s – made no impression. In the meantime, a large number of tanks which had not yet been approved stood ready for loading.

Hauptmann Günter, our 'tea merchant', shook his head like a stubborn mule. He wasn't interested in any explanations, nor in the progress of events on the front line, and insisted on his 'bond' just like the creditor in the Merchant of Venice. As a final resort, after more than eight days pointless negotiation, it occurred to me to phone Minister Speer personally. However, I only managed to reach Herr Saur to whom the matter explained itself and who promised that a decision would soon follow. In just half an hour he called back and said that of course the Tigers should be accepted and that we – in case *In. 6* still continued to refuse – should send the tanks without them being officially accepted. If this happened, he said, the whole '*Heeresabnahme*' ('army acceptance') section would be superfluous and handed over for service on the front line and that I should make this clear to their lordships!

I then told Herr *Hauptman* Günter this and, as expected, this triggered a whirlwind of enthusiasm. His men sprang onto the finished vehicles which were all accepted that very day. Our financial office was also delighted by this turn of events; *In. 6* now received the invoices and then the acceptance certificates and at last these could be submitted to the authorities.

Of course Kassel, which had an array of armament factories since 1942, increasingly became a target for enemy air attacks. The first significant one took place on the night of 28 August 1942. The largest 35 of these are noted in two record sheets (see photograph below) which list the number of participating aircraft, the tonnage of bombs dropped, the target area and the number of aircraft lost. There were also numerous attacks by fighter-bombers which were directed essentially against the western zone of the railway station.

"RAID DATA SHEETS."
(EX. 'HARRIS' BLUE BOOKS: DAMAGE DIAGRAMS.)
FOR
KASSEL.

SHEET Nº 1
Nº OF SHEETS 2

BOMBER COMMAND				8TH USAAF.			
RAID DATE	AIRCRAFT ATTACKING	TONS CLAIMED	OBJECTIVE	RAID DATE	AIRCRAFT ATTACKING	TONS CLAIMED	OBJECTIVE
1942				1943			
27/28-8	256	563	TOWN AREA	28-7	54	129	FIESELER BETTENHAUSEN
1943				30-7	94	222	" "
3/4-10	501	1616	" "	30-7	37	87	FIESELER WALDAU.
22/23-10	486	1824	" "	30-7	3	7	TOWN AREA.
26/27-11	1	5	" "	1944			
1944				19-4	106	246	KASSEL/WALDAU
18/19-3 to 15/16-10	119	145	" "	19-4	51	121	"/BETTENHAUSEN/ -/ALTENBAUNA
1945				19-4	52	114	-/ALTENBAUNA
6/7-1 to 2/3-3	170	193	" "	22-9	602	1667	HENSCHEL AFV & M.T. FACTORY.
8/9-3	268	1142	" "	27-9	248	705	" " "
16/17-3 to 20/21-3	36	29	" "	28-9	138	385	HENSCHEL TANK FACTORY.
				28-9	104	315	HENSCHEL AFV & M.T. FACTORY.
				2-10	106	258	BETTENHAUSEN ORDNANCE DEPOT.
				2-10	551	1370	HENSCHEL AFV & M.T. FACTORY.
				7-10	67	188	ALTENBAUNA AERO-ENGINE FACTORY.
NUMBER OF AIRCRAFT MISSING FROM R.A.F ATTACKS -101				NUMBER OF AIRCRAFT MISSING FROM 8 U.S.A.A.F. ATTACKS - see page 2 J.S			

"RAID DATA SHEETS."
(EX. 'HARRIS' BLUE BOOKS: DAMAGE DIAGRAMS.)
FOR
KASSEL.
CONTINUED

SHEET Nº 2
Nº OF SHEETS 2

BOMBER COMMAND				8TH USAAF.			
RAID DATE	AIRCRAFT ATTACKING	TONS CLAIMED	OBJECTIVE	RAID DATE	AIRCRAFT ATTACKING	TONS CLAIMED	OBJECTIVE
				1944 CONTINUED			
				7-10	153	450	HENSCHEL TANK FACTORY
				18-10	297	799	" "
				4-12	221	615	M/YD.
				15-12	304	898	HENSCHEL LOCOMOTIVE WORKS.
				30-12	319	889	M/YD.
				1945			
				1-1	309	708	"
				29-1	71	192	HENSCHEL AFV & M.T. PLANT.
				29-1	176	512	M/YD.
				28-2	360	1217	"
				9-3	80	158	STATE RAILWAY REPAIR SHOPS.
				9-3	110	314	HENSCHEL LOCOMOTIVE WORKS.
				9-3	76	162	M/YD.
				9-3	64	183	HENSCHEL AFV & M.T. WORKS.
NUMBER OF AIRCRAFT MISSING FROM R.A.F ATTACKS - 1				NUMBER OF AIRCRAFT MISSING FROM 8 U.S.A.A.F. ATTACKS - 37.			

Regarding these attacks, Herr Pertuss recalls:

As far as I can recall, Kassel had to endure a total of 120 bombing attacks the aim of which was also to strike at the production of the Tiger. They did not succeed. A few of the air strikes that hit Werk Mittelfeld were effective to a limited extent. But I also know for certain that just three to five hours – at the most – after such an attack, production was up and running and most of the worst of the damage had been repaired. During the last winter of the war, we had hardly any roofs left and the walls of the workshops were only partly intact. But the steel frames of the workshops survived and were still able to support the cranes without which it would have been a bit awkward. We learned how to endure the cold and the snow from our Russian personnel. They each organized for themselves a metal pot, bucket or barrel and knocked holes in the sides of them. They gathered coke from the work's foundry and in this way boiled water in containers placed on top. For one thing, this coke-oven warmed their backs and for another thing, after using their hands to splash ice-cold water onto the steel on the lathes to keep it cool, they would immediately plunge them into the hot water on their makeshift oven. This alternating bathing in hot and cold water was the 'medicine' that enabled them to continue working. Necessity is the mother of invention. None of the air attacks – even those carpet bombing raids that were exactly on target – distracted us from our task. Not a single employee, nor foreign worker, perished in these attacks.

The last Königstiger was collected by *Major* Scultetus and his men from Padderborn. The Americans were already in Wildungen. We only had shipping tracks – there were no battle tracks left. There was little fuel and as far as shells were concerned, we had only 'Beschussmunition', that is to say *Patronenmunition* [with the propellant and shell as a single item] which was used only for testing finished gun barrels – amongst other things we also built 8.8 cm anti-aircraft and anti-tank guns. For reasons of fuel economy, the tanks had for some time been run-in using bottled gas. Eight gas containers were sufficient for one test drive.

The degree of destruction during the air attacks varied. This picture below shows the gear-manufacturing area in the old part of the hall areas after being hit on 28 September 1944. (Henschel Museum)

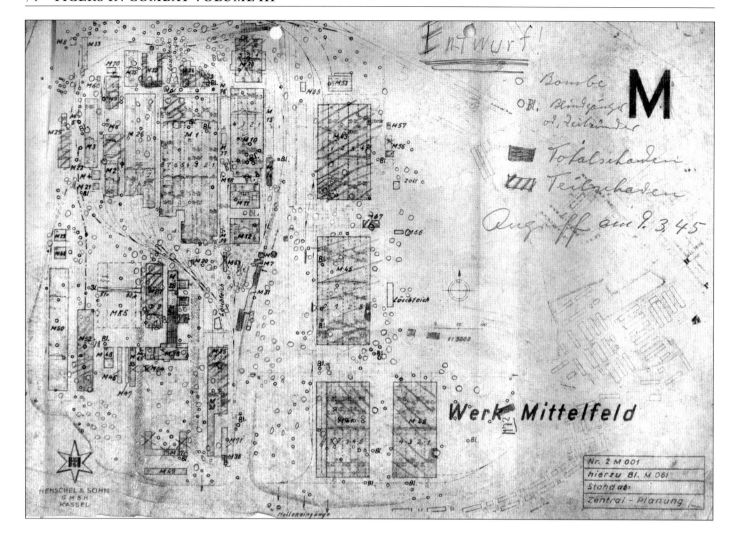

After devastating attacks, such as the one shown above in a contemporary sketch from 9 February 1945, a significant amount of clearing up and reconstruction work was required. The picture to the left shows the target map of the attack on 7 November 1944 with the *Halle 3* still completely intact. (NARA)

The picture below, taken on 2 October 1944, shows the extensive damage to *Halle 2*. (Henschel Museum)

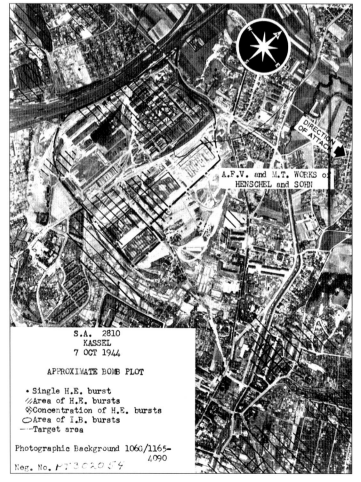

Before the finishing work was completed, the acceptance test-drive of the hull was conducted using bottled gas for reasons of fuel economy. (photos: Pertuss)

At the railway sidings inside the construction area, the tanks that had been accepted were loaded onto rail trucks. Usually they were then transported to the dispatch depot in Burg (near Magdeburg).

Delivery directly from the factory to the troop units generally did not take place. 'Roll outs' such as the one shown in the picture to the right (taken during the summer of 1943) were only conducted for propaganda reasons.

The Tiger manufacturing plant was the destination for many prominent figures. Here we see the *Generalinspekteur der Panzertruppen*, Heinz Guderian, making a courtesy call...

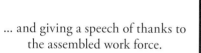

... and giving a speech of thanks to the assembled work force.

On the *Führer's* birthday in 1944, *SS-Hauptsturmführer* Michael Wittmann, a battle proven *Kompanieführer* (company leader), visits the Henschel factory to thank the workforce for their efforts in the production of these outstanding armoured fighting vehicles. The gentleman wearing the hat (on the extreme right of the picture) is Chief Designer Erwin Aders

2 Training

In-depth training forms the basis of the combat effectiveness of units (and individual crews). There exists in the literature an abundance of proof that the German Panzer units, though outnumbered, were frequently superior at a tactical leadership level or in local duels because of their high level of training. This applied to both the 'manual' crew training and their mastery of the weapons systems as well as to the professional skills of the leaders at all levels.

The training of crews – a focal point of this documentation – will be considered in detail. However, for the sake of completeness, the training of the leaders should be described briefly, too.

Besides the obligatory advanced training in the individual units, such training was essentially through courses delivered at officer/NCO schools.

Leadership Training

In contrast to the training of troops – this was the responsibility of the unit leaders at *Kompanie* and *Batterie* level – leadership training took place at courses either at brigade level (or higher) or in special schools for non-commissioned and commissioned officers. Training specific to the branch of the service of the officer cadets generally took place alongside NCO candidates. This had great advantages in terms of unity and strengthening the *esprit de corps*.

Army schools for non-commissioned officers from particular branches of the service were in existence from 1 March 1940. Those of the motorised troops originated at the barracks at Putlos, among others, with a *Kompanie* for tank personnel. Previously there were general schools, that is to say ones that covered all branches of the army but with a focus on the infantry. On 16 August 1942, the armoured section at Putlos was restructured and transferred to the *Heeresunteroffizierschule (Panzer)* (*HUS*/ Army School for NCOs) for motorized units at Eisenach. From 1 November 1943, the *HUS (Panzer)* at Eisenach consisted of three training companies for NCO candidates and one training company for officer candidates. Previously, officer candidates had been trained at troop training units. Later, *HUS* acquired a *Stab (Gruppe Führer)* and a *Stabskompanie*. Accommodation was in the Prittwitz-Kaserne. In addition, in autumn 1942, *Feld-Unteroffizierschulen* (schools for NCOs) for the separate branches of the army were established in order to prepare the way for privates and NCOs of the reserve to enter into service as NCOs on active duty. For this, a minimum service period of one-and-a-half years was stipulated. An equivalent school for mobilized troops – from April 1943 for the tank personnel – was established in the former Polish War Academy in Rembertow, close to Warsaw, in September 1942.

From 23 December 1942, the three previous officer-candidate courses for mobilized troops were consolidated in the officer candidate school for motorized troops in Zossen. This was later renamed *Schule für Fahnenjunker der Panzertruppen* (Officer Cadet School for Armoured Units). From March 1944, because of the greater number of applicants for the armoured units – a consequence of the educational pre-requisite of completion of the *Abitur* having been withdrawn – four officer cadet schools in Groß-Born, and later in Wischau, Ohrdruf, Könbrück and Bamberg, and two senior officer cadet schools (in Groß-Glienecke and Wischau) were established. As a result of the territorial losses during 1944/45, the schools were transferred, in part, to other locations. For example, the *HUS* was relocated to Erlangen. The officer cadets were then taught the tactical elements of the course in the *Kriegsschulen* (military academies).

Future gunnery instructors (a *Feldwebel* in each company or instructors at the training schools) were trained at the gunnery school for tank personnel in Putlos.

In 1940, the separation of maintenance training from the army training schools was seen as problematic. This was to some extent quickly corrected when special technical courses – which soon expanded to three teaching groups – were set up at the *Panzertruppenschule* (armoured troops training school) in Wünsdorf. As a consequence of this, from April 1943, all armour repair services were reassigned to the armoured units and were no longer ranked among the *Versorgungstruppen* (supply troops). The training of *Panzerwarte* for the repair and maintenance detachments of the armoured companies took place in the technical teaching groups within the tank-training courses. Craftsmen for the newly established repair and maintenance detachments of the armoured units were already qualified vehicle technicians and trained in the manufacturer's designated repair works in Vienna. However, in the last phase of the war these craftsmen were trained in the appropriate manufacturing plant which for Tiger tanks was the Henschel factory in Kassel. For tank repair and maintenance personnel of the *Werkstattkompanien* (workshop companies), specific training courses were run in Coesfeld, Krems, Kressborn and Kuttenberg.

A *Kompanieführerschule* (company-leader school) was established in Versailles for prospective company chiefs and a school for unit commanders was set up in Paris. In the early part of 1944, these were transferred to the newly established tank-training unit at Bergen.

The *Panzer-Ersatz-Abteilung 500* (a replacement unit) was first set up at the end of 1942, initially at Putlos, before being moved to Paderborn. (Strenge)

The Panzer gunnery school was located in Putlos. It was here that future gunnery instructors and tank commanders were trained; at first on *Pz.Kpfw. III* and *IVs* and later on the type in which they were destined to serve. (Strenge)

The first commander of *Pz.Ers.Abt. 500* was *Hauptmann* Hannibal von Lüttichau, an experienced frontline company commander with *Panzerregiment 31*. He was later to become the commander of *s.Pz.Abt. 509*.

Tank Courses at Paderborn

As a result of the expansion of the army in general and the armoured units in particular, the capacity of *Panzertruppenschule I Wünsdorf* was predictably exceeded when the new Panther and Tiger armoured fighting vehicles were introduced. Given this situation, tank-training courses for Panther crews were established in Erlangen and for Tiger soldiers in Paderborn. This was preceded on 20 December 1942 by the formation of *Panzer-Ersatz-Abteilung 500* in Putlos, the location of the gunnery school for the armoured troop units. From the very beginning, the lack of suitable terrain for thorough combat training proved to be something of a problem. Also, the distance from the factory support headquarters, for example in Kassel, was considerable. For these reasons, the commander of the *Abteilung*, *Hauptmann* Hannibal von Lüttichau, requested relocation to Paderborn which took place on 22 February 1943. The *Abteilung* was accommodated in the barracks in Driburger Straße, the former home of *Panzerregiment 11*. Gunnery and combat training could then take place either on the local exercise area, '*Auf der Lieth*', or on the neighbouring exercise area at Senne (Sennelager). Near Staumühle, a fenced equipment parking place was established so that heavy equipment did not have to be driven through Paderborn, Schloß Neuhaus or Schlangen. Driving instruction took place to the north of the army camps. Gunnery practice was conducted on the ranges in Senne.

In Haustenbeck, a four-metre-deep pond was dug and a gas testing hall was constructed specifically for the *Pz.Kpfw.* Tigers (see separate section).

After a devastating aerial attack on Magdeburg and the main ordnance depot in Burg on 5 August 1944, the auxiliary ordnance depot Sennelager was set up in the motor vehicle hall on Küglerweg opposite the '*Alten Waldlager*' and was in operation from 15 August 1944. Under great time pressure, the office and guard rooms were built and parking areas for use by heavy vehicles prepared.

The establishment of a facility for providing tank courses in Paderborn *(Panzer-Lehrgänge Paderborn)* followed in accordance with official orders *(OKH/Chef Heeresrüstung u. BdE/AHA/Ia(II) Nr. 1237/43 g.Kdos.)* as of 12 March 1943 as part of *Pz.Ers.Abt. 500*.

The commander of *Pz.Ers.Abt. 500* was also the commander of *Panzer-Lehrgänge* Paderborn.

On 1 April 1943 (effective from 10 April) *Panzer-Lehrgänge* Paderborn was set up as follows:
- Stab Panzer-Lehrgänge consisting of *Gruppe Führer* and a *Pionier Zug* (engineer platoon) in accordance with *K.St.N. 10 1150 /15.02.1943*
- two retraining and instruction companies (each with three platoons) in accordance with *K.St.N. 10 1176 /05.03.1943*.

- a *Panzerwerkstattkompanie/Panzer-Lehrwerkstatt* (tank apprenticeship workshop) in accordance with *K.St.N. 10 1185/ 15.02.1943*.

The core of the key personnel was drawn from
- *6./Pz.Ausb.Abt. 5* (*Wehrkreis* (W.K.) III)
- *6./Pz.Ausb.Abt. 4* (W.K. XVII)

The *Panzer-Lehrwerkstatt* was formed from personnel from *Pz.Ers.Abt.500*.

The *Pionier Zug* was assembled from the engineer reserve units in W.K.VI.

The role of *Panzer-Lehrgänge Paderborn* was to provide tactical, technical and gunnery training for the new Tiger units. Setting up the courses and selecting personnel remained the responsibility of *Pz.Ers.Abt. 500*.

At the *beginning* of March 1943, the first Tiger I tanks for *Pz.Ers.Abt. 500* were sent to Putlos. Of these six vehicles, three were taken by the *Abteilung* to Paderborn, while the other three were left with the *Panzerschießschule*. More tanks were delivered later; one on 27 May and seven on 6 June.

Between 25 and 30 August 1943, another six Tigers arrived and in September, nine more. In October, just one Tiger was delivered. Three refurbished Tiger Is arrived on 14 and 20 April 1944; another three on 1 May 1944. On 21 November 1944, two previously knocked-out Tiger Is were delivered; on 6 January 1945, the last Tiger was delivered.

In July 1943, *Oberstleutnant* Hans-Georg Lueder became the new commander, bringing the experience he gained in Tunisia as the commander of *Schwere Panzerabteilung 501* to the training. From this point in time, the training establishment was also referred to as '*Panzerlehrgänge Tiger*' or, more succinctly, as '*Tiger-Lehrgänge.*'

The first fully trained Tiger recruits were dispatched to their units in late autumn 1943. This is apparent from the new *Kriegsgliederung des Ersatzheeres Stand* (order of battle strengths of the reserve army) of the end of December 1943:

Stab Kdo. Pz.Lehrg. 'Tiger' Paderborn (note the designation is like that of a Panzer regiment) with:
- two tank instructor companies
- a tank apprentice workshop 'Tiger'
- an instructor group for technical training.

Stab Pz.Ers.u.Ausb.Abt. 500 with:
- four tank training companies
- a convalescent/basic training company
- a *Marschkompanie* (march company)

In July 1944 *Oberstleutnant* Lueder handed the training facility over to *Oberstleutnant* Erich Hoheisel, the former commander of *Schwere Panzerabteilung 502*.

The first two Tiger II tanks were delivered on 1 April 1944; eight more followed on 30 June. Of this delivery, four were handed over to *Schwere Panzerabteilung 506* for deployment in Arnhem but these were later returned. Further deliveries took place on the 3 July (one tank) and 10 August (two tanks). Two Tiger IIs (with Porsche turrets) then arrived from the *Ersatzheer* (reserve army) on 5 December with another one following on 6 January 1945.

In September 1944, 15 Tiger I tanks were taken from the strength of the *Panzerlehrgänge* for the establishment of *Panzerkompanie 'Hummel.'*

According to the *Kriegsgliederung des Ersatzheeres Stand* on 10 August 1944, the *'Tiger-Lehrgänge'* then acquired its own *Stabskompanie*. The *Marschkompanie* was removed from *Pz.Ers. und Ausb.Abt. 500*. Due to the many convalescent soldiers who were not yet fit for active duty, the *Abteilung* swelled to a strength of around ten companies.,

Paderborn and Seenelager were temporarily overcrowded with numerous Tiger units so that alternative locations for training on Tigers were maintained in Mailly-le-Camp (France), Wezep/Oldebrook (Netherlands) or Ohrdruf. In addition, many units were trained on the extensive military-exercise area near Bergen and these were, for example, accommodated in Fallingbostel. The exercise area there had capacity for up to two divisions. Demonstration exercises and courses for aspiring regimental and division commanders were also held there. The training detachments were also involved with carrying out technical tests. As the training detachments were withdrawn (amongst other things for the formation of the *Panzerlehrdivision*, such tasks had to be taken over by *Schießschule Putlos*.

By December 1944 the command of the *Tiger-Lehrgänge* was transferred again, this time to *Major* Werner Freiherr von Beschwitz, a former commander of *Schwere Panzerabteilung 505*.

Because of the latent danger of air attacks, the companies of the *Ersatzabteilung* (replacement battalion) were billeted in villages in the vicinity of Paderborn and this made both supervision and the provision of supplies more difficult.

On 8 February 1945, at the suggestion the new commander, the regimental *Stab* was dissolved. The *Panzerlehrgänge*, together with the technical training unit and the much reduced *Pz.Ers.u.Ausb.Abt. 500*, were combined to form *Panzer-Ersatz- und Ausbildungs-Abteilung Tiger'* (without a number).

The picture to the left shows the transfer of command by *Oberstleutnant* Lueder; above is *Oberstleutnant* Hoheisel (beside him is *Hptm.* Thieme); in the centre is *Major* Freiherr von Beschwitz, the commander succeeding von Lüttichau. (Photos: Lueder)

Panzerersatz- und Ausbildungsabteilung 500 / Tigerlehrgänge

Panzerersatz- und Ausbildungsabteilung 500

Tank Inventory

Deliveries / Dispatches:

Dates	Tiger I	Tiger II	Inventory	
March 1943	6		3	*3 for Schießschule Putlos*
27.05.1943	1		4	
06.06.1943	7		11	
25.-30.08.43	6		17	
September 1943	9		26	
Oktober 1943	1		27	
November 1943	1		28	
01.04.1944		2	30	
14.and 20.04.44	3		33	used tanks
30.06.1944		8	41	
01.05.1944	3		44	used tanks
27.05.1944	1		45	used tanks
03.07.1944		1	46	
10.08.1944		2	48	
September 1944	-15		33	to *Pz.Kp. Hummel*
21.11.1944	2		35	used tanks
05.12.1944		2	37	from *Ersatzheer*
06.01.1945	1		38	used tanks
06.01.1945		1	39	from *Ersatzheer*
Grand Total:	41	16		

The tank inventory of the *Tiger-Lehrgänge* show tanks with varying specifications. For example, the two Tiger Bs delivered from the *Ersatzheer* on 5 December 1944 were models equipped with the so-called Porsche turret. Older vehicles (used tanks) were added from the repair and maintenance organization. The three damaged tanks delivered in early 1943 are not listed.

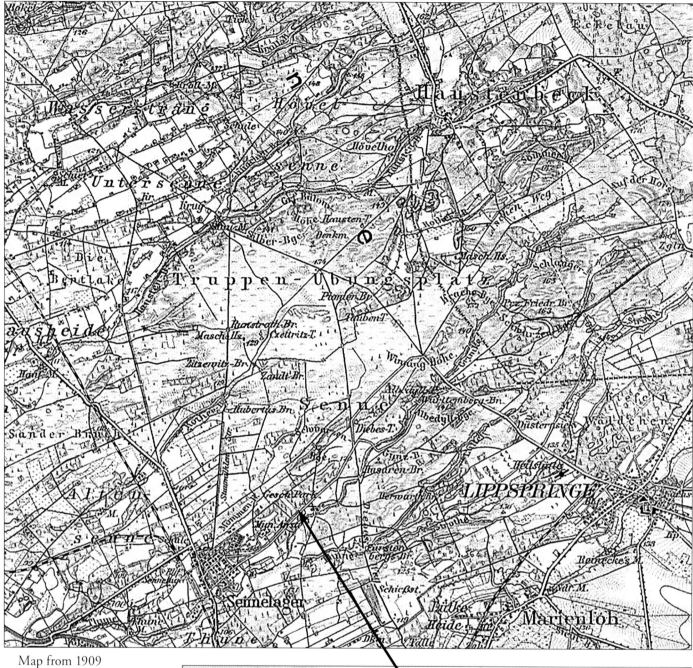

Map from 1909

An dem Teutoburgerwalde
Wo sehr heiss die Sonne brennt,
Liegt 'ne riesig grosse Heide
Welche man die Senne nennt.
Hier aus dieser grossen Heide
Wo man uns hat einquartiert
sendet Grüsse

Truppenübungsplatz Senne
Altes Lager

The Senne military training area had been in existence from 1892. The postcard to the right shows the so-called *'Altes Lager'* ('old camp') in 1906 which was gradually expanded over the years. This 'old' Senne camp provided accommodation for units that were to be newly set-up or refitted. Because of the lack of capacity in Sennelager, other camps were also used; for example, the *'Neues Lager'* ('new camp') in Augustdorf.

The accommodation for personnel belonging to the armoured units in the barracks in Driburger Straße, which had been newly built in the 1930s, was incomparably more comfortable than in the army camps. (Photos: Lueder)

At roll calls, for example for the declaration of oaths, there was a large assembly area in front of a multi-purpose hall.

The picture to the right, taken in June 1943, shows the commander of a parade detachment reporting to the unit commander.

From the troops' quarters, it was only a short distance to the technical area where all the tanks could be parked in hangers to protect them from the weather. (Photos: Britsch – Collection Münch)

The technical area was modern and built for purpose; the workshops are in the background and in front of them the garage and maintenance halls; in the foreground sits the fire-fighting water tank.

The technical area, located in the northern part of the tank barracks, was of generous proportions with halls in which effective equipment-based training was possible if the weather conditions were unsuitable for training outside. Most of the movements made by the tanks were powered by means of bottled gas to save fuel.

The workshop personnel worked under ideal conditions – when they were not breaking safety regulations (working under suspended loads!)

Coming from the technical area, it was possible to drive onto the road leading to Senne or to the nearby railway siding

The *Tiger-Lehrgänge* identified its tanks with three digits – the last numerals of the tank's chassis number were painted in white in the middle of its front panel. Tank '273', delivered on 6 June 1944, is shown in this picture.

Reconditioned tanks were also used. This picture shows tank '002' which was delivered in the early part of 1944. This tank had originally seen service with *Schwere Panzerabteilung 502* with the turret number '111'. (Leffers)

The drivers completed their familiarization and training on what was for them new tanks with or without 'recovery incidents.'

The Sommerberge was an area with steep slopes and ditches which made it a challenging area for vehicle trials and driving instruction.

When short instruction drives were undertaken in the local exercise area, the tanks were fuelled by gas.

An important part of the drivers' tuition was loading their tanks onto a rail lorry using end-loading ramps. This picture, taken at the beginning of July 1944, shows the tank with hull number '002' and soldiers of the '510'. (Leffers)

According to safety regulations instructors were not supposed to stand on the same rail truck as the tank; but soldiers too learn from mistakes. Notice the rather unconventional position of the gas bottles on the rear of the tank. (Heimberger)

With the '155' from the first delivery to the '500', soldiers of s.Pz.Abt. 508 are instructed in the correct procedures for loading onto rail lorries. (Heimberger)

Of course training for loading onto rail lorries also took place in winter; this picture shows Tiger '245' which was delivered on 27 May 1943 (Haas)

Tiger '447' struggles up the ramp. The two photographs below show the gas bottle fastening brackets and gun tube tensioner on the rear of the tank. (Weller from collection Münch)

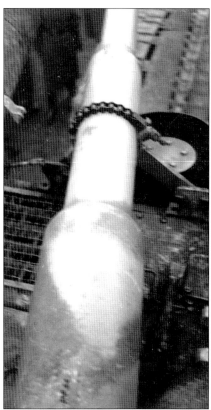

Soldiers from other companies had the gunnery ranges or, for example, the Haustendorf urban warfare training area at their disposal.

The *Flakzug* (flak platoon) could be trained at the nearby *Ersatzabteilungen*; the same applied to the *Pionierzug*.

As the training centre for the Tiger, Paderborn was also visited by the *Generalinspekteur der Panzertruppen* (inspector general of the armour forces). The picture below shows Guderian on 26 July 1943; the CO is on his right hand side.

The '*500*' was also involved in the life of the garrison as shown in this picture, taken on 12 March 1944, at the cathedral square in Paderborn on the occasion of the '*Heldengedenktag*' (memorial day for fallen heroes). (Lueder)

A parade passing through the market square in Paderborn in July 1944; the tank is number '445' (delivered in September 1943). In the background stands Paderborn's town hall. (Lueder)

'Open door days' were also held by the *Tiger-Lehrgänge*; as the placard declares…trips on board the Tiger were on offer! (Weller)

In the camps, the newly fitted-out units organized their own daily activities outside their course work. In this picture, taken in Sennelager on 26 October 1944, *Feldwebel* Litzke of the *'509'* has just been awarded the Knight's Cross. (Litzke)

After setting up the secondary arsenal on Küglerweg, new tanks were also handed over there. Hopefully, this radio operator will somehow manage to stow his accordion…

Gunnery training was also conducted under own responsibility of service units, here by *'506'* with a tank of the *Tigerlehrgänge* at the beginning of 1944 (due to high threat of air attacks the tank is equipped with an anti-aircraft machine gun. (von Römer)

The military training area at Sennelager according to the official map of 1938. The author has highlighted the tank training area with light and the infantry training area in dark lanes. The 'Fuchsbau' and 'Silberberge' areas (between 'Hubertus' and 'Dörenkamp') were added later. The firing range used for aerial target practice is marked in grey.

Panzerkaserne Paderborn   8 km

Gradually, on most of the firing ranges, a cable system was introduced to raise plates or to pull moving targets. The cables were actuated either manually or by motors.

This picture shows a difficult-to-hit tank turret target which mimics an enemy tank in a partially concealed position. If possible the hits were checked directly at the plate to verify the score with unequivocal results.

During gunnery practice, target observation was carried out using *Scherenfernrohre* ('scissor'-binoculars) or range finders borrowed from air-defence units.

The most suitable tank gunnery range was the 'Dörenkamp.' This allowed two units to fire side-by-side (on Dörenkamp Ost and D. West). It was used in its entirety, for example, during firing under combat conditions by a deployed company. The depth of advance was more than 3km. In the rear area, a 'terrace' was raised to allow groups of instructors a good view of the gunnery range. This photograph from 2 April 1945, taken from the Diebesturm [a stone-built tower on the Sennelager exercise area that was blown up 2 April 1945] shows the terrace with a Tiger in position on either side of it. The white rectangle top right is another tower, the Albedyll-Turm.

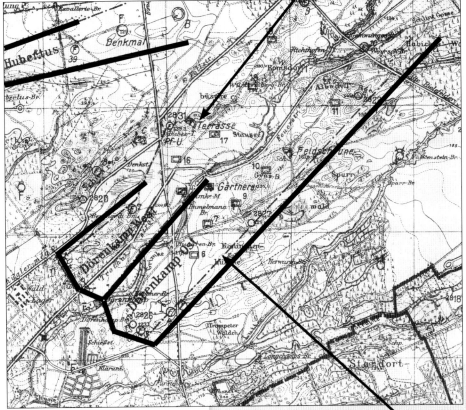

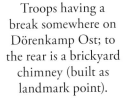

Troops having a break somewhere on Dörenkamp Ost; to the rear is a brickyard chimney (built as landmark point).

The picture shows a Tiger on the right-hand-side of the 'Czettritz.' The white spot in the background near the woods on the right is a ruin that was once a tavern. It seems strange that the recruits have not been taught how to handle ammunition properly!

Tiger powered by bottled gas on the Hubertus firing range; it has just crossed the 'Diebes-Weg'. Behind the woods lies the neighbouring firing range, the 'Dörenkamp.' (Weller)

The first practice shots fired by the recruits were initially conducted from stationary positions at the start of their respective ranges. These positions were marked by wooden balustrades. The gas provided was just sufficient fuel for the march to and from the shooting ranges or to the tank barracks in Paderborn.

The *Tigerlehrgänge* were frequently visited by generals and high-ranking delegations. A particularly notable visit was made by a delegation of the Japanese military attaché under the direction of the Japanese ambassador, General Oshima, on 18 November 1943. This picture shows the Japanese guests at a briefing by *Oberstleutnant* Lueder in a *Sandkasten-Hörsaal* [an auditorium in which a sandbox is used for demonstrating military manoeuvers and so on]. (Photos: Lueder)

The guests were then briefed on the equipment (above) and were given the opportunity to travel on a Tiger (here Tiger '055') at the Senne military training ground.

This Japanese delegation had already visited *1./s.Pz.Abt.* 502 at the front, near Siewerskaja on 6 July 1943. Here they receive an in-depth briefing about the [weapons] system from *Oberleutnant* Diehls and his crew. (Photos: Lohmann)

A very boldly camouflaged, factory fresh Tiger I of s.Pz.Abt.502 is demonstrated to the Japanese Ambassador to Germany, General Oshima and his aide, in June 1943, near Siverskiy. They were impressed enough that, after a meeting and tour of the Henschel works in Kassel in July, an agreement was reached to send a dismantled Tiger I to Japan by submarine. This plan, however, never came to fruition which is just as well, as the jungles of the Pacific islands were as unsuitable for the Tiger as the forests of Northern Russia.

The commanding general of the sector, *Generaloberst* Lindemann, is in conversation with General Oshima. The newly delivered tank was painted in crude camouflage modelled on the Japanese style.

The day closed with a brief combat exercise and cannon firing demonstration.

Also in July 1943, the delegation visited the Henschel factory. On the left we see Heydekampf in conversation with General Oshima. On the right of the picture, the gentleman with the hat is the owner of the company, Oskar Henschel. (Photos: Pertuss)

In a posed 'roll out' for the cameras, a new Tiger and Panther are handed over to a troop unit in front of Werk 3. Evidently at this time there was no danger of an air attack on the factory.

Afterwards, the guests – using several tank hulls – were driven out to the company's own testing grounds.

They drove a few cross-country laps. *Ingenieur* Pertuss (standing behind the driver's hatch) provides explanations. The protocol officer listening to him seems to be afraid of his cap flying away.

Then the mobility of the
Tiger – better without the
turret – was demonstrated
on a test track. The Panther
hull was also presented to the
Japanese delegation.

From a hill with a commanding
view, General Oshima observes
the demonstrations; beside
him are Pertuss and *Ingenieur*
Köhler, the 'test driver boss.'

Köhler performed part of the demonstration himself; in the picture above he is about to dismount from the hull of a Tiger…then it's time for a souvenir picture with Heydekampf standing between two of the Japanese visitors in the demonstration area.

Japan bought a Tiger and was billed for it (see the *Rechnung* to the right). It is interesting to note that they were charged about three times the amount charged to German users. A Tiger was then to have been shipped via Bordeaux but that never came to pass. Instead it was then 'snapped up' by the *13./SS-Pz.Rgt.* 1.

Besides Putlos and Paderborn, a Tiger was used in the engineer school in Dessau. This was evidently delivered from the repair and maintenance organization with steel bogie wheels but the old style cupola. Here it is approaching a pontoon ferry. (Collection Münch)

Early in February 1944, after the defection of Italy, newly formed Italian units loyal to Mussolini (*Repubblica Sociale Italiana*) were equipped and trained in Senne. On the occasion of a visit by Mussolini, a large-scale exercise took place on 19 July 1944 on the 'Augustdorf' firing range with parts of the *2. Divisione Granatieri 'Littorio'* for which tanks of the *Tiger-Lehrgänge* had been set aside.

Tigers crossing in front of one of their own positions (a 7.5 cm *Pak*) join the attack and take up positions at infantry cover position no.4 where they wait for the accompanying infantry to close up. This somewhat unrealistic scenario arises because of safety regulations.

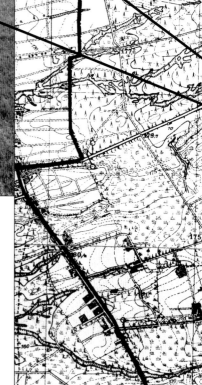

The infantry make a wrong move by clumping behind the tank for protection.

Under covering fire provided by the Tiger, the infantry launch their attack. They carry planks with them to surmount ditches and wire obstacles. (Photos: BA 675-7902-4 to -11)

To bridge dried-out water courses, planks were brought for laying over the obstacle. Diagonally to the right, cover position no.6 can be seen.

Smoke candles are lit in response to 'enemy' fire. Security assistants wearing white armbands run behind the units and detonate exercise pyrotechnics. A radio detachment can be seen in the foreground while in the middle distance a column of cars carrying the guests is visible.

Il Duce on top of a viewpoint on the Augustdorf firing range on 19 July 1944. On the left of the picture stands Marschall Graziani. General von Tschudi, the German leader of the liaison unit responsible for equipping the Italians, stands at Mussolini's left shoulder.

At the end of the exercise Mussolini speaks to his troops. In the background, the German leadership group and other onlookers watch events while, at the front of the picture, a stressed-out visitors' guide stands wearing a (green) armband.

Technical Trials at Senne

From 1935 there was already a tank research facility in operation on the area once occupied by the former village of Haustenbeck. This was used for the development and testing of the Tiger armoured fighting vehicle (the Henschel variant). To avoid the disruption of the exercise and firing operations, a tank driving area of around 20 hectares was sought in the northern part of the then military exercise area which was to be put at the permanent disposal of the Henschel company. Consequently, the neighbouring 'Kampmeiers Stätte' (the most southerly farm in Haustenbeck) was bought and the land between Roter-Bach and Grimke, from the tank road in the west to the Sommer-Bergen in the east, was designated as running-in zone for armoured vehicles. The area was fenced off and access strictly prohibited, even for soldiers.

The permanent staff at this time consisted of around 20 persons under the direction of *Oberingenieur* (chief engineer) Arnoldt and were accommodated in a converted farmhouse, 'Kampmeiers Hof'. Arnoldt was a very creative developer who not only worked closely with the project but also had a rich imagination. He built cars and racing cars to his own design and independently developed the idea of a one-man combat vehicle.

Other technicians were added to the experimental/testing facility.

Service, workshop and living quarters were built in the former farm buildings and stables. In 1940 an assembly workshop – which would later become known as the 'Tiger-Halle' – with a 6.5 m ceiling height and gantry crane was added because a lifting capacity of 15 tons was required. From the Sennelager – Haustenbeck road, a solidly constructed approach road with a new bridge across the Roter-Bach was built. South of the Roter-Bach, in the direction of Aschenweg, a tank access route was constructed. Electricity was drawn from Wesertal by means of a mast transformer at the production facility. Telephone and teleprinter connections were securely laid underground. But it was not only Henschel designs that were tested. The *Heereswaffenamt* increasingly awarded assignments to the research and development sections of many other firms. Trials were conducted with, among other things, communication-trench ploughs, an entrenching device, with truck-mounted cranes, turret rotary assemblies, vehicle transmissions, running gear, tracks for vehicles, air and water-cooled motors and also on captured armoured vehicles.

On 20 April 1942 the Henschel version of the Tiger was sent by rail to Rastenburg for the demonstration of the two competing types of Tiger tanks (the other version was from Porsche).

In Fallingbostel, on 19 and 20 August 1942, the first four Tigers were handed over to *Schwere Panzerabteilung 502*. Kurt Arnoldt and his technicians were sent there to provide support. Until their transport to the Leningrad on the Eastern Front on 23 August 1942, the Tigers were run-in, their guns tested and minor faults repaired.

In autumn 1942, the army requested that the Tiger should be submersible to a depth of 4.5 m. At the beginning of 1943, between the Tiger-Halle and the Roter-Bach, a concrete submersion tank measuring 60 m by 18m with a water capacity of 2,200 qm, was built. The volume of water required was taken from a pond created by damning the Roter-Bach. The water reserves in the pond amounted to 60,000 qm. Two 40 HP electric pumps were installed to supply the submersion tank with water from the reservoir. Also, to simulate the natural winds above a river, a fan was placed on a bridge spanning the middle of the submersion tank which could be filled to a depth of 6.66 m by means of pumps. If a dangerous situation arose it could be emptied within eight minutes by means of two 50 cm-diameter outflow pipes by activating lifting-disc valves.

After completing all technical measures for engineering the fording ability of the Tiger, the first success-ful submersion test was carried out on Tiger 'V3' on 24 May 1943. Other tests followed on 26 May 1943 and in June. In an important trial crossing of the Boelke-Stausee carried out on 12 July 1943, Georg Schönbach, the driver, gave a good impression of the event with this description:

Everyone was a little excited to see how our Tiger would behave in unknown waters. Leading engineers from Henschel and experts from the *Heereswaffenamt* attended the event to witness the demonstration. The reservoir had already been sounded out a few days earlier but this did not establish that felled or fallen trees lay on the bottom and these were nearly fatal for us. An armoured recovery vehicle equipped with thick steel cables was on the shore. Divers in full kit waited in a state of readiness. Wearing a special army submerged-escape apparatus, I stepped into the Tiger. The turret hatch was closed. I was alone in the tank and made the last radio test with the call, 'Jacob, Jacob'. Slowly, I put the heavy vehicle into motion. The bank of the lake was steep. The front of the Tiger slipped on the ground as soon as it was submerged. By grinding the tracks I managed to get the tank in a nearly horizontal position. Through deep mud the vehicle probed its way forward. I couldn't see a thing; I received my instructions by radio. After crossing the lake I was supposed to drive out onto the opposite bank. It didn't turn out like that. The gun barrel buried itself in the steep embankment. I feared it would be ripped off. So...a turn underwater and head back to take a new run ashore at a different place. I managed to find a way out. The order came [on radio]... 'Turn around and go back into the lake.' Then it happened, in the water. The hull hung up on a tree trunk. The tracks were unable to find a grip and went crazy. A question came over the radio... 'Do you need to be rescued?' I replied, 'Not yet, I'll try again.' My main concern was to keep the engine running; if it stopped there was a possibility of water entering. Keep calm! Slowly, I let one track run forwards…the other backwards. Centimetre by centimetre the heavy vehicle overcame the obstacle. Despite the chill air I'm sweating. But I did it.

For around one-and-a-half hours, under instruction by radio, I cruised back and forth under the water. Everyone breathes a sigh of relief when the turret heaves from the water at the bank of the lake. I drive the vehicle, which is now covered in thick layer of mud, once more on to the land.

The Tiger had passed its submersion test. We are all rather proud…months of works have ended successfully.

Another trial of this sort took place on 14 October 1943. In summer 1943, gas trials were carried out in a pentagonal, reinforced-concrete 'Gashalle' built in the north-eastern sector of the station. In addition to tests using exhaust gas, others were carried out using hydrogen cyanide and mustard gas. At first, these tests were performed without a crew on board but instead used several cats as 'warning sensors.'

Climatic studies were also conducted. For this purpose the temperature in the hall could be varied between -20°C and +66°C. Using artificial rain it was possible to achieve a humidity of almost 100% – sandstorms could be simulated up to wind force 9. From the tank inside the test hall to the external measuring point, up to 85 cable connections were made to enable remote measurements to be taken. Some of the gas trials were also conducted outdoors.

All further essential changes to the specifications of the Tiger armoured fighting vehicle were tested in Haustenbeck. Other vehicles, such as the Panther tank, were also tested. Tests on *Pz.Kpfw.* Tiger II (*Ausf. B*) began immediately after this. Purely firing tests were in part conducted at Putlos. On 26 January 1944, trials of an entrenching device for the Tiger were carried out.

At the end of 1944 several other prototypes were examined including the *E-100* [a super-heavy tank] and a *Geschützwagen* [artillery carrier] with a 17 cm gun mounted on a stretched Tiger II chassis. Other designs (such as, for example, a one-man tank) did not progress beyond the drawing board.

On 2 April 1945 the facility was occupied by the Americans. Within a few days they recognised not only its value but also that of the documents that had survived.

Kurt Arnoldt – on behalf of the US Army – continued his work. In the summer, when the British took over responsibility, General Hobart and Arnoldt arranged for the continuation of operations. Accordingly the hull of the *E-100* was completed and then transported to England. In addition, a number of captured vehicles were also repaired in the workshops; a *Jagdtiger* brought in by the French was repaired and sent back to them.

The work went on until the end of 1945 when the factory was put out of operation. However, the British continued using the building until September 1946. In the summer of 1948, the facility was blown up.

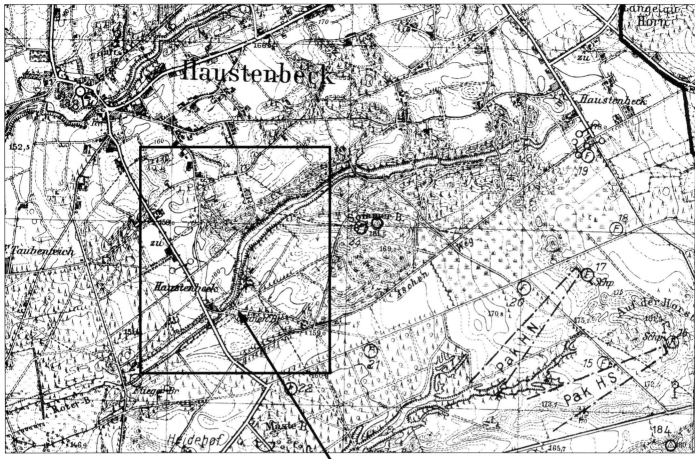

To the south of the evacuated village of Haustenbeck, the tank testing station was gradually expanded. It is noteworthy that the existing house No. 96 (formerly that of Hagemeier) was included in the naming of the station. Building No.86 (once the home of the Brinkmann family) also retained its number. The testing grounds around the Sommerberge were immediately to the east.

Legend:

1. Accommodation building with canteen and recreation room
2. Accommodation for station members
3. Station leader
4. Visitor quarters
5. Fuel pumps
6. Small submersion pond
7. Workshops
8. Corrugated iron hall
9. Air raid shelter
10. Hall with 15-ton crane
11. Tigerhalle
12. Garages
13. Workshops
14. Large submersion pond
15. Small pumping station with pipes connection to the pond
16. Dam wall for the Roter Bach
17. *Gashalle*; gas testing hall

Sketch: Walter Göbel

View from the bridge on the large submersion pond (14) towards the north and the *Gashalle* (17). (Photos and sketch: Walter Göbel)

The real estate of *Panzerversuchsstation 96*. (Tank Experimental Station 96)

View from the north towards building 1 with the extension for Arnoldt's office (3); immediately to the left is the northern side of building 4.

A Tiger in front of a workshop (7) after a successful immersion test in summer 1945; in the background are the two accommodation buildings (1 and 2); in the background on the right is the crane hall (10).

Looking towards the Tigerhalle (11) from the submersion pond; to the left are the adjoining workshops (13) and to the right the garages. In the foreground is the hull of the *E-100*.

Mechanics Finis and Wagner at work on a final drive component in front of the east side of the crane hall (10).

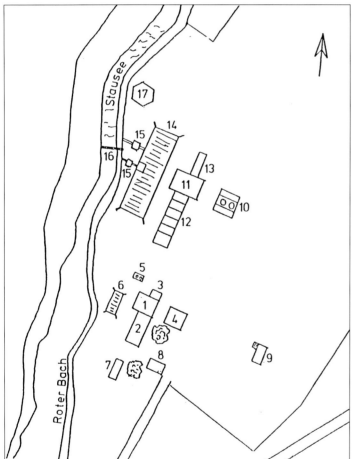

Tiger after an immersion run in front of the garages (12); to the left is building (1)

On the left of the picture is the extension with Arnoldt's office; to the right is the start of the garage block (12); in the space behind (but not visible in this picture) is the fuelling point (5).

The west side of accommodation building 4.

On the ground belonging to Henschel in Kassel (see Chapter 1), and in Senne, intensive driving trails were conducted. Because no turrets were at first available, the hulls were loaded with weights (as in the picture on the left) or a ballast ring. (Pertuss)

Inside and outside the gas testing facility many airtightness tests and decontamination activities were carried out on the interior and exterior of the tank.

Almost all new tank models were tested at *Versuchsstation 96* (Experimental Station 96). In January 1944 the first Tiger II arrived. Here – in front of the fuel pumps – it is carefully examined by members of the *Tiger-Lehrgänge*.

A side interest for Arnoldt was designing a one-man combat vehicle of which a wooden model was partially built before the end of the war. Developed in isolation from its tactical value, the concept nevertheless had some very innovative components including running gear that could be lowered from a cross-country driving mode to a 'duck' position. Furthermore, the vehicle, with a total weight of 0.78 tons, was supposed to be capable of being driven underwater. For power, Arnoldt suggested 11HP motors (?), one on each side, which could give the vehicle a top speed of 75km/hr (!) and a range of 300km.

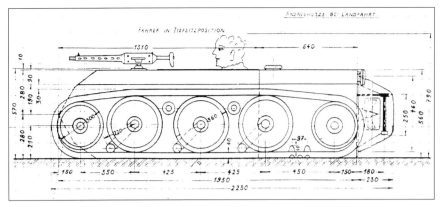

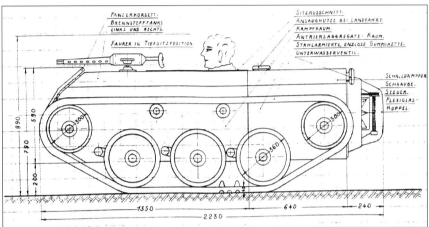

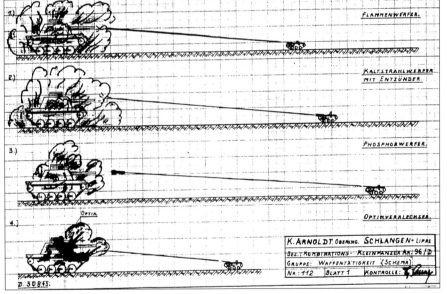

Of course, Arnoldt was well aware that this lightweight vehicle could never have at its command weapons that would be decisive in combat. In two sketches he illustrated unconventional weaponry solutions (left) and 'normal' ones (below).

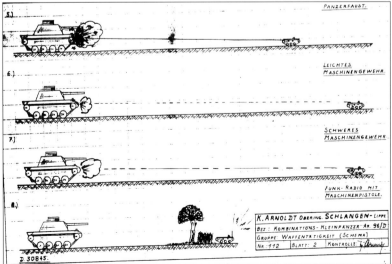

When the British took over the station, Arnoldt explained his concept to the amazed guests on 9 June 1945. The British made faithful copies but that was the last he heard from them. This is an example of how gifted technicians, completely at the demands of the military (and in a tactical sense) could blossom.

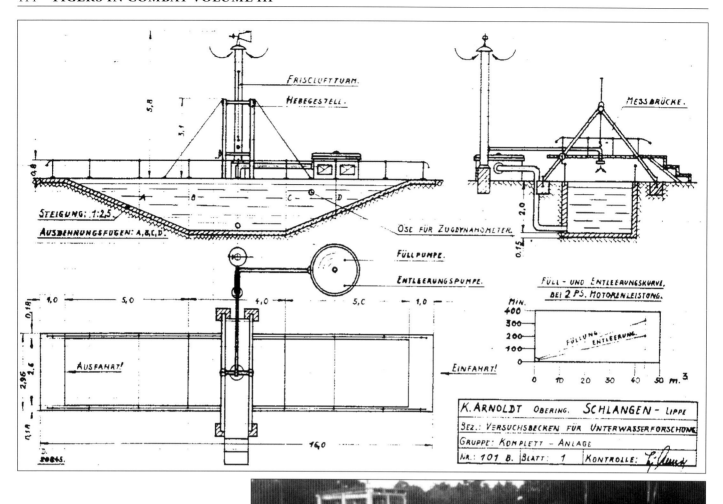

At the beginning of May 1943 the facility was completed but with a shorter command bridge; the picture shows the first transit attempt by a Tiger 'V3.'

From 24 May 1943 a whole series of trouble-free transits were made thus proving the Tiger's technical reliability.

Drivers and other crew members were equipped with life jackets and breathing apparatus.

A submerged crossing of the Boelke-Stausee was undertaken to document a transit in a natural waters (east of the 'terrace' on the Dörenkamp firing range). In fact, this never took place in an active deployment.

It was not only production series vehicles that were tested; here an entrenching device mounted on a *VK 30.01 (H)* is watched as it is put through its paces east of the crane hall.

In January 1944 the *Laufgrabenpflug LP 500* (a connection-trench-digging machine) was also tested on the rear of a *VK 30.01*. In the picture it sits in front of building 1 with a raised plough on its rear.

After occupation by the Americans and the takeover by the British at the end of the war, the remaining personnel continued operations at the facility for some months.

The Tiger was constantly under close attention from the highest levels. *Reichminister* Speer frequently kept an eye on the progress of both design types – at the Nibelungen factory (right) or in Kassel in the Senne region. (Pertuss)

The tank was also demonstrated several times to Hitler – for the first time in Rastenburg on 20 April 1942 and (in the picture to the right) at the beginning of December 1942 at his headquarters in Winniza – and likewise to Speer and generals Ramke, Schmundt and Thomale. In the picture above, a winter test is being conducted in July 1942, on the Großglockner, Austria's highest mountain.

16 Granaten mehr im »Tiger«

Eine Halterung aus einfachem Bandeisen

Die 2. Panzer-Lehrkompanie regt zur Ausstattung des Pz. Kpfwg »Tiger« mit zusätzlicher Granatenmunition eine Halterung an, durch die die Mitnahme von weiteren 16 Schuß ermöglicht wird.

Hierzu sind 8 Eisenbügel nach folgender Skizze anzufertigen. Zwischen Panzerwanne und den Senkkästen (in denen sich die Panzergranaten befinden) setzt man 2 Bügel und ist somit in der Lage, hinter diesen 4 Granaten zusätzlich unterzubringen. Da sich im Panzer 4 dieser Senkkästen befinden, ergibt sich eine Gesamtzahl von 16 Granaten.

Nachdem die zusätzliche Munition zuerst verschossen ist, werden die Bügel herausgenommen, und der Ladeschütze ist in der Lage, auch die Munition aus den Senkkästen herauszunehmen. Außerdem besteht die Möglichkeit, an je 8 Granaten in den Nischen zu gelangen, wenn sich auch hinter den Bügeln die zusätzliche Munition befindet.

Das Schwenken des Turmes um 360 Grad ist durch diese Halterungen nicht beeinträchtigt.

Die in der letzten Zeit bei der 2. Panzerlehrkompanie umgeschulten Truppenteile haben sich je Einheit einen dieser Bügel mitgenommen, um sich von ihren Panzerwarten die benötigte Zahl aus einfachem Bandeisen herstellen zu lassen.

Stark,
Hauptmann und Kompaniechef.

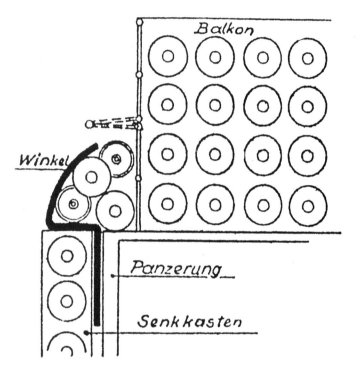

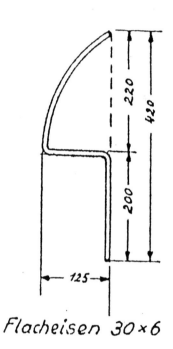

Flacheisen 30×6

The *Tiger-Lehrgänge* did not only carry out training for Tiger troop units but also conducted – mostly in conjunction with personnel from the Henschel testing station at Haustenbeck – technical appraisals and tests. In this context they also submitted suggestions for improvements to the *Heereswaffenamt* or the staff officer for armoured warfare at the *OKH*. Shown above is an example which describes a method for accommodating additional ammunition in the im *Pz.Kpfw.* Tiger I. This example was distributed by the *OKH AHA-Stab* (*Sonderstab A*) on 19 March 1944 to troop units. However, by this time, being supplied with sufficient ammunition was already the exception so this suggestion was already 'dead.' This solution was finally distributed in an army technical regulations sheet on 3 September 1944.

These information sheets and their valuable instructions for training and deployment were always well received by the troops.

Combat Operations to the End of the War

At the beginning of January 1945 there were isolated fighter bomber attacks on the rail facilities at Sennelager and against the engineering warehouses. Consequently, 25 *flak* cannons provided by the *Ersatzabteilung* were deployed along the stretch of railway and these brought down several of the attacking aircraft. Late in the afternoon of 27 March there followed a large-scale aerial attack by the British with 270 Lancaster bombers. In the troop area only around 30 bombs struck, causing only minor damage. In contrast, the town of Paderborn itself was heavily damaged by air attacks on 17 January, 23 February and 10 and 22 March 1945. On the morning of 28 March 1945, the *Standortälteste* (garrison commander) of Arnsberg reported to the *Wehrkreiskommando* (command authorities of the military district), that the enemy was close to Siegen and advancing in a south-westerly direction. At 1900 hours the chief of staff, *Oberst* Eichert-Wiersdorff, drove to Sennelager to take stock of the forces located there. However, because in the previous weeks many of the trainers who were fit for active service, and also the replacement soldiers, had been pulled out in the course of the alert warnings with the codenames 'Gneisenau', 'Leuthen' and "Goten-Bewegung', only partially operational units could be mustered. This made it difficult to man the 18 Tiger I and nine Tiger II tanks that were still operational.

In the night leading to 29 March 1945, after obtaining the approval of the *Oberbefehlshaber des Ersatzheeres* (supreme commander of the replacement army) the *Oberbefehlshaber* of *Heeresgruppe B*, *Generalfeldmarschall* Model, ordered the deployment of 'Panzergruppe Paderborn' together with other forces –including four *Panzerkampfwagen III* and five Panthers – that were in, or close to, Paderborn for refitting. The leader of this group was *Hauptmann* Rudolf Uckert. Two Tiger I tanks, one Panther and a *Sturmgeschütz* were manned by crews from *3./s.Pz.Abt. 501* and several Tiger II tanks by soldiers of the '508.' The remaining soldiers, together with *Abteilung 504*, were deployed as infantry.

The deployment of this *Panzergruppe* is described in Volume II of *Tigers in Combat*.

The re-established *Schwere Panzerabteilung 507* was subordinated to *SS-Panzer-Brigade 'Westfalen'* (see Volume I of *Tigers in Combat*).

Fighting in the vicinity of Paderborn ended on 3 April 1945 when the American 49th Mechan. Inf. Bn. occupied the training area. The Soviet prisoners of war released from the camp at Staumühle immediately set about plundering the area before they were 'interned' by the Americans in the Südlager which had been newly fenced for the purpose. Later, this facility was used to detain 'politically suspicious' people.

Having lost contact with its unit during the combat around Borchen, this Tiger belonging to '*Panzergruppe Paderborn*' joined with the forces of s.*Pz.Abt.507*. It was disabled on 2 April 1945, during an attack on Willebadessen.

On 4 July 1945 British soldiers performed several firing and driving trials. First, a Tiger II with a blown-off gun-barrel end is driven through the immersion pond…

…then its ability to topple trees is demonstrated…

…and it's faster than the British 'Archer' or 'Valentine' armoured fighting vehicles.

Finally, it is driven around a target tank, another Tiger, positioned in open countryside…

…before an 'Archer' anti-tank vehicle shoots at it from an unfairly close distance.

The target Tiger is carefully examined and several shell-penetration sites are pointed out. (Photos: NARA)

In October 1945, at the request of the British, the final submersion test is carried out on a Tiger in front of a large audience. A whole series of pictures of this event can be found in Arnoldt's collection and the Tank Museum in Bovington.

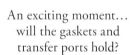

An exciting moment... will the gaskets and transfer ports hold?

Illustrious guests on the bridge... Field Marshal B. Montgomery, carrying his field marshal's baton in his left hand, is on the right in the picture.

Breathing air for the crew and combustion air for the engine are drawn in by a telescopic tube on the commander's hatch. The initial solution of supplying air through a telescopic tube on the rear of the tank was found to be defective and not without risk after the first submersion test.

Made it! As the tank surfaces at full speed, water in the hot exhaust turns to steam.

A souvenir picture taken with the tank still not dried off. The *Gashalle* can be seen in the background. The gentleman on the right with a hat and coat is Arnoldt; on the extreme left is the driver, Georg Schönbach.

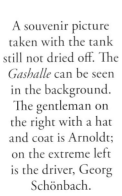

Lectures were kept as brief as possible during troop training and usually only during the initial briefing.

Learning in the open air was more fun, even for dry themes such as 'internal and external ballistics.' In this picture the instructor points out the maximum height attained during the trajectory of a shell. On the blackboard this is indicated by 'GP' (the *Gipfelpunkt*).

Oberleutnant Scherf (of the '503') supervises radio communications training.

The troops too were provided with training at every opportunity; here troops of the *Großdeutschland Division* receive machine-gun training in May 1943, in Achtyrka.

Training Course Content

The first important task was to provide initial training for the new tank personnel destined to serve in Tiger units following their basic training as recruits. This lasted three – and then later barely two – months. During this time the focus was on the basic infantry training that all troops underwent; shooting with rifles and assault rifles, formal training and physical training. In the last year of the war, basic recruit training was increasingly combined with training for tank service.

Secondly, at Paderborn crews already trained on other tanks were retrained. This generally applied to whole units (with reserves) that were intended for the establishment of new heavy tank units. According to their lack of personnel they were supplemented by newly trained Tiger personnel.

This meant that there were two training routes: a longer course for prospective tank men and a shorter one (approximately three weeks) for those who were merely unfamiliar with the Tiger.

Basic training included that of individual trainees and (towards the end of the course) whole crews.

Individually trained crew members included the gunner, loader, tank driver and radio operator. Commanders that had not been trained on Tigers completed the gunnery course. The tank repair and maintenance soldiers were taught in technical training groups and completed a factory based secondment with Henschel in Kassel which lasted for several weeks.

The technical instruction of officers was somewhat insufficient; firstly because there was a lack of training capacity and, secondly, because it was mistakenly thought that officers had no need for extensive technical knowledge of weapon systems and equipment. The result was often a lack of ability to analyse faults or recognise the overloading of equipment. This misconception was unfortunately widespread and was never properly corrected. A striking example of this lamentable lack of knowledge was demonstrated by *Oberst* Graf von Stauffenberg who, during his assassination attempt on Hitler in the *Wolfsschanze*, did not know that he merely had to place the second explosive charge close to the first, primed charge so that it too would detonate when the first charge exploded.

Even at the beginning of the *Bundeswehr* (post-war German Army) the author can personally attest to the fact that company commanders had little idea of weapon systems and only went near them during military exercises. Also, in the technical service of the unit, they strutted around in a service uniform wearing a tie and suede gloves

– that is, if they could be seen at all. However, in the course of the 1960s, this was sustainably corrected.

It must be clearly stated that in Paderborn the duration and content of training was due to the requirements of war. That is to say, the ideal 'peacetime training' of tank troops (described in my book *Panzertaktik*) with a minimum duration of a whole year could (for new) tank troops in 1943/44 never have been an achievable benchmark.

The specific training of individual crew members, as well as of the crew as a unit, is described in individual chapters that follow. Training content was guided by sections contained in the regulations beginning with '*Bedienung* von…(Operation of…)

Technical descriptions were of lesser importance and provided only insofar as they were relevant to correct operational procedures.

The training, only a small part of which was in the form of lectures, was predominantly practical in nature and included the use of working and cut-away models, illustrated charts and sand boxes to demonstrate combat scenarios but to a large extent was conducted on the tanks themselves. From 1943, tactical elements of the training included the use of the increasingly widely distributed *Merkblätter* (information sheets), issued by the *OKH*, which included combat experiences.

After the delivery of their own tank, the focal point of crew training was gunnery practice. It was for this reason that there were at Sennelager a series of gunnery ranges some of which had target distances of 3,000m or more and these were still in use until 1945. For example, a firing order shows that gunnery ranges Dörenkamp, Hermanns-berg, Hubertus, Stapelage and Silberberge were assigned to *Schwere SS-Panzerabteilung 502* from 15 January to 9 March 1945. *Schwere SS-Panzerabteilung 503* had used these ranges from 15 January 1945 until their transfer to *Heeresgruppe Weichsel* (Army Group Vistula) on 16 January 1945. On 8 and 9 February, and also on 20 February 1945, gunnery ranges Dörenkamp and Czettritz were assigned to *Schwere Panzerabteilung 510*. From 25 to 29 January 1945, *Unteroffizierbewerberkompanie 'Tiger'* [a company for officer cadets who were prospective members of SS units] shot on the Dörenkamp and Hubertus ranges. *Panzerlehrgang 'Tiger'* used the Horst-Süd range on 18 February 1945. The last registered users were *1.* and *2. Lehrkompanie Pz.E.u.A. 'Tiger'* (from 26 February into March 1945). *Schwere Panzerabteilung 507* also used the ranges in March 1945.

Inside a weatherproof building, demounted turrets, turret mantlets, guns with breeches and such like were mounted on stands for use during the first briefings dealing with turrets and weaponry.

Training courses for drivers included briefings in the engineering workshops using cut-away models of drive units, illustrated charts on the walls and such like. Here they learn about the steering mechanism, transmission, final drive, disc brakes and driving wheel.

In later phase of training, the crews received instruction on the tank. The instructors mostly wore the black *Panzeruniform* and the recruits drill suits.

Weapons and Equipment Training

This is was a prerequisite for the use and deployment of the tank.

Every soldier learned the movements and actions necessary for the smooth fulfilment of his tasks. This applied not only to operational actions but also to the care and maintenance of the vehicle as well as to the recognition and, if appropriate, the correction of faults. The latter of these tasks were confined to the replacement of defective fuses and gaskets and such like. Serious faults had to be formally reported and were fixed by the company's repair and maintenance personnel or specialized repair facilities.

As already mentioned, training was at first performed in separate classes before proceeding to working within the framework of a crew. Finally, specific parts of the training programme could only be taught to the whole group:

    Training of the gunner and loader
    Driver instruction
    Radio operator instruction
    Common course content

This concerned the following themes:
- Establishing operational readiness
- Tank gunnery
- Working in the tank

The training of 'old' and 'new' tank crews together proved its worth because of the *'Vordermann Effekt'* in which the young soldiers learned more quickly by observing and emulating more experienced tank men. However, this method was also necessary because it was not possible to fill either replenished or newly established units with soldiers that already had front-line experience. The picture to the right shows training in the technical area of the Paderborn barracks with recruits practising re-arming of the tank.

In the spring of 1943, three Tigers that were no longer repairable were sent to Paderborn, among them a badly shot-up vehicle belonging to *Leutnant* Zabel of the '*503*'. Behind it is the '121' of the '*509*' and the '121'of the '*503*.'

The turrets, including the slewing rings, of both tanks belonging to the '*503*' were set on concrete pedestals. This allowed them to be turned manually so they could be used for training loaders and gunners. The tank commander in the cupola conducted aiming at targets using curved trajectories and at miniature ones.

Later, the turrets of other damaged tanks were installed on the other two concrete pedestals. (Britsch – Collection Münch)

Tank Firing Practice

Gunnery training is an essential component of the training of prospective tank crews. With this, the foundation stone for successful deployment in combat is laid. Only crews that carry out the correct activities before and during the firing procedure, and confidently apply the gunnery regulations in a firefight, will prevail in a duel between tanks and turn their vehicles' technological superiority into tactical dominance.

Although tanks such as the Tiger possessed firepower and ideal characteristics, mistakes by the crew could lead to the success of a better trained crew of an enemy tank.

The *Merkblatt* (information sheet) entitled *Schieß-anleitung und Schulschießübungen für den PzKpfw Tiger* (Gunnery Instruction and Practice for the Tiger Armoured Fighting Vehicle) clearly stated that: 'Deviation from the gunnery regulations leads to missed targets, the loss of time and to the unnecessary expenditure of ammunition.'

The high standard of gunnery training was maintained to the last days of the war. An essential prerequisite was the successful completion of weapons and equipment training and the reliable mastery of individual control components (see Chapter 3, 'Operating the Tiger').

Gunnery training took place after the completion of crew training in accordance with the school's predetermined, standardized shooting practice. Every member of the turret crew was clearly instructed in gunnery and gunnery regulations during training. Drills in the tank practice-guns and aiming exercises ensured that the crew confidently recognised and set targets of every sort and that, before firing their first live round, all training deficits were eliminated and the best gunners selected.

The exercises for gunnery training with live rounds were, in the course of time, aligned to the experience gained in combat and the technical capabilities of the tank. As of 7 August 1944 the following shooting exercises were carried out:

1st Exercise: Cannon; ranging-in on targets with *Sprenggranaten* (high explosive fragmentation shells) at distances of under 1,200m.
Exercise: static tank; cannon; target at unknown distance at 800-1,200m, four *Sprenggranaten*.
If the crew hits the target with fewer rounds than envisaged by the exercise a second target will be assigned. The number of targets hit is to be entered in the firing list under the heading, 'Remarks.'
Requirements: one hit.
Objective: to learn ranging-in on point targets with *Sprenggranaten* at an unknown range of under 1,200m.
Shooting: tank crew.
Location: open ground.

Target: *Pak* plate (front).
Tank: the tank stands at combat readiness with aiming direction at 12 o'clock at an unknown distance from the target. The tank's cannon is unclamped. From his seat, the commander oversees the activities of the crew.
Execution: the commander orders the loader: '*Sprenggranate*! Load and lock!'
After executing the instruction the loader responds: '*Sprenggranate* loaded and locked!'
The commander orders the gunner:
'12 o'clock…*Sprenggranate*…900!' (the commander gives the range)…
Pak…Fire!'
The loader unlocks the cannon.
The gunner fires the first round. (*Achtung!*), observes the strike and reports his observation to the commander, for example, '*weit!*' (overshoot). The commander orders the correction.
The following rounds are to be fired according to the gunnery regulations for ranging-in with the commander issuing the firing order.
Before firing the last round the commander gives the order '*Rohr frei!*' (barrel empty).
After firing the last round, the loader leaves the gun unloaded and, with the breech open, reports: '*Rohr leer!*'(barrel empty).
The commander gives the order '*Mündung hoch!*' (raise muzzle).

2nd Exercise: Cannon; ranging-in on targets with *Sprenggranaten* at unknown ranges more than 1,200m.
Exercise: static tank; cannon; target at unknown distance greater than 1,200m, six *Sprenggranaten*.
If the crew hits the target with fewer rounds than envisaged by the exercise then the exercise is complete.
Requirement: one hit
The process in analogous to the first exercise using the gunnery regulations for long range.

3rd Exercise: Cannon; ranging-in on targets with *Panzergranaten* (armour piercing shell) at unknown ranges more than 1,200m.
Exercise: static tank; cannon; target at unknown distance greater than 1,200-2,000m, four *Panzergranaten*.
If the crew hits the target with fewer rounds than envisaged by the exercise then the exercise is complete.
Requirement: one hit.
Target: tank plate (front).
The process is different from the first and second exercise in that it is not the impact (explosive flash) but first

and foremost the tracer path in relation to the target that is observed.

Lateral and elevation corrections are carried out by realigning the weapon using the crosshairs with respect to the reticules, not by adjusting the range mark.

4th Exercise: Cannon; shooting at laterally moving targets with *Panzergranaten*.

Exercise: static tank; cannon; distance greater than 800-1,200 m, 3 rounds *Panzergranaten* against target moving laterally at 20 km/hr. Distance of travel for target: 150 m. Time for firing: 30 seconds.

Requirement: one hit.

Objective: to learn the lead and re-alignment required when aiming at a laterally moving target and how to correct the aiming point based on observation.

Target: tank target on sled (length approximately 4m and height, including turret, around 2m).

The process is analogous to the 3rd exercise but the commander gives the aiming lead in reticule lines as well as the target distance.

In addition, shooting practice was carried out with the coaxial turret machine gun as well as the anti-aircraft machine gun. Depending on the ammunition situation and the availability of a suitable firing range, small-scale combat shooting was conducted within the framework of a platoon – or even company – in order to give the leader schooling in fire control under combat conditions.

The exercises just described were referred to as 'dry' or 'aiming' exercises the intention of which was to practice shooting without hesitating to think when it came to firing live rounds.

Initially, individual shots were fired on order of the commander. However, after completion of their training at the gunnery school, the gunners were drilled to open fire autonomously.

A common sight in tank companies during training and on active service; this picture, taken in May 1943 in Coetquidan (a French military training facility), shows the '*502*' on a training exercise. With views across open terrain, a whole range of topics can be taught: battlefield observation, reconnaissance, target practice, the terminology of combat, optimising the interaction of crew members and the sighting-in of turret weapons. (Vennemann)

Combat Training

Combat training was carried out in several consecutive stages.

To begin with the crew, that is to say individual tanks, were taught the essential elements of tactically appropriate conduct in combat situations. The knowledge gained during tank gunnery training was now used to focus on:

- battlefield observation
- the rapid identification of targets
- effective target engagement
- the appropriate choice of position
- exploitation of the terrain.

These themes were quickly integrated into the training procedures in the form of an obstacle course. Placed in a simulated tactical situation, the crew fulfilled small missions in varying terrain where they were confronted with unpredictable threats and types of target. Examples include stumbling upon a *Pak* position, an enemy tank approaching from the flank, penetrating hostile artillery fire, driving over an anti-tank mine and such like. The 'enemy' was represented by troops acting in that capacity, targets and the presentation of scenarios by means of radio.

The benefits of such procedures included drill reinforcement, refreshing training, comparing the ability of crews and facilitating the organization and standardization of training.

In the following stage of training, the fulfilment of appropriate tactical missions was practiced with the individual crew elements working within the framework of platoons. This step was the focal point for the tankers because the majority of their tasks were executed at the tactical level. A well-drilled tank platoon could react appropriately within the framework of a company, that is to say with two further tank platoons. The fulfilment of tactical missions at the company level, and up to unit level, is a leadership responsibility, particularly with regard to the appropriate application of basic tactical principles (see Chapter 5 'Tactics').

The training content for the Tiger was in principle identical to that of 'normal' tank troops. This was also reflected in reality. Well trained and organically integrated units, after retraining on the Tiger tank, adapted to their new weapon system without difficulty and were just as successful in combat. Tiger-specific training content was therefore not required except for, of course, knowledge of the technical and tactical possibilities and, very importantly, the limits of the vehicle in terms of its weight and manoeuvrability. These factors had a significant effect on the tank's mobility on, for example, muddy or especially swampy ground and on overcoming or driving over obstacles and bridges. Such knowledge concerned principally the tank drivers and commanders.

Combat exercises are indisputably desirable for the training of leaders and command posts at company level and within the framework of larger units, particularly in combination with other weapons and branches of the military. However, the scope of such exercises was limited in the second half of the war by an environment governed by a lack of fuel and repair and maintenance capacity.

This was to some extent overcome by the sensible use of teaching aids or other methods of training. Sand boxes, in which various tactical situations could be simulated, were widely used for training the crews and their commanders. Gunners and drivers were instructed in the appropriate exploitation of the terrain and choice of static positions, radio operators in voice traffic and commanders in the processes of decision making and the issuing of orders. The crew practiced repetitive procedures primarily when engaging targets.

The same procedures could be practised in greater depth during so-called *Geländebegehungen* ('area inspections') alongside other training content such as signalling, selecting roads and assembly points, range estimation and the dissemination of observations and reports and so on.

At meetings to discuss the terrain, tank commanders, platoon leaders and company leaders were briefed in tactics by the chief instructor's descriptions of various situations in differing sectors of the terrain or by enemy roleplay and practice targets. They learned to assess the enemy's military situation and resolve possible outcomes and finally issue orders. Other means of training included planning exercises using maps or leadership training at command posts and radio stations but without complete troop units.

In surprisingly clear terms, the tank training school in Paderborn addressed training requirements in a paper on the principles and application of training issued 28 May 1943:

> As the, most valuable and best German tank, the Tiger, requires the most tried and tested tank soldiers. Commanders, gunners and drivers must be men with practical experience on tanks.
>
> Therefore the retraining of other branches of the military and service grades is not appropriate for the Tiger.
>
> Until now the time spent in all areas of training before deployment has been far too short. There must be sufficient scope available for the thorough training of the *Kampfstaffel, I.-Gruppen* and the *Werkstatt*. It is expected that after the receipt of their last Tiger, a unit should receive at least three or four weeks for consolidation and training to attain the highest level of dependability. As practical experience has proven, any excessive haste leads

to a lack of success in operations and to the premature breakdown of the tank because of insufficient expertise. There is also the slight danger, given the vehicle's technical shortcomings because of inadequate development, that technical failures caused by the improper operation by the troops can, in certain circumstances, damage their trust in the Tiger.

Individual training: for commanders, gunners and loaders it is demanded that they can use their weapons and equipment with somnambulistic certainty and eliminate each fault that occurs, by the crew itself as far as this is possible. The estimation of range, gunnery practice, target recognition and designation, and teamwork within the crew, can never be practiced too much. Enemy tank recognition is a particularly important topic. Because armoured combat is generally conducted over large distances, the crew must always be in the situation of being able to immediately recognise the most dangerous of the hostile tanks. Thorough training in ballistics, the considered use of ammunition, the correct choice of weapons and knowledge of their effect are prerequisites for resounding success. Commanders are required to have a tactical and intuitive understanding of their respective situations. Advance assessment of the terrain and enemy forces, map-reading and taking bearings – which should be able to be taken for granted – is still poor among non-commissioned and young officers. For the commanders of Tigers these points are of crucial importance. For the drivers of Tigers, a lengthy spell on the front line as a driver of a light tank is absolutely necessary. Only drivers with a good feel for their vehicle are equal to demands of the delicate Tiger. Retraining them requires long distances across mostly open terrain. Tiger drivers and *I.-Gruppen* must be so thoroughly trained in technical matters that they are able to remedy most faults and so free-up the workshops for major repairs. General basic training principles apply to loaders and radio operators.

More time must be spent training tank and truck drivers, which means that more fuel needs to be made available for this purpose. It is a question of investment; of whether more is spent on this or whether bad driving methods lead to the premature breakdown of vehicles in the field. Ninety percent of the distances travelled are cross-country. If a driver is capable of driving off-road, he is also able to drive on roads.

Combined arms unit training: generally the same principles apply as for medium-sized units. Today more than ever with the Tiger, the mantra of forwards, onto the enemy, must be repeated. On no account allow the long 'arm' of the 8.8 cm [gun] to seduce one into standing still. Recently, movement itself has brought success. Carry out combat shooting practice, lots of it, at dusk too. In this way firing discipline and distribution can be thoroughly practiced. When doing this, use the smoke-laying equipment in order to familiarize the crew with it. Conduct night marches and find assembly areas under the most difficult conditions. Training should certainly be only undertaken in difficult terrain.

These sometimes fascinating assessments hit the nail on the head. However, they include demands that could not be met considering the personnel available and the miscellaneous bottlenecks and limiting factors that could not be changed. Longer preparation times for newly equipped, larger units, as well as the placement of personnel that already had front line experience within them, was simply not feasible. That was certainly the reason why the 'old' Tiger units were clearly more successful than the later, frequently thrown together, units. This explains the limited success of the SS units which predominantly consisted of semi-skilled crews and non-commissioned officers... and inexperienced leaders.

Training at the level of large, combined units was seldom carried out simply because there was no time to do so. Moreover, making Tigers available for active deployment was a matter of priority. Preparations for *Unternehmen 'Zitadelle'* in the summer of 1943 were an exception. Here, the assault divisions took part in several exercises which were also used for the further training of the leaders, delegations of whom observed the large-scale troop exercises from vantage points. There was also the so-called *'Türkenübung'* (Turkish exercise) carried out by *s.Pz.Abt. 503* on 27 June 1943 in which a high-ranking Turkish delegation was supposed to have witnessed the superiority of the Tiger armoured fighting vehicle in a demonstration within the framework of ongoing (but unsuccessful) efforts to persuade Turkey to become allies [of the Germans].

Because the capacity for the formation and training of units was insufficient in Senne, other training areas such as Coetquidan were used. This picture, shows tanks from *2.* and *3. Kompanien s.Pz.Abt. 502* in front of Chateau du Bois du Loup, which served as their accommodation. (Vennemann)

On 20 June 1943, an ongoing course for the leadership offered a close look at the still 'new' Tiger at the Malakoff Porcaro mill, which had been converted to a *Wehrmacht* memorial. (Fischer)

At this time in occupied France, war service could be spent in peace…

…or undergoing march training under threat from the flank…

…or maybe gunnery training. Here *Hauptmann* Radtke explains the significance of the green and the red flags used in firing practice. (Photos: Vennemann)

Mailly-le-Camp was another training area in France. Here it is being used by 3./s. Pz.Abt. 503 at the start of August 1944 (BA 721-399-17)

There were also training areas in the Netherlands (the picture above shows s.SS-Pz.Abt. 103 on Oldebroek near Zwolle in February 1944) and in Belgium (to the left is a picture of tanks belonging to s.SS-Pz.Abt. 101 on exercise in the area around at Amiens). (Photos: above Kothe, left BA 288-1805-17)

Troops in the field provided training support sometimes, too. Shown here, in pictures taken between 6 and 15 May 1944, are Tigers belonging to *s.Pz.Abt. 503* (formerly *Kampfgruppe* 'Mittermeyer') being used to train Hungarian crews in Kolomyjo. Later, the Hungarian Army received 14 Tiger I tanks from the inventory of the '*509*.'

Tigers in Hungarian Service

In light of Soviet preparations for an offensive operation in the spring of 1944, *Generalfeldmarschall* Model had grave concerns that the Hungarian forces operating under his command as part of *Heeresgruppe Nordukraine* would not survive for long because of their second-class equipment. As a matter of urgency, he requested the *OKW* to make German armoured vehicles available to them.

In 1943, in order to improve the assertiveness of the forces at their command, Hungary had indeed began to acquire German armoured vehicles. By the middle of 1944 Panthers and Tigers had been added. Accordingly, in May 1944 in Kolomyjo, crews of the 1st Battalion / 3rd Tank Regiment /2nd (Hungarian) Armoured Division were trained by elements of *s.Pz.Abt. 503* and others. The Tigers were then transferred to *s.Pz.Abt. 509*. When the latter shortly afterwards received six new Tiger I tanks, arrangements were made to hand these, and eight other Tigers, over to a Hungarian collection detachment. At that time Kolomyjo was within the combat sector of the 2nd (Hungarian) Armoured Division (attached to the 1st Hungarian Army), which had been deployed between the Dnjestr and the Carpathian Mountains. However, contrary to orders, the Hungarians were supplied with used tanks rather than the new ones. According to official sources, the Hungarian division had ten Tigers at their disposal in May to which a further three were added in July. However, the transfer of a total of 14 vehicles was confirmed independently (without dates) to the author by several participants in the Kolomyjo training programme. Using one of each type of tank, a training unit was formed under the leadership of *Leutnant* Máthiás Eszes. The 14th Tiger evidently does not appear in the 2nd (Hungarian) Armoured Division's reports.

In total, from May 1944, the Germans also supplied 74 *Pz.Kpfw. IV* (G and H variant) tanks, 50 *StuGesch III* assault guns, 100 *Panzerjäger* 'Hetzer' tank hunters and 5 Panther ('G' variant) tanks. The transfer of the equipment to the Hungarian *I./3 Battalion* took place in Nadworna. The division reported an inventory of four Tigers on 15 May 1944 and ten Tigers on 26 May 1944. The 3rd Battalion had a dubious mixture of equipment split into four armoured companies. One of these had eleven *Pz.Kpfw. IV* '*lang*' tanks and one had nine StuGesch III assault guns. One of the remaining two companies had six

Tigers and the other initially only four. The commanders of the two Tiger companies were *Oberleutnant* Ervin Tarczai (2nd Company of the 1./3rd Battalion) and *Hauptmann* János Vedress (3rd Company).

In July, on the birthday of the Hungarian inspector of the pioneer troops, *Gen.Maj.* Hollosy-Kuthy, three more Tiger I tanks were handed over.

When, in June 1944, the battalion deployed these vehicles for the first time (for a period of just several days) with the 24th (Hungarian) Infantry Division, they shot-up three T-34 tanks and numerous anti-tank guns and annihilated a dozen bunkers and an ammunition dump. According to an inventory status report of 11 July 1942, a total of six Tigers were in combat-ready condition.

The inventory report of the 2nd (Hungarian) Armoured Division on 16 July 1944 mentions seven combat-ready Tigers.

On 23 July 1944 the battalion was deployed to the east of Stanislau. On the road to Nadworna, on 26 July 1944, a single Tiger annihilated eight enemy tanks together with numerous trucks and artillery guns. One group (with several Tigers) captured Cziczow, a settlement lying to the north of Stanislau. There was no further breakthrough to Jessupol. Instead, the Soviets penetrated the Hungarian front line at Otynja. One group under the leadership of *Hauptmann* Mátyássy of the 1./3 was ordered to proceed to there and joined combat at the settlement of Zhyrowa (south of Otynja) with only moderate success.

While the retreat towards the Carpathians was underway, the Tigers usually formed the rear guard. Near Saturnia, two Tigers destroyed 14 T-34 tanks in the vicinity of Hill 514.

Between 24 and 27 July 1944, during withdrawal manoeuvers via Czuczylow – Grabevjec – Horodische – Saturnia – Rosulna – Kraszna – Dolina and Rozniatów, seven Tigers were lost. On 10 August 1944 only three Tigers were still serviceable. According to reports issued on 14 September 1944 two Tigers were still combat ready; by 5 October 1944 none were (of a total of three). Later, these three were lost in Transylvania because of lack of fuel and a means of recovering them.

Apart from that, the Hungarian logistic units' biggest problems were supplying and maintaining the foreign vehicles.

In the first combat missions, tanks (here the '214') were used on a daily basis by the 24th Hungarian Infantry Division for the bombardment of enemy positions.

This picture (below) shows one of the few brand new Tigers that were delivered with the chief of the 2nd Company, *Oberleutnant* Tarczai.

The picture above shows vehicle '212' at the end of May 1944 as it crosses the River Prut near Szoldvina.

A late photo from July; wounded soldiers brought in on the back of a tank are evacuated by a Fieseler-Storch plane.

3 Operating the Tiger

The two service manuals describing the equipment and operating instructions for the *Pz.Kpfw.* Tiger, D 656/21 (chassis) and the D 626/22 (turret), were not entirely suitable for the initial training of crews nor for subsequently keeping them up to date. They were incomplete and also contained too many instructions for the maintenance personnel making them too confusing for the tank crew.

The interaction of the crew members was seldom adequately described, if at all, and the descriptions of the handling procedures that had to be performed in sequence at the individual crew stations was simply insufficient. In addition, there were numerous, and often conflicting cross-cutting regulations (for example, for the radio communications equipment) and instructions (see bibliography in the appendix). Before the issue of the final regulations document there was, for each vehicle, a so-called *'Firmen-Sammelmappe'* (construction-company collection folder) which contained much of the contents that would appear later.

Because the above mentioned deficiencies were detected immediately by the training organisation, attempts were made to remedy the situation. This was done through the publication of additional operations manuals and data sheets. The *Tiger-Lehrgänge* created their own handouts for the instructors. The D 656/27 regulations booklet, *'Tigerfibel'*, was a remarkable step forward for its time. *Oberstleutnant* Hans Christern, formerly of *Pz.Rgt. 31*, was responsible to the *Inspekteur der Panzertruppe* for the management of training and was himself an experienced tank commander and holder of the Knight's Cross. He established a team that was given the task of creating an easily understandable, and above all instructive and methodical *'Fibel'* (primer book) that was humorous and based largely on images so that the crews could quickly assimilate the content. But first this concept had to overcome the resistance of old-fashioned traditionalists and then ultimately meet the approval of the new *Generalinspekteur der Panzertruppen, Generaloberst* Heinz Guderian – and meet the requirement that it had to be easily stored in a trouser-leg pocket and be no more than 100 pages in length.

This basic training and service manual found immediate acceptance amongst the troops – as did the concept of the *Fibel*. As a result, similar documents were produced for other *Wehrmacht* units such as, for example, document D 655/27, the *'Pantherfibel'*, for other armoured units.

In the following sections the service training regime will be explained. For this, it is appropriate firstly to deal with the individual operator's station and thereafter that of the whole crew.

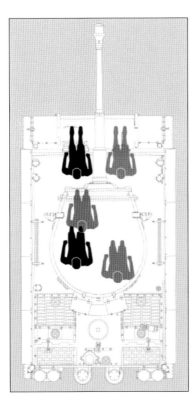

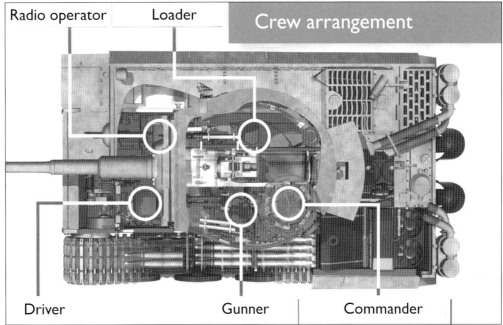

The arrangement of the crew positions in the *Pz.Kpfw.* Tiger I (a similar arrangement was to be found in the Tiger II) with driver, gunner, and commander sitting one behind the other on the left-hand side and the radio operator and loader on the right-hand side. (Harada)

The cover page of the legendary 'Tigerfibel' which immediately found full acceptance by the crews because – unlike various other 'dry' regulation documents – it was well illustrated and presented humorously everything that was important for the operation of the tank.

A peculiarity of the armoured units is that leaders at all tactical levels (platoon, company and battalion) are also tank commanders. In this picture, taken in May 1944, we see *Leutnant* Röder, a platoon leader with *s.Pz.Abt. 506*. (Röder)

Commander's Operating Tasks

In the regulations at that time, the tank commander was referred to as the *'Panzerführer'* (tank leader). Because of this, there was a conceptual association with the leaders of larger military units, who were also referred to by the term *'Führer'* and soon tank commanders were referred to only by the term *'Panzerkommandanten.'*

For the *Panzerkommandanten* there were a number of Tiger-specific duties to fulfil.

These were:
- operation of the commander's cupola
- operating the anti-aircraft carriage
- operating the machine-pistol port.

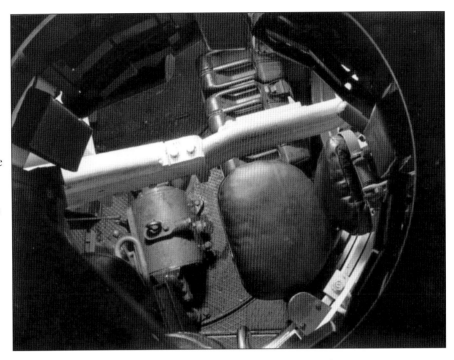

A view into the interior of the tank through the commander's hatch. Below and to the front of the seat, the cover of the turret-drive can be seen; this transmitted power from the engine to the turret-rotation mechanism. Three water canisters are stored to the right of the seat.

Drawing of the commander's side of the turret. In front of the seat is the handwheel for the auxiliary drive of the turret. If, for example, the engine-power to the turret failed, the commander could use this to assist in the rotation of the turret. (Trojca)

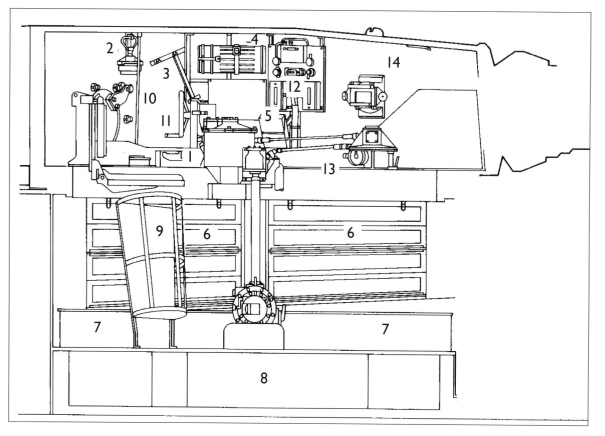

Internal
storage
on the
commander's
side

1	binoculars	9	wire basket (for flags/maps)
2	MG sealing plugs	10	drive of cupola direction indicator
3	signal pistol	11	handwheel cdr
4	gas mask cdr	12	socket for radio headset cdr/gunner
5	gun documentation book		battery for emergency firing above
6	ammunition rack, 16 rounds	13	turret direction indicator
7	ammunition rack, 4 rounds	14	gunner's window
8	luggage box		

Internal storage
turret rear

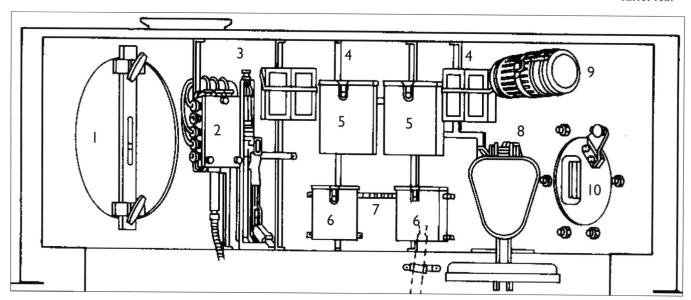

1	escape hatch	6	flares, 24 rounds
2	fuse box	7	hatch wrench
3	machine pistol	8	cdr's water flask
4	spare windows for observation slits	9	gasmask
5	headset, microphone	10	MP firing port

Operation of the commander's cupola

The tank commander's cupola consists of a cylindrical casing with five welded-in boxes for laminated glass, a graduated ring and a cupola hatch. There are five observation slits in the casing behind which, for the protection of the eyes from lead fragments and rifle shots, a 90mm-thick, laminated-glass block lies. The glass, which is located in a frame with a latch, can easily be replaced. The observation slits are made watertight by means of seals installed at the front of the protective boxes, against which the laminated glass is pressed. Protection for the forehead and nose is provided at each opening.

At the front of the forward-facing observation slit are aiming indicators while the rear sights are fixed to the underlying framework. Using this device the commander of the Tiger can, in combination with the 12-hour-divisions on the graduated rim, identify the direction in which the turret weapons point and correct the gunner during target allocation.

D 656/22 S. 27/28)

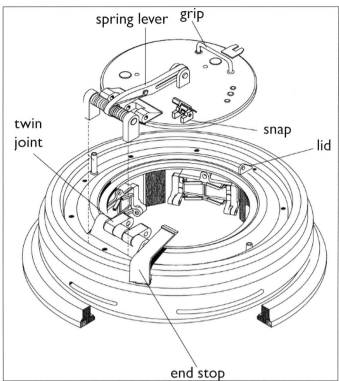

Because it had the form of a vertical cylinder the hatch initially installed on the Tiger I offered a good target which, in combat, was shot at by weapons of every calibre as a matter of priority in order to blind the commander. It usually had to be unscrewed (see picture on left) to repair damage.

The cover of the new hatch (below) was swung to the side when opened and could be positioned above the opening to protect the commander from above.

The cupola hatch cover was opened from the inside and remained – fixed by a bracket – in a vertical position. This restricted vision to an extent. In addition, with the hatch open, it was possible for hand grenades to be thrown in.

Because this 'old' type of cupola was rather prone to damage, and was sometimes even sheared off by a serious hit, a new design was installed as of March 1944. In this new cupola design, the rim had seven prismatic mirrors under a welded cover that could easily be removed from the inside by loosening a clamping device. The new cupola was also flatter and welded rather than screwed to the turret roof. The 12-hour engraved ring was also dropped. In practice it was found to be of little use because the commander more or less had all-round vision when sitting in his seat.

Internal
storage:
turret roof
(underneath)

1	ventilation fan with switch	8	loader's prism
2	MG sealing plug	9	balancer for loader's hatch
3	cdr's cupola	10	breathing tubes
4	prism bracket	11	gun travel lock
5	switch for smoke dischargers	12	telescopic sight (*TZF*) lock
6	cdr's handgrip	13	socket for firing device
7	reading light	14	socket for *TZF* and gun elevation indicator light

View of the commander's seat from the front. The MP opening is on the turret wall to the left of the seat; the handwheel for the auxiliary drive for the turret is on the right of the picture.

Operation of the anti-aircraft MG carriage

A mounting bracket for a machine gun served as a central support for the MG 34 (and later the MG 42) when used for firing at aerial targets. It was held securely to the tank commander's cupola by means of a clamping device. For aiming to the side, the swivel arm could be rotated on a steel ring on the cupola. Rough aiming at high targets could be achieved by pulling on the support arm. Otherwise the machine-gun operator could rest the butt of the weapon on his shoulder and aim by moving the upper part of his body. For shooting at aerial targets, there was a special sighting device mounted on the weapon. However, this combat method was seldom used in practice; firstly because there was little chance of success unless several machine guns were firing at a slow moving aerial target, and secondly because in doing so the tank would have revealed its position unnecessarily.

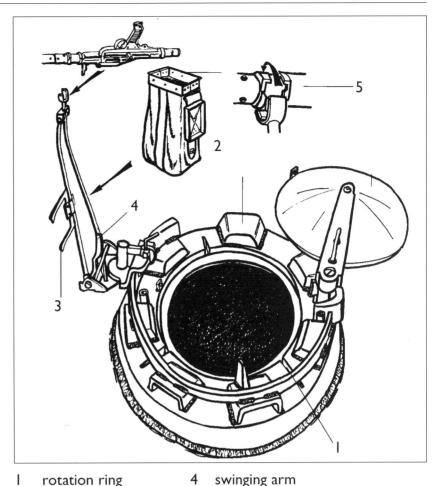

1	rotation ring	4	swinging arm
2	ammunition-belt bag	5	clamping mechanism
3	belt bag holder		

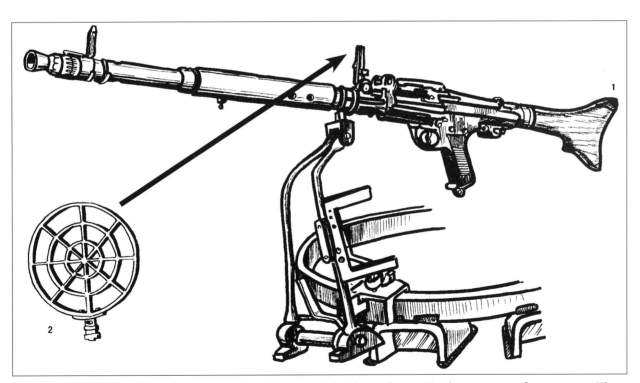

The ground-target sighting device was replaced by an aerial sighting device (2) when engaging flying targets. The three circles were used for head-on attack (inner), slow moving and fast moving aircraft (outer circle) respectively.

Using the MP port

In the turret side-wall behind and to the left of the commander there was a machine-pistol port which was closed by a plug with a short chain attached to retain it after it had been pulled out and a long one for pulling it back in. The first production vehicles had an MP port on each side (right) at the rear of the turret but from chassis no. 250046 (December 1942) the one on the right was instead replaced by an integrated emergency escape hatch.

Of course nothing much could be targeted from the remaining port. However, the Tiger II had one installed in the centre of the rear of escape hatch on the rear of the turret.

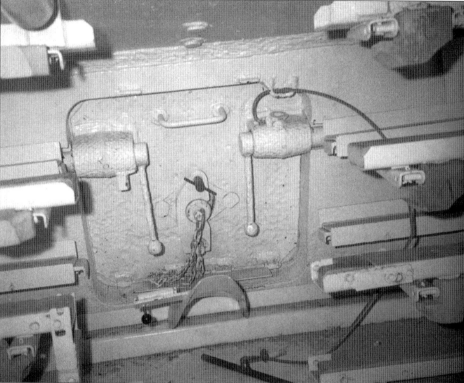

In the Tiger II the MP port was integrated onto the emergency exit hatch on the rear wall of the turret.

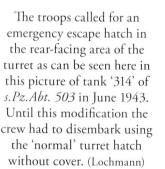

The troops called for an emergency escape hatch in the rear-facing area of the turret as can be seen here in this picture of tank '314' of *s.Pz.Abt. 503* in June 1943. Until this modification the crew had to disembark using the 'normal' turret hatch without cover. (Lochmann)

Gunner's Operating Tasks

In order to fulfil his main task – to engage targets of every kind using the on-board cannon and turret mounted machine gun – the gunner had also to be able to deal with specific subtasks:

- using the turret's telescopic sight
- aiming
- operating the travel lock
- firing the cannon and turret machine gun
- learning the firing regulations

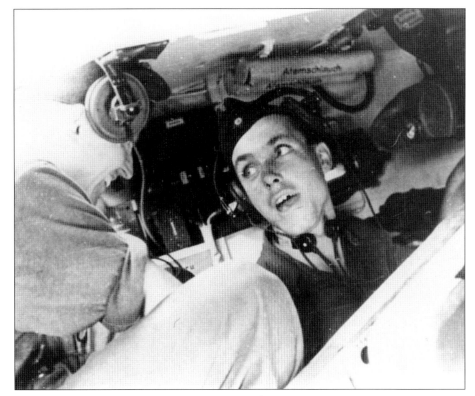

The gunner, in this case *Obergefreiter* Otto of *s.Pz.Abt. 502*, was the key to success in firefights if he could react instinctively and with cold blood. He was often given instructions through shouts by the commander (that's why he's keeping a 'free ear'). (Rosenburg)

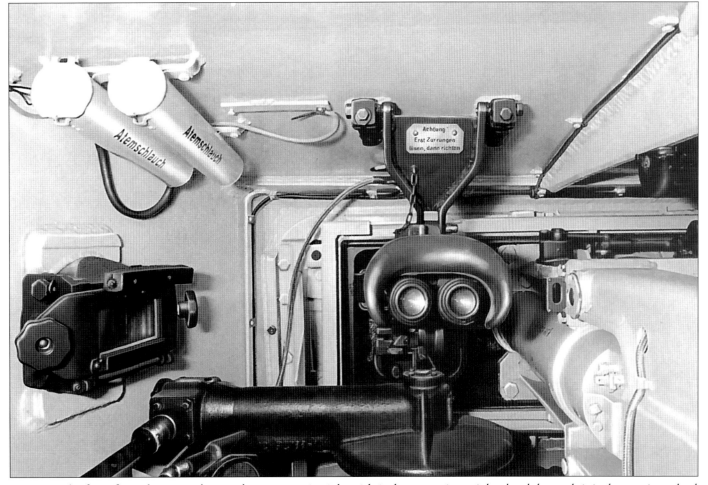

A view to the front from the gunner's seat; the turret main sight with its brow rest is straight ahead; beneath it is the turning wheel for the fine adjustment of the turret direction. On the turret wall to the left, is the gunners observation slit. (Trojca)

The gunner's seat with the gun-elevation adjustment wheel and beneath it the foot-operated steering controls, the foot-operated lever for firing the machine gun and, to the left, the clutch levers on the turret rotating-mechanism drive with its two positions 'Aus' (downwards) and 'Ein'. The gunner's upholstered seat was fixed but the back rest was adjustable for height.

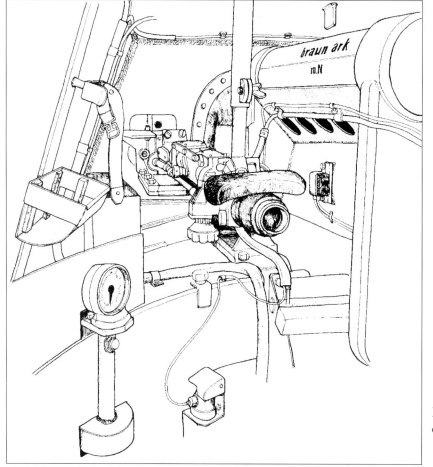

Due to the sloping wall the gunner's position was certainly narrower to his left on the Tiger II than on the Tiger I. Only the *TZF 9d* monocular sight was installed there.

Using the gunner's sight (*TZF*)

The gunner had to take a series of steps when commissioning and while using the *TZF*. By means of a clamping screw the gunner set the position of the headrest and eye cups. The telescope linkage allowed the eyepieces to be swung in the range +30° to -20°. By turning the eyepiece ring, the image clarity could be adjusted when making observations at a large distance.

> In the dark, the reticules are illuminated by a plug-in light on the swallowtail guide of the illuminated window on the reticule box. Inside the lamp housing there is a covering shield with which the brightness can be adjusted down to total darkness.
>
> (page 44 of D 656/22)

On the *TZF 9d* monocular sighting device, which was installed later, the gunner set the magnification to x 2.5 by moving a lever on the left side to the forward position; when engaging targets the magnification could be increased, if necessary, to x5 by setting the lever to the rearward position. The bulk of the *TZF 9b* devices installed in the Tiger I were binocular with a magnification power of only x 2.5. Using a binocular telescopic sight is less tiring and the picture (subjectively) clearer. The field of view covered 25° which corresponds to 444 reticule marks; with the *TZF 9d*, the field of view was 28° or 14° which respectively corresponds to 488 m and 244 m at a distance of 1000 m.

When a target was identified it was now the gunner's essential task to precisely adjust both of the moving parts of the reticule according to the type of ammunition being deployed and the sighting distance. Two semi-circular distance scales were engraved on the reticule; on the left was the scale for the MG and armour piercing shells and on the right, the scale for use with high explosive shells. These scales took the form of small circles the first and every second of which were numbered. This scale was rotated according to the (known) target distance. With the distance scale set to zero, the *Strichplatte* (aiming plate) was located centrally.

On the *Strichplatte*, at the centre of a row of six small inverted 'V's, was a triangle indicating the main aiming point. The distance between the points of these indicators was four *Strich* (a unit of measurement based on the radian) and it was these that were used to engage targets moving across the line of vision (see diagram below). Turning the adjustment knob to set the desired target distance moved the *Strichplatte* vertically downwards (less if the target was nearer and more so if the target was more distant). The cannon was then raised or lowered manually as required until the aiming indicator was on the target.

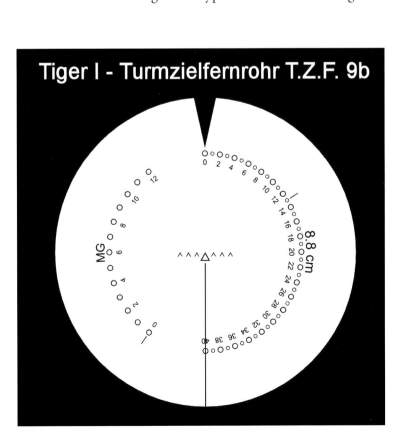

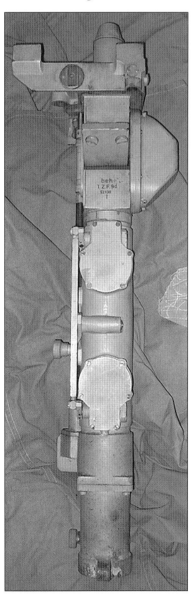

TZF 9d (dismantled from tank).

Aiming at targets

Learning to sight-in targets rapidly required some practice which on the Tiger was originally regulated with a high degree of effectiveness. The gunner could operate the turret traversing mechanism (**Turmschwenkwerk**) either hydraulically – by a motor powered by the running gear drive shaft – or manually. The hydraulic system was actuated by means of pedals. (see diagram)

Page 23 of the instruction manual for the operation of the turret gives an exact description:

> During actuation the pedal footplates and the appropriate hand lever remain in their central positions and the hydraulic drive control lever in its leftmost position. As soon as the pump is started by engaging the clutch, a suction effect that fills the pump and the hydraulic drive that rotates the drive shaft is achieved by slowly pressing on the footplate. **The further the footplate is moved from its zero position (central position), the higher is the speed of rotation of the drive shaft and therefore the traverse rate of the turret.**
>
> After starting, the hydraulic-drive motor can be set to its highest speed by moving the control lever to its furthest right position. Following this, the footplate controls and control lever can be used without damaging the transmission drive whether it is stationary or running. By turning the drive off or on, the footplate is brought back to its central position by a supporting spring.
>
> **All adjustments are to be performed quickly and smoothly.**

The elevation of the cannon was achieved by means of a handwheel that was connected to the elevation mechanism by a transmission rod. Both of these operations, aiming to the side or adjusting elevation, could of course only be carried out if both the barrel and turret travel locks had been released.

It is important to note that the traverse speed of the turret depended on the speed of rotation of the tank's engine. If the gunner had to traverse the turret quickly, the driver was ordered to increase the engine speed. Page 62 of the *Tigerfibel* (see the top of the following page) describes the interaction between the crew members.

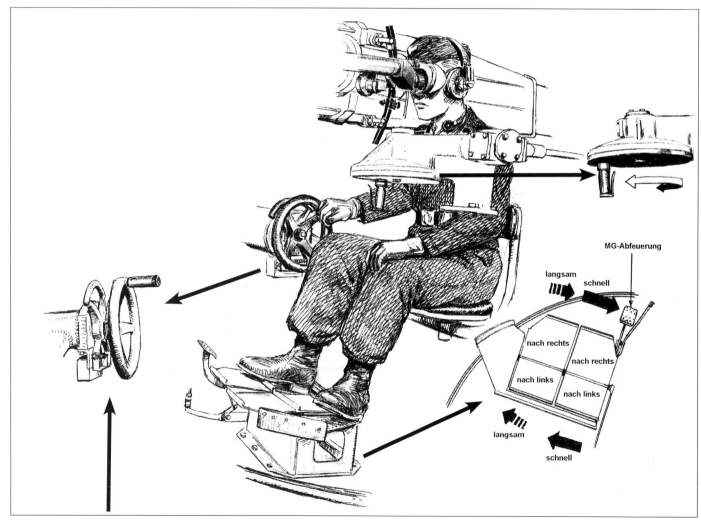

The gunner, keeping a watch through the telescopic sight in the turret, turns the handwheel used to adjust the gun's elevation with his right hand and by rocking both feet engages the motor-driven turret traverse drive. Fine adjustment is carried out with the manual drive (using the left hand). A lever mounted behind the elevation handwheel fires the cannon.

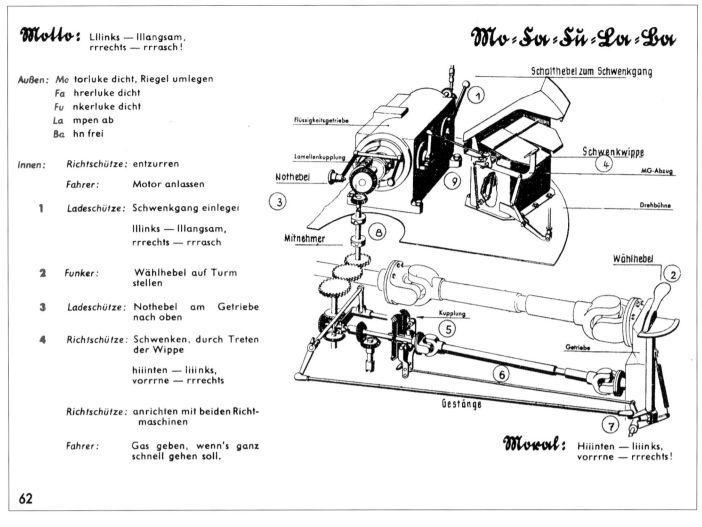

The relative position of the turret – in relation to the tank's hull – was visible to the gunner on a numbered clock-dial direction indicator (*Zwölfuhrzeiger*). This indicator was used only intermittently, for example when the commander was assigning targets or when resetting the 12 o'clock position for the continuation of a roadmarch following an exchange of fire to the side. It was also used when fire-plan diagrams were required (see Chapter 4, on 'Deployment').

The turret could be turned manually if the hydraulics for the turret traverse mechanism failed or when making fine adjustments to the aiming direction. The tank driver, and later the commander, could if necessary assist the gunner by means of an auxiliary drive if, for example, the tank was standing on a steep slope. In the Tiger II, the loader could assist mechanically.

The relevant description page 21 of D 656/22 states:

> The hand drive is located to the front left in the bevel drive housing which is bolted to the turret reinforcing ring. When not in use the handwheel is secured by a spring-loaded locking pin that is set in a drilled hole in the bevel drive housing. To turn the handwheel, the locking pin is released by pulling the lever. The rotation of the handwheel is transmitted via the handwheel shaft, bevel gear 4, shaft, bevel gear 5, drive shaft and the worm of the upper worm wheel.
>
> The auxiliary drive and it bearing is bolted to the gearbox housing for the turret traversing mechanism.

The turret was locked in position by turning the locking wheel clockwise; this pressed a toothed segment into the turret gear rack.

Firing the gun and the turret machine gun

To fire the tank's cannon the gunner pulled on the firing lever (*Abzugshebel*) located behind the handwheel that operated the elevation mechanism (on the Tiger II this was on the hand-wheel itself). This completed the circuit on the firing switch which sent an electrical impulse to the firing circuit on the cannon's breech ring.

In the event of the failure of the electrical power source, the emergency firing system (*Notabfeuerung*) was activated by means of which a short duration current was generated by magnetic induction. However, early models had an emergency battery instead of the emergency firing system.

The turret machine gun was activated by means of the MG firing device (*MG-Abzugsvorrichtung*). This was connected to the foot pedals for the hydraulic turret traversing mechanism (*Turmschwenkwerk*). Aiming was achieved by means of the turret traversing mechanism and the gun elevation gear. Corrections were made based on the position of the fire dispersal cone relative to the target as viewed through the gunner's telescopic sight. It the firing mechanism failed, the machine gun could be fired manually by the loader.

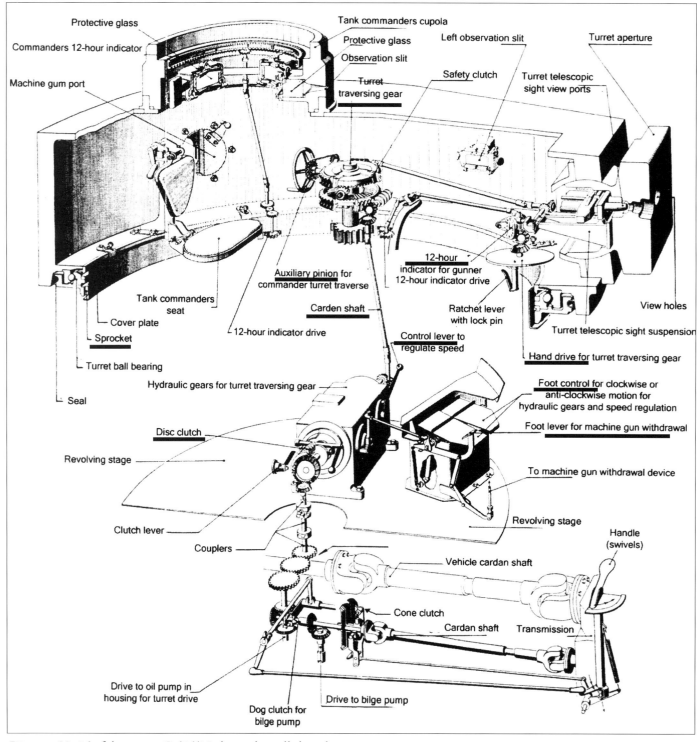

Protective glass

Commanders 12-hour indicator

Machine gum port

Tank commanders cupola

Protective glass

Observation slit

Turret traversing gear

Left observation slit

Safety clutch

Turret aperture

Turret telescopic sight view ports

12-hour indicator for gunner 12-hour indicator drive

Auxiliary pinion for commander turret traverse

Carden shaft

Control lever to regulate speed

Ratchet lever with lock pin

View holes

Turret telescopic sight suspension

Hand drive for turret traversing gear

Tank commanders seat

Cover plate

Sprocket

Turret ball bearing

Seal

12-hour indicator drive

Hydraulic gears for turret traversing gear

Disc clutch

Revolving stage

Clutch lever

Couplers

Foot control for clockwise or anti-clockwise motion for hydraulic gears and speed regulation

Foot lever for machine gun withdrawal

To machine gun withdrawal device

Revolving stage

Handle (swivels)

Vehicle cardan shaft

Cone clutch

Cardan shaft

Transmission

Drive to oil pump in housing for turret drive

Dog clutch for bilge pump

Drive to bilge pump

Diagram Nr.36 of document D656/22 shows the well thought out arrangement of the turret traversing mechanism. The parts mentioned in the text are underlined.

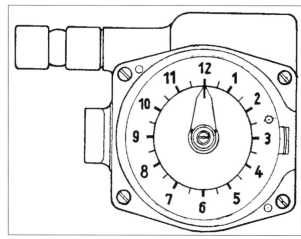

The diagram on the right shows the *Turmstellungsanzeiger* (turret position indicator). In this diagram the 12 o'clock position is shown. As the turret is rotated the pointer on the dial turns accordingly. Later a second indicator with intervals of 1 to 64 was added to the left side.

Learning the firing rules

This part of the training (see Chapter 4, 'Deployment', 'Applying the firing regulations') was very time consuming because the precise determination of the distance of a target and the lead angle required was of crucial importance for the success or failure of a shot because the tanks at that time still had not been equipped with rangefinders. These were first installed only in a few models of *Ausf. F* of the *Pz.Kpfw.* Panther. On 28 February 1945, the *Waffenprüfstelle* (Weapons Testing Office) asked Henschel to test the installation of an optical base-rangefinder in the turret of a Tiger II. The first turret was supposed to have been converted by 31 March 1945. Krupp, as the manufacturer of turrets, pledged to provide the necessary drillings for the rangefinder mountings as from the 601st vehicle produced in the middle of July 1945.

All tanks and other gun platforms therefore determined the distance to a target by means of an engraved scale method (see *Tigerfibel* diagram). Using this method, a whole range of factors could exert a negative influence on aiming. These concerned the gunner's ability to concentrate after long periods of stress as well as the lighting conditions under which the target was viewed and the way this affected the optics, for example glare from sunlight and such like. Moving targets presented a particular difficulty because choosing the necessary lead angle on the target – which depends on its speed – had to be carried out by adjustment of the position of the aiming mark by moving the turret, and in the case of an oliquely moving target also by adjusting the elevation of the gun.

It is obvious that it took a great deal of time to train gunners to achieve the highest levels of certainty of action. On the grounds of capacity, the training content (the loaders and new commanders were also trained in this) was taught not only in the tanks themselves but also with the assistance of artillery observation telescopes, optical rangefinders and 'scissor' binoculars. Target areas were real open spaces but there were also scaled-down target zones (so-called *Kleine Zielfelder*) and gunnery sandboxes were also used.

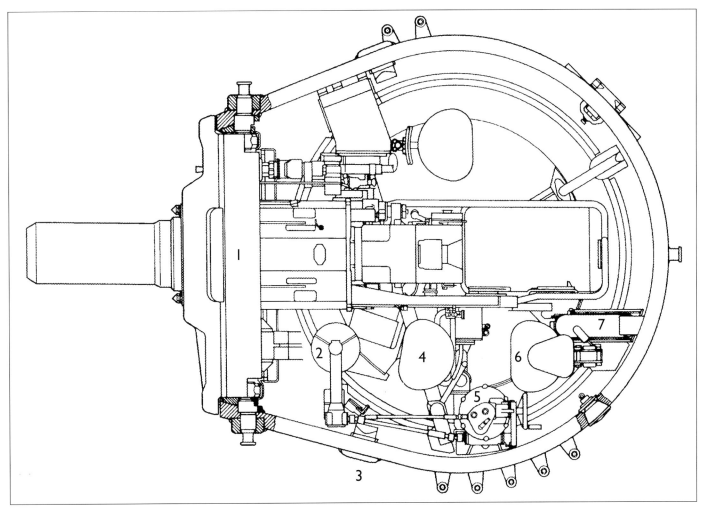

This plan view of the turret shows just how cramped the gunner's seat (4) was.
Legend: 1 gun mantlet, 2 traverse hand wheel, 3 gunner's observation slit, 5 traverse mechanism and auxiliary manual drive, 6 cdr's seat, 7 balancing spring.

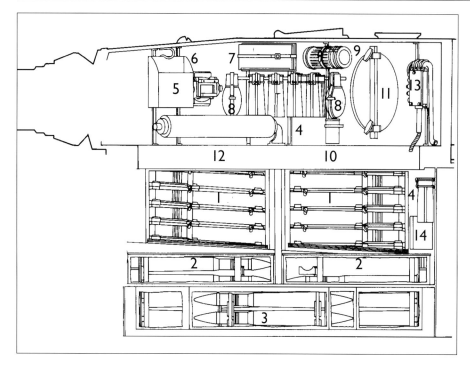

5   luggage box
6   smoke discharger switch
7   MG bipod and shoulder brace
8   drinking bottles
9   gas masks
10 ejector tool
11 escape hatch
12 spring ballancer
13 turret fusebox
14 MG tools

Stowage arrangement
(loader's side and hull/floor)

Ammunition racks
1   for 16 rounds
2   for 4 rounds
3   for 6 rounds
4   MG ammunition bags

15 luggage box
16 ammo-stowage flap
17 storage for small parts
18 replacement breeches
19 fire extinguisher
20 water canister
21 wire basket for flags
22 turret traverse motor
23 foot pedals for turret
    traverse mechanism
24 turret drive
25 rack for turret MG when
    submerged

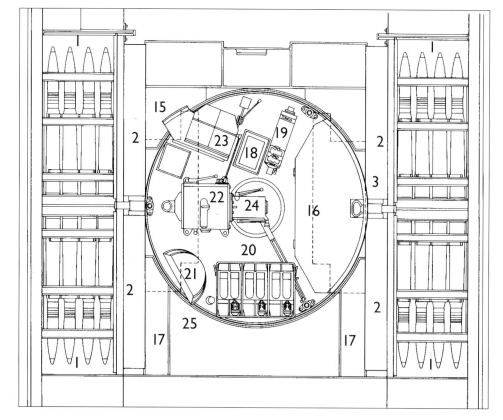

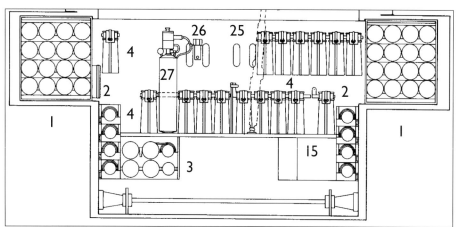

26 mine release switch
27 autom. fire extinguisher

Loader's Operating Tasks

As the name clearly implies, the loader's main task was to load the on-board cannon as quickly as possible with the requisite type of ammunition. In addition, he monitored the operational readiness of the turret machine gun.

Gunners were taught the following essential training points:

- re-arming the tank
- loading procedure for the tank's cannon
- procedure for installing, demounting and loading the machine gun
- securing the cannon
- operation of the close defence weapons
- loading the mortar equipment
- dealing with problems

A view to the left of the cannon's breech block (locked) with the safety switch above the recoil damper. Below right on the breech is the breech-opener in the 'on' position and above it the mechanical safety catch in the '*sicher*' position, that is to say the breech-block cannot be closed. This area was mistakenly painted in this restored Tiger.

A loader sweats as he fulfils his main task – loading the cannon.

The view from the loader's seat towards the front with the built-in MG and the barrel of the cannon to the left; beneath this the upper part of the toothed arch that is part of the elevation mechanism can be seen; to the right is the spring balancer with its linkage parallelogram. (Trojca)

The breech of the main gun with the breech-wedge in the upper (closed) position.

Re-arming the tank

Restocking the tank with ammunition was strenuous work for the whole crew but especially for the loader in the tank. However, it was only in a few cases that the full battle complement of 92 shells and 39 bags of machine-gun ammunition (each with 150 rounds) had to be loaded into the Tiger I – or 84 rounds of 8.8 cm shells and 32 bags of machine-gun ammunition in the Tiger II. In the majority of cases only the amount used during the last engagement had to be added. The procedures are described in detail in the series of pictures in this chapter; the position of the ammunition racks can be seen in the sketches of the interior of the tank and in the pictures.

Training for this activity was carried out using inert shells so that no damage occurred to expensive ammunition. It was particularly important that the ammunition was correctly installed in the racks and locked in place by the lifting yokes so that they did not slip or get damaged when the tank was in motion.

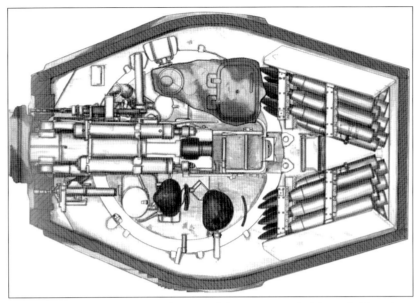

The ammunition racks in the rear of the turret on the Tiger II (above) were usually not used by the troops because a hit could cause a devastating explosion. The cannon ammunition in the Tiger I was stored only in the hull and in four different types of rack.

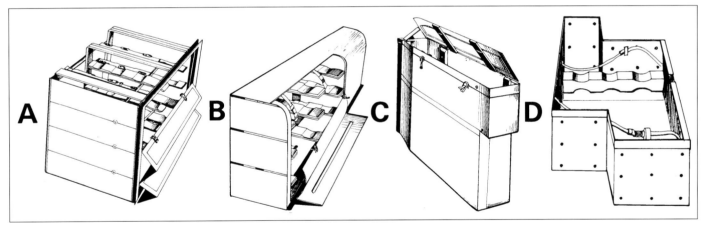

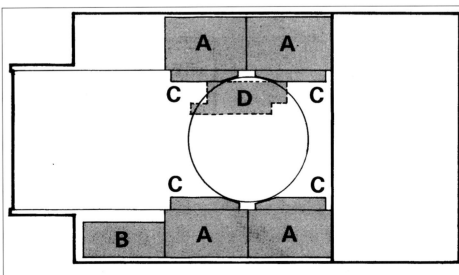

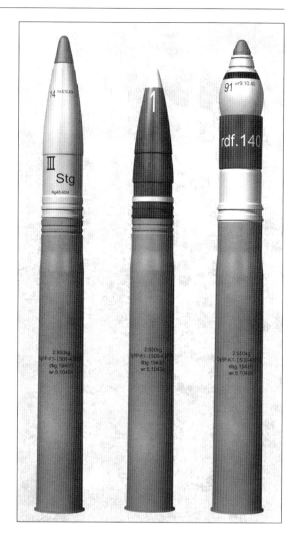

The three most used type of ammunition were the *Sprenggranate* (yellow), *Panzergranate 39* (*Pz.Gr. 39-1* is shown in the centre) and the less frequently used *Panzergranate 39* (Hl). (Drawings by Harada)All types of ammunition could be stored in the racks at the hull sides but the floor storage area could accommodate only the shorter *Pz. Gr.*

Storage on the turret roof was more likely to be criticized! (Wunderlich) The empty shell cases were packed into wooden boxes and the storage racks taken away by the munitions detachment. (BA 22-2948-38)

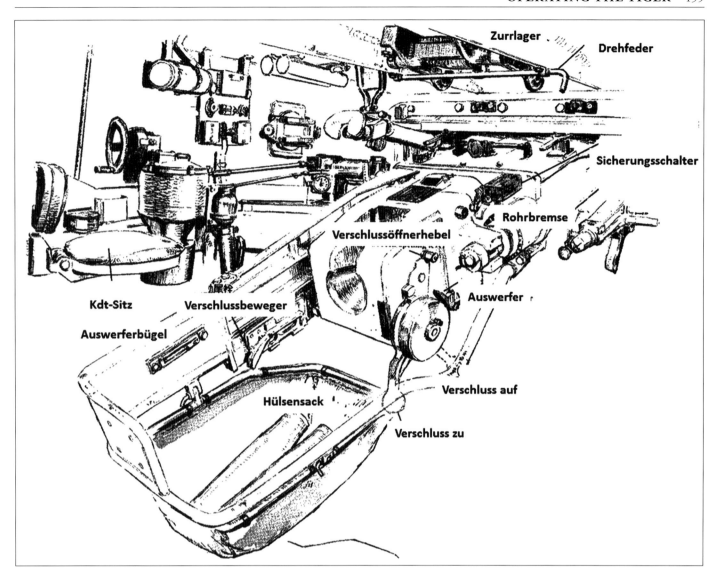

Zurrlager

Drehfeder

Sicherungsschalter

Rohrbremse

Verschlussöffnerhebel

Auswerfer

Kdt-Sitz   Verschlussbeweger

Auswerferbügel

Verschluss auf

Hülsensack

Verschluss zu

Gun loading procedure

Apart from the physical effort of handling the heavy shells, loading the cannon was functionally straightforward. Only when the cannon was loaded for the first time did the loader have to manually open the breech (*Verschluss*). When firing the cannon, the recoil automatically opened the breech and ejected the empty shell casing and held the breech block in the (open) loading position. The loader promptly pushed the shell into the chamber and gave it a final push with the heel of his hand. The ejector (*Auswerfer*) was released by the rim at the bottom of the shell casing so that the breech block slid up under pressure from a spring and this closed the breech chamber.

The loader opened [the breech block] by hand by releasing a catch and turning the crank handle to the rear.

> With this the crank rotated the pinion and crankshaft. The crank then released the breech block and pushed it down to its limit past the ejector. The pinion pulled the gear rack in the breech trigger to the rear and this stretched the closing spring. At this point the opening spring was not under tension. However, as soon as the crank handle was released the spring under tension tried to close the

breech but the retracted ejector held the breech block in the loading position.

> (D 2061/1 '8.8-cm-Kampfwagenkanone 43 (L/71)')

Closing was easy:

> Press the handgrip on the ejector shaft forwards and at the same time lift the hand crank a little and let it go. The hook on the ejector is then pulled from the breech block and the breech closes automatically.

This procedure was the same on both Tiger models. After loading the shell, the loader immediately pressed the button on the electrical safety switch (*Sicherungsschalter*) and called out: 'Loaded!' The indicator lamp on the left-side wall shone red. He grasped the next shell and kept it clear of the recoil area of the breech to avoid injury and damage to the shell.

During breaks in firing he filled the racks nearby with shells so that they were instantly available. There was a special tool for removing jammed shell-casings. Occasionally the assistance of the barrel cleaning rods was also required.

A view of the turret MG (cannon elevated); to the right is the spring balancer [for the weight of cannon]. The number '8' on the viewing slit refers to the water tightness procedures of the seals when submerged; this was omitted on later models.

Installing, disassembling and loading the MG

The MG 34 was installed to the right of the mantlet in a gimbal mounting in an adjustable housing and was secured by a spring-loaded clamp. The loader could pull back a fork on the MG support to his rear and fold it to the right in order to either change the barrel of the MG (using an asbestos cloth if the barrel was hot) or when installing or dismounting the MG. The forked piece was secured by a removable pin.

A machine-gun ammunition-belt holder was attached to the MG support.

It holds two ammunition-belt sacks on support frames that can be swivelled backwards and forwards each of which is held by a sprung safety catch that enables it to be easily replaced and moved to the side. Hanging to the left is the ammunition-belt sack containing a belt with 150 rounds; to the right is an empty sack used to catch the cartridge cases. The rear panel of the sack holding frame is designed as a flap. The flap stays in the vertical position when firing. When changing barrels the flap is fastened to the front in the horizontal position using the knob located on the right side of the ammunition-belt sack support frame so that the housing for the MG 34 can be swung free. A lever securely locks the flap to the sack support frame in the 'vertical' and 'horizontal' positions.

(D 656/22 pages 16 and 17)

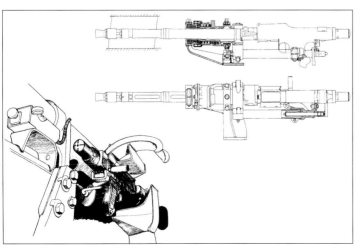

The drawing to the right shows the modified MG installation in the Tiger II with a curved bridge for the ammunition belt feed and the funnel underneath that led the ejected cartridge casings down to the spent-cartridge box.

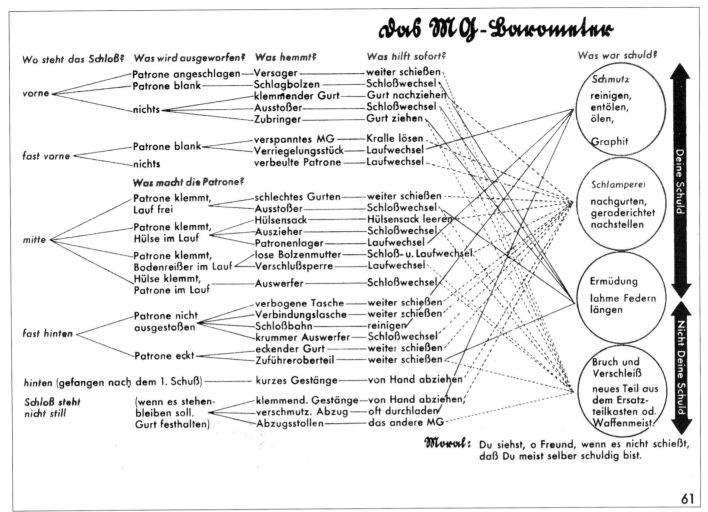

Das MG-Barometer

Wo steht das Schloß?	Was wird ausgeworfen?	Was hemmt?	Was hilft sofort?	Was war schuld?

vorne — Patrone angeschlagen — Versager — weiter schießen
— Patrone blank — Schlagbolzen — Schloßwechsel
— klemmender Gurt — Gurt nachziehen
— nichts — Ausstoßer — Schloßwechsel
— Zubringer — Gurt ziehen

fast vorne — Patrone blank — verspanntes MG — Kralle lösen
— Verriegelungsstück — Laufwechsel
— nichts — verbeulte Patrone — Laufwechsel

Was macht die Patrone?

mitte — Patrone klemmt, Lauf frei — schlechtes Gurten — weiter schießen
— Ausstoßer — Schloßwechsel
— Patrone klemmt, Hülse im Lauf — Hülsensack — Hülsensack leeren
— Auszieher — Schloßwechsel
— Patronenlager — Laufwechsel
— Patrone klemmt, Bodenreißer im Lauf — lose Bolzenmutter — Schloß- u. Laufwechsel
— Verschlußsperre — Laufwechsel
— Hülse klemmt, Patrone im Lauf — Auswerfer — Schloßwechsel

fast hinten — Patrone nicht ausgestoßen — verbogene Tasche — weiter schießen
— Verbindungslasche — weiter schießen
— Schloßbahn — reinigen
— krummer Auswerfer — Schloßwechsel
— Patrone eckt — eckender Gurt — weiter schießen
— Zuführeroberteil — weiter schießen

hinten (gefangen nach dem 1. Schuß) — kurzes Gestänge — von Hand abziehen

Schloß steht nicht still — (wenn es stehenbleiben soll, Gurt festhalten) — klemmend. Gestänge — von Hand abziehen
— verschmutz. Abzug — oft durchladen
— Abzugsstollen — das andere MG

Schmutz
reinigen, entölen, ölen, Graphit

Schlamperei
nachgurten, geraderichtet nachstellen

Ermüdung
lahme Federn längen

Bruch und Verschleiß
neues Teil aus dem Ersatzteilkasten od. Waffenmeist.

Deine Schuld

Nicht Deine Schuld

Moral: Du siehst, o Freund, wenn es nicht schießt, daß Du meist selber schuldig bist.

61

Operating the turret MG was complex and the firing mechanism prone to failure. The *Tigerfibel* took account of this by dedicating a whole page to this problem ('*MG Barometer*' on page 61) with important advice for the loader thoughtfully divided into events for which was he was, or was not, at fault!

Loading the mine discharger

If the tank was equipped with this device (on the turret or the rear deck), it was the task of the loader to arm it before the tank was deployed. The mine (6) was placed in its respective container fixed to a support plate (3) on the base of which was an electrical firing contact fuse (5), the ignitor (4) was then screwed into place, the ignition wire connected to the discharger contact and the plug inserted (this was removed before loading) into a socket on the turret (2). Finally, the protective cap (1) was flipped up.

It was triggered by opening the control box in the turret and briefly pressing the button corresponding to the appropriate mine discharger. Ignition occurred after approximately four seconds by the activation of the ignition rod (7) in the body of the smoke mine.

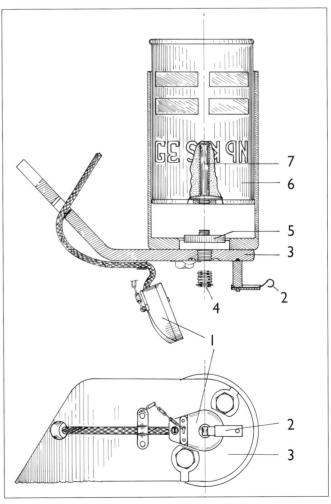

Gun lashing (on Tiger II 'turret lashing')

On long marches in the battle zone, the cannon was fixed in order to protect its trunnion and bearing from mechanical damage by reducing vibration. The description on Page 14 of the turret regulations states:

> The gun-cradle lock is screwed under the turret roof. On its shaft are two hooks and a swivel-mounted clamping device consisting of a spindle and threaded shaft. To lock the gun, it is elevated to 15°. The hooks are then placed over the spigots on the breech and pressed against the breech by turning the spindle on the shaft of the clamping device.
>
> When not in use the hooks and clamping device, held together by a bar, are folded back under the turret roof

and held in place by a retaining device consisting of a shaft, torsion spring, two cranks and two latches.

This foregoing is a good example of how the actual operation of the device was clearly more straightforward than the description.

After releasing the turret travel lock, the loader set the clutch hand lever for the multi-disc clutch to the '*Ein*' position, otherwise power assisted traversing of the turret was not possible.

From November 1943, Tiger I tanks were equipped with a barrel clamp on the rear of the hull (see picture).

On the Tiger II, there was a barrel traverse lock to the right of the loader that when screwed in blocked the rotation of the turret.

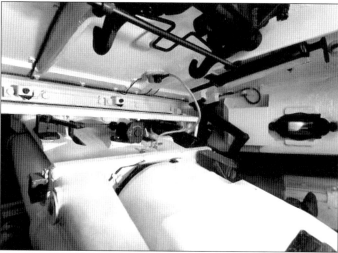

Lashing the gun in the Tiger I with the hooks in the raised (see above) and the fitted position (see left).

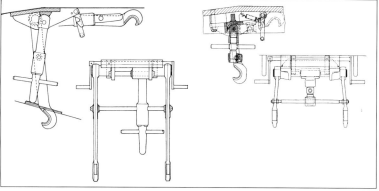

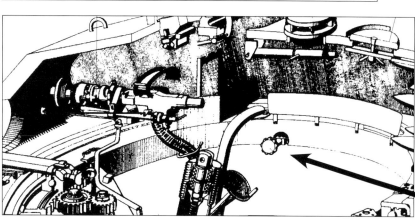

Turret lashing in the Tiger II.

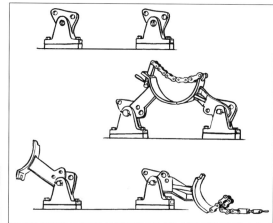

Tube lashing on the hull rear of the Tiger I (was omitted later).

Operation of the close combat weapon

The close-combat weapon system on the turret behind the loader's hatch (installed on the Tiger I as from March 1944) fired *Schnellnebelkerzen 39* (rapid deployment smoke candles) to obscure the tank, mortar shells for engaging nearby hostile troops, *Rauchsichtzeichen orange 350* (orange smoke canisters) as an identification sign for the *Luftwaffe* as well as flares or was used for firing various munition with the aid of a flare pistol.

The operation of the close-combat weapon system is fully described in the Turret Regulations (page 33 and onwards):

1. Open the cover by turning the bayonetted lock to the right and remove the sealing plug. Load the ammunition into the breech. Replace and lock the cover.

2. Insert the Zündschraube C43 (ignitor screw) into the opening for the firing pin. Pull the firing pin back against the pressure of the firing spring until it clicks and place the ignitor screw in the recess. Pull back the firing pin slightly then release the safety catch on the firing lever and push the firing lever upwards. The device can be reset from new.'

A description of the operations for using various kinds of ammunition follows. In addition, a flare pistol could be inserted into the opened close-combat weapons facility and from it any kind of flare could be fired, including, amongst others, the new *Sprenggranatpatrone* (high explosive fragmentation grenade) with a time fuse. These grenades detonated 0.5 m to 2 m above the ground scattering shrapnel up to 100 m.

On older tanks, on orders from the commander, the loader was also responsible for firing the machine pistol through the machine-pistol port at nearby attackers.

The machine-pistol opening in the tank wall is closed by turning the flap using the knob on the pivoting lever. The knob sits on a spring-loaded bolt that springs into recesses in the turret casing so that the flap can be held securely in the open or closed position.

(Turret Regulations, page 30)

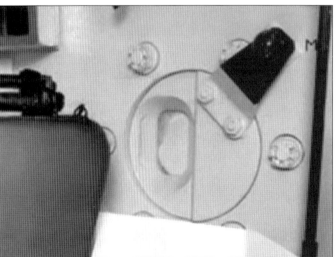

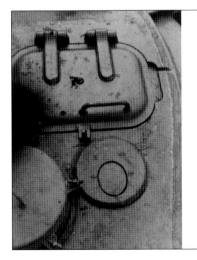

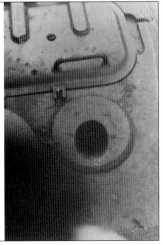

Close-defence weapon installation as seen from the outside (shown here on a Tiger II), open on left picture resp. closed.
The picture below shows a flare pistol ready for use in the close-combat weapons port.

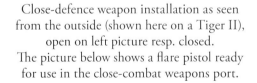

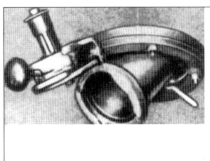

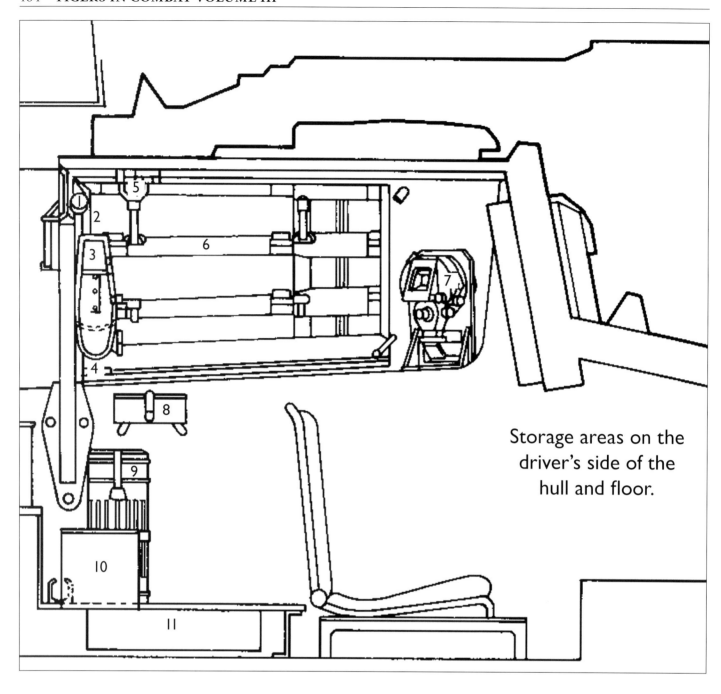

Storage areas on the driver's side of the hull and floor.

 1   breathing tube
 2   prism insert
 3   water bottle
 4   magnetic inspection lamp
 5   front headlight
 6   ammo rack for six 8.8 cm rounds
 7   gyro compass
 8   binocular holder
 9   gasmask
10   headphones and microphone
11   driver's tool box

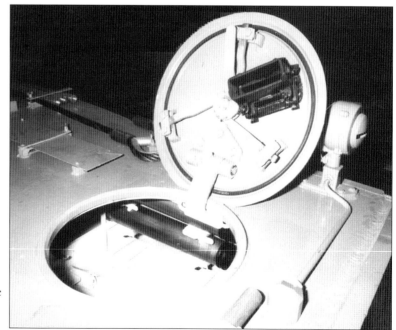

Open driver's hatch with integrated periscope. A storage rack for ammunition for the cannon can be seen to the left of the driver's position.

Driver Operating Tasks

Tiger-specific operating elements

The following descriptions are quoted in part word for word from the regulations

- D656/43 for the Tiger *Ausführung B*, Handbook for the Tank driver from 1.9.44
- D656/23 for the *Pz.Kpfw.* Tiger *Ausführung E*, Handook for the Tank driver from 10.5.44 as well as the previously mentioned *Tigerfibel*.

Large parts of the text in the first two of these sets of regulations coincide but the regulations for the Tiger II are more extensively and consistently illustrated.

Important variations and differences of both types are discussed separately.

Because of its ability to operate under water the Tiger I at first had additional controls for the ventilation of the engine and warm air extraction as these had to be properly controlled to prevent it from overheating. Changes had already taken place after half a year as a result of the changeover to the HL 230 power plant with its different ventilation drive.

Driving the vehicle was made easier by using the modern gearbox and steering system as in the later Leopard I armoured fighting vehicle but the safe commissioning, servicing, operation in emergencies and maintenance of the vehicle required an extensive knowledge of the technical processes involved. In order to avoid incorrect operation under the stress of action it was important to have calm and level-headed drivers. Overall, the operations involved in driving the vehicle were clearly more extensive than for other operating elements.

The driver's seat in the *Pz.Kpfw.* Tiger Ausf. E showing the more important controls.
(Bovington Tank Museum with ammendments by the author)

Drawing from the driver's position in the Tiger I with the original instrument panel. In some of the later-built vehicles other displays were installed. (Trojca)

Bow compartment and driver's seat in the Tiger *Ausf. B* (Tiger II). Except for the up to date ability for the driver to adjust the height of his seat and controls during marches so that his head was above the hatch opening, there were no essential differences between driving the Tiger II and Tiger I. (D656/43)

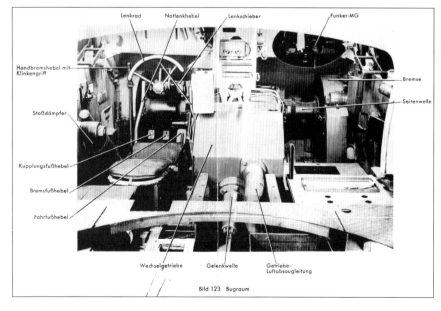

Service entry and basic handling

(according to D656/27, D656/43, various articles in HtVBl 1943 and 1944)

It took the driver about two hours to prepare the vehicle if he took the matter seriously. According to page 13 of the *Tigerfibel* the driver was supposed to attend to the following points before starting the vehicle: '*Sprit-Strom-Wasser-Starten-6 x Ölstand-Öldruck-Warten*'. [a mnemonic for checking the fuel, electrical system, water level before starting and then checking the six oil levels and waiting for correct pressure] Because the Tiger driver had to have mastery over the relatively sophisticated and temperamental vehicle technology he could in no way be considered simply a 'driver' or 'grease monkey.'

However, it is doubtful if the many modifications influencing the operation of the Tiger that had been made within just a few months could be taught in detail, and mastered, during active service.

Checks prior to mission start

1) Check and top up fuel level.
2) Check and top up cooling liquid level.
3) Tiger II: check and top up oil level in both fan drives. The engine cover of the Tiger II can only be opened when the turret is traversed to the side, in an emergency by a strong man if necessary.
4) Check and top up oil level in both final drives with gear oil.
5) Is the track damaged, are there any links broken?
6) Are any track-bolt securing devices missing? (below)
7) Is the track properly tensioned (hand width; see below)?
8) Are the screws on the drive and running wheels secure?
9) Does the on-board intercom work perfectly?

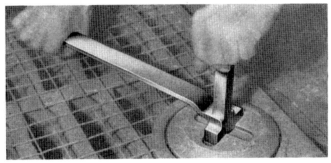

Noch Sonderwerkzeug 021 D 2799 U 16

Anwendung: Der Schlüssel 021 D 2799 U 16 findet Anwendung zum Öffnen und Schließen der Deckel über den Kraftstoffbehältern.

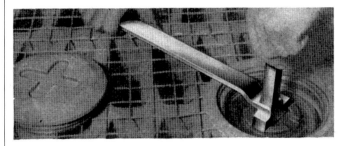

Anwendung: Der Schlüssel 021 D 2799 U 16 findet Anwendung zum Öffnen und Schließen der Deckel der Kraftstoffbehälter.

Opening the cap on the radiator. (D674/180)

Filler on the coolant expansion tank on the Tiger II (D656/43, pic. 18)

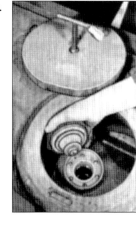

(D656/43, pic. 95)

(D656/43, pic. 83)

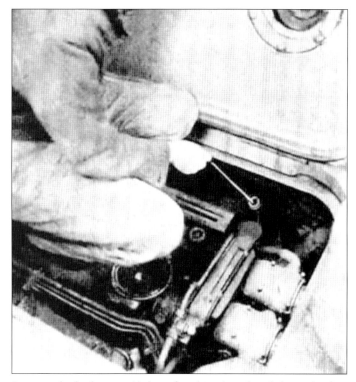

Loosen the lock-screw(s) (two fan drives) and withdraw the dipstick and top up if necessary using a funnel. This picture shows the procedure on the right-hand-side of a Tiger II. (D656/43, pic. 24 a. 25)

Starting the engine

1)   Open the floor vent and rear hood (on the engine compartment hatch) for ventilation.
2)   Tiger I, two fuel cocks open; Tiger II, open the fuel control lever located behind the driver.
3)   Turn on the accumulator (battery) main switch.
4)   Turn off the fan drive using the hand lever (only in the cold part of the year).

On the Tiger I with the HL 210 power plant: set the two levers on the partition wall to 'air in' and 'land.' When stationary two fan motor speeds are available on the ventilation gear.

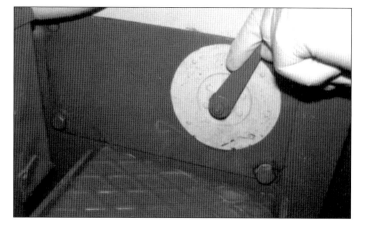

The battery main switch of a Tiger II on the instrument board on the partition wall of the engine compartment. Disengaging the fan drive on a Tiger II by pulling the hand lever through an aperture in that wall (left). (D656/43, pic. 104, left 21)

Fuel pump and hand lever with floor plate removed. Manual operation of the automatic fuel shut-off valve for bleeding in the Tiger II (below) (D656/43 pic. 38, above pic. 39)

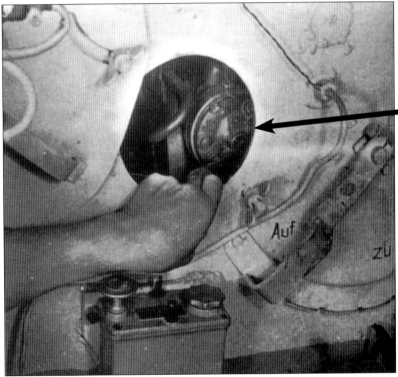

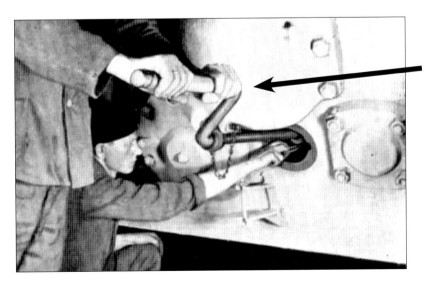

5) Tiger I: Set the fuel tank extractor fan to the 'land' position for venting to the outside.

6) Tiger I: Set the flow control lever on the partition wall for the warm air ventilation duct between the gearbox and exhaust fan to the 'under' position (on).

7) Tiger I (deleted later): Set transmission venting lever to 'land' position (through the manifold cover in the radiator housing to the fans).

8) Tiger I: Set both venting levers in the up position to expel hot air and flammable vapours from the radiator compartment.

9) Tiger I: Slide the vent cover to close the ventilation slit in the partition wall.

10) Tiger I: Turn the electric fuel pump on briefly to prime the fuel.

11) Tiger II: after prolonged periods of stopping fill the fuel lines and carburetor by means of the manual pump with the fuel shut-off valve open.

12) Disengage the clutch (pedal fully depressed).

When cold the engine should only be started by the vehicle's inertial starter or by using the starting handle and muscle power to conserve the battery and electric stating motor so that they function reliably when on active service. The inertial starter consists of a mechanically complex flywheel drive and must be revved up by two soldiers with the starting handle. This system works well on an engine that is fault-free. The starting handle is more simply constructed and turns the engine directly.

13) The inertial starter or starting crank should be engaged at first with the ignition switched off and this is confirmed by the radio operator and loader. Check if excessive water is expelled through the exhaust pipes as this is indicative of a defective cylinder head gasket. To avoid further damage through 'hydraulic knocking' the engine must not be started. If only a small amount or none is expelled the engine may be started. (HtVBl 1943, Article Nr. 432, issued 1 November 1944)

14) Insert the ignition key and turn on the ignition.
15) Disengage the clutch by fully depressing the clutch pedal.
16) Operate the carburetor (only pull the choke lever if the engine is cold).
17) Engage the inertia or starting crank after having been operated by radio operator and loader.

Only if the engine is warm: press the starting button for the electric starting motor.

In no circumstances should the accelerator be operated when starting; the fuel mixture is too 'rich' and this 'floods' the engine. The result is that all the spark plugs must be removed, dried and cleaned before reinstalling them: an hour's work.

18) Switch off starting motor and press the accelerator.
19) Allow the engine and transmission to warm up. Set the direction of motion lever to neutral and engage the clutch using the foot and allow the engine to idle. Keep the engine at 1,000-1,200 revolutions per minute until the cooling water has reached a temperature of 50°. If the tank has been standing for a long time, particularly when the outside temperature is low, the transmission must be allowed to run until it is warm to the touch. This allows the oil in the transmission to become fluid enough to allow the steering and gears to work faultlessly.
20) Tiger II and Tiger I with HL 230 engine: Switch on ventilator fans (see 'switching off' above).

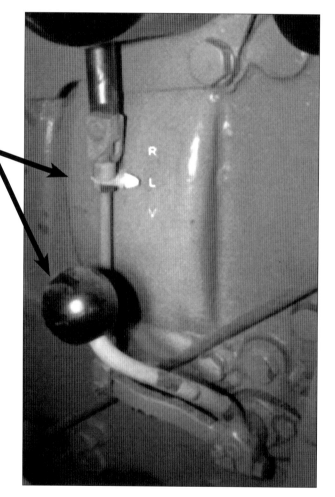

If the tank is standing on a slope the handbrake should be applied.

Sonderwerkzeug 021 D 2799 U 16

Schlüssel für Klappen über dem Motor

Testing with the engine running

Opening the engine compartment cover on the Tiger I (below) was both cumbersome and difficult because of its size and weight. Also, the turret had to be turned to the side. Firstly, a special tool (see the picture on left – taken from page 48 of D674/180) was used to turn the locking lever on the engine cover to the side. The weight of the cover, around 240 kg, was not balanced by a sprung torsion bar or any other such device.

Opening the engine cover required an initial force of 120 kg on the handgrips, a task for at least two men – or for safety reasons three or four men. (See picture below taken on 16 July 1943, at *s.Pz.Abt.503*) The open cover was secured by a ratchet lever.

1) Check the engine oil level daily with engine idling.

The picture to the left shows the dipstick of a Tiger II in use. (D656/43, pic. 2).

2) Check the transmission oil level daily with engine idling. The picture to the right shows the dipstick for the transmission oil level in use. (D656/43, pic. 58)

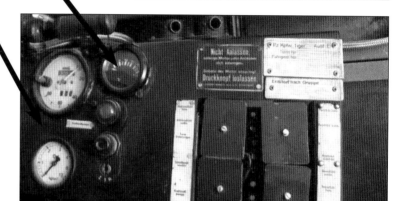

3) Does the charging indicator light go out at around 1,000 rpm at the latest?

4) Check the engine oil pressure. At 2,000 rpm the pressure should be at least 3.5 bar, otherwise shut down the engine and establish the cause.

5) With the vehicle stationary and the engine running make sure that the steering wheel is not displaced from the central position when the driver enters or leaves the vehicle as the Tiger will begin to turn on the spot even if the gear selector lever on the transmission is in the neutral position.

6) Test the hand- and footbrakes by driving a short distance forwards and backwards.

Changing gears

1) Moving: disengage the main clutch by depressing the clutch pedal.
If necessary set the pre-selector gear lever to the desired position between first and fourth gear – for example, third gear should be selected for driving on roads – and press this lever to the right to select the gear.

Set the driving levers from the mid position (idling) to the desired driving direction, accelerate the engine revs to around 1,600 rpm and slowly engage the clutch.

Note: Selecting and engaging gears are two independent operations. A gear is selected as long as the gear lever is in a notch and until a reverse pressure is detected. Depending on the terrain and running resistance a single, or several, gears can be skipped. However the gear will only change when the vehicle reaches relevant speed by braking, freewheeling or accelerating.

2) Changing gear when in motion: Select the desired gear by pushing the pre-selector lever to the right. It is not necessary to disengage the clutch.

With the engine running at 2,500 rpm the respective speed of Tiger II is:

1. Gear	2 km/hr
2. Gear	3 "
3. Gear	4 "
4. Gear	7 "
5. Gear	10 "
6. Gear	16 "
7. Gear	23 "
8. Gear	34 "
1. Reverse gear	3 "
2. "	4 "
3. "	7 "
4. "	9 "

Note: To avoid serious damage to the gears select only the gear that corresponds to the speed of the tank at the moment the gear is changed.

The most suitable engine speed for changing up gears is around 2,300 rpm and for changing down gears around 1,700 rpm. Changing gears must always be carried out when the engine speed is greater than 1,600 rpm otherwise the oil pressure is insufficient to keep the main coupling in the disengaged position and the clutch engages during gear selection causing severe damage to the transmission.

3) Stopping: Disengage the clutch, brake, change down to one of the first four gears, set the direction of motion lever to neutral and engage the clutch. The direction of motion lever cannot be set to neutral when higher than fourth gear is engaged.

To be able to stop suddenly when driving in 5-8th gear, disengage the clutch and brake until the tank comes to a halt. While doing this keep the clutch foot pedal pressed until one of the first four gears are engaged and the direction of travel lever is set to neutral.

4) Reversing: reversing is only possible in 1st to 4th gear (5th to 8th gear are locked). Select gear 1, 2, 3 or 4 according to the terrain and ground resistance, disengage the clutch and set the direction of travel lever to 'reverse' (rückwärts). Accelerate and slowly engage the clutch.

When reversing over longer distances up to 4th gear can be selected. When reversing, the steering must be turned in the opposite direction to the desired direction of travel.

Operating and driving the *Pz.Kpfw.* Tiger (the picture shows a vehicle belonging to *s.Pz.Abt. 503* on 5 June 1943) was clearly more straightforward than most of its contemporary equivalents. If the driver adhered to the operating requirements and exercised due care its susceptibility to damage was comparatively low. (Lochmann)

Steering

Steering is performed by means of a steering wheel attached to a steering valve. The travel on the steering wheel is around 90° clockwise and anti-clockwise. The force required to turn the steering wheel increases as the steering wheel is rotated. The steering valve controls the flow of oil to the relevant couplings and causes the tank to move in a curve corresponding to the chosen amount of rotation of the steering wheel.

The dual radius steering gear is flange-mounted to the transmission and makes it possible to drive in a curve with a large or a small radius in every gear. The result is a minimum turning circle of 2.4 m in 1st gear and a maximum turning circle of 114 m in 8th gear.

Note:
The higher the gear, the smaller the decrease in the speed of the inner track and the greater the radius of the curve travelled.
Curves should be driven without jerky operation of the steering wheel in order not to overload the multi-plate clutch. (HtVBl 1944, Article Nr. 714 issued 21 September 1944)

In contrast to other tanks of the period, which were simply turned by steering brakes on each side, the Tiger had a steering rack with two radii which could be controlled by turning the steering wheel. Also, the pedal arrangement was the same as in a car.

Turning on the spot

Turn the steering wheel to the left or to the right, depress the clutch or set the direction of travel lever to neutral and accelerate. The tank then turns on the spot, that is to say one track runs forwards and the other backwards. If the steering wheel is turned halfway, the turning motion is slower than with the steering wheel turned to its full extent. With the transmission in the neutral position and the engine at a standstill the steering wheel must always be in the central position, otherwise the tank will turn on the spot when the engine is started. If the steering wheel does not go into the central position of its own accord the I-Staffel (Instandsetzungs Staffel/repair detachment) or the Werkstattkompanie (Workshop Company) must examine the steering valve.

Note: If you do not intend to drive keep your hands off the steering wheel! If the engine is running and the transmission idling, especially in confined spaces and between vehicles where people could be endangered, the slightest turn of the tank places them and men working on the suspension in deadly peril.

Always keep the steering wheel turned until the end of the curve being travelled. Do not repeatedly pull on and let go the steering wheel as this will cause excessive wear on the couplings.

When reversing there is a change in steering direction, that is to say when the steering wheel is turned to the left, the tank turns backwards to the right and vice versa.

In order to avoid the tracks overriding and damaging the idler and the final drive, the greatest caution was ordered when driving in reverse. At the same time, turning in heavy ground and loose sand was to be strictly avoided. (HtVBl 1944, Article Nr. 430 issued 9 June 1944)

Essential driving skills
(D656/43, pages 88-89)

a) On roads

Starting:
1) Release handbrake.
2) On level ground start with 3rd gear.

Driving and changing gear:
1) Change gear in good time. Accelerate vigorously before changing up gears.
2) Keep the engine at around 1,800 to 2,000 rpm in each gear.
3) Change to a higher gear when the engine is at 2,300 rpm; a lower gear when the engine is at 1,600 to 1,700 rpm.
4) Keep the foot away from the clutch pedal when driving.

Braking and stopping:
1) Brake using the footbrake and handbrake.
2) Disengage the clutch shortly before stopping.
3) Set the direction of travel lever to the neutral position and apply the handbrake.

b) In open terrain

Starting:
1) On upward-sloping gradient release the handbrake while simultaneously engaging the clutch and accelerating. Start with the handbrake going downhill.

2) Start in 1st or 2nd gear when on an upward slope.

Driving and changing gear:
1) Do not over rev the engine. Pay attention to the rev counter! Do not exceed the limit of 2,500 rpm.
2) Before starting on an upward-facing slope select the appropriate low gear.
3) Start off downhill in the same gear that could be used for going upwards on the same slope.
4) If driving downhill while braking with the engine operate the footbrake from time to time.
   Do not over rev the engine; the engine rev limiter does not work while driving downhill.
5) Avoid turning while climbing! Approach slopes head on and begin steering movements only if the vehicle tips back to the horizontal position.

Braking and stopping:
1) Both the footbrake and the handbrake can be used for stopping.
2) After stopping the vehicle select 1st,2nd, 3rd or 4th gear otherwise the travel of direction lever cannot be moved to the neutral position.
3) Disengage the clutch and set the direction of movement lever to the neutral position. If stopping for an extended period switch off engine and set the direction of movement lever to 'Vorwärts' (forward).'

Slightly undulating, dry ground was the ideal surface for the Tiger such as the one belonging to *s.Pz.Abt. 505* in this picture taken on 4 June 1943. (Lochmann)

Things to monitor during travel

(D656/43, D656/23 and HtVBl 1944)

- The engine tachometer pointer should not enter the red area.
- The oil pressure gauge should display 3.5 bar at 2,000 rpm.
- The cooling water temperature should be around 80-85° C. The fine adjustment of the cooling water flow can be carried out by means of a valve lever on the bulkhead or the driver's seat and/or – in the Tiger II – by adjusting the flow of air by means of a lever operating the ventilator cover on the bulkhead.

The turret crew was instructed accordingly if operated when in motion. The ventilator cover was later dropped.

- If a fuel was running low the turret crew could turn a fuel cock to 'Reserve' (Tiger I) or the driver (Tiger II) could switch to 'Hilfsbehälter Motorraum' (engine compartment auxiliary tank).

The range on reserve fuel was approximately 30 km on roads.

Emergency operation and towing

(as in D656/43, pages 53-55)

Emergency operation of gears (Tiger II)

In order to change gears if the oil pressure regulator is damaged, the forked lever can be moved with an emergency spanner. To carry out an emergency gear change the oil-pressure control valve must first be removed (see section on cleaning operations) and the drilled hole in the transmission housing from which the valve was removed sealed by means of the flange on the top of the pressure control valve. The pump is short circuited to prevent oil entering the gear selector. Open the dust cover on the forked lever with the emergency spanner. If one of gears 5 to 8 are engaged or should 5th, 6th, 7th or 8th gear be selected, the direction of travel lever must be brought to the 'Vorwärts' position and the clutch disengaged by moving the forked lever with the foot. If any of the four lower gears are selected in an emergency, the direction of travel lever must be set to 'Leerlauf' (neutral). Using the emergency spanner move the forked lever to the desired position. The position for the emergency selection of each gear is indicated on the plate on transmission cover.

Throttle position (G): Emergency spanner to the front.
Brake position (B): Emergency spanner to the rear.

Note: Move the forked lever to its furthest extent.
If this is not possible briefly turn the engine with the starter motor and at the same time let the clutch slip gently and press the forked lever to the end position with the emergency spanner.

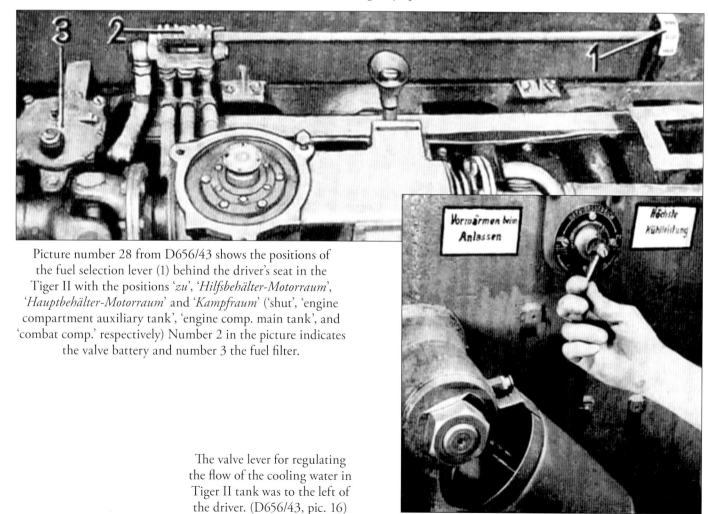

Picture number 28 from D656/43 shows the positions of the fuel selection lever (1) behind the driver's seat in the Tiger II with the positions 'zu', 'Hilfsbehälter-Motorraum', 'Hauptbehälter-Motorraum' and 'Kampfraum' ('shut', 'engine compartment auxiliary tank', 'engine comp. main tank', and 'combat comp.' respectively) Number 2 in the picture indicates the valve battery and number 3 the fuel filter.

The valve lever for regulating the flow of the cooling water in Tiger II tank was to the left of the driver. (D656/43, pic. 16)

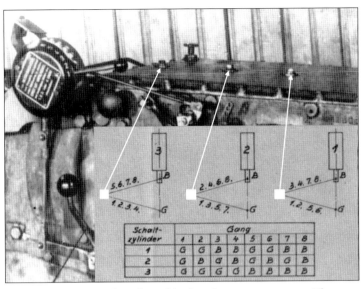

Schalt-zylinder	Gang							
	1	2	3	4	5	6	7	8
1	G	G	B	B	G	G	B	B
2	G	B	G	B	G	B	G	B
3	G	G	G	G	B	B	B	B

Every gear can be selected by hand in an emergency. The corresponding control lever positions are shown on the gearbox (Maybach-Olvargetriebe OG 401216 repair manual and technical description with further amendments)

Tow start

If the engine has to be put into gear during towing then 7th gear should be used. This has to be carried out according to the emergency procedure described previously. Towing is however expressly forbidden, for example, for the purpose of starting in cold weather.

Emergency steering

Besides the superimposed steering system, the vehicle is also equipped with brake-operated steering that is activated by means of an emergency lever. These brakes are to be used only in the case of an emergency, for example when the vehicle is being towed. If an emergency steering brake lever is pulled, all connections to the hydraulic steering gear are detached by means of a shut-off valve.

Each emergency driving lever is connected to a brake by means of a rod assembly. To achieve a steering effect without overusing the brakes the emergency brake levers must be operated jerkily. The planetary gears on the main shaft work such that the track that is not braked is accelerated by the support shaft and runs quicker.

Note: Steering with the driving brake is intended only as an emergency steering method when the steering gear fails or when being towed.

This tank belonging to *s.Pz.Abt. 503* had a defective starter motor in July 1943 before being towed back the workshop. In order to have the towing cables immediately to hand, the crew left them in the forward cable coupling hooks. Nevertheless, several prisoners of war were happy to travel on it (Rubbel)

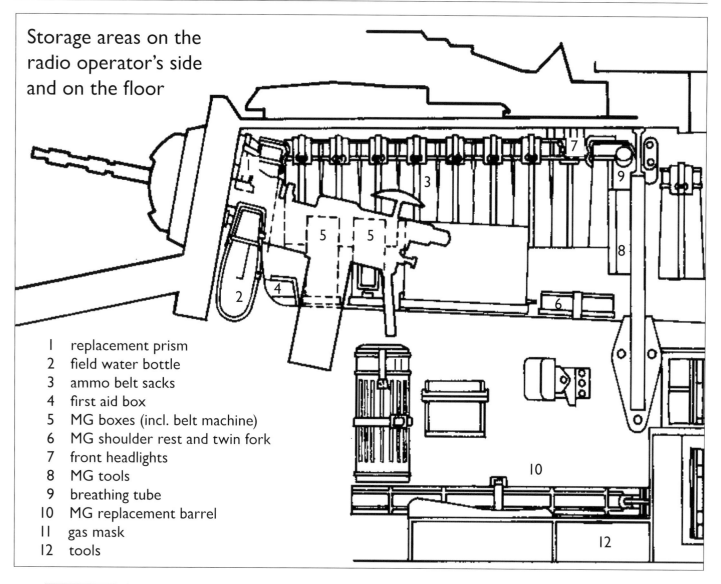

Storage areas on the radio operator's side and on the floor

1 replacement prism
2 field water bottle
3 ammo belt sacks
4 first aid box
5 MG boxes (incl. belt machine)
6 MG shoulder rest and twin fork
7 front headlights
8 MG tools
9 breathing tube
10 MG replacement barrel
11 gas mask
12 tools

The radio operator's seat with a view of the bow MG. To the left of it is the KFZ 2 with its headrest with head protection above. Below the MG is the handgrip for aiming; a spent cartridge sack can be seen to its left. (Trojca)

Twelve ammunition-belt sacks hung to the right of the radio operator. The spent cartridges and belts were emptied from the spent cartridge sack into the MG boxes. The MG ball mantle (below) could be moved in any direction.

Radio Operator's Tasks

The commissioning, tuning, operation and maintenance of the radio equipment required no tank-specific technical training because they were standard devices installed in other vehicles. This also applied to the operation of the antenna rods and the screw attachment on the base of the antenna. In general it was fully trained radio operators that were transferred to the Tiger units. They already had at their command all the necessary hand movements and servicing and repair skills – for example the ability to replace fuses. It was then the responsibility of the company to which they were sent to train them in crew-relevant tasks.

Also the use of the bow MG by the radio operators required no special training because the weapon, which was mounted in a ball mantle, could be pointed in any direction with the aid of a handgrip although it was aimed using the nearby optical sighting device. Its operation and aiming was therefore similar to that of weapons employed by the infantry (loading procedures, changing barrels and so on). The bow MG (below) was merely for close range use (maximum 200 m) and had a very limited radius of fire.

The activities of the crew consisted of repetitive routines such as the 'well-loved' barrel cleaning after every deployment as demonstrated in this picture of a crew belonging to *s.Pz.Abt. 508* (taken on 3 February 1944).

At cold times of the year or in unfavourable weather conditions the crews were happy to be able to carry out their work under cover. This picture, taken in spring 1943, shows a crew from *s.Pz.Abt. 502.*

But there was always something to do during the marches such as the preparation of meals as shown here on a tank belonging to *s.Pz.Abt. 503* in April 1943.

Whole Crew Operating Tasks

A whole range of activities and work were only achievable collectively by the whole crew:
- Zeroing of the turret weapons
- Replenishing the tank with ammunition
- Refuelling the tank
- Establishing states of readiness (ready for movement, ready for combat, ready to load, recovery and towing, (deep-)wading or submerged driving)
- Crew and routine maintenance
- Work related to deployment in winter
- Work on running gear

Zeroing of the turret weapons

The successful deployment of weapons, that is to say the reliable hitting of targets within combat range, depended (and still does) on a whole series of factors. These are referred to with the terms 'internal and external ballistic influences'. External ballistic factors refer to all influences acting on the projectile when it is in flight (primarily rifling, speed, the force of gravity, air resistance, side wind, the temperature of the projectile and the ambient temperature, scattering rates). Internal ballistic factors refer to, amongst other things, recoil behaviour of the weapon mounting, pitching movements during firing, set up on the tank (tilt angle?), the internal pressure profile of the barrel, the temperature of the barrel, and – to a decisive extent – the precision of the aiming device(s). In purely ballistic terms the enemy's cannons that were encountered (for example the 85mm gun of the T-34 and the 122 mm weapon of the Joseph Stalin tank) were good. The latter of these was frequently prevented from operating successfully by inadequate means of aiming, particularly at long range. This was due to the limited ability to range the distance to the target and also to the crude means of setting the angle of elevation (see sections 'Using the *TZF*' and 'Conducting firefights' in Chapter 5, 'Tactics').

Therefore, within the framework of weapon adjustments, the checks undertaken as well as – if necessary – any corrections were of fundamental importance. With the elevation and traverse of the weapons and aiming devices correctly set, targets could usually be hit. These important activities were conducted only by an experienced commander or a *Waffenmeister* (armourer sergeant) and needed special care. This is also the reason why the turret regulations specify every single step down to the last detail on pages 46 onwards (or page 25 and onwards in the case of the Tiger II regulations).

The zeroing checks and corrections were carried out most precisely with the assistance of targets at short ranges. If these were not available on active service then a suitable landmark in terms of aspect and height (for example the top of a church spire or chimney) and at a distance of at least 1,000 m was chosen as a target.

Zeroing in the field by *3./s.Pz.Abt 503* in June 1943. (Rubbel)

The instructions in the regulations demonstrate to the reader the care and effort that went into the zeroing of the weapons:

1. Align the armoured fighting vehicle in the direction of travel and horizontally (applies to both procedures). (…)
2. Place the calibration testing panel at a distance of 50 m – measured from the gun cradle – and erect it vertically to the axis of the barrel of the combat vehicle; the string of the plumb bob must cover the vertical line on the target panel, that is to say the target panel must be hung horizontally.
3. Insert the aim verifier and bore-sight tester (in the mouth of the cannon's barrel and turret MG respectively).
4. Set the turret sighting telescope (*TZF 9b* or *TZF 9c*) to the 'zero' mark on the distance divisions for the 8.8 cm (for the *TZF 9b* of the Tiger II: use the zero mark for *Pz Gr 39/43*).
5. Align the 8.8 cm *KwK 36* (or *43*) [cannon] at the calibration testing panel by turning the turret and gun cradle such that the aiming cross-hairs of the aim verifier covers the appropriate cross on the calibration testing panel. (…)
6. The top point of the large aiming triangle in the right hand side of the turret sighting telescope must now point to the centre of the right hand half of the double cross for the turret sighting telescope.
7. If this is not the case then proceed as follows:
   a) Unscrew the end caps on the adjusting screws of the right-hand telescope.
   b) Adjust the turret sighting telescope with the attached spanner until requirement 5 is satisfied.
   c) Screw the end caps back into place. The telescopic sighting device is constructed in such a way that it is necessary to set the azimuth before the elevation. Setting the azimuth also simultaneously moves the height of the aiming triangle; therefore setting the elevation first and then the azimuth misaligns the previously set elevation.
8) Set the *TZF* to mark '10' (to '15' in the Tiger II) on the distance divisions for the 8.8 cm (this applies to the Tiger II when using *Pz Gr 39/43*).
9) Turn the lever on the end of the objective lens on the left half of the telescope upwards until it stops and then screw tight.
10) Now, with the right-hand-side of the telescope, aim at the centre of the right half of the double cross again.
11) The top point of the large aiming triangle in the left-hand telescope of the turret sighting device must now point at the middle of the left half of the double cross.
12) If this is not the case then proceed as described in Nr. 7.

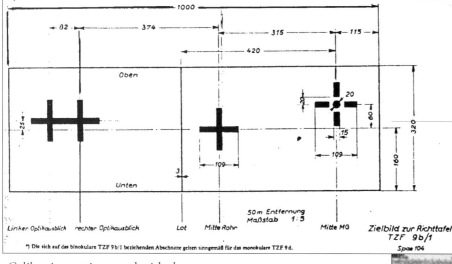

Calibration testing panel with the two aiming crosses for the optical sighting device (left), the bore axis of the main gun (centre) and the mid-line of the turret machine gun.

A look through the aim verifier at the end of the barrel of the Tiger 'von Eschnapur' of *s.Pz. Abt. 508* (previously *Kompanie 'Meyer'*) after maintenance work on the weapon systems.

Finally, the calibration operations for the turret MG were described which follows the same procedure but with the difference that the mounting of the MG on the clamp bearings on the mounting bracket had to be adjusted by loosening the necessary clamp screws.

> By this procedure the bore axis and the axis of the right-hand half of the sighting telescope were kept parallel to each other with respect to both their elevation and azimuth. The aim of the left-hand telescopic sight is set to a range of 1,000 m (or 1,500 m in the Tiger II).

Adjustment on active service without the use of a testing panel was conducted according to the same principals but over a greater distance with the difference being that the *TZF* was set to the position 'zero' because the left-hand half of sighting telescope calibration conformed to the required shooting distance.

This is known as 'parallel calibration' and is, in conjunction with high performance optics and weapon mounting, the optimal system because it works equally well for targets at any range. In general, Soviet tanks and tank-destroyers used the so-called 'point calibration' method. Here the bore of the gun and the axis of the optics were set to a specific target distance (for example 800 m) with the serious disadvantage that at target distances much greater or less than this, the cross hairs of the sighting optics were in the wrong position. Additionally, the quality of target ranging was negatively affected because, in contrast to the Tiger, the sighting telescope could not be set cleanly and continuously but could only be very roughly calculated with the aid of a vertically oriented, non-linear scale.

With the aid of another calibration testing panel (below), the MG in the ball mounting was calibrated in the same way as the turret MG for parallel alignment with the aiming cross of the ball-mounted sighting telescope (KZF 2/ *Kugelzielfernrohr* 2).

If there was no aim verifier readily available, an aiming cross was formed on the end of the muzzle by means of threads. The firing bolt on the breech block was removed. The calibration target was then sighted by looking through the barrel with the correct target distance setting. Deviations in the elevation or azimuth indicated that the calibration of the *TZF* was skewed.

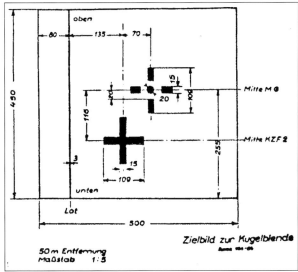

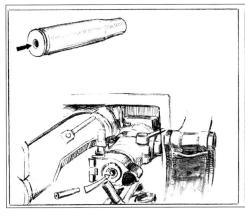

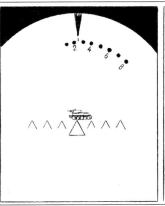

Provisional calibration of the turret MG: Remove the MG butt and bolt, insert a spent cartridge without its primer into the barrel, set the target range to 250 m, aim at the target and adjust the MG sight calibration.

Replenishing the tank with ammunition

The activities of the crew in the fulfilment of this routine task can be best illustrated by the following series of snaps.

A series of pictures taken in the vicinity of Gatschina in September 1943 shows the crew rearming Panzer '312' of *s.Pz. Abt. 502*. The ammunition was delivered packed in pairs inside wooden boxes. A member of the crew stands beside the turret and takes the shells as they are passed up to him. He then passes them in to the loader who is inside the tank and who then stacks them one after the other into the storage racks. (BA 4309-461-25/27/32/34)

Chaotic times for *s.Pz.Abt. 503* on 23 August 1943 after a battle at Gonki; apparently there is no danger of attack from the air. (BA 22-2948-22)

Two examples of incorrect handling of the shells; the body of the projectile – not the detonator – should be supported by the hand and the projectile should be held so that it does not tilt.
(BA 22-2948-30 and 461-213-35)

The correct receipt of the shell into the tank by the gunner; the soldier on the outside prevents the tip of the projectile from hitting against the tank.
(BA 22-2948-28)

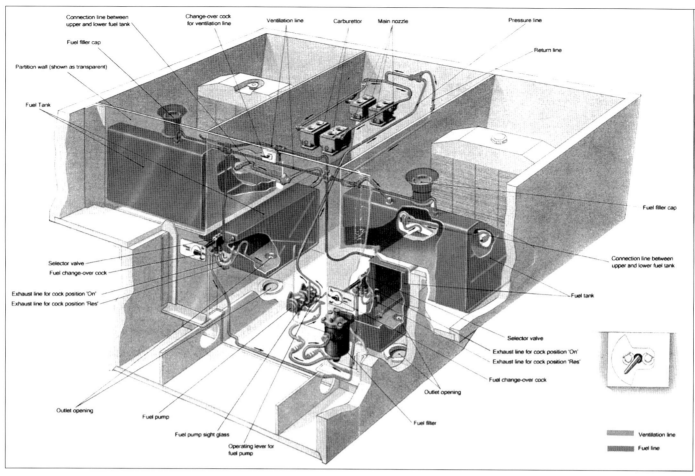

Picture Nr. 13 of D656/12 shows a good overview of the fuel storage layout in the Tiger I with the two filling points on the main tanks as well as the two fuel selection levers.

Refuelling was a task for the crew; as is shown in this picture taken of a tank belonging to *s.Pz.Abt. 501* on 13 January 1943. It was the task of the battalion's supply units to deliver the fuel for the tanks. (BA 788-19-1)

Refuelling the tanks

The *Pz.Kpfw.* Tiger I had a maximum fuel capacity of 534 litres in four tanks (two external and two in the engine compartment). The *PzKpfw.* Tiger II on the other hand could accommodate 860 litres in total distributed amongst seven tanks. There were two under each of the two ventilation units, one on the rear wall as well as two in the fighting compartment, all of which were switched from the valve manifold.

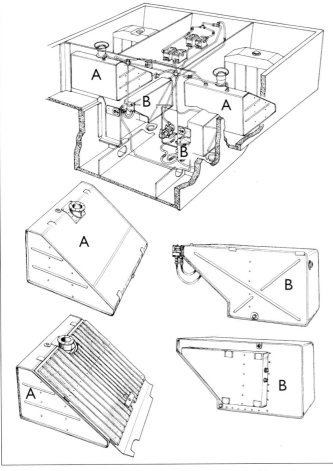

Arrangement of the four fuel tanks in a Tiger I

In normal circumstances the fuel was taken continuously from the main tanks by means of a mechanical pump. By means of a fuel selection lever behind the driver's seat or on the bulkhead the driver could control the remaining fuel tanks by selecting the *'Hilfsbehälter'* (auxiliary tank) position only if the main tanks had been emptied in order to be able to respond even if the tank was at a standstill. A switchable electrical fuel pump supported the start-up procedure but this was turned off as soon as the engine fired.

Spilled fuel and water that had entered the hull could be pumped out with the assistance of a self-priming bilge pump. It forced the fluids through a pipe system that ran above the right upper fuel tank to the outside through a self-closing external flap.

Refuelling was carried out while observing important safety regulations – no smoking, no naked flames, a carbon tetrachloride fire extinguisher at the ready and normally with the engine switched off. Despite the various fuel tanks, the tank was refuelled centrally through just two filling points situated on the rear part of the hull (see diagram).

Driving until the fuel tanks were empty was not recommended! If this happened the power plant could not be simply started after refuelling; first the air in the fuel lines had to be removed.

The *Tigerfibel* addressed this point succinctly on page 15:

> *Look out!* If the fuel is reaching the last drop, immediately change to the reserve; if the reserves are nearly done switch off the engine and stop. Thirty seconds work!

> *Otherwise* the fuel lines and pump are emptied and will not allow fuel to pass through after refuelling: unscrew the air filter and housing, remove the hollow screws on the carburetor, run the electric pump until fuel appears (do not allow it to overflow). Reinstall all components.
> *One hour's work!*

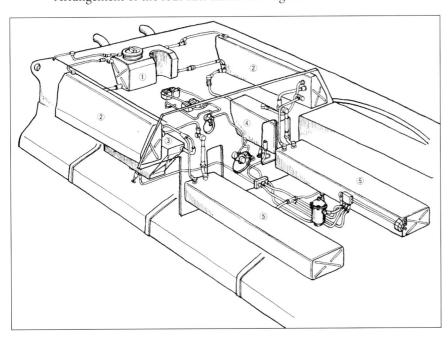

Layout of the seven fuel tanks in a Tiger II:
1 carburettor; 2 fuel pump; 3 fuel filter; 4 fuel tanks; 5 fuel tanks (side)

If no encounters with the enemy were expected during a march the protective covers remained on the muzzle, bow MG and smoke grenade launchers to protect them from the ingress of dirt as shown here on a tank belonging to *s.Pz.Abt. 501* on 24 November 1942. Notice too that the headlights have not been removed. (sketch for removal procedure)

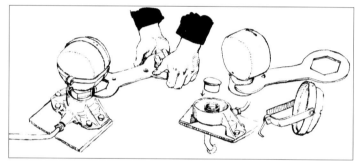

Location of external equipment

1. close combat weapons
2. towing cable
3. 15mm wire cable for removing tracks
4. barrel cleaning equipment
5. cover for air intake to the engine compartment
6. sledge hammer
7. shovel
8. winch base
9. spades
10. axe
11. wire cutters
12. luggage store
13. carbon tetrachloride fire extinguisher
14. protective cover for antenna
15. spare track links
16. 15 ton winch
17. track tools
18. towing shackles
19. starting handle for inertia starter
20. crowbar
21. spotlight
22. smoke grenade launchers
23. attachment points for a camouflage screen (for example as a truck or a bus)

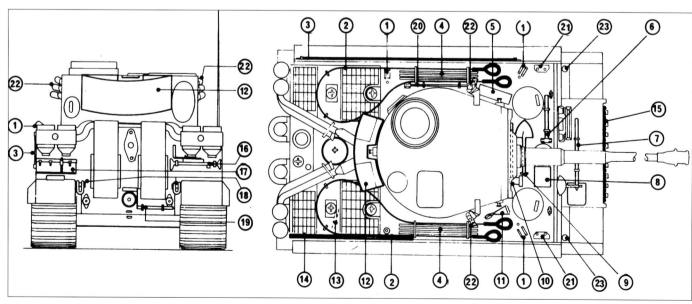

The layout for the storage of the tools, equipment and towing cables varied to some extent because of the numerous changes made to the Tiger I.

Establishing States of Readiness

There were no clear descriptions for this in the contemporary tank regulations even though such instructions are particularly important for the deployment readiness of armoured fighting vehicles. However, in the Tiger training courses appropriate guidelines were created for use in the training of the Tiger crews.

The following readiness levels were ordered by the commander:

- March readiness
- March and combat readiness
- 'Ready for combat!'

There were also other states of readiness relating to recovery of the vehicle, readiness for transport by rail and of course withdrawal from service.

March readiness was so to speak the basic instruction as this order was given before every relocation of the vehicle, even over short distances. The tasks undertaken by the driver (see the section 'Operating tasks of the driver') were rather extensive and time consuming and were during times of constant deployment all too often neglected. Trusting in the steadfastness of the technology under his control, he often had to set off without carrying out most of the checks. Indirectly this favoured the scrupulous adherence to the activities for decommissioning resulting in the detection of operational damage where circumstances required this, topping up oil and fluid levels and remedying mechanical faults. If, for example, during the hasty commissioning of the tank no leaks or other visible defects were detected, the crew in most cases could assume the operational fitness of the vehicle. Often the driver and the commander were also in the position of being able to assess the indicators of the trouble-free running of the tank (no significant oil loss, unusual noises or temperature readings) and recognise defects at an early stage.

In addition to the procedures carried out by the driver, the remaining crew members also had important duties to perform. These included the proper stowage of equipment both within and on the exterior of the vehicle (including the crew's hand-held weapons), checking the storage racks and their contents, cleaning optical aids and (if circumstances required it) clearing snow and/or ice from the running gear and making sure the engine compartment cover was clear. Other tasks of the remaining crew members included installing the protective covers on the turret, bow machine-gun and muzzle-brake to protect them from contamination and then securing the cannon. The radio operator then selected the operating mode (transmitting or ready to receive) and the frequency according to orders and tested the radio apparatus having previously screwed the antenna onto its mounting and checked its condition. Depending on the situation, the tank's camouflage covers were attached for the march. All of these preparative actions and checks were referred to as '*Tätigkeiten vor der Benutzung*' (activities prior to use).

When a march was ordered to stop (or, in the final analysis, during any interruption) all round visual and 'hands-on' checks were made for the proper operation of the vehicles. As far as the tracks and suspension were concerned, mechanical problems and consequential leaks and such like could usually be detected by touching the hub plates on the bogie wheels as these could become very hot before a fatal fault arose.

In addition, the establishment of **combat readiness** included all weapons-based checks as well as checks on the optical sighting devices, the turret traversing mechanism and the instant availability of ammunition for the cannon and the ammunition belt sacks for the MG. The latter of these had been partially loaded with all the protective caps removed. Basically, the cannon should have remained secured but in practice this rule was increasingly ignored.

With the command '*Klar zum Gefecht*' (**ready for combat**) all hatches were closed except for that of the commander. The cannon was unlocked. A round was loaded, usually a *Panzergranate*. The gunner set the 'battle sight' as ordered, for example according to the command '*Panzergranate 800*' ('armour piercing round 800 m'). With this setting on the sighting device an unexpected appearance by the enemy would be fired upon without further assessment of the range. Due to the relatively straight trajectory of the armour-piercing shell, targets could be hit at distances from around 500 to about 950 m with this setting. Experienced gunners aimed a little higher for targets that were further away and lower for more closely located targets.

When a tank was withdrawn from service the above mentioned procedures were annulled and the driver's checks carried out in a manner similar to the commissioning process. Every crew member checked the performance of the moving parts within his area of operation or registered defects and damage. The amount of ammunition used and fuel consumed was reported to the platoon leader who then passed on an informal report of the ammunition and fuel consumption of his platoon, together with a list of known technical defects, to his company commander. He then summed up this information in the form of a request for replacement materiel and had a damage report drawn up and these were passed on via the *Versorgungsunter-offizier*, and later the *Geräteunteroffizier* to the unit's command authority. If there was an urgent need for ammunition or fuel, the company commander passed on his requirements by telephone or radio.

Immediately after parking their vehicle the crew – with the support of their *I-Gruppe* – attended to all damage and deficiencies that did not fall into the area of responsibility of the workshop. In addition, the weapons were cleaned.

Tank '312' of the *3./s.Pz.Abt.502* in September 1943 is in march and combat readiness and moves out. The muzzle and bow MG covers have been removed, the tools are on their storage brackets and the antenna is attached to its mounting. (BA 461-212-8)

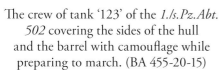

The crew of tank '123' of the *1./s.Pz.Abt. 502* covering the sides of the hull and the barrel with camouflage while preparing to march. (BA 455-20-15)

'*Klar zum Gefecht'* – this tank belonging to *2./s.Pz.Abt. 502* observes the approach of other forces on 6 April 1944 on the '*Ostsack*', a Soviet bulge in the German lines near Narva. The commanders hatch cover is raised to give him a view over the edge of the hatch.

Tank '131' of *s.Pz.Abt. 503* in June 1943 with its breakdown flag hoisted by the crew and its turret turned to the side to allow the assessment of damage in the engine compartment.

There was no formal ***Bergebereitschaft*** (state of readiness for recovery of a vehicle). However, the crew of a vehicle that had come to a standstill or had become bogged down did use the time it took for the recovery team to arrive to prepare for their rescue. This involved the attachment of the towing cables and, if necessary, shovelling earth that had bulged up in front of the tracks away from the anticipated towing direction. In the event of a breakdown the crew raised the breakdown flag (yellow ground with a black cross). Away from roads, the turn-off towards a broken tank was marked or a soldier posted to direct the recovery platoon.

The recovery of a tank from ditches or bogs and such like was sometimes extremely expensive in terms of time (see Chapter 4) but required no further technical measures because this only involved pulling the tank to drivable ground so that it could again move under its own power. In contrast, the preparations required for towing a tank over longer distances were extensive and are described below.

On long marches the companies sometimes carried towing scissors to clear the way with the help of other vehicles in the event of a breakdown. Here *Unteroffizier* Seiffert of the *2./s.Pz.Abt. 503* awaits assistance on 17 September 1943 in Krassnograd. (Heier)

Preparations for Towing and Recovery

(in accordance with D 656/43 and the Maybach factory manuals for OG 401216 and OG 401216B)

1) Towing during engine, transmission or steering mechanism damage is carried out with poles. For this both half-shafts are removed.

2) If the engine is damaged but the transmission and steering mechanisms are trouble-free, cables can be used for towing if no poles are on hand. To do so on the Tiger II disconnect the claw coupling on the gearbox (on the Tiger I dismount the drive-shaft from the gearbox), select the gear appropriate to the towing speed, push the direction of motion lever forwards and steer with the steering mechanism. If it is necessary to steer with the brakes these should be operated in jerky movements.

3) Drive sprocket and final drive damage
a. on the left side: dismantle the first swinging arm and remove the required number of links from the track. Reconnect the track over the second track roller.
b. on the right side: it is not possible in this case [to follow the procedure described in 'a'] because the track does not pass by the designated swinging arm. Tow on a sound road surface, if necessary without tracks.

4) Idler wheel damage
a. on the left side: dismount the idler wheel. It is not possible to shorten the track because of the guiding swinging arm arrangement.
b. on the right side: dismount the idler wheel and close the shortened track over the last bogie wheel.

5) Bogie wheel damage
Remove the defective bogie wheel, protect the hub area from ingress of dirt. It is only necessary to tie up or remove the first swinging arm to prevent damage from the track's teeth.

If the engine and transmission are damaged refer to the device description and operating instructions OG 401216 (Tiger I) and OG 401216B (Tiger II) provided by the Maybach factory regarding the different measures required for towing over long and short distances. In doing so it should be noted that both transmission systems have the same basic construction but that in the case of the Tiger II some improvements have been incorporated:

Towing over short distances (up to 2 km)

1. Damage to the steering system: remove both side shafts.

2. Damage to the engine: select gear 1, 2, 3 or 4 (if necessary using the emergency spanner) and set the direction of motion lever to neutral.

3. Transmission damage: select gear 1, 2, 3 or 4 (if necessary using the emergency spanner) and set the direction of motion lever to neutral.

Towing over long distances (more than 2 km)

a. Damage to the steering system: remove both side shafts.

b. Damage to the engine:
• Disengage the drive shaft from the gearbox. On the Tiger II simply disconnect the claw coupling by means of the hand lever
• Set the gear selector (if necessary with the emergency spanner) for slow towing in open country to 4th gear and to 6th gear for fast towing on roads and in each case dismount the valve plate on the lubrication valve.
• Set the direction of motion lever to 'forward' if being towed forwards and to 'backward' if being towed backwards.

In this way the gear selector mechanism, powered by the tracks, supplies hydraulic fluid to the steering mechanism and lubricating oil to the gears.

c. Damage to the gear selector: remove both side shafts otherwise further damage will result because of a lack of lubricating oil.

The recovery and towing of the tank presented the crew, particularly the driver, with the task of getting the vehicle to safety without causing further damage. The *Tigerfibel* advocated the following division of tasks:

Driver: Freeing the tracks or opening them, removal of the side shafts.

Radio operator and loader: Removing blockages ('*Schanzen*') in front of the tracks and hull.

Commander: Searching for attachement points and making ready the tools, towing poles, ropes, S-hooks and winches.

The activities in the vehicle, such as disconnecting the drive shaft on the transmission and the removal of the side shafts, were sometimes difficult and physically demanding and had to be carried out as quickly as possible out of necessity under very cramped conditions inside the tank's smeared-with-oil and dirty 'bilges.' Stowing cumbersome cables or heavy towing poles likewise required great physical exertion in all weather conditions, and possibly while still within sight of the enemy. So it was work for everyone. In this regard the *Tigerfibel* states:

> Don't start smoking or smearing sandwiches or you'll get one on the roof!

And furthermore:

> The moral: Recovery is an exhausting but unfortunately indispensable job.

Of course nothing much functioned without the vehicle recovery squads and their towing vehicles. Before the introduction of the *Bergpanther* recovery tank, which was never delivered in sufficient numbers, two or three *Sd.Kfz. 9* 'Famo' half-track vehicles with a pulling power of 18 tonnes each were used for towing but these were also in scarce supply. If they were available, captured tanks were also used as towing vehicles after their turrets had been removed. Towing one Tiger with another over-stressed the towing vehicle and could easily lead to engine damage.

Removing a side shaft: there were four 10 mm screws for the cover and eighteen 14 mm screws on each side shaft to loosen (the picture below shows a side shaft that has been removed from the tank). The brake drums were attached again with three of these screws to prevent them from sliding off. On the left side, the pedal connections added further space restrictions. (D 656/30 b u. c, page 143)

This picture of a tank belonging to *s.Pz.Abt. 505* offers a good view of the arrangement of the running gear and the different bogie-wheel hubs during August 1943. (Neubauer)

The spaces between the interleaved running gear components could become blocked, particularly when driving across muddy ground. This could cause the track to lift when the tank was travelling in a curve making it possible for it to run off the driving sprockets. The crew cleared away such clumps when they stopped, as shown in this picture of a tank from *s.Pz. Abt.503* in Bogo-duchow on 12 April 1943.

For this reason the forward-most bogie wheel was removed in many instances without affecting the tank's mobility (such as in this tank belonging to the *13./Pz.Rgt. 'GD'*).

Work on the Running Gear

(Spielberger, Jentz/Doyle, Fletcher, diff. parts of
HtVBl 1944, D656/27)

In total three running gear layouts were used in the Tiger I and Tiger II. All had interleaved bogie wheels but their layout was different. The tracks were composed of hinged links with small components which meant that each track contained a very large number of components. The links were joined by track pins with locking rings secured with hollow dowel pins or alternatively by pieces of strong, bent wire. In addition on the hull deflector plates pushed back the track pins when passing by. Until the end of production of the Tiger II there were three different types of track each of which required driving wheels with either nine or eighteen sprockets. The final version was only introduced sporadically. In addition to these there were narrower tracks used during transport by rail. The transport and combat tracks of the Tiger I had 96 links while the Tiger II tracks had 90 links.

Until the start of 1944 the Tiger I had three bogie wheels with solid rubber tyres or bands on each swinging arm. Because of the limited weight bearing capability of the rubber tyres, the weight increase during the development of the Tiger I meant that one of the original two bogie wheels per swinging arm was replaced by a double wheel. This increased the maintenance and repair effort and made the replacement of bogie wheels more difficult. Furthermore, this required the removal of the sixteen outer bogie wheels when the track used for transport by rail was fitted. Occasionally, in certain types of terrain, the frontmost group of three bogie wheels was completely removed to prevent jamming of the driving wheel with mud and so on.

The arrangement of the bogie wheels and their swinging arms as viewed from below with the tracks removed. The outer wheels, shaded grey in the drawing, had to be removed when the transport track was fitted.

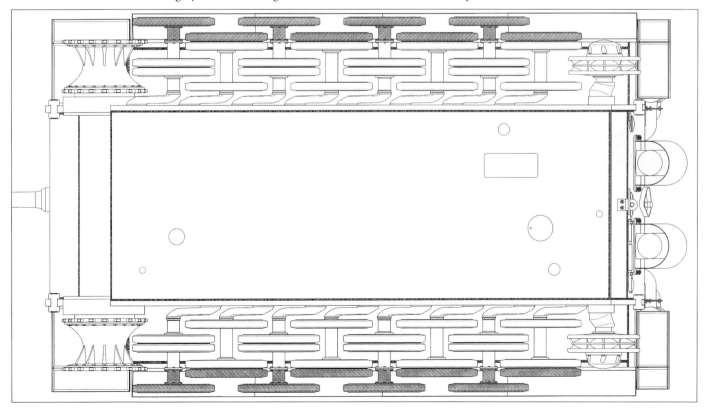

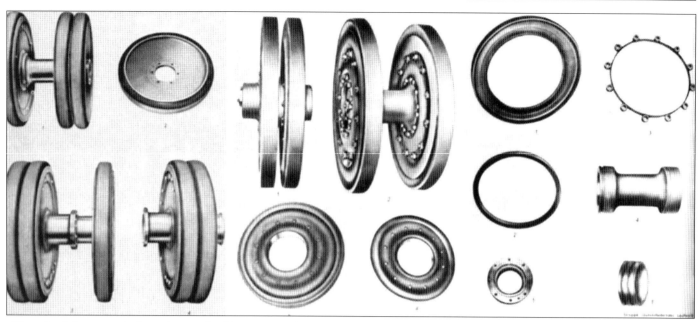

The wheel design with the vulcanised rubber tyres is shown on the left with the rubber sprung wheel for comparison to its right.

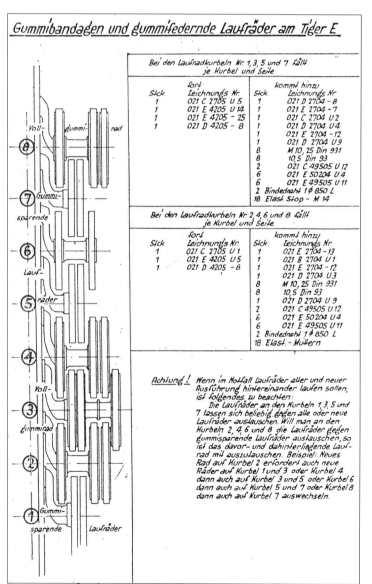

Instructions for the correct installation of mixed old and new bogie wheels. (*Heerestechnisches Verordnungsblatt* of 07.06.44, section 427, drawing 5, page 250)

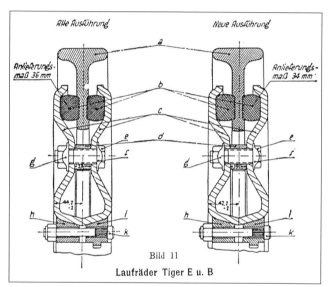

This drawing shows the cross section of the old and new versions of the steel wheel. The internally clamped rubber ring shock absorbers are indicated by label 'b' and the steel wheel by label 'a.' (*Beiblatt zum Heerestechnisches Verordnungsblatt* of 29.10.44, page 9)

From February 1944, the conversion to rubber-saving running gear with just two rubber-sprung steel wheels on each swinging arm took place.

Fundamental changes to the swinging arms and the suspension were not required and many parts were interchangeable. The replacement of the old wheels was approved in the event of damage but only for the whole of the running gear. The installation of mixed old and new bogie wheel groups was only allowed in an emergency but the substitution of single wheels on the same axel was not possible.

The elaborate removal and installation of bogie wheels when changing between transport and combat tracks was no longer necessary.

The changeover to rubber-sprung steel bogie wheels must have been a considerable relief to the crews especially since the frequent changing of wheels (because of damaged tyres and when loading for transport) was no longer required. However, the change attracted some criticism because the clearance between the bogie wheels and the track guide teeth compared to the old running gear was too narrow and the uneven loading through the staggered bogie wheels unfavourable in that (in the Tiger II) it often led to the bending of the track pins and the consequential jamming of the track links.

In November 1944 it was announced in the *Heerestechnisches Verordnungsblatt* (the army's technical journal) that new, 4 mm narrower, bogie wheels were to be introduced. Also, the Tiger II was provided with running gear that had two rubber-sprung steel bogie wheels on each swinging arm that were not interleaved but arranged in staggered pairs.

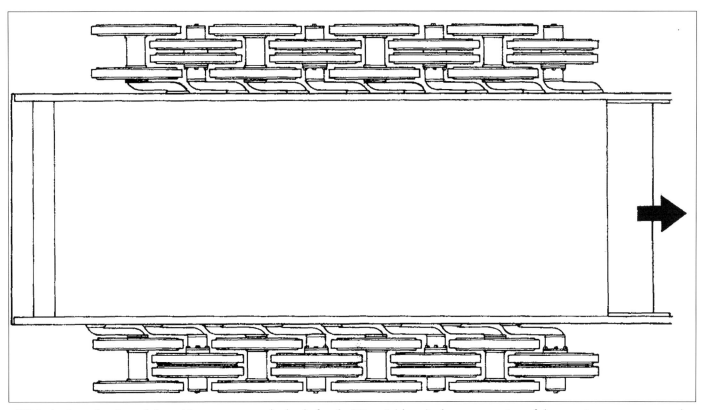

With the introduction of the rubber-sprung steel wheels for the Tiger I (above), the construction of the running gear was greatly simplified and it was also more stable. The arrangement of the running gear in the Tiger II was different again (below).

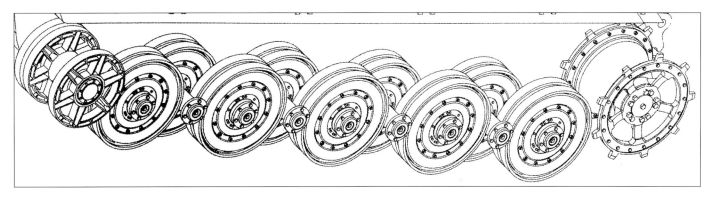

The new steel bogie wheels – as shown here on a vehicle belonging to *s.Pz.Abt. 507* – were laid out in a completely different arrangement and easy to distinguish from the earlier wheels.

The torsion bar suspension system was common to all versions of the Tiger, a reliable and maintenance-free system that is widespread even today. The torsion bars ran across the floor of the hull and were connected on one side to the swinging arms and on the other side to the wall of the hull.

The torsion bars formed a sort of steel grid on the floor of the hull. Only the Tiger II had a floor hatch as an emergency exit and this was situated to the right of the radio operator and in front of the first torsion bar.

For reasons of space, the swinging arms on the right side were directed towards the front (leading swinging arms) and on the left side towards the rear of the tank (trailing swinging arms) – a more suitable arrangement in terms of suspension technology.

Adjusting and fitting the torsion bars was not problematic when the bogie wheels were removed, other than when the floor of the hull had been distorted by hitting a mine or something similar.

Inboard shock absorbers were fitted to the front and rear swinging arms because they were under higher load. These positions also had stronger torsion bars.

The torsion bars themselves were only a problem with the Tiger units until the crews had learned to handle them *'wie ein rohes Ei'* (literally 'like a raw egg') in the vehicle and when carrying out any repair and maintenance work. Even a tiny amount of damage to the polished surface could lead to the torsion bar breaking after a short time. For example when welding in the hull, every effort had to be made to avoid hot beads of welding spatter falling onto the torsion bars. (HtVBL Art. 362,25.09.43)

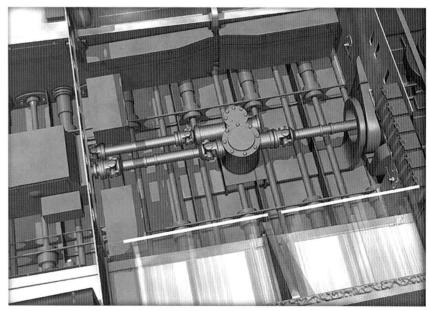

The layout of the torsion bars in the floor of the hull of the Tiger I. (Harada)

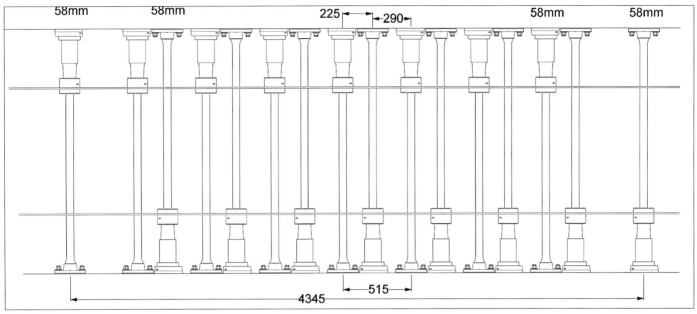

This drawing shows the layout of the torsion bars of the Tiger I with dimensions. It was clear that individual torsion bars were unequally loaded (the front considerably more so than those in the middle of the hull) and that cracked or distorted rods or bearing sleeves could cause consequential mechanical damage. (David Byrden)

Damage by mines or explosions made it necessary for the repair and maintenance service to undertake torsion bar replacement in the field, as shown here on a tank belonging to *s.Pz.Abt. 505* immediately after *Unternehmen Zitadelle* in July 1943. (Neubauer)

Running gear repair after mine damage on 29 February 1944 at *s.Pz.Abt. 508*. Distorted swinging arms and damaged bogie wheels needed to be replaced. (BA 32-0898-24)

Pure enthusiasm prevailed if work had to be done in the biting cold, as shown here at *s.Pz.Abt. 505* in February 1944. (Krönke)

Often tanks had to drive long distances after having a bogie wheel ripped off before there was time to carry out repairs, as in the case of this vehicle belonging to *s.Pz.Abt. 503* in summer 1943.

Handling the components of the running gear

(taken from Spielberger, Jentz/Doyle, Fletcher, diff. sections in HtVBl 1943/44, D656/23, D656/27)

Bogie wheels

The interleaved running gear with its relatively high number of bogie wheels – developed for reasons of weight bearing – had several advantages in terms of driving performance but also significant disadvantages when in operation. The novel, highly stressed, hard-rubber tyres with bead wires had a much complained about short lifetime and were attached over a screwed-on tensioning ring and therefore could not be replaced without changing the bogie wheel. Also, to replace the more inward of the bogie wheels because of damaged tyres (or mine or shell damage) could require up to 13 of the neighbouring wheels of the rubber-sparing running gear to be removed and then reinstalled. Bogie wheels that had been allowed to collect dirt tended to freeze-up during the winter which meant that the crew had to take appropriate precautionary measures.

It is easy to imagine that this bogie wheel design created heavy, and at the same time responsible, work for the crew and tank mechanics – particularly in in open country

– during which other components of the tank's undercarriage could be adversely affected. Even the *Tigerfibel* commented:

> if it's dark as a dungeon, cold, wet and dirty; if the winch, hammer, spanner can't be found; if rods break and [swinging] arms hang loose; if three wheels are missing and five are jammed and if the jack sinks in the muddy ground; just think to yourself in such misfortune what would the constructor do in such a situation?

There was nothing else for it but to get on with the job and in spite of the difficult conditions keep everything clean while working; to attach the bogie wheels to the intermediate flanges without stressing them, and then tighten and secure the nuts and bolts 'correctly' in order to prevent damaging components. The fastenings on the wheels tended to loosen during use because of the high lateral forces and the rubber tyres were prone to detachment from the wheels. The critical inspection and re-tightening of the screws on the running gear, which had to be cleaned whenever necessary, was a never ending task. 'Watch out for loose and torn bandages, for loose bolts, cracked wheel discs, broken torsion bars and cranks (of the swinging arms), replace them in good time, said the *Tigerfibel* by way of a reminder, 'otherwise the damage just gets bigger and bigger.'

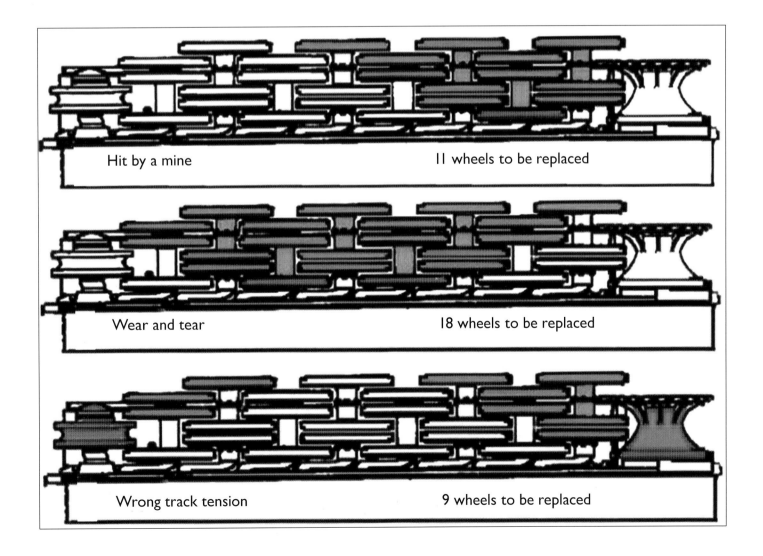

Hit by a mine   11 wheels to be replaced

Wear and tear   18 wheels to be replaced

Wrong track tension   9 wheels to be replaced

Working on the tracks was a recurring routine, as shown here on a vehicle belonging to *s.Pz. Abt. 506.*

The sheer weight of a track weighing more than two tonnes was too much for a five man crew to move and required the assistance of the whole platoon as shown in this picture taken in February 1944 of a tank belonging to *s.Pz.Abt. 505.*

Opening both tracks, as shown here with tank from '*506*', had the disadvantage that the tank could not be moved under its own power.

It was particularly precarious for the tank's crew if bogie wheels had been partially torn off and had wedged themselves in the running gear. The tank was immediately immobilized and it took a considerable effort by the crew to free them. (Wunderlich)

It took at least two soldiers to lift the heavy idler wheels. Here, work is carried out on tank '334' belonging to s.Pz.Abt. 503 on 22 July 1943. (BA 22-2948-05)

Because the bogie wheels did not wear evenly during use, the crew always took care to re-install them in their original positions to prevent them distorting the swinging arms. (Zorn)

If the final drive was damaged the drive sprocket had to be removed, as shown in this picture of tank '234' belonging to *s.Pz.Abt. 503* taken in April 1943.

Even if only a few of the teeth on the sprocket wheels were broken (centre left), it could only be removed and replaced by opening the track (above) as is shown in this picture, (taken on 12 November 1943 in Orscha) of a tank belonging to *s.Pz.Abt. 505*. (Boche)

Manoeuvring the heavy drive sprocket was best accomplished with the help of a crane, as shown here in a picture taken at *s.Pz.Abt. 503* on 20 July 1943. (Wolff-Altvater)

A mountable device that, when combined with a pulley block, made the removal and installation of the drive sprocket and the subsequent removal of the final drive easier was sent to the repair and maintenance detachments in spring 1943. To accommodate the device, a 60 cm mounting socket was attached to both sides at the front of the hull on every tank.

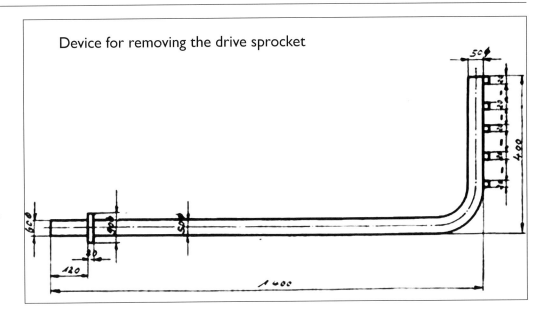

Device for removing the drive sprocket

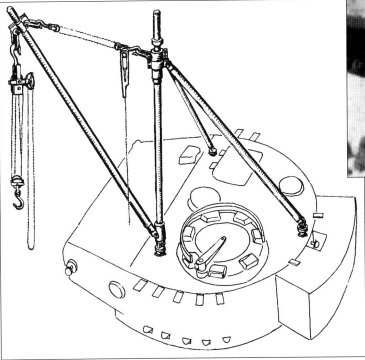

From April 1944 three attachment points for makeshift cranes with a lifting capacity of up to two tonnes were added to the turrets. Using this device enabled a great deal of work to be undertaken on tanks (for example, lifting the engine covers) without the need for trucks with cranes.

Work on the tracks was often required, for example following damage by a shell or mine as in this example which shows a vehicle belonging to *s.Pz.Abt. 501* on 15 January 1943.

Changing the tracks for transport by train was routine work as this picture from *s.Pz.Abt. 506* taken on 20 September 1944 as it travelled to Arnheim shows.

Another reason was abrasion, for example to the bogie wheel rubber tyres or, as shown here, wear and tear of the sprockets on the drive wheels.

Working on the tracks

The tracks required just as much attention; setting the correct track tension and the tightness of the track pins to prevent them from moving laterally were high on the list of routine tasks. For example, the correct track tension for an unbraked Tiger I was reached when the span between the upper edge of the first bogie wheel and the track measured four fingers. Too little track tension increased the danger of the track being thrown off the driving wheel. If a track was too tight, this overloaded the track tensioner and also the bearings in the final drive and bogie wheels which increased abrasion and could result in breakage. Bent track pins due to the high loading on the tracks created a high rolling resistance in the drive and problems during the disassembly of the track or when the track was broken. Removing a link from a track that had been stretched during use and which could no longer be tensioned sufficiently made it serviceable again.

Wear on the track links, track pins and drive wheels had to be monitored in order to avoid the track breaking or derailing in use. But even without operational errors being made during service, the tracks could rise up onto the driving wheel sprockets when reversing on heavy ground or loose sand – a weakness in the design of the Tiger I suspension. The high tensile forces in the then overstretched tracks made it impossible to disconnect the links by normal means and they had to be cut open with a welding torch or blown apart with an explosive charge.

A vehicle that had suffered such a malfunction could certainly be towed slowly before opening the affected track but this imposed a heavy load on the track drive (final drive) and required a powerful towing vehicle.

Changing the track was therefore – like changing the wheels – a recurring duty for the entire crew. Organizing and using a suitable means of recovery to position the heavy track or track components correctly in front of the tank and pulling the vehicle onto them was a matter of practice and experience as was the final pulling together of the upper length of the track with the aid of the driving wheel and a steel rope (acting as a capstan) or hooking the track onto the drive wheel and reversing.

In an emergency the track had to be dismantled into small lengths in order to be able to position it manually. Closing the track with a *Kettenschließer* (a special track-closing tool) and striking in the track pins was certainly no more difficult than attaching the end connector on modern tank tracks.

It was common practice to open just one of the tracks as this picture of a tank belonging to *s.Pz.Abt. 503* shows, taken on 30 July 1943. (Wolff-Altvater)

The mobility of a tank could be restored with a makeshift method of shortening the track. Here a tank belonging to s.*Pz. Abt. 505* is shown with a defective right-hand-side driving wheel.

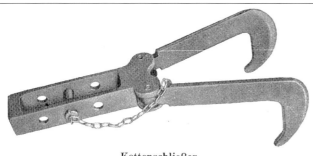

Kettenschließer

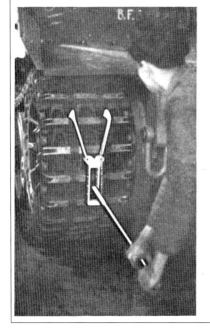

Anwendung: Der Kettenschließer 021 C 39 399 U 9 findet Verwendung zum Zusammenfügen der beiden zusammenzuschließenden Enden der Gleiskette in Verbindung mit einer Brechstange, mit der das von unten angebogene Ende der Kette dem von oben herabhängenden Ende genähert wird, bis es möglich ist, einen Kettenbolzen durch beide Kettenenden hindurchzustecken. Der Kettenschließer wird auch als Bordwerkzeug beim Panzerkampfwagen mitgeführt.

Vortreiber für Kettenbolzen

Track pins were hammered in using the *Vortreiber* (driving chisel) (above). Closing the chain was best done using the special *Kettenschließer* tool (left) otherwise this had to be done with a wrecking bar. (D674/180)

Carrying out the work using the Tiger I as an example

(D656/23, pages 36-37)

Installing the track

1. Open the chain tensioner cover on the rear wall.
2. Turn the chain tensioner as far as possible to the left using the hexagonal spanner.
3. Lay the tracks at the correct gauge, with the track-pin heads to the inside.
4. Drive or tow the tank onto the tracks until there are still four links in front of the first bogie wheel.
5. Hook the 14 mm steel cable to the rear end of the track and coil the front end of the 2-3 times around the body of the drivr sptovket and secure it.
6. In first gear, pull the track over the idler wheel and bogie wheels until the drive sprocket engages with the track. During this procedure keep the cable taut as it comes off the drive sprocket and pull on the emergency steering lever on the opposite side to apply the drive sprocket brake.
7. Remove the steel cable and move the track further to the front using engine power until the two ends of the track can be gripped with the *Kettenschließer* and brought together.
8. Strike in the track pins and secure them.
9. Tension the track by turning the adjusting spindle on the track tensioner.
10. Screw on the track tensioner cover.

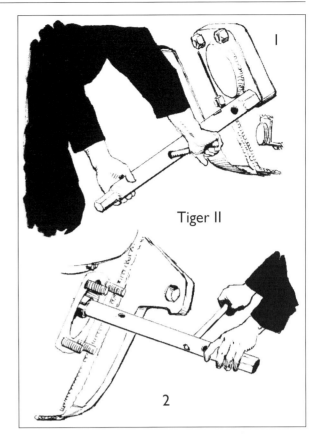

Tiger II

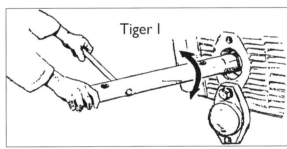

Tiger I

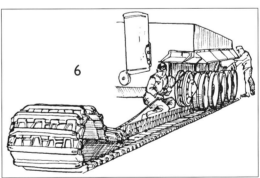

The various different types of bogie-wheel hubs can be clearly seen in this picture of a tank belonging to *s.Pz.Abt. 506.*

A damaged track link has been replaced on this tank belonging to *s.Pz.Abt. 508.* Picture taken on 3 February 1944. (BA 311-0904-21)

Abziehvorrichtung für Außenradflansch

Pullers for removing the outer flange on a bogie wheel (left) and (on the right) the bogie and the idler wheels. (D674/180 resp. D655/21, pic. 52)

Replacing a track pin

1. Drive the tank forward so that the track pin to be replaced lies on the idler wheel and the hull of the tank is not an obstacle.
2. Release the tension on the track.
3. Strike out the dowel securing the track pin and remove the ring.
4. Relieve the load on the track pin by using the *Kettenschließer* to draw the two links joined by the track pin together.
5. Strike out the damaged track pin from the outside to the inside using the driving chisel, then insert the new track pin from the inside to the outside.
6. Push on the track pin ring and strike in the securing dowel.
7. Tension the track

Replacing a track link

1. Drive the tank forward until the damaged track link is under the drive sprocket.
2. Release the tension on the track.
3. Tighten the upper span of the track with the engine so that the track hangs under the drive sprocket.
4. Strike out the track pins on each side of the damaged link from the outside to the inside – see previous section.
5. Insert the new track link and strike in and secure the track pins.
6. Tension the track.

Removing and mounting the supplementary bogie wheels when installing and removing the transport tracks (first version of suspension).

The easy way under favourable conditions:
1. Separate the combat tracks under the idler wheel.
2. Drive the tank straight forwards until the track runs off to the front of the tank and if necessary immobilize it with wedges.
3. Lay out the transport tracks in line with the combat tracks and join them.
4. Drive or tow the vehicle onto the transport tracks.
5. Install the transport track as described above.
6. Remove the supplementary wheels on the inner bogie wheels. Loosen the nuts on the wheel studs and remove the bogie wheel using the jacking screws (M12).
7. Remove the supplementary wheels on the outer bogie wheels. Loosen the screws and locking clips and draw off the bogie wheel with the jacking screws (M12). The spacer ring, secured by three countersunk screws, remains on the hub of the outer bogie wheel.

8. Remove the flange for the supplementary wheel from the inner bogie wheels. Loosen the screws and locking clips and remove the flange.
9. Fitting the supplementary bogie wheels for installing the combat track is carried out in the reverse order. Replace the locking clips, tighten all nuts and screws and examine at the next break in the march. At every pause in the march, check the fastening screws on the hub and the tyre rim of the bogie wheels for fastness.

Vehicle-specific tools

Without vehicle specific tools there was a higher danger of damage to components by potentially rough installation and dismantling with inappropriate tools. It all depended on the individual skill of the crew.

Torsion bar installation with bar holder, winding handle and adjusting gauge for removing the torsion bar and the setting the correct (unloaded) angle of the swinging arm. (D655/21+, pic. 51)

Hier ist eine Übersicht über die Arbeiten, Schlüssel und Sonderwerkzeuge, die nötig sind, um eine Laufrolle, ein Triebrad, Leitrad oder einen Flansch zu wechseln.

Laufrolle Reihe	1	2	3	4	5
Wie bocke ich die Schwing-arme hoch?	Auflaufbock vor innerstes Laufrad des zu hebenden Armes legen, Pz auffahren **1** Am besten mit 2 soliden Stützplatten, 2 Ölhebern zu 30 t eine Längsseite hochbocken **2**		Kette aufmachen. Mit Winden eine Pz-Seite über Kettenzahnhöhe hochheben		
Wieviele Rollen müssen ab?	1	3	4	8	13
Welche Steck-schlüssel, Son-derwerkzeuge brauche ich?	27	27	27	10 (2799/5) 70 50 C 2798 U5 **4** Gew. Zapfen M 39 × 1,5 Schraube 18 × 35	15 (2799/5) 70 50 C 2798 U5 **5** Gew. Zapfen M 39 × 1,5 Schraube 18 × 110
Wieviele Rollen müssen ab?	1	3	3	5	
	Außen-flansch	Innen-flansch	Leitrad	Triebrad	
Welche Steck-schlüssel, Son-derwerkzeuge brauche ich?	27	27 2798 U10 Schrauben-zieher **3**	22 50 C 2798 U5 Schrauben M 14 × 90 Gew. Zapfen M 39 × 1,5 Rohr mit 15 mm Innen-⌀, 75 mm lang **6**	Schlüsselweite 50, 46 Triebrad mittels Abdrück-schraube abdrücken, Kolben mit Feder entfernen, Vorrich-tung C 2798 U3 mit Spindel und Mutter, Steckschlüssel 27, 46, Kopfschraube 50, Mitnehmer abnehmen, ge-teilten Ring abnehmen, Filz-ring erneuern **7**	

On pages 36 and 37 of the *Tigerfibel* there is an overview of work on the bogie wheels and the tools required.

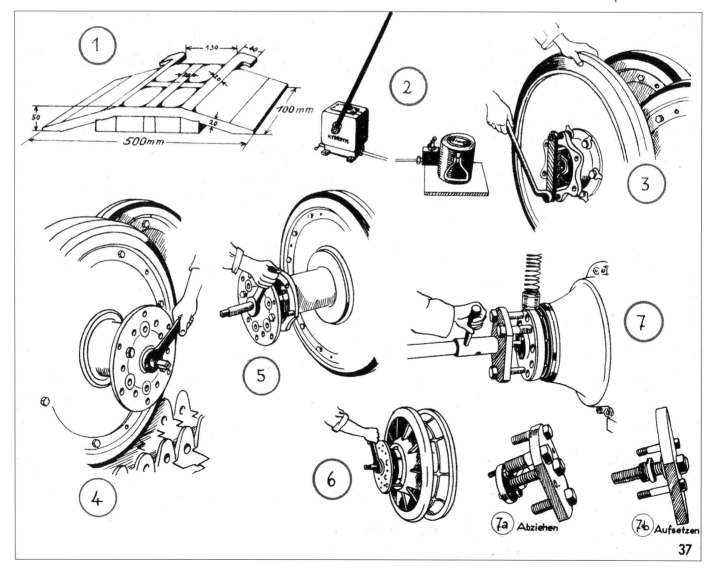

Care, Maintenance and Preservation of Operational Readiness in Extreme Environmental Conditions

For the crew, the majority of routine activities were limited to: cleaning the optics and mechanical parts under stress; attending to the storage of items and to gaskets with oil, grease and talcum powder and following the instructions for taking care of the tank's equipment. During operational service, constant checks were made for damage, abrasion, wear and tear on moving parts and, of course, on the fluid levels of the turret hydraulics, engine, gearbox and cooling system. This was done by visual inspection (looking for marks and leaks) or by feeling with the hand, for example for the overheating of components such as bogie wheels (which might have been caused by damage from projectiles). It is beyond the scope of this publication to list the details of all of the checks that were carried out.

The constant inspection of the suspension components and maintenance of the tank's weapons was absolutely essential. These had to be cleaned after intensive use to keep the tank in a state of operational readiness. Even the smallest traces of burnt-on powder residue, or dirt that had entered from the outside (which could also occur when the weapons were not being used), could cause irreparable damage to the inside of the gun tube or to its recoil device. This of course was the reason for covering the muzzles of weapons during marches. In an imminently dangerous situation these could be shot through. The individual steps for cleaning the barrel of the cannon are shown in a series of pictures later in this chapter.

It was the duty of the company and battalion commanders to plan time for carrying out these technical procedures in advance, for example during stops on long marches.

Work was carried out regularly according to elapsed time intervals (so-called *Fristenarbeiten*). This work was partly the responsibility of the crew but was carried out under the guidance of the repair and maintenance personnel. The necessary tools, means of cleaning and lubricants were held in readiness for use. The procedures were set out in the regulations in the form of a '*Fristenplan*' (maintenance schedule) as is shown in the pages that follow. During the actual work, the commander or the repair and maintenance mechanic ordered the implementation of individual activities and checked the work that had been done.

If technical defects or damage became evident during routine inspection or in service, these were reported informally or on standardized damage reports which then – after first being examined by specialists – formed the basis of a detailed workshop order (see illustration).

Smaller defects such as damaged prisms, blown fuses or bent storage racks were in general dealt with by the crew. In connection with this it was also important to select and remove any damaged ammunition.

The following section is concerned with the important work of the maintenance schedule.

Cleaning the machine guns and other weapons was also important. Here this work is being carried out by the crew of tank '832' of the *8./SS-Pz.Rgt. 2* at the beginning of February 1943. (Mittelstaedt)

OZ	Bezeichnung	Tätigkeit	Mittel	Frist alle 250 km	Frist alle 500 km	Frist alle 1000 km	Frist alle 2000 km	Frist alle 4000 km	Sonst.
1	Schrauben und Muttern am Triebrad (n. n.) .	prüfen					x		
2	Triebrad	schmieren	Fett		x				
3	Stoßdämpfer-Aufhängung vorn	schmieren	Fett	x					
4	Gelenkwellen am Turmantrieb	schmieren	Getriebeöl				x		
5	Turmantrieb Ölstand	prüfen	Getriebeöl			x			
5	Turmantrieb	Ölwechsel	Getriebeöl				x		
6	Bodenventile	prüfen			x				
7	Motor: Wasserpumpe	schmieren			x				
8	Anlasser und Anlasserritzel (n. n)	schmieren	Motoröl						Bei herausgenommenem Motor, da sonst nicht möglich.
9	Anlasser und Anlasserritzel (n. n).	prüfen							Bei herausgenommenem Motor, da sonst nicht möglich.
10	Motor: Ölbadluftfiler	reinigen	Motoröl	x					
11	Motor: Ölstand	prüfen	Motoröl	x					
11	Motor HL 210 im Tiger I	Ölwechsel	Motoröl				x		Bei 250 km, 500 km, 1000 km, dann alle 2000 km
	Motor HL 230 im Tiger II	Ölwechsel	Motoröl			(x)	x		Bei 250 km, 1000 km, dann alle 2000 km. Bei starkem Staubanfall (Tropen, Osten) alle 1000 km
12	Laufräder	schmieren	Fett	x					
13	Kühlwasserstand (n. n.)	prüfen		x					
13	Kühler: Überdruckventil (n.n.)	prüfen					x		
14	Leitrad	schmieren	Fett		x				
15	Lüfterantrieb (Tiger I mit Motor HL210)	schmieren	Getriebeöl	x					
	Lüfterantrieb-Zwischengetriebe Ölstand (Tiger I mit Motor HL 230)	Prüfen (?)	Getriebeöl						Nicht verzeichnet
	Lüfterantrieb-Zwischengetriebe (Tiger I mit Motor HL 230)	Ölwechsel (?)	Getriebeöl						Nicht verzeichnet
	Lüftergetriebe –Ölstand (2 x) (Tiger II)	Prüfen	Getriebeöl	x					
	Lüftergetriebe (2x) (Tiger II)	Ölwechsel	Getriebeöl				x		Bei 250 km, 500 km, 1000 km, dann alle 2000 km
16	Gelenkwellen am Lüfterantrieb (Tiger I mit Motor HL 210)	schmieren	Fett				x		
	Lüftergelenkwellen Motorseite (Tiger II)	schmieren	Fett	x					
	Lüftergelenkwellen Lüfterseite (Tiger II)	schmieren	Fett				x		
17	Kettenspannvorrichtung (n.n)	schmieren	Fett						Vor jeder Kettennachstellung schmieren
18	Rutschkupplung für Lüfter Tiger I bei mangelhafter Kühlleistung prüfen	prüfen.	n. n.						Nicht verzeichnet
19	Lichtmaschine (n. n).	Prüfen							Bei herausgenommenem Motor, da sonst nicht möglich.
20	Motor: Magnetzünder (n. n.)	prüfen					x		
21	Motor: Vergaser (n. n.)	reinigen		x					
22	Vergasergestänge	schmieren	Getriebeöl		x				
23	Motor: Kraftstoffpumpen	reinigen		x					
	Motor: Kraftstoffilter (Tiger II)	reinigen	P3	x					
24	Motor: Ölfilter	reinigen			x				
25	Motor: Zündkerzen: Elektroden-Abstand (n. n.)	prüfen			x				
26	Motor: Zündkerzen: Entstör-Sammelhaube	reinigen		x					
27	Vergasergestänge	schmieren	Fett	x					
28	Batterien	prüfen		x					
29	Turm: Schleifringübertrager	schmieren	Motoröl		x				
30	Gelenkwellen	schmieren	Fett				x		
31	n. n., fehlt								
32	Schwingarme und Stoßdämpfer-aufhängung hinten durch Schmierbatterie	schmieren	Fett	x					
	Vordere Stoßdämpfer: Ölstand	prüfen	Stoßdämpferöl				x		
	Hintere Stoßdämpfer: Ölstand	prüfen					x		Bei Ausbau des Motors
32	Leitradkurbel durch Schmierbatterie	schmieren	Fett			x			
33	Lenk- und Schaltgetriebe: Ölstand	prüfen				x			
33	Lenk- und Schaltgetriebe (Tiger I)	Ölwechsel					x		Bei 250 km, 500 km, 1000 km, dann alle 2000 km
	Lenk und Schaltgetriebe (Tiger II)	Ölwechsel							Bei 250 km, 1000 km, 5000 km, bei normalem Betrieb alle 5000 km
33	Lenk- und Schaltgetriebe: Ölfilter (Tiger I)	prüfen				x			Erstmals nach 2000 km, dann alle 1000 km
	Lenk- und Schaltgetriebe Ölfilter (Tiger II)	reinigen	P3		x				
34	Kupplungsgestänge	schmieren	Fett	x					
35	Bremsgestänge und Hebellenkung	schmieren	Fett	x					
36	Seitenvorgelege: Ölstand	prüfen	Getriebeöl		x				
36	Seitenvorgelege	Ölwechsel	Getriebeöl				x		
37	MG-Lagerung (n.n.)	schmieren	Öl						Vor jedem größeren Schießen
38	MG-Lagerung (n.n)	schmieren	Fett						Vor jedem größeren Schießen
39	Zwölfuhrzeigertrieb (n.n)	schmieren	Fett						Alle 2-3 Monate
40	Turm: Flüssigkeitsgetriebe (später weggefallen))	schmieren	Getriebeöl				x		
	Turm: Flüssigkeitsgetriebe	Ölwechsel	Getriebeöl						Arbeit der Waffenmeisterei
41	Turmschwenkwerk	schmieren	Fett				x		
42	Turm: Höhenrichtmaschine	schmieren	Fett				x		
43	Rohrwiege		Fett						Vor jedem größeren Schießen
44	Turmzurrung	schmieren	Fett				x		
45	Schildzapfen	Schmieren	Fett						Alle 2-3 Monate
	Motor: Leerlauf	prüfen				x			
	Motor: Zylinderkopfschrauben (später Arbeit der Panzerwarte)	prüfen (anziehen)				x			
	Motor: Ventilspiel (später Arbeit der Panzerwart)e	prüfen					x		Erstmals nach 2000 km, dann alle 4000 km
	Motor: Zündeinstellung (später Arbeit der Panzerwarte)	prüfen					x		Erstmals nach 2000 km, dann alle 4000 km
	Kühlwasserstand	prüfen		x					

A revised and expanded list (prepared by the author) of the numbered maintenance point locations (OZ/Ortszahlen) is shown in the diagram on the following page.

Schedule Related Work

The schedule of work carried out on the *Pamzerkampfwagen* Tiger Ausf. E (Tiger I) is described in accordance with
• maintenance schedule booklet D 626/24 and
• handbook for the tank driver D656/23 of 10 May 1944

and on *Pz.Kpfw.* Tiger *Ausführung B* (Tiger II) in accordance with the following regulations
• Tiger *Ausführung B*, handbook for the tank driver D 656/43of 1 September 1944.

These are quoted in part literally or with relevant additions.

The first mentioned set of specifications are without doubt based on the initial vehicle series with the Maybach HL 210 engine that was made entirely of aluminium and differed from the HL 230 engine with respect to the layout and performance of its air filter, magneto and ventilator drive unit. For the driver, it served as the basis for the necessary

and regular maintenance work that had to be carried out in order to prevent premature wear and subsequent failure of components and was written in a commanding tone.

The maintenance schedule booklets used by the *Bundeswehr* (German Army) are very similar in style and cannot deny their 'ancestry.'

This booklet, issued at the time when the Tiger tank was first deployed, gives the impression of being incomplete and is afflicted by the confusing allocation of numbers regarding the servicing points. It is based on the lubrication diagram – with erroneous handwritten entries – in the factory device description and operating instructions for the chassis (D656/21), one of the first makeshift collections of various company regulations issued in March 1943 for construction groups working on the Tiger I.

On a separate page at the end of the booklet the exchange and overhaul of the engine and gearbox were to documented.

Overview of the maintenance points with so-called *Ortszahlen* (see the table on the previous page).

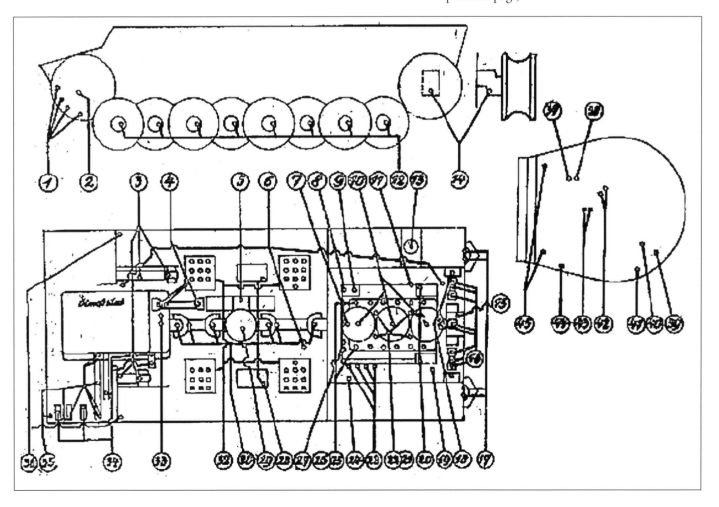

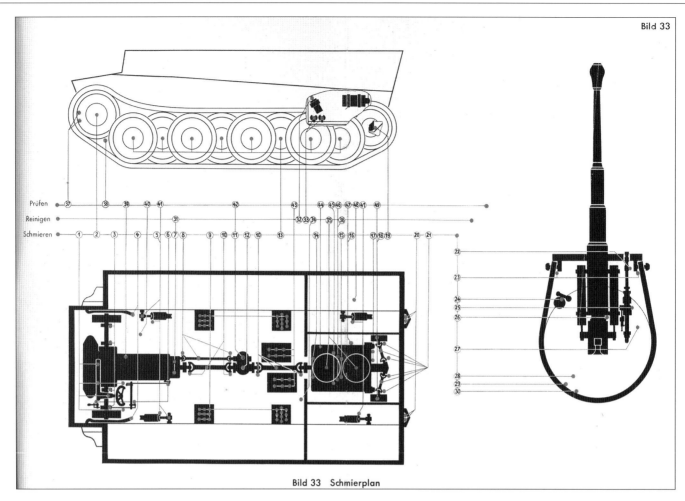

Bild 33   Schmierplan

The lubrication diagram for the Tiger Ausf. E in the handbook for the tank driver (D656/23) looked much more professional. The diagram below, taken from the servicing schedule for the hull of the Tiger II in D656/44, and the corresponding overview (on the following page) show the lubrication points and items requiring maintenance.

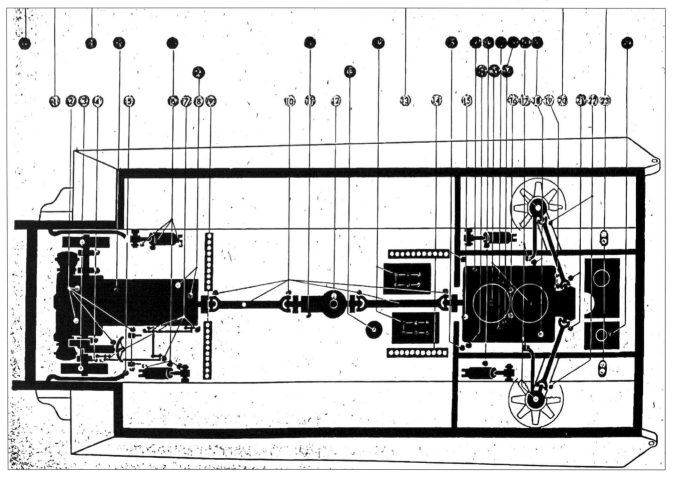

Mö	Motorenöl der Wehrmacht	
Gö	Getriebeöl der Wehrmacht	
F	Einheitsabschmierfett	
Sö	Stoßdämpferöl nach TL 6027 (violett)	
KF	Korrosionsschutzfett	
R	Reinigungsflüssigkeit, notfalls Kraftstoff	
K	Kraftstoff	
W	Wasser	
DW	Destill. Wasser	
1	nur beim Einfahren	2 nur bei starkem Staub

Schmier- und Pflegestellen am Pz.Kpfw. Tiger Ausf. B

Fristenplan nach dem km-Stand

Note: Stoßeinsatz für Fettpresse U 549/13 (zu Nr. 10/11)

Nr.	Benennung	Anz.	tägl.	250	500	750	1000	1250	1500	1750	2000	2250	2500	2750	3000	3250	3500	3750	4000	4250	4500	4750	5000
	Schmieren																						
1	Triebräder	2			F		F		F		F		F		F		F		F		F		F
2	Bremsgestänge und Hebellenkung	8		F	F	F	F	F	F	F	F	F	F	F	F	F	F	F	F	F	F	F	F
3	Bremsen	2			F		F		F		F		F		F		F		F		F		F
4	Seitenwellen	4			F		F		F		F		F		F		F		F		F		F
5	Seitenvorgelege Ölw.	2				Gö				Gö				Gö				Gö					Gö
6	Stoßdämpfer vorn	4		F	F	F	F	F	F	F	F	F	F	F	F	F	F	F	F	F	F	F	F
7	Kupplungsgestänge	5		F	F	F	F	F	F	F	F	F	F	F	F	F	F	F	F	F	F	F	F
8	Wechselgetriebe Ölw.	1		Gö	Gö						Gö				Gö				Gö				Gö
9	Schmierbatterie vorn	22		F	F	F	F	F	F	F	F	F	F	F	F	F	F	F	F	F	F	F	F
10	Hauptgelenkwellen	6				F				F				F				F				F	
11	Turmantrieb Ölw.	1					Gö									Gö							Gö
12	Schleifringübertrager	1			F		F		F		F		F		F		F		F		F		F
13	Laufräder	18		F	F	F	F	F	F	F	F	F	F	F	F	F	F	F	F	F	F	F	F
14	Schmierbatterie hinten	20		F	F	F	F	F	F	F	F	F	F	F	F	F	F	F	F	F	F	F	F
15	Vergasergestänge	1		F	F	F	F	F	F	F	F	F	F	F	F	F	F	F	F	F	F	F	F
16	Vergaserbetätigung	8		F	F	F	F	F	F	F	F	F	F	F	F	F	F	F	F	F	F	F	F
17	Lüftergetriebe Ölw.	2			Mö		Mö				Mö							Mö					
18	Motor Ölw.	1		Mö			Mö				Mö					Mö							Mö
19	Gestänge z.Durchdrehvorr.	1 / 1	nur bei herausgenommenem Motor schmieren, da sonst nicht zugänglich; von Heckwand aus zugänglich																				
20	Leiträder	2			F		F		F		F		F		F		F		F		F		F
21	Lüftergelenkwellen Motorseite	2					F				F				F				F				
22	Lüftergelenkwellen Lüfterseite	2	Düsenrohr 73.1.00/018 nur bei herausgenommenem Motor, da sonst nicht zugänglich																				
23	Kettenspanner	4					F				F				F				F				F
24	Rohrwiege	2	vor jedem größeren Schießen				F				F				F				F				F
25	MG-Lagerung vorn	1	vor jedem größeren Schießen				F				F				F				F				F
26	Schildzapfen	2									F							F					
27	Turmschwenkwerk	1									F												F
28	Zwölfuhrzeigertrieb	1									F							F					
29	MG-Lagerung hinten	1	vor jedem größeren Schießen				Gö				Gö				Gö				Gö				Gö
30	Flüssigkeitsgetriebe	1																					Gö
31	Drehkranz	2			F		F		F		F		F		F		F		F		F		F
	Reinigen																						
32	Wechselgetriebe-Ölfilter	1			R		R		R		R		R		R		R		R		R		R
33	Kraftstoff-Filter	1		R	R	R	R	R	R	R	R	R	R	R	R	R	R	R	R	R	R	R	R
34	Motor-Ölfilter	1		R	R		R		R		R		R		R		R		R		R		
35	Luftfilter	2	beim jeweiligen Kraftstofftanken																				
36	Zündkerzen	12			R		R		R		R		R		R		R		R		R		R
	Prüfen																						
37	Schrauben am Laufwerk		.			O					O							O					
38	Seitenvorgelege Ölst.	2			Gö		Gö		Gö		Gö		Gö		Gö		Gö		Gö		Gö		Gö
39	Wechselgetriebe Ölst.	1	O																				
40	Stoßdämpfer vorn Ölst.	2			Sö		Sö		Sö		Sö		Sö		Sö		Sö		Sö		Sö		Sö
41	Turmantrieb	1			Gö		Gö		Gö		Gö		Gö		Gö		Gö		Gö		Gö		Gö
42	Sammler	2		DW	DW	DW	DW	DW	DW	DW	DW	DW	DW	DW	DW	DW	DW	DW	DW	DW	DW	DW	DW
43	Bodenventile	2			O		O		O		O		O		O		O		O		O		O
44	Schrauben am Zyl.-Kopf	28					O				O				O				O				
45	Stoßdämpfer hinten	2	nur bei herausgenommenem Motor, da sonst nicht zugänglich																				
46	Ventilspiel	24					O				O				O				O				O
47	Zündkerzen Elektr.-Abst.	12					O				O				O				O				
48	Lüftergetriebe Ölst.	2			O		O		O		O		O		O		O		O		O		O
49	Motor	1	Mö																				
50	Kühlerüberdruckventil	1																					O

The servicing schedules appear to have been set up for peacetime operations and seem somewhat theoretical and optimistic: the service interval only went as far as 4,000 km whereas the following versions of the schedule booklet provided for service intervals up to 24,000 km. The servicing booklets were to be kept by the *Schirrmeister* (maintenance sergeant) and handed out to the driver for vehicle servicing but they were taken with the vehicle when it went into action. The *Schirrmeister* then had to verify that the work had been completed according to schedule on a weekly basis. Towards the end of Tiger I production eighteen months later, driver handbook D 656/23 appeared which contained a simplified overview of the lubrication and maintenance schedule based on the HL230 engine. It seems to have been updated in the light of operational experience and the locations (*Ortszahlen*) on the technical drawings, which are easier to distinguish, are clearly divided according to the type of servicing work required: '*Prüfen, Reinigen, Schmieren*' (check, clean, lubricate). However, it should be pointed out that it is still an open question as to whether the service booklet carried on the vehicle was the abovementioned D 656/24.

With a few exceptions, the service schedule D 656/44 for the Tiger II contains the same service location points but is it is more clearly organized. In addition there is a clear, colour-coded division into 'check, clean, lubricate' and, in contrast to the Tiger I service schedule, the person (or the position of the person) that carried out the work is identified. However, a new service routine for 'every 4,000 km' was issued. In the driver's handbook for the Tiger II (D 656/43) there was no separate listing of the maintenance activities but an explicit reference was made to work schedule D 656/44.

Lubrication and maintenance work was carried out by the tank driver and a mechanic. During difficult operating conditions the driver autonomously, or on orders, carried out the lubrication and maintenance work correspondingly earlier. It was also the intention that in the tropics or other especially difficult conditions the service intervals should shortened on the decision of the unit commanders. The target service intervals were supposed to be valid only for 'normal' operational conditions and could probably only be applied to replacement units. Because postponement during military operations couldn't be avoided the appropriate work was, as the situation allowed, either anticipated or caught up upon.

The driver had to certify the work had been carried out by signing the schedule booklet. In a separate column the driver's supervisor was supposed to sign and date the work but this was often omitted.

The careful execution of the maintenance work, and therefore the technical reliability of the tank in combat situations, was in the best interests of the entire crew. For technical problems that arose during deployment the driver first had to face the commander, even if he was not directly responsible for them. Tiger commander, *Oberfeldwebel* Krebs, the leader of tank '112' of the *s.Pz.Abt. 501*, made the following remark to the author about his first hour in Tunisia:

> I took as a driver the one who knew how to get the engine running at its best!'

The activities that were described were basically to be regarded as of equal status to the traditional regulations. However, it should not be assumed that in every case the ideal maintenance schedules – as practiced by the peacetime or replacement units – could be conducted according to plan in units that were on the front line. Work on heavily used vehicles was more likely to be carried out at an opportune moment by the workshop or during the infrequent refitting or reorganization stops.

It was however certain that the driver, from experience, assiduously attended to important matters such as

- checking the levels of engine oil and coolant
- checking the condition of the electrical installations, particularly the batteries
- examining the power unit components, fuel and cooling system for leaks
- monitoring the serviceability of the fire extinguisher equipment
- cleaning the air filter, engine oil filter and fuel filter
- checking the spark plugs and carburettor if the engine was running rough
- lubricating the drive shafts and running gear components

Changing the oil

(taken from D 656/23, D 656/43, D 635/5, diff. articles in HtVBl 1944)

Changing the oil in the engine and transmission of a tank under field conditions at that time was not done under the conditions we are familiar with today for dealing with fluids that are environmentally harmful and dangerous to health. However, used oil was a valuable raw material and it was collected for recycling. Refilling the oil bath air filter was an important daily task.

Apart from the *Kameraden* who carried out this work in unbelievably (and previously mentioned) cramped conditions and who because of their intimate contact with lubricants were not infrequently and mockingly referred to as '*Ölis*' (oilies) – the fighting compartment itself often became a greasy place during deployment if the oil contaminating the 'bilges' – that is to say the space between the floor and the armoured bottom of the hull where the torsion bars were housed – could not be satisfactorily cleaned. Such unpopular work was however of pressing importance – particularly if there was contamination with fuel – in order to keep on top of the lurking danger of fire and the unpleasant oil and fuel fumes rising up from below.

In the *Tigerfibel* (below) there is a summary – at least for the Tiger I – that made it unnecessary to search for information regarding this theme. This summary clearly describes what to lubricate ('*Wo füllen*'), the specified lubricant ('*Was füllen*'), the quantities to be used ('*Wieviel füllen*') and the consequences of failure to adhere to the lubrication regime (under '*Sonst passiert was*' there a list of unpleasant things would happen!).

However, the table does not include oil filling in the fan drive (angled drive) of the HL230 engine on the right and left, each with 3 litres of gear oil (only to the upper level-mark) while the engine is at a standstill.

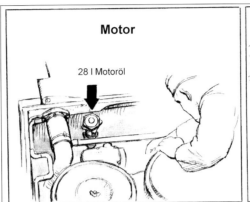
Motor
28 l Motoröl

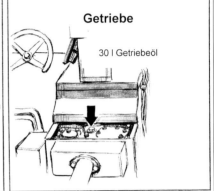
Getriebe
30 l Getriebeöl

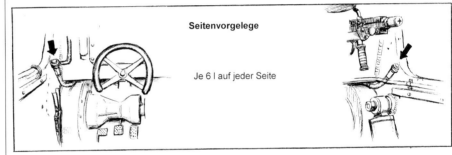
Seitenvorgelege
Je 6 l auf jeder Seite

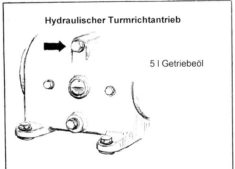
Hydraulischer Turmrichtantrieb
5 l Getriebeöl

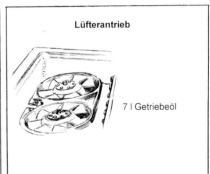
Lüfterantrieb
7 l Getriebeöl

Topping up the oil in a Tiger I.

Wo füllen?	Was füllen?	Wieviel füllen?	Sonst passiert was?
1. Motor	28 Liter Motoröl	höchstens obere Marke mindestens untere Marke	Sonst verölen die Zündkerzen, brauchst Du viel Öl und Motoren
2. Wechsel-Getriebe	30 Liter Getr. Öl	bis Meßstab gerade eben eintaucht	Sonst kannst Du weder schalten noch lenken.
3. Vorgelege (rechts)	6 Liter Getr. Öl	kleine Prüfschraube (nicht die große Schraube) abschrauben	Sonst füllst Du zu viel oder zu wenig. Beides ist schlecht.
4. Vorgelege (links)	6 Liter Getr. Öl	nachfüllen bis Öl überläuft	
5. Turmantrieb	5 Liter Getr. Öl	füllen bis Spiegel 1 fingerbreit unter Füllöffnung steht	Sonst kannst Du den Turm nicht schwenken.
6. Lüftertrieb	7 Liter Getr. Öl	nur bis oberste Marke, bei stehender Maschine auffüllen.	Sonst wird es auf den Auspuffmantel geschleudert.

Changing the engine oil

Oil changes are to be carried out when the engine is warm so that the contaminated used oil runs out completely.

1. Remove the cover in the tank hull bottom.
2. Remove the drain plugs on the sumps (1) and on the oil reservoir (2) – let the oil drain out.
3. With the ignition switched off, turn the engine with the cranking device to pump the remaining oil from the engine.
4. Clean the oil filter.
5. Replace drain plugs with gaskets and screw tight.
6. Open the filler cap on the left side of the engine cover.
7. Fill with 30 litres of fresh oil to the upper mark on the dipstick, measured while engine is idling.
8. Close filler opening and bottom cover.

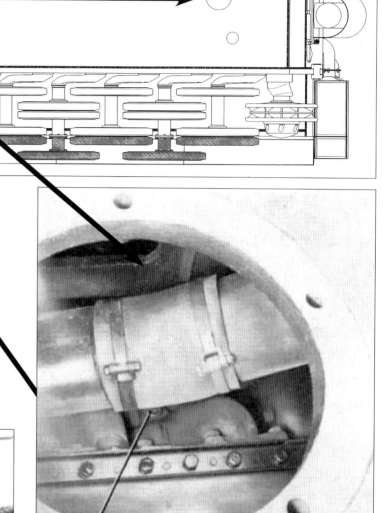

(D656/43, pic. 3, 5 and 6)

Gear selector and steering drive

Tiger I:

1. Allow the gearbox to warm up.
2. Open the bottom cover in the hull bottom.
3. Remove the radio equipment and control panel, to expose the gearbox flashing.
4. Remove the upper cover of the metal flashing and open the gearbox cover below. Unscrew the oil drain plug so that the oil reserve in the gear se-lector oil tray above the gear train flows out.
   (In the Tiger II simply remove the rear cover of the transmission).
5. Open the two drain plugs on the gearbox oil sump.
6. Remove the cover on the sheet metal cladding and unscrew the oil filter.
7. Remove the oil filter, dismantle and clean it. Leave to dry before reinstalling, scoop the oil from the housing and clean the housing.
8. To empty the pipes let the engine run for a short time with the gear selector in neutral.
9. Reassemble in reverse order.
10. Fill with about 30 litres of fresh oil (38 litres in the Tiger II).
11. Test the oil level with the dipstick.

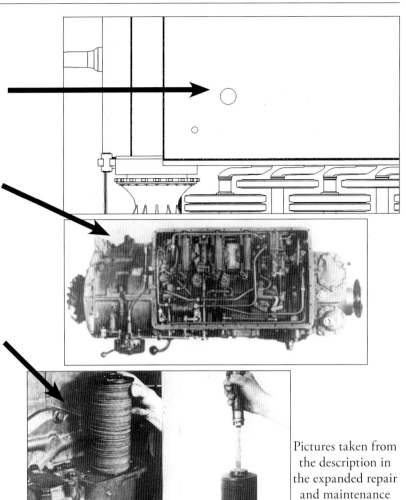

Pictures taken from the description in the expanded repair and maintenance regulations and the instructions for Olvargetriebe OG 401216A gearbox.

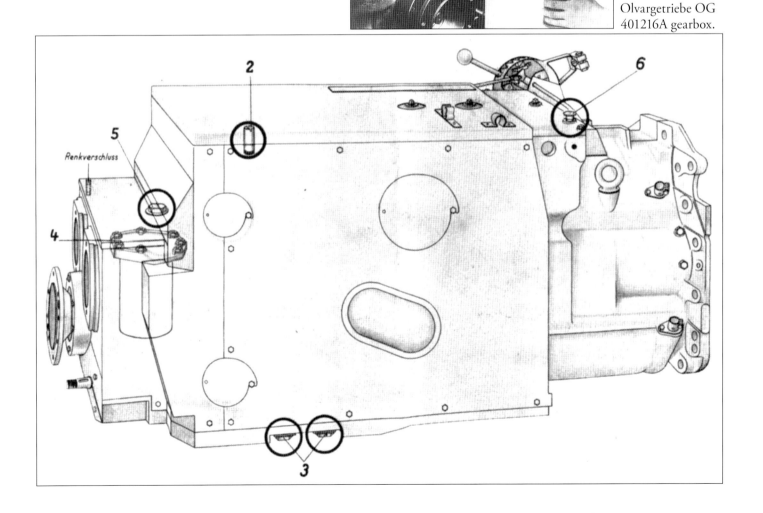

Ventilation fan drive Tiger I

(HL 210 engine)

Lubrication of the ventilator drive also provides lubrication for the drives below the fan.

1. Open the oil drain plug and collect the oil.
2. Close and tighten the oil drain plug.
3. Pour 6-8 litres of fresh oil (*Wehrmacht* summer, winter or 8E) though the filler cap and check the oil level with the dipstick while the engine is running.

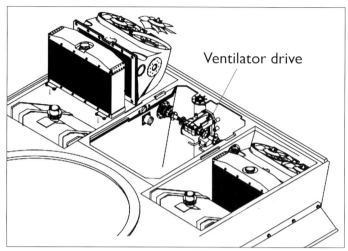

The picture to the left shows the limited accessibility of the ventilator drive unit in the space between the engine and the rear wall of the hull. (D656/22, pic. 33)

Ventilation fan drive Tiger I

(angular gearbox, HL230 engine)

Lubrication of the ventilator drive also provides lubrication for the drives below the fan.

1. Open the oil drain plug at the lowest point in the housing and collect the oil.
2. Briefly run the engine with the ventilation switched on.
3. Close and tighten the oil drain plug.
4. Pour 3 litres of fresh oil (*Wehrmacht* gear oil 8E) into the oil inlet and check level with the dipstick.

Remark: oil change of the fan drive in the Tiger II was only possible with fan removed and should be done during repair work on the engine.

One of the two ventilator drives (intermediate gear); this one is on the right side of the engine compartment and is partially obscured by the (white) cooling water pipe to the HL 230 engine. (BWB WTS)

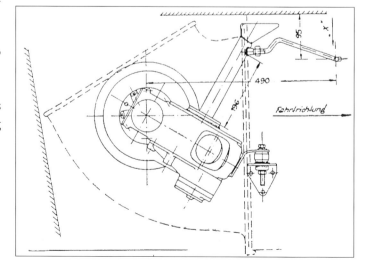

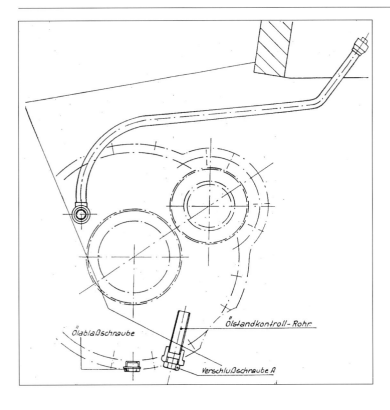

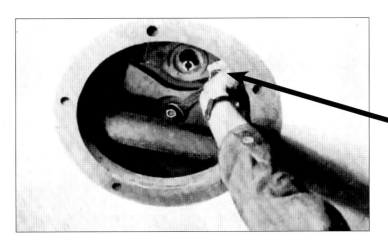

Only easily visible with the turret removed: at the bottom edge of the picture the turret drive is visible while at the top of the picture is the rear end of the gear selector unit. Between them are the drive shafts for the main drive (left) and the turret drive (right). (D656/22+, pic. 32,

Final drives

In the final drive the correct oil level was determined not by a dipstick but by an oil overflow tube. It was closed down by a screw. Oil was poured into the final drive from above until it ran out of the open oil overflow tube.

1. Open the oil drain plug and closing screw (left) on the oil level tube and allow the oil to run out.
2. Close the drain plug. Pour fresh oil into the oil inlet pipe (Z) using a funnel until it over-flows from the oil-level tube. The oil capacity amounted to 7 litres. Using the green 'all year round' 8E oil of the *Wehrmacht* – introduced in autumn 1943 – it took just four minutes at room temperature to fill the final drive whereas it took seven minutes using the summer grade oil, 1.5E. In the latter case, it took nine minutes if the oil-level tube was closed.
3. Screw in and tighten the filler screw and closing screw on the oil level tube.

Turret drive

Example Tiger II:
1. Unscrew the oil filler cover.
2. From below, open the lid in the centre of the tank's hull. According to regulations there is no floor lid in the Tiger I. Changing oil in this case is much more cumbersome.
3. Unscrew the oil drain plug on the turret drive.
4. Collect the oil in a container.
5. Screw in the oil drain plug.
6. Pour 4 litres of *Wehrmacht* gear oil 8E into the oil inlet.
7. Check the oil level on the control screw (1).
8. Refill with oil up to the control screw.
9. Screw on the oil filler cover screw.

This photograph of a vehicle belonging to *s.Pz.Abt. 504* taken on 7 March 1943 in Trapani clearly shows the preparations for cleaning the barrel. The poles of the barrel cleaner are already joined and the oil brush is screwed on; cleaning cloths are laid out on the barrel and are ready for use.

Inside the tank the loader wraps the rags around the brush before the crew pulls it forward in the barrel to remove powder residue. It was possible to lower the barrel even lower…

Barrel cleaning is fun…well that is the (unconfirmed) rumour…

It certainly wasn't so in winter…

To finish the work, the inside of the barrel was given a thin coat of oil with the aim of preventing corrosion.

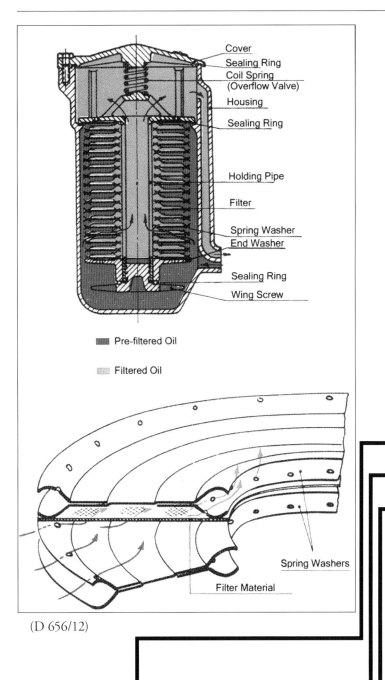

Pre-filtered Oil

Filtered Oil

Spring Washers

Filter Material

(D 656/12)

Cleaning work

(from D656/21+, D 656/23, D656/27, D 635/5, D 656/43, diff. articles in HtVBl 1944)

This was by far the most time consuming work between missions and was intended to maintain the combat readiness of the tank. Initially it concerned the equipment, the running gear and the weapons. Amongst the latter of these activities, cleaning the barrel of the gun tube was the most important task because otherwise serious damage could occur when firing.

Engine oil filter

At every engine oil change, the more frequent the better, the oil filter is to be cleaned. If it is allowed to become clogged, unfiltered oil passes through the overflow valve and reaches the engine bearings. The engine oil filter is to be found behind the left bulkhead cover.

1. Unscrew the oil filter cover; watch out for the tensioned spring on the screw.
2. Pull out the oil filter cartridge.
3. Loosen the wing screw on the filter cartridge.
4. One by one carefully slip the fabric washers and spring washers from the slotted retaining tube and wash them out using P3, – Cehapon cleaning fluid or such like; fuel can be used in an emergency.
5. Rinse out the filter housing with cleaning fluid or, if necessary, with fuel. Fuel must not be spilled inside the hull – danger of fire!
6. Rebuild the filter in reverse order. Tighten the screws evenly.
7. Top up the oil.

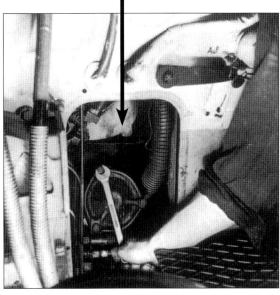

(D656/43, pic. 7)

(D656/43, pic. 8)

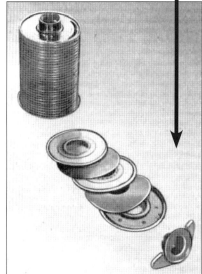

(D656/43, pic. 10)

Gear selector oil filter

The transmission oil filter required special attention because the pre-selector control valves were sensitive to contamination. The main 'wet' multi-disc clutch and freewheeling clutches built into the gearbox were immersed in the gearbox oil and subject to surface abrasion so contamination of the oil was unavoidable. In addition, the oil circuit in the gear pre-selector drive included the steering drive with further oil-cooled multi-disc couplings. As in any transmission system, this meant that there was the potential for the abrasion of metal components. Valves that had been jammed by dirt inevitably led to faults in the gear selector mechanism that could only be resolved by undertaking complex and time-consuming repairs.

1. Remove the sheet-metal transmission cover above the oil filter.
2. Unscrew the eight hexagonal screws on the oil filter cap and remove the cap.
3. Lift out the coil spring and filter cartridge and clean as described previously for the engine oil filter.
4. Scoop the oil from the filter housing and clean the filter housing.
5. Reinstall the filter paying careful attention to the reassembly of the compression spring.

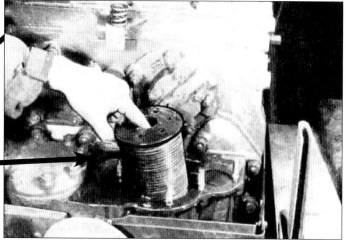

Steering gear oil filter

A separate oil filter for the steering gearbox is only provided in the more advanced gearbox and steering gearbox of the Tiger II. This is built into the gear selector drive and it too must be cleaned regularly.

1. Remove the metal cover.
2. Unscrew the eight hexagonal screws on the oil filter lid and steering valve flange and remove the cover with the attached steering valve.
3. Pull out the spring and the filter cartridge and clean the filter housing in the manner already described.
4. Reassemble and install the filter cartridge.

Gear selector drive and pressure control valve

The oil pressure control valve was prone to contamination and this could lead to malfunctions in the transmission components. On the gearbox of the Tiger II it was possible to reach this from the outside and it was easy to clean. Two different versions were built but these differed only in the way they were attached.

1. Remove the metal cover on the transmission.
2. Unscrew the two hexagonal screws on the flange of the pressure control valve.
3. Using two screwdrivers with even pressure, lever out the pressure regulation valve on its flange.
4. Turn the pressure regulation valve upside down and open the valve disc using a screwdriver with downward pressure; blow out any contamination.
5. Reinstall in the reverse order.

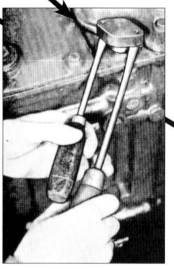

Steering gear and valves

In the gear selector drives of the Tiger I and II, an externally accessible valve that controlled the hydraulics was installed and this was cleaned if faults developed in the steering. In the Tiger I this was located behind and above the driver's side of the transmission (see under 'Checking and adjustment'); in the Tiger II it was located at the top of the transmission to the right of the steering drive oil filter cover.

Cleaning the steering valve from the outside (Tiger II):
1. Remove the sheet metal cover.
2. Remove the screw plug in the middle of the steering valve.
3. Open the valve by pressing down with a screwdriver while the transmission is running to allow the oil to flush out contaminants from the valve.
4. Screw in the plug again.

If simply cleaning does not lead to the successful remedy of the problem, or damage to the valve is suspected, it is to be removed. This is done according to the method used for the removal of the gear selector drive valve (see above). It is then disassembled into individual components and cleaned before reassembly and installation.

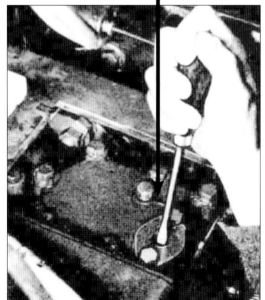

Engine air filter

If the oil bath in the cyclonic air filter was too tacky, the filter insert gradually became clogged and this had harmful consequences for the engine. Every 250 km in normal service the air filter had to be cleaned and the oil changed but this was done at every fuel refill if the terrain was particularly dusty, however, in such conditions, the air filter in the Tiger I was cleaned after merely 50 km, or even sooner. Page 29 of the *Tigerfibel* warns:

> With your Maybach you can travel smoothly for 5,000 km in combat, if you give it clean air to breathe. Otherwise not even 500 km.

The initially installed Feifel pre-filters installed on the rear of the Tiger I were cleaned daily when operating in dusty areas by opening the bottom cover to let the dust flow out.

Procedure when working on, for example, the Tiger II:

1. Lever off the cover above the tommy screw.
2. Unscrew the tommy screw.
3. Using the two handgrips pull out the filter assembly.
4. Remove the oil filler cover.
5. Remove the filter element.
6. Rinse the filter element with fuel.
7. Pull out the oil reservoir.
8. Pour out the oil.
9. Clean out the reservoir using cleaning fluid or fuel.
10. Fill up to the mark with engine oil.
11. Assemble in the reverse order. Make sure that the arrows on the filter housing point in the direction of travel. The seal between the air filter and the air intake of the carburettor must be properly seated so that no unfiltered air can be drawn into it.
12. Clean the second air filter using the same procedure.

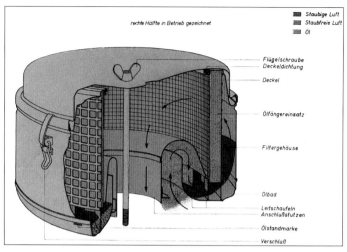

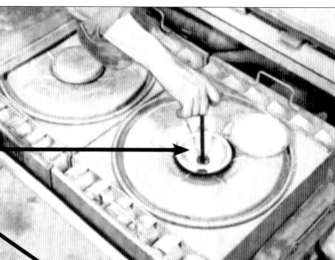

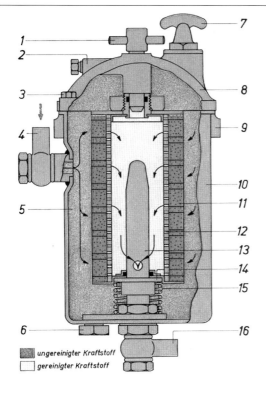

1 Entlüftungsschraube
2 Entlüftungsleitung
3 Befestigungsschrauben
4 Filtereinlaufstutzen
5 Zulaufraum
6 Schlammablaß
7 Einfüllschraube
8 Deckel
9 Befestigungsflansch
10 Gehäuse
11 Filtereinsatz
12 Filterrohr
13 Spannbolzen
14 Verschlußbuchse
15 Schraubenfeder
16 Filterauslaufstutzen

ungereinigter Kraftstoff
gereinigter Kraftstoff

Bild 12a. Kraftstoffilter

Fuel filter

The fuel filter element had to be cleaned every 250 km and the sludge removed from the housing. A fuel filter was first provided for the Tiger I from September 1943 and was located in the corner of the rear fighting area on the bulkhead. In the Tiger II it was to be found under the turret on the leftside of the fighting compartment. Cleaning it was something of an effort as it had to be done in an uncomfortable position. Spilling the fuel had to be avoided as far as was possible because of the danger of fire.

1. Turn the turret to the 3 o'clock position, remove the turret platform flap.
2. Unscrew the four screws on the fuel container cover and remove the cover.
3. Remove the filter cartridge.

4. Place a small bowl under the filter housing, unscrew the debris run-off plug (1) and allow the mixture of fuel and debris to run out. Clean the filter housing with fuel.
5. Screw in the debris run-off plug.
6. Unscrew the hexagonal screw on the filter cartridge and remove the cover plate with felt washers (see picture below).
7. Wash out all parts with cleaning fluid or, if necessary, with fuel.
8. Reassemble the filter element in the reverse order.
9. Open the fuel selector lever and bleed screw until fuel flow escapes.
10. Close the fuel selector lever and bleed screw.
11. Remove the filter assembly and the fuel pump through the cover in the floor of the hull and clean them. When reassembling, make sure the seal sits properly in position otherwise there is a danger of poor pump performance and the danger of fire because of escaping fuel.

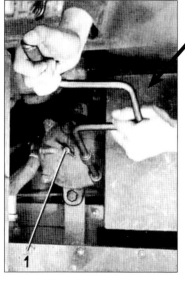

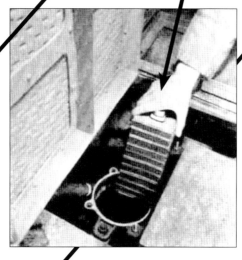

Carburettor main jets

According to the instructions in the last handbook for drivers of the Tiger, issued in September 1944, cleaning the carburettor main jets was the only task he had to carry out on the carburettor.

But this was contrary to the instructions in the still-valid *Tigerfibel* according to which the carburettor cover had to be removed in order to test the carburettor and to monitor the fuel level in the float (*Schwimmer*) housing.

1. After removing the air filter loosen the two hexagonal screws on the air collecting box.
2. Remove the air collecting box.
3. Unscrew the jet retainer screw in the carburettor.
4. Blow through the main jet (*Hauptdüse*). If this does not clear any contamination that is present, use a screwdriver to unscrew the main jet from its housing and if necessary clean it with the jet-cleaning needle.
5. Assemble in the reverse order.

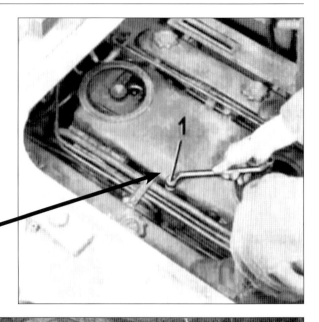

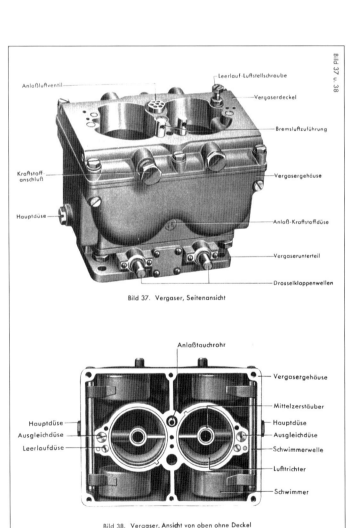

Bild 37. Vergaser, Seitenansicht

Bild 38. Vergaser, Ansicht von oben ohne Deckel

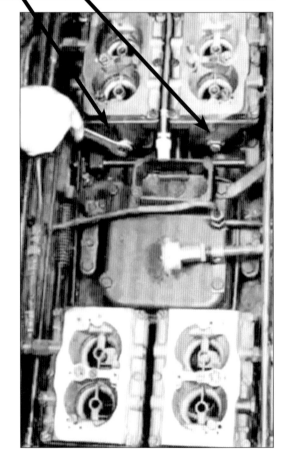

Cleaning and checking the spark plugs

Nowadays, cleaning spark plugs and checking their electrode gap has almost passed into obscurity but for the Tiger the frequent checking and renewal of spark plugs was necessary – as was the need to solve ignition and carburation problems. The spark plugs in particular were at the centre of the driver's attention. The experienced driver or tank mechanic was in the position of being able to assess the tank's performance, the fuel-to-air ratio, the ignition timing and the fuel combustion process and could therefore assist in avoiding possible future damage to the engine. However, in a large-capacity twelve cylinder engine it was not always easy to recognise or localize any misfiring to a particular cylinder during operation. Poor combustion in a cylinder led to a lack of performance and subjected the cylinder wall to greater abrasion because the oil film had been washed off and this in turn could lead to piston seizure. Checking the condition and cleanliness of the ignition system to avoid flashovers, and consequential misfiring, was therefore work related to this.

The Tiger driver only attended to cleaning the carburettor jet and sparkplugs and to setting their electrode gap as described above. Work on the ignition contacts in the magneto and setting the ignition timing was not his remit.

The servicing of the sparkplugs was carried out pragmatically when the main jets on the carburettors were being cleaned because then only two radio-interference suppressor covers still had to be removed in order to reach the spark plugs.

1. Remove the air filter and air collection box, as described in cleaning the carburettor main jets.
2. Loosen the three handgrip screws with the 'Maybach' logo and remove the left and right radio-interference suppressor covers.
3. After pulling off the spark plug leads, unscrew the twelve recessed spark plugs using a socket spanner taking care not allow the spanner to tilt in order to prevent damage to the insulator. After removal check the thread for damage and contamination, particularly if resistance was encountered.
4. Assess the spark plug's appearance and clean sooty or wet spark plugs with spark plug cleaner or a small piece of wood or if necessary with fuel and a hard brush. Replace the spark plug if the thread is damaged or the electrode is burned. Check the space between the electrodes of 0.4 mm on new or cleaned spark plugs with a feeler gauge and readjust if necessary.
5. Assemble in the reverse order. Inserting the deeply recessed spark plugs must be done by 'feel.' Misaligned spark plugs results in extensive repairs to the cylinder head.

Because the radio set was very sensitive to the ignition system, its components were screened and 'encapsulated.' Therefore during assembly, special attention had to be paid to the sealed and metallic connection, by means of an interference-supressing braided cable, between the interference suppressor covers and the engine block.

A *Werkmeister* and a soldier inspect the ignition system. The left radio-interference suppression cover, the 'cap' over the sparkplugs, has been removed. (BA 022-2936-27)

Checking and/or adjusting

(D 656/23, D 635/5, D 656/43, H. Dv. 471)

The gear selector and clutch free travel

The play in the clutch must be checked and adjusted so that the clutch, when engaged, is not destroyed by slipping.

The discs of the main clutch must be replaced when it is no longer possible to set the required free travel of 50-60 mm on the clutch pedal.

Procedure on the Tiger II:
1.   Loosen the lock nut on the adjusting screw (1).

2.   Loosen the adjusting screw until an 8 mm feeler gauge can be pushed into the gap between the screw and the lower lever on the clutch shaft (2).
3.   Tighten the lock nut again.

The amount of wear on the clutch can be determined by means of two marks and a pointer on the clutch pedal.

Ensure that the clutch linkage operates smoothly, otherwise lubricate with a few drops of engine oil.

(D656/43, pic. 57)

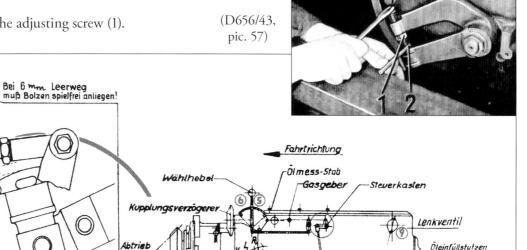

Darum:

Wechselgetriebe: 1. Ölstand öfter überprüfen, Ölfilter reinigen.

2. Griffmutter so lange nach rechts drehen, bis die Kupplung erst nach einem toten Gang von 6 mm gelöst wird. Mach Dir aus Holz ein Stichmaß von 6 mm Breite.

3. Anschlag für den Fußhebel so einstellen, daß die Griffmutter noch einen Weg von 10 mm nach oben macht.

4. Der Winkelhebel zum Steuerkasten muß spielfrei anliegen, wenn der Kupplungs-fußhebel seinen 6-mm-Leergang zurückgelegt hat. (Siehe „2".)

Pages 32/33 in the Tigerfibel give instructions for adjusting the free play on the clutch of a Tiger I. (The free travel is indicated by the number '2' on the drawing.)

5. Den Hebel auf der Gasgeberwelle so einstellen, daß der Motor auf die höchste Dreh-zahl kommt, wenn man das Gasgestänge von Hand bis zum Anschlag zieht.

6. Das Gestänge des Wählhebels muß den Gang sicher auslösen.

7. Die Gestänge ölen und leicht gangbar machen, damit sie schnell und sicher in die Ruhelage zurückgehen.

8. Die Telekinzüge zu den Lenkhebeln müssen stets etwas Spiel haben.

9. Lenkventil reinigen, wenn Du Lenkstörungen hast. Die Dichtflächen werden von Staubkörnchen befreit, wenn Du den Ventilteller hineindrückst.

10. Befestigungsschrauben des Wechselgetriebes nachziehen,

Free travel on the brakes

If the brakes heat up and smoke when not in use they are binding and the free play must be adjusted. At the end of the operating pedal the play must amount to 13 mm. If oil is leaking out of the final drives onto the brakes this can be recognised by oil stains and reduced effectiveness. The workshop will then seal the final drive and clean the brakes.

Example Tiger I:

1. Pull the handbrake up to the fifth ratchet and tighten the turnbuckle until the handbrake engages. Release the handbrake.
2. In the event that such adjustment is not possible remove the connection bolt in the perforated section, separate the turnbuckle and hook it the next hole in the perforated section.
3. If the last adjustment has been reached the brake unit must be exchanged for a new one.

Shock absorbers

A shock absorber that was working properly could be recognised by the fact that it became hotter during operation (to the right is picture 84 from D656/43). Only the shock absorbers next to the driver and his adjacent crew member were freely accessible and easily checked. The rear shock absorbers could only be reached by removing the engine and were always checked on such occasions. The oil level was supposed to have been checked every 3,000 km:

1. Park the tank on a flat surface.
2. Unscrew the oil filler screw (1) and the air bleed screw (2).
3. Fill up to the edge of filler opening with 'violet shock absorber fluid.'
4. Insert both screws.

Lubrication

Every former motor vehicle apprentice knew about it – lubrication! This involved looking for grease nipples, cleaning them thoroughly, attaching the grease gun securely and pumping it until fresh grease appeared at the greasing point. If it didn't appear, the grease nipple had to be replaced or a bigger repair to the bearing assembly was due. There are 'good' vehicles with few, easily accessible grease nipples and 'less good' vehicles with many greasing points in dirty and difficult to access corners.

Greasing was carried out using a hand or foot pump or most conveniently by utilizing a 'lubrication battery' – an array of grease nipples in an easily accessible, central location.

In some instances cavities – such as between the drive sprocket and the drive flange – were filled with grease to prevent the ingress of water and dirt. The hinges on the hatches and numerous small linkages were oiled using an oil can to prevent them from becoming stiff or seizing due to corrosion or frost in winter.

The maintenance schedule gave precise information regarding the location of the lubrication points.

Batteries (lead accumulators)

Modern motor vehicles can no longer run without a properly functioning battery and a faulty battery, even after the vehicle has been started using jump leads, can result in a breakdown. The Tiger, thanks to its magneto ignition system – a system still occasionally used in two-wheeled vehicles – and the muscle power applied externally to the mechanical starter could be made to start without a battery. Neither the fire control system nor the telescopic sighting device, required an electrical supply. Of course in the event of an emergency, or when restarting during a mission, the engine had to be started electrically. In addition, the radio and communication system was supposed to work under battery power when the tank was parked with the engine switched off and, without the electrical smoke-extractor fan, the turret would quickly become unbearable for the crew when firing with the hatches closed.

The on-board electrical system ran at 12 volts but the 6 horse power starter required 24 volts. By means of an electromagnetic switch, the two 12 volt batteries were temporarily connected in series to supply the 24 volt starter. A voltage regulator controlled the output voltage of the engine-driven generator to provide the electrical supply and charge the batteries.

The weighty (approximately 45 kg) 12V/150 Ah lead-acid batteries were fitted under the turret floor flaps (the picture at the top right shows the right-hand battery). The charge status and acid level of the batteries had to be checked at least once a week.

Checking the sufficient output voltage

With the headlights turned on, the battery voltage had to be at least 11 volts.

Checking with a meter:

1. Switch on main battery switch; turn off all other electrical devices in the vehicle.
2. Connect a voltmeter terminal to earth, that is to say to any bare metallic point on the tank's hull.
3. Connect the other terminal to the headlight fuse in the fuse box on the dashboard.
4. Turn on the headlights and read the voltmeter.

(D656/22+, pic. 30)

(D655/1b)
Battery with its heatable isolation box.

Bild 110. Sammler mit heizbarem Isolierkasten

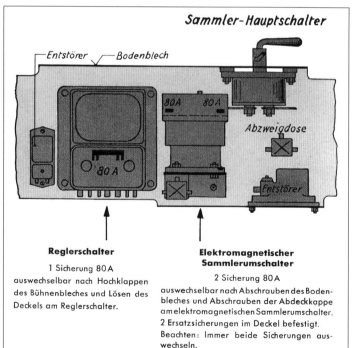

Sammler-Hauptschalter

Entstörer   Bodenblech

Abzweigdose

Reglerschalter

1 Sicherung 80 A auswechselbar nach Hochklappen des Bühnenbleches und Lösen des Deckels am Reglerschalter.

Elektromagnetischer Sammlerumschalter

2 Sicherung 80 A auswechselbar nach Abschrauben des Bodenbleches und Abschrauben der Abdeckkappe am elektromagnetischen Sammlerumschalter. 2 Ersatzsicherungen im Deckel befestigt. Beachten: Immer beide Sicherungen auswechseln.

Major electric hull-based components on the base plate underneath the floor in front of the partition wall on the left side (forward looking). (D655/5, pic. 37)

Checks on the batteries

1. Open the turret floor hatch above the batteries.

2. Remove the insulated container cover. Do not place tools on top of the battery. Never short circuit the positive and negative terminals – danger of accident.

3. Open the battery cell plugs.

4. Check the acid level: the acid in the individual cells must be 10-15 mm above the upper edge of the plate; test with a clean wooden stick. A metallic tool must not be used. During operation, the continued charging of the battery produces water vapour and elemental hydrogen and oxygen – an explosive mixture! If the electrolyte level has dropped below the upper edge of the plates, distilled water must be used to top up the battery. Although the *Handbuch für Kraftfahrer* (handbook for vehicle drivers) issued in 1939 expressly prohibits the use of boiled water or rainwater, the Tigerfibel allows this or melted snow. (It seems questionable to me whether a long battery life can be presumed according to the still valid operational regulations for lead batteries).

5. Check the density of the electrolyte with a hydrometer: suck up enough electrolyte from a cell until the float is free then read the density on the scale:

   Charged: 1.285 (Tropics 1.23)
   Discharged: 1.14 (Tropics 1.1)

6. Return the electrolyte to the cell.

7. The lead poles on the battery must be kept free of acid. Oxidized poles are to be cleaned as required with the cleaning brush, acid protection grease applied and the screws on the pole clamps made secure in order to ensure the smooth flow of electrical current. To prevent damage to battery's soft poles, no force is to be applied while installing or dismantling them.

8. Reassemble in the reverse order.

In winter note (see also the following section relating to winter operation):

A charged battery freezes and bursts at -65° C, a discharged one by -10° C. It should be noted that that in winter the voltage and the capacity of the battery reduces and this increases the freezing point. If the voltage falls under 11 V or the vehicle is standing for a long time in the cold, the battery should be taken from the vehicle and maintained.

The previously mentioned electrically heatable isolation box (see 'Bild 110' on previous page) was supposed to counteract this behaviour of the batteries in cold weather and associated circumstances. A more detailed description follows in the section about handling batteries at extremely low temperatures.

Comments relating to handling the batteries

In motor vehicles nowadays, very few problems are encountered with starter batteries that have sealed – and often maintenance free – cells inside a robust housing. However, a treacherous point in those days was, for example, the exposed connecting bars between the in-series cells (see picture 110 on p228). This method of construction made it possible to identify 'dead' battery cells but at the same time it was imperative to avoid placing electrically conducting tools on the battery (for example during maintenance work), as this could potentially trigger an increasingly violent short circuit that could initiate a fire, cause painful burns or damage the battery.

In extremely cold weather the battery housing broke easily and it had to be removed and reinstalled with great caution – easier said than done given the weight of the batteries and the cramped conditions inside the tank.

If a battery leaked inside the vehicle it had to be drenched with copious amounts of water to avoid damage by the escaping sulphuric acid. This treatment was (and still is) applied to splashes on the skin and in the eyes. Splashes on clothes also had to be washed out immediately; if at first they went unnoticed, they shortly afterwards formed unsightly holes.

This photo shows the '113' of *s.Pz. Abt. 502* on the 12 January 1943 in Putoschka. Towards the end of winter the old paint has washed off to reveal that the tank had once been the '04' and before that the '03.' (BA 457-56-6)

In Mailly-le-Camp during early August 1944, prior to their deployment on the Seine bridgeheads, a crew of the *3./s. Pz.Abt 503* sprays brown patterns on the primer coat of a newly supplied tank. (Wunderlich)

It was difficult to touch up the white camouflage with brushes in the bitter cold, as in this picture of a vehicle belonging to *s.Pz.Abt. 502* taken at the end of 1943 shows. (BA 458-76-31)

Camouflage and the Application of Camouflage Paint

(from Deneke, TL 6352, TL 6355, diff. sections in H.M. 1943)

Camouflage and the application of camouflage paint by the Tiger crews was not different from that of other tank types.

The early Tigers deployed in 1942/43 in Tunisia already had their battlefield camouflage paint applied by the manufacturer or before being shipped.

From spring 1943 until autumn 1944 the camouflage colours yellow, brown and green were applied as a relatively high quality 'Gerätanstrich' (equipment paint) in the form of camouflage paste – a water soluble emulsion or dispersion fluid – possibly according to a camouflage scheme specified at unit level. The design of this camouflage pattern was at the discretion of the troops with the work usually being carried out within the framework of the unit away from the front line.

The camouflage pastes were constantly in short supply and so had to be used sparingly.

The seemingly trouble-free application of these colours, that among other things had to be workable after three days of storage at below -40° C and subsequent thawing at temperatures above freezing, is interesting.

The instructions for the use of these colours – taken from the provisional technical delivery conditions for the use of coloured camouflage paste – give a good impression of the steps necessary during their application.

A. Applying the paste
1. Remove coarse dirt from the surface.
2. Thoroughly stir the paste as delivered and use brushes or cloths soaked in water or fuel to spread lightly and thinly on the equipment to be camouflaged.
3. If water or fuel are not on hand the paste can be applied lightly and thinly on the equipment to be camouflaged without being diluted using dry brushes or cloths.
4. To increase its coverage and improve its workability the paste can be diluted with 10-20% water. Only the required quantity of paste should be diluted in a special container. The paste cannot be stored for long periods when diluted.
5. For spray application the paste must be diluted with as much water or fuel as is necessary (use smaller quantities and stir for a longer time!) to reach the desired consistency.
6. Small amounts of lubricants or moisture remaining on the surface to be camouflaged are unimportant.

B. Re-camouflaging equipment already camouflaged with the paste.
7. Camouflage paste can be applied over equipment already camouflaged with camouflage paste. If the old coat of paste has softened due to insufficient curing time (due to frequent temporary re-camouflaging) the new paste must be applied without dilution or the old paste first washed off with fuel.

C. Removing camouflage paste
8. Camouflage paste can be rubbed off using fuel-soaked cloths.

D. Safety regulation
9. Safety measures must be observed when using leaded fuel (HDv 179) to remove or apply the paste..

The use of water as a thinner was somewhat controversial. It was reported that the camouflage paste, after having been diluted with water, supposedly quickly washed or ran off during damp conditions.

Thinned camouflage paste could be applied using spray guns (see picture below) supplied with compressed air provided by small workshop compressors.

Water-soluble white emulsion paint – and later white camouflage paste – was applied by the troops as winter camouflage. Vehicles that were delivered in the winter months arrived at the units with the necessary camouflage already applied.

From summer 1942, a move was made towards supplying new vehicles with factory-applied camouflage paint in uniform patterns.

It is worthy of note that safety advice was always provided regarding the danger to health when handling leaded fuel.

Because of the shortage of tetraethyl lead, a high percentage of equally toxic benzene was added to fuel and the warnings about the careless handling of fuel therefore remained valid although it clearly might be doubted that compliance with the appropriate protective measures actually took place under combat conditions.

In extremely cold conditions, the tanks became ice-cold heaps of steel. In February 1944, the crew of this vehicle belonging to *s.Pz.Abt.505* have removed the machine guns to prevent them from freezing. Perhaps they should also have put on the muzzle cover…

New snow overnight…this had to be been promptly removed otherwise the hatches and covers could freeze up; this photograph shows a tank belonging to *s.Pz. Abt. 502* in January 1944.

Snowstorms were also a problem because the snow could penetrate even narrow gaps and could, for example, block the turret traversing ring. Here a group of vehicles of *s.Pz.Abt. 509* in January 1945 in Hungary. (König)

Operation in Winter

(D632/17, D632/21, D 635/5, D635/16a, D 656/21+, D 656/43, D 659/51. diff. sections in HtVBl 1943 and 1944)

As the Tiger was being developed, the German Army was enduring the catastrophic Russian winter of 1941/42 during which defects in German motorized battlefield equipment often came to light.

Safeguarding and maintaining combat readiness in extremely low temperatures therefore assumed absolute priority.

The hazards of winter experienced in Germany such as
- freezing coolants that could destroy engines, radiators and poorly charged batteries
- increased viscosity of lubricating oil that made starting difficult and could break engine components
- inhibition of fuel-air mixing required for starting and for a clean-running engine
- reduced performance of components of the starting system including the electric starting motor, inertia starter and batteries
- frozen running gear that made progress through snow and ice difficult

were compounded on the front line and this, in some instances, made operating motor vehicles and tanks dramatically more difficult. Thawing and heating engine components over an open fire or with a blowtorch were among the improvisations used to get vehicles started. What it was like to work at such low temperatures under field conditions in, or on, steel tanks that seemed to radiate coldness, can perhaps only be appreciated by today's construction machinery or vehicle mechatronic engineers who have to work the whole year round on construction sites.

For subsequent cold periods, 'winter kit boxes' containing various special devices – in part these were designed for specific models of motor vehicle – were put together for the troops. These might contain, for example, special apparatus for heating the coolant with heat lamps (blow-torches). The retrofitting of heating for the driver's cab also became an issue. Installation instructions, device descriptions and user instructions were attached in each case. The techno-logistical effort that lay behind this can be easily imagined.

From the outset the Tiger was equipped with special facilities for operation at extremely low temperatures and these were either further developed during the course of time or were dropped. The external auxiliary starting equipment that was later introduced suited both the Tiger and the Panther tanks.

At the Tiger instruction courses in Paderborn in the winters of 1943/44 and 1944/45, vehicles with full winter equipment were supposed to be on hand for the purpose of instruction, together with the additional necessary winter equipment that was not specific to individual vehicles.

The diverse knowledge needed to overcome the difficulties of winter described in this work closely follow the service regulations for winter operations and give a good impression of the tasks, the mastery of which ultimately probably could only be fully achieved by experience.

In its early years, the *Bundeswehr* benefited from these painful experiences when equipping its first generation of vehicles. 'Preheating with a swingfire heater ' [a small petrol combustion heater], 'turbo-heater' and a 'cold-start device with a trembler coil' are key terms that every vehicle driver serving in the *Bundeswehr* before 1980 can relate to.

Preventative measures and maintaining the tank in winter

Who would have thought that 'Glysantin', the colloquial synonym for antifreeze, had already been used in the Tiger? In severe winters nowadays we have to make sure that there is enough frost protection in our windscreen washers and radiators but in the Tiger such preventative measures took on a completely different dimension.

During the Second World War, diesel and even lubricating oil had to be diluted with a significant proportion of petrol. It should be expressly noted, that this had no significant consequences for the operational reliability of the Tiger engine. This statement is somewhat surprizing given the rather mediocre quality of the German lubricating oils and the problems with the connecting rod bearings in the Maybach HL 230 engine until the end of 1943, quite apart from the increased susceptibility of the oil additive to ignition.

Operating liquids
Anti-freeze liquids

The mixing of antifreeze with the cooling system water was not required in summer but the anti-corrosion chemical 'Akorol' could be added. However, before the frosty weather set in, it was necessary to add the frost protection agent Glysantin to the cooling water. If that was not possible, the cooling water had to be drained from the vehicle before turning off the engine.

In severe frosts, even if the engine was running, cooling water without antifreeze could freeze in the radiator preventing its circulation and this in turn led to overheating of the engine. To avoid this problem care had to be taken to cover the radiator and fan if the cooling water temperature was low, for example when the engine was idling.

The Glysantin-water mixture in the Tiger was supposed to, as far as possible, consist of

- 60 parts Glysantin to 40 parts water (as of March 1943 and July 1943 for the winter 1943/44) or
- 50 parts of Glysantin and 50 parts water (for the 'Eastern Army' as of 1 September 1944) or
- a mixture depending on the expected degree of frost (outwith the 'Eastern Army' as of 1 September 1944).

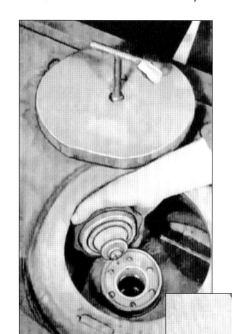

(D656/43, pic. 18 and 19)

Adding more than 60 % Glysantin gave poorer protection against frost. Pure Glysantin froze between -11° and -14° C and turned into a jelly. Because of the fire risk it was supposed to have been warmed up in its container without exposure to a naked flame.

A sample of engine coolant had to be taken each week and tested with the Glysantin hydrometer for the correct mixture ratio.

Glysantin had a descaling effect which could result in leaks in coolant hoses, gaskets and radiators. The cooling system was therefore checked every day for leaks and sufficient coolant level.

The corrosion inhibitor Akorol was never, under any circumstances, allowed to be added to the Glysantin-water mixture.

Anti-freeze liquids are harmful to health! Mixing cans and equipment had to be rinsed with warm water prior to further use.

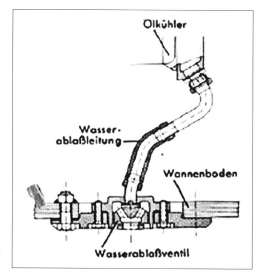

(D656/43, pic. 15)

Draining the cooling water and filling with antifreeze liquid

1. Open the coolant filling cap.
2. On the Tiger I: Open the access cover for coolant drainage and maintenance of the fuel pump in the bottom of the hull.
3. On the Tiger I: Open the drain valve on the oil cooler. On the Tiger II: Open the integral rapid-drain valve on the floor of the hull.
4. If necessary collect the escaping water in a container so that it does not cause the tracks to freeze to the ground.
5. Flush the cooling system several times with fresh water. This is not necessary if Akorol has been added to the cooling water.
6. Close the drain valve.
7. Fill with a prepared antifreeze mixture until it is a distance of two fingers wide below the overflow pipe; this prevents the coolant overflowing when it heats up. Tiger I: ca. 114, Tiger II: ca. 148 litres.

Fuel for winter use

Different winter fuels were delivered in accordance with the area of operation. For operations '*im Osten*' (in the East) the violet coloured winter petrol had the greatest resistance to cold and could withstand temperatures down to −40° C. Great care had to be exercised when refuelling because contamination with rain, snow, ice or condensation decreased the fuel's ability to withstand low temperatures. The formation of ice crystals could cause blockages in the fuel system that were time-consuming to remedy. The filling ports had to be kept free of ice and snow and covered with cloths when it snowed or rained. Containers that had just been emptied had to be closed immediately.

Leichtbenzin ('Gasolin') (a petroleum spirit composed of low molecular weight hydrocarbons) was available for the starting injector as this allowed the formation of an easily combustible fuel mixture to enable starting even at very low temperatures. *Leichtbenzin* was highly inflammable and care was needed when filling up; it also had to be kept away from naked flames. Containers of *Leichtbenzin* had to be protected from excessive heat and direct sunshine.

Engine oil

Initially, petrol was added to the engine oil used by the *Wehrmacht* – in winter temperatures down to -30° C 15% of the mixture was petrol; below this temperature 25% petrol was added.

With the existing '*Fuchs*' coolant heater first built into the Tiger I from January 1944, winter oil was used at temperatures under -10° C and at temperatures below -30° C the oil was diluted with 15% petrol.

Until the changeover in the dilution method and the addition of extra marks on the engine-oil dipstick, restoring the correct mixture after deployment was, by necessity, carried out using a bubble viscosity meter to establish the degree of dilution required – a cumbersome and complex process.

Carrying out the first oil dilution to 15% or 25% (as of March 1943):

1. Before the admixture of oil, the engine should be hand warm (around 40 ° C).
2. In conditions down to -30°C, 15% is petrol which corresponds to 2.5 litres; under -30° C 25% of the mixture is petrol which corresponds to 6 litres to be added to the engine oil.
3. Run the engine at a moderate speed, around 800 to 1,000 revolutions per minute, for 1 or 2 minutes to completely mix the oil.

Repeating or complementing the oil dilution (as of March 1943).

At engine temperatures of more than 60° C petrol that was mixed with the oil evaporates completely inside three or four hours of continuous driving, otherwise only partially. On each occasion, the evaporated petrol was replaced with the aid of a bubble viscosity meter after stopping the engine.

Carrying out the first oil dilution to 15% (as of September 1944) under the supervision of the *Schirrmeister* (NCO in charge of technical matters):

1. Park the tank on a horizontal surface with hand-hot oil, not over 40°C.
2. In external temperatures below -30° C drain off 15% of the oil content down to the (additionally added) dilution mark on the dipstick; see under 'changing the engine oil.'
3. Fill up to the 'full' mark with petrol.
4. Allow the engine to run at moderate speed for three or four minutes to mix the oil. Do not allow the temperature of the engine to exceed 40° C otherwise some of the petrol will evaporate again.

Restoring or supplementing the oil dilution (as of September 1944).

As already mentioned above, the mixed-in petrol evaporates within three to four hours at engine temperatures of more than 60°C in continuous operation, otherwise only partly.

The petrol lost by evaporation has to be replaced after stopping the engine:

1. Allow the engine to cool until it is lukewarm, about 30-40° C.
2. If the oil level has sunk to below the 15% mark add engine oil until the level is at this mark. If according to the weather conditions further dilution is required, add petrol up to the 'full' mark.
3. If the oil level is found to be between 'full' and the 15% mark, top up to the 'full' mark with petrol if further dilution is required.
4. Run the engine as described above to mix.

After diluting between five and six times, the *Schirrmeister* checked the solution with a bubble viscosity meter to exclude any possible over-dilution that might prove harmful to the engine.

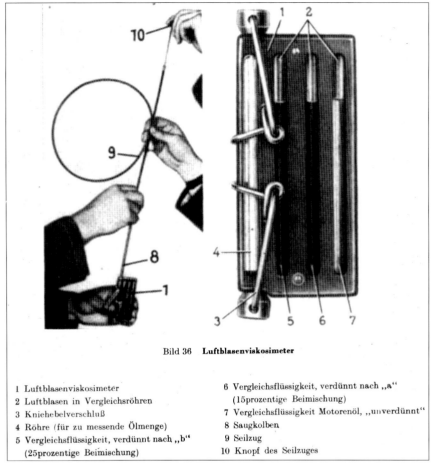

Bild 36   Luftblasenviskosimeter

1 Luftblasenviskosimeter
2 Luftblasen in Vergleichsröhren
3 Kniehebelverschluß
4 Röhre (für zu messende Ölmenge)
5 Vergleichsflüssigkeit, verdünnt nach „b"
  (25prozentige Beimischung)

6 Vergleichsflüssigkeit, verdünnt nach „a"
  (15prozentige Beimischung)
7 Vergleichsflüssigkeit Motorenöl, „unverdünnt"
8 Saugkolben
9 Seilzug
10 Knopf des Seilzuges

Bubble viscosity meter for checking the grade of dillution of the engine oil.
(D 635/5)

Gear oil

Until the introduction of the 'Wehrmacht winter gear oil' in autumn 1942, the gear oil was diluted with 20% diesel fuel. In March 1943, for temperatures below –30 ° C, diluting the gear oil with 20% diesel fuel was made mandatory.

The green 'Wehrmacht gear oil 8 E' introduced in autumn 1943 usually did not need dilution with 15% diesel fuel until temperatures fell below –30°C. The unusual designation '8 E' indicated the contemporary requirement for gear oil with a viscosity of not below 8° Engler at +50° C (this is comparable to oil with a viscosity rating of 75W/80W).

However, the semi-automatic Olvar gear selector required a mixture consisting of 15% diesel fuel at temperatures below –20°C in order to avoid damage to the hydraulic selector mechanism by sticking when the transmission was cold.

Lubrication oil diluted with petrol led to higher oil consumption. The diesel fuel in the mixture evaporated after 5 or 6 hours at an operational temperature of more than 60° C. Any loss of diesel fuel by evaporation had to be replaced after stopping.

Carrying out oil dilution with 20% diesel fuel at below -30 ° C (as of March 1943):

1.   With the transmission warm (about 40° C) drain off 15% of the properly filled oil; see section on changing oil in the appropriate assemblies.
     Transmission and steering 6.0 litres
     Final drives each   8.0 litres
     Turret drive   0.8 litres
     Fan drive   1.6 litres
2.   Replace the amount of oil removed with diesel fuel and refill.
3.   Check the oil when the transmission is running.

Carrying out oil dilution on the Olvar gear selector with 15% diesel fuel at temperatures below -20° C (as of September 1944):

1.   With the transmission handwarm (about 40° C) drain off 15% of the oil; see section on changing oil in the transmission.
2.   Replace the amount of oil removed with diesel fuel and refill.
3.   Check the oil when the transmission is running.

Lubrication grease

All lubrication points which were lubricated by hand had to be greased thoroughly with the beginning of the frosty period with a mixture of 1:1 grease and engine oil. If necessary the filled grease gun was warmed.

Shock absorber oil

The violet shock absorber oil was operational down to -40 ° C.

Oil in the oil-bath air filter

Although oil that was too viscous impaired the efficiency of the oil bath air filter, diluting it was strictly forbidden because of the risk of fire, for example if the engine misfired.

Components and equipment
Turret bearings

The use of force to turn a turret that had been immobilized by frost was not allowed. Ice in the gap between the hull and the turret had to be melted with a blowtorch and the melt water removed. The turret's ball bearings were lubricated with a mixture of 1:1 lubricating grease and engine oil.

Tank flaps and covers

The hinges and covers on the on the observation slits, hatch covers and engine covers were greased and cleaned so that they did not freeze and then have to be forced open. At the same time the ingress of water, snow and slush was avoided. During long halts even the brakes, throttle controls and clutch linkages could freeze solid.

Leather components

Leather parts had to be kept dry and supple by the application of leather oil or engine oil.

Optical equipment

Seized optics had to be heated with a hot cloth before moving them. Protective glass fittings were rubbed with a thin film of 'Glasil' to prevent them misting up and freezing.

Optical devices marked with a blue circle next to the manufacturer's name could be moved at temperatures down to -40 ° C without special heating.

Batteries

If no distilled water was on hand, the battery acid could be topped up using clean, melted snow (!). Before switching off, the proper mixing of top-up water with the battery acid had to be ensured, possibly by using the hydrometer or by driving, so that the upper layer of water did not freeze.

The severe cold placed great demands on men and equipment. This crew member of *s.Pz.Abt. 501* is looking forward to a plate of 'warmth' on 26 February 1944. Due to lack of heating, the crews wore thick winter clothing which was not conducive to freedom of movement!

Starting the engine

At low temperatures, almost all efforts revolved around getting the engine up and running. Preparatory procedures that might impair the lifespan of the components, and at the same time increase the already great operational dangers, had to be applied. These procedures – mixing petrol with engine oil, cylinder wall 'rinsing' (the deliberate washing off of the film of engine oil on the cylinder walls to the prevent the pistons sticking when starting) and topping the battery with rainwater or melted snow – were all borne of necessity and demonstrated the inadequate preparation for the conditions in the operational zone and the suitability of the technology for these conditions.

A central issue was the pre-heating of the engine and coolant, if necessary in conjunction with the dilution of the engine oil. Initially the use of coolant transmission (from one vehicle to the other) and heating devices had their own troubles, but with the introduction of the 'Fuchs' device a practical coolant heater device could at last be spoken of.

It can be assumed that, at least theoretically, the Tiger and Panther had adequate, easy-to-use winter equipment only from early 1944.

Chroniclers remain politely silent about whether the jumble of detailed regulations in force for the conduct of winter operations mentioned here were understood and applied – or even if they could be applied.

Preparations for starting at the conclusion of a mission

Taking the correct measures during and after the termination of a mission had a significant influence on the successful starting of a chilled power plant at a later time.

As the engine was switched off the preparations for starting it later had already begun. The dilution of lubricating oil and the emergency draining of coolant are considered in other parts of this work.

Switching off

- Protect the tank from the cold, wind and aerial reconnaissance by parking it close to the edge of wood, bushes, in the shelter of a wall or railway embankment or in hollows such as the valley of a stream. Build snow up to the level of the track covers or dig the tank into a snowdrift. Clear track marks.
- Place brushwood, planks or straw underneath to avoid getting stuck by freezing. Roughly clean off any mud in the running gear (the picture to the right shows tanks belonging to s.Pz.Abt. 505 in January 1944).
- Remove snow from the vehicle and park with the engine close to the wall when parking in heated areas but make sure it remains accessible.

- Release all brakes to prevent them from the possibility of freezing solid. Keep the clutch pedal in the disengaged position by jamming with a block of wood.

Keeping the tank warm

Cover the tank with tarpaulins, blankets, bags, straw or reed mats to help retain the heat produced during operation in the engine assemblies, the cooling water and batteries for as long as possible. Protect the engine compartment from draughts using covers that reach down to the ground and weight them down with stones. Fill the space under the hull with straw or hay. Take care to insulate the batteries.

Insulation is to be removed before restarting to avoid the risk of fire. Additional heat retention measures, such as putting the coolant heater into operation, are to be undertaken according to location and weather conditions.

Refuelling

After completing a journey (if sufficient fuel is on hand) refill the fuel tank in order to prevent the formation of internal condensation and ice. Empty water traps frequently. Thaw frozen parts of the fuel system using warm water – never use a blowtorch.

Cylinder rinsing

At temperatures under 0° C the oil film on the cylinders had to be softened by flooding the cylinder bores with a rich fuel-air mixture without the ignition being switched on – in normal operation this caused the dreaded '*Versaufen*' (flooded carburettor). This was done by momentarily revving up the engine and, at the moment of switching off the ignition, operating the choke – a procedure that had to be repeated 2 or 3 times.

General information for starting the engine with and without aid

Aimlessly trying out all possible starting procedures was pointless and a waste of time and energy. In cold weather only the correct approach led to success. For starting, a sufficiently high engine speed and the correct fuel-air mixture was essential and warming the engine and cooling fluids created the best conditions for this.

Whether the engine started or not depended of course on the prevailing temperature and the condition of the engine. An engine that was hesitant to start was often difficult to get running properly in very cold weather.

Starting without aids

1. Use only the inertia starter or cranking handle. Winter engine oil on its own is sufficient when using these starters down to -10° C. The fuel injector and priming fuel is to be used for every cold start. If the temperature is below -10° C, the engine must be heated using the built-in '*Fuchs*' heating device.

2. The simultaneous use of the inertia starter device or cranking handle with the electric starter is forbidden, as is towing, which can lead to severe damage to the starters or clutch, steering gear and final drive.

3. In order to break the tenacious film of oil, turn the engine over with the ignition key inserted and the clutch pedal depressed, or with the transmission and steering disengaged (in the Tiger II pull the release lever on the gearbox beside the driver). The gearbox must be disengaged so that it is not 'dragged' by the engine as it turns over which might possibly prevent the engine from reaching the speed required for starting. If disengaging the clutch is not possible in the Tiger I disconnect the drive shaft on side closest to the engine.

4. Sequence of measures:
   a. Turn off the ventilation drive.
   b. If necessary refill the carburettor and empty fuel lines by manual operation of the fuel pump.
   c. Fill the starter fuel container with priming fuel.
   d. As the inertial starter engages, quickly apply five strokes of the pump to spray priming fuel into the carburettor air inlet (picture 44 from D656/43).

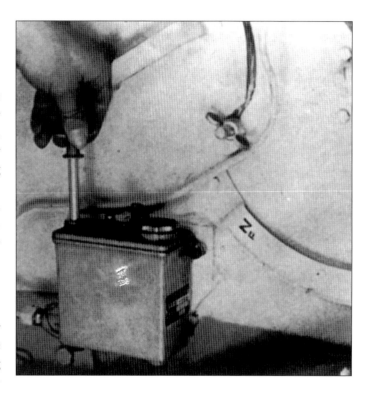

If equipped with a cranking handle starter:
   When cranking, press the pump about every six seconds to inject priming fuel until the engine begins to start.
   e. If the engine begins to start apply another two or three strokes of the pump.
   f. Without pressing the accelerator, activate the choke without further application of the pump. Engage the inertial starter and at the same time operate the hand pump until the engine runs smoothly.
   g. If the engine is running smoothly, accelerate a little and disengage the starting device. With the engine running, pump the priming fuel device until it is empty
   h. If no priming fuel is on hand use petrol.
   i. If equipped with a cranking handle starter device, the coolant should be preheated for 30-40 minutes if the temperature is below -20°C; see the following section
5. The priming fuel injector device is an important aid to starting the engine. It is therefore important to ensure that the hand pump is in good working order.
6. Personnel requirements: two soldiers working the inertial starter, one at the priming fuel pump and the driver.

Starting with the assistance of auxiliary equipment

Warming the batteries

In cold weather, the performance of lead-acid batteries falls away strongly and their ability to charge is impaired. In this condition the batteries can only support the operation of the radio apparatus. Before driving the batteries must therefore be warmed to enable them to work at full capacity.

In the Tiger I, if no insulated battery box with electrical heating was installed, the batteries had to be removed and warmed as described in the section relating to carrying out routine maintenance work. They then had to be placed in a warm room, but not near an oven.

From the end of December 1943 every Tiger was equipped with a factory-fitted battery heater.

The insulated boxes prevented excessive cooling of the batteries for up to 12 hours.

When driving in temperatures below 0°C the batteries were kept warm with a 100 watt heating element and recharged with an external charging unit (rectifier, external power source) while the engine was switched off in which case they were warmed with a 300 Watt heating element. For this purpose, there was a terminal box with actuating switches and indicator lights installed beside the control panel.

By connecting an external charging device to the negative terminal (-) and the central positive terminal (+), the batteries were charged slowly and each was warmed by a 100 watt heater.

This circuit provides for the charging of the batteries of a parked tank at normal operating temperature. In this case the green indicator light was illuminated.

When the connection was made to the negative terminal and positive terminal on the left hand side – the SH+ (*Sammler-(Batterie-) Heizung'*) terminal – the batteries were heated quickly with a power of 300 watts but not charged.

When tank had completely cooled down at an ambient temperature of -30° C, the battery, after charging and being and kept warm for 2-3 hours, could be reconnected.

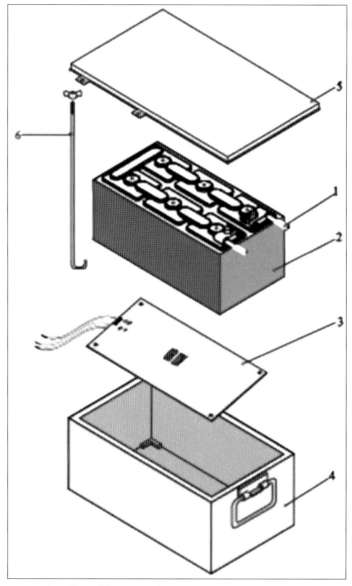

Insulated battery box
1 Battery cables
2 12 volt battery
3 100/300 watt heating plate
4 Heater box
5 Cover
6 Securing hooks

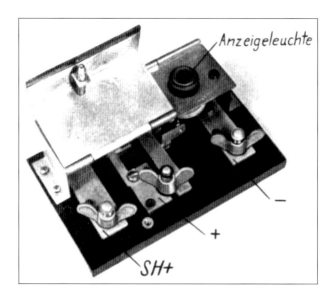

Connecting plate for external power source with cable clamps. (D655/5, pic. 109)

Coolant transfer and coolant heater device

The transfer of coolant and the coolant heater devices had the aim of bringing the engine being warmed to a temperature at which it was possible to start it without trouble in the severe cold. Coolant transmission devices and the first of the coolant heaters were costly in training terms and in use and – following the introduction of the 'Fuchsgeräte' in December 1943 – were officially designated as 'emergency measures' in June 1944 and subsequently abolished. Devices still in use had to be returned by autumn 1944. This concerned uneconomic measures that used up fuel and shortened the life expectancy of expensive engines to warm up vehicles.

Coolant transfer in the Tiger I (until the introduction of the *Fuchsgerät*)

This was the transfer of warm coolant from the running engine of one vehicle to the one to be warmed. Special connections were installed on the vehicles and hoses that had self-sealing, easily made connections were carried so that no coolant loss occurred when coupling and decoupling them. The connections were sealed by protective caps that could be easily opened and closed by hand.

Coolant transfer was allowed only if oil dilution had been carried out and the coolant in the engine to be warmed had not become viscous or icy because of a lack of Glysantin.

The transfer hoses were filled once and carried in the filled state.

The initial filling of the hoses

1. Unscrew the blanking cap on the red connection on the coolant pipe and securely connect the end of the hose with union nut.
2. Open the engine cover, see under 'Operation – Driving.'
3. Close the throttle valve, open the radiator cap.
4. Hold the free end of the hose up high.
5. Press the plunger on the blanking cap on the free end of the hose to open the valve. Run the engine at around 2,000 revolutions per minute until the coolant comes out of the free end of the hose. Release the plunger, the hose is now filled.
6. Stop the engine and open the throttle valve.
7. Remove the hose and screw the blanking caps onto the red connection and the end of the hose.
8. Make up any losses to the Glysantin-water mixture and close the radiator cap.

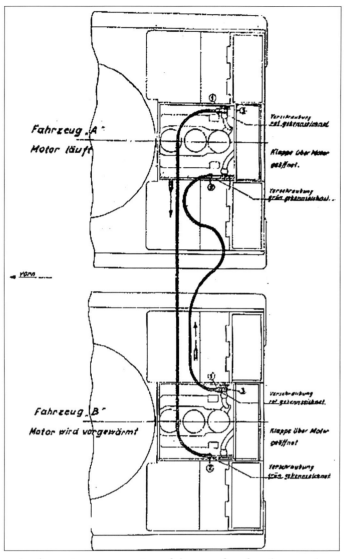

A schematic representation of the transfer of coolant on the Tiger I. (D656/21+, drawing HSK J2933)

Hose connections for coolant transfer (black and light arrows) and throttle valve (dark arrow) to close off the flow of coolant to the radiator on a Tiger I. (Köhler)

Carrying out coolant liquid transfer

1. Park the already warm tank rear to rear or side by side with tank to be warmed.
2. Switch off the cooling fans in the warm tank and allow the engine temperature to rise to 60°C before switching off.
3. Open both engine covers.
4. Shut off both ventilation fans.
5. Open the screw connections on the radiator of the warm tank otherwise the transfer will not take place.
6. Close the throttle valve.
7. Connect the hoses so that each tank is linked to the other by the black and light arrows (picture on previous page).
8. Run the engine of the warm tank at 2,400 rpm for the first minute then at around 2,000 rpm. Monitor the coolant temperature. If the transfer cycle progresses without fault the temperature at first falls. Under no circumstances must it be allowed to approach boiling point. If water flows from the radiator pressure relief valve on the vehicle being warmed the engine speed must be reduced. If that does not work, the pressure relief valve is defective and the overflow pipe must be temporarily closed with a plug.
9. At and ambient temperature of -30°C, it takes around 15 minutes to warm the cold engine to 50°C. At this temperature an attempt can be made to start the machine, otherwise continue heating.
10. After starting, open the throttle valve immediately and turn of the engine [of the heat supplying tank].
11. Disconnect the transfer hoses and store them.
12. Screw on the blanking caps on the vehicle supplying the heat, close the screw on the radiator and turn on the cooling fan.
13. Likewise, when the second vehicle has warmed, screw on the blanking caps and remove the plug (if fitted) from the radiator overflow. Switch on the cooling fans and close the engine cover.

Rectifying faults

If no circulation of coolant occurred and the temperature of the engine supplying the heat did not drop, it could be because
*   the union nuts on the hoses had not been tightened sufficiently and the valves did not allow the coolant to flow or
*   the Glysantin content of the water in the engine being warmed or in the transfer hoses was too low and the coolant too viscous.

In the first case, the connections were tightened in order to allow the valves in the hoses to open completely. In the second case, the hoses were placed on the warm engine; if this was insufficient, a single hose was connected to the red and green connection on the tank supplying the heat to close the throttle valve and by means of this short circuit each hose was filled with warm coolant.

If the engine to be warmed was affected, the whole cooling system, with particular attention paid to connecting pipes, had to be thawed out using a warm-air blower until the Glysantin-water mixture had become fluid.

Handling instructions

*   Tighten the blanking caps securely so that they do not loosen when driving
*   Do not damage the threads when mounting the hoses
*   Check that the hoses are seated correctly and do not leak
*   Do not step on the hose
*   Do not attempt to break ice in a frozen hose with a hammer.

In the winter of 1944/45, the command group of *s.Pz. Abt. 510* used a generator mounted on a single-axel trailer (parked in front of a second tank in the background) to provide electrical current and to reduce the load on the batteries during starting. (Gilbert)

The heating lamp ('*Lötlampe*')

Amongst the following coolant heating devices the nowadays almost forgotten 'blowtorch' was of crucial importance. In winter 1943/44, along with spare parts, it belonged to the equipment carried by every vehicle. In the Tiger I and II it was kept in the fighting compartment beside the radio. The device was built by several manufacturers to a similar design and quickly asserted itself as the most important means of heating. The lamp was powered by petrol and when correctly used produced a large amount of heat on a small area. Various specifically designed coolant heaters were mounted externally or built into the vehicle.

The blowtorch was however anything but harmless and maintenance-free in operation. Because it was fuelled by petrol, careless handling could result in fires, burn injuries and poisoning by carbon monoxide. There was therefore a whole list of safety regulations regarding its use.

The hot-air blower

The hot-air blower, produced by various manufacturers, provided hot air through a hose that could be directed towards places that needed to be thawed or warmed up. The device had different modes of function. These too required care when in use. The hot-air blowers did not deliver heated fresh air but exhaust gases so there was a danger of poisoning when used inside a vehicle without sufficient ventilation. Its use was therefore banned in rooms used for accommodation and in the fighting compartment. For the winter of 1943/44, each unit was equipped with an HB 50 coolant heating device, each tank workshop with a Kärcher-Zwerg and each tank workshop company with two Tecalmite devices. In winter 1944/45, every tank workshop platoon and every *I-Staffel* received a Volkmar Hänig hot-air blower.

HB50 on the cargo deck of a Berge-panther recovery vehicle. On top is the round cover for the hose connection.

Heating equipment with integrated hand pump for the Tiger I (until the introduction of the *Fuchs* device)

A heating device with a hand pump (picture top right) – temporarily installed on the rear of the tank – was coupled with the coolant transmission connections instead of the second Tiger. The heat was provided by a 2-litre blowtorch produced by various manufacturers and was later installed on the *Fuchs* heating device.

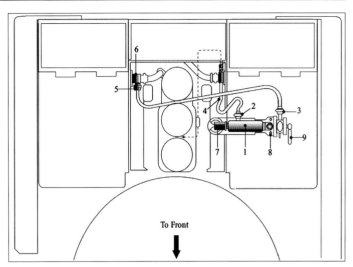

To Front

Heat exchanger (1); Blowtorch (7); Pump lever for the hand pump (9). Right – connected and ready for use. (D656/21, pic. 41)

Operation

1. Open the engine cover and turn off the cooling fans.
2. Fasten the heating device with two hook bolts on the rear.
3. Attach the short and long coupling hoses.
4. Close the throttle valve.
5. Light the blowtorch and operate the hand pump lever to circulate the coolant.
6. When the engine starts, open the throttle valve and remove the connection hoses.
7. Remove the heating device.
8. Switch on the cooling fans and close the engine cover.

Heating equipment without hand pump for the Tiger I (until introduction of the *Fuchs* device)

A heating device without a manual pump was attached below the opening for the inertia starter during preheating. It consisted of a boiler heated by a built-in blowtorch. In vehicles set up for this device, two coolant hoses with quick release connectors that attached to certain points on the cooling system led to the rear of the tank. These hoses could be pulled out through the opening for the inertia starter and connected to the boiler. Circulation of the coolant during preheating then took place automatically by thermosyphonic action. Here too, the radiator throttle valve was closed for the duration of preheating. The other procedures were carried out as previously described.

So far, no images for this (probably rare) device are available.

Panzer-Kühlwasserheizgerät 42

This universal heating device used the previously described red and green hose connections on the cooling system and was attached to the tank by the same means as the heating device without a hand pump. It did however have a lever-operated hand pump to circulate the coolant during heating. It was operated in the same way as the heating unit with a hand pump as previously described. Every tank workshop company and every tank repair and maintenance unit was supposed to have two of these devices on hand in the winter of 1943/44. Towards the end of 1944, tanks were no longer provided with this device.

Blowtorches, hot-air blowers and also the *Kühlwasserheizgerät 42* were extensively used pieces of equipment delivered to other German Army units but their function is not described in this publication.

The *Fuchs* coolant heater for all Tigers and Panthers from around 1944

This device was attached to the HL230 engine and connected to a blowtorch on the outside through a gap in the armour that was closed by an armoured cover when not in use. In order to avoid the danger of fire, the boiler was covered with a wire mesh that could be removed for cleaning.

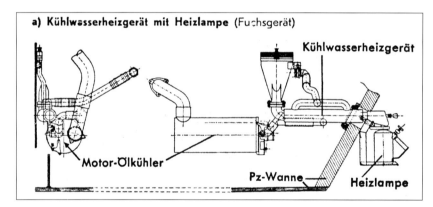

Diagram of the *Fuchs* device with the accompanying blowtorch. (D635/5)

Operation

- During heating the crew is not permitted to remain in the fighting compartment.
- If the coolant is too viscous (this can determined by stirring the coolant through the filling opening) it should not at first be heated with a small flame in order to avoid damage to the hoses and the boiler by the formation of steam bubbles
- Before inserting the blowtorch check that the heating fins on the boiler are free of dirt. Take care not to bend the heating fins when cleaning them.
- Open all hatches and close off the heating in the fighting compartment (if fitted).

- Fill the blowtorch to three quarters capacity, put it into operation and keep on full power (blue flame and buzzing sound) by continual pumping.
- Close the cover in the coolant riser pipe if still installed.
- Set the manually operated coolant temperature control (beside the driver or on the rear wall) to the closed position ('Zu') – for warming up. After starting open it immediately and regulate the coolant temperature according to instructions.
- A wrongly set pressure relief valve risks the danger of a build-up of steam and the destruction of the boiler.
- Mount the blowtorch so that the flame is directed towards the centre of the boiler and does not overheat one side.
- If the coolant thickens up at temperatures below -40° C with the correct amount of Glysantin (50 parts water to 50 parts Gylsantin – see above) apply heat carefully

because the heat circulation is impaired and a damaging build-up of steam in the boiler is possible.
- Apply heat for about 1 minute for every 1° below 0°C. The fuel in the blowtorch lasts for approximately 30 minutes. Quickly refill if necessary and continue to heat.
- In severe cold: After heating for 20 minutes spin the engine using the inertia starter or crank handle to break the congealed oil film in the engine.
- After 30 minutes heating start the engine by operating the primer fuel injector device as described above.
- After starting, if the engine runs, remove and switch off the blowtorch and replace the cover on the boiler to prevent the entry of dirt and projectiles, make sure that the seal is properly seated.

External starter

It was possible to use jump leads to make starting the Tiger easier if the inertial starter or cranking handle failed to sufficiently raise the engine speed. Towing was banned because of the risk of damage to the clutch, gearbox and final drive.

While the *Kurbelwellenbenzinlasser* had already been available from 1942, it was only later used in conjunction with a VW *Kübelwagen* as a starting gearbox (Porsche) Typ 198.

Kurbelwellenbenzinanlasser

A *Kurbelwellenbenzinlasser (KBA)* was a small power unit consisting of a two cylinder, two-stroke petrol engine attached to the two protruding, smooth retaining pins on the crankshaft cover on the rear of the tank and was thus connected to the tank's crankshaft. The use of a pawl mechanism made it possible to withdraw the starter when the engine was running without encountering any problems. In the winter of 43/44, every Tiger unit was equipped with this device – following that none were provided.

This 66 kg, maintenance-intensive device required a strenuous effort by hand to get it running.

If it was not possible to store it in a cold-protected environment during frosty weather before being called into use, it too had to be pre-warmed using a blowtorch.

KBA mounted on the rear of a Panther.
(D659/51, pic. 8)

A *Kurbelwellenbenzinlasser* as viewed from the right:
1 carrying frame
2 clamping screws
3 selector rod
4 locking bar
5 connecting shaft
(D635/5, pic. 53)

Operating the *Kurbelwellenbenzinlasser*

1. Using two men, attach and secure the *KBA* to the retaining pins.
2. Set the selector rod to '0'.
3. Open the fuel cock on the *KBA* and 'tickle' the carburettor float to enrich the starting mixture.
4. Swing the starting handle out to the right and allow the chain to retract.
5. Allow engine to warm up at medium speed.
6. Push the *KBA* against the tank and turn the shaft by hand until the coupling claw engages with the crankshaft. Secure the starter to the mounting frame with clamping screws.
7. Push the selector rod forwards to its limit of travel (1st gear). Allow the engine to run for a short time then pull the selector rod backwards to its limit of travel to engage 2nd gear.
8. When the engine is running, loosen the clamping screws and pull the *KBA* backwards, set the selector rod to '0' and then remove the *KBA* from the tank.
9. If no other vehicle is to be started, press the short-circuit button to turn off the engine. If the device is to be switched off for a lengthy period, close the fuel cock and empty the carburettor.

Starter Typ 198 for Tiger and Panther

The starter gearbox could be installed on the rear of a VW *Kübelwagen* which was fitted with mounting bolts that were used in the same way as with the *KBA*. The drive linkage was attached to the rear of the tank and to the starter gearbox by a driveshaft. The advantage of this system was that it did not require a special starter motor and used a reliable and popular vehicle. However, the space taken up by the bulky components that had to be transported with the gearbox was something of a disadvantage.

For the winter of 1944/45, the starter gearbox Typ 198 was intended only for use by the Tiger and Panther units.

Operation

1. Reverse the Volkswagen, with a warmed engine and starter gearbox attached, to within about three or four metres of the rear of the tank.
2. Mount the pipe supports of the guide bridge on the support bolts on the tank and tighten.
3. Push the guide bridge forwards, insert the claw coupling and secure the guide bridge with the clamping screws.
4. Insert the short splined shaft into the starter gearbox. An angle of up to 30° between the Volkswagen and tank is permissible.
5. Disengage the starter gear clutch.
6. Start the Volkswagen engine.
7. Engage 1st gear on the starter gearbox.
8. Turn on the tank engine ignition.
9. Engage the starter gearbox clutch and increase the speed of the Volkswagen engine.
10. If the tank engine fails to start, repeat the attempt with the starter gearbox in 2nd gear.
11. When the tank engine is running, disengage the starter gearbox clutch and turn off the Volkswagen engine, remove the drive shaft, pull the guide bridge and shaft from the tank and dismount the device.

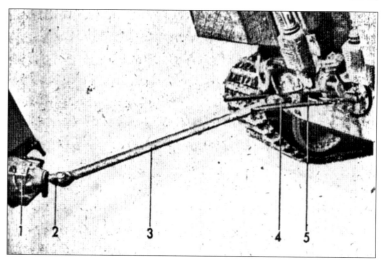

Picture 10
Starting gearbox Typ 198 attached to Volkswagen and Panther tank
1. Starter gearbox; 2. Splined shaft (short); 3. Drive shaft; 4. Splined shaft (long); 5. Universal joint

Picture 11
Sliding guide bridge with universal joint
1. Guide bridge support pipes; 2. Adjustable guide bridge; 3. Clamping screws; 4. Universal joint; 5. Long splined shaft; 6. Splined power transfer shaft

Details of the component parts of the connections to the tank.
(D659/51)

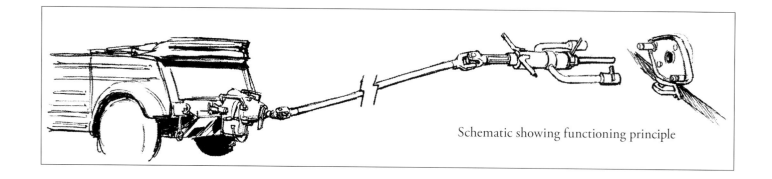

Schematic showing functioning principle

The hood for transferring warmed air from the radiator to the ventilation system for submerged driving. (D656/21+, pic. 40)

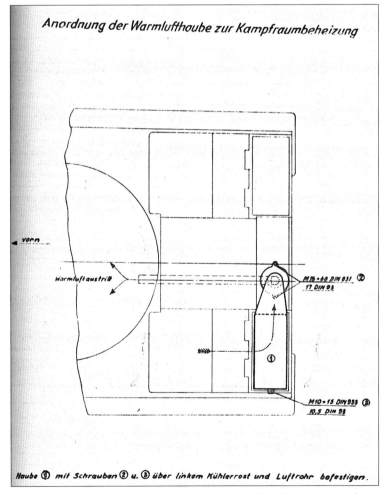

Anordnung der Warmlufthaube zur Kampfraumbeheizung

vorn

Warmluftaustritt

M16×60 DIN 931 ②
17 DIN 93

①

M10×15 DIN 933 ③
10,5 DIN 93

Haube ① mit Schrauben ② u. ③ über linkem Kühlerrost und Luftrohr befestigen.

Details of the air ducting that was supposed to have increased the danger of fire in the engine compartment and was therefore abandoned. Source: (D656/21+, drawing HSK-J2934)

Heating in the fighting compartment of the Tiger I

(winter 1942/43 only)

All Tigers delivered to *Heeresgruppe Süd* (Army Group South) until February 1943 were equipped with heating in the fighting compartment.

Warm air was conducted from the left-side radiator over an attached hood, through the air intake duct and ventilation shaft for underwater driving, through the engine compartment and into the fighting compartment. The demountable air ducting was supposed to be taken out and stored by the repair and maintenance squad by spring.

It was reported through a Maybach representative that all fighting compartment heating systems had been removed in order to avoid an addition risk of engine fire.

On 1 June 1944 it was officially announced that the Tiger I would no longer be equipped with a heating system for the fighting compartment.

Carbon monoxide indicator

(CO indicator)

On long marches, the air inside the enclosed fighting compartment was supposed to have been checked frequently with the *CO-Anzeiger* (carbon monoxide indicator) for the dangerous gas. This involved sampling the air in various locations in the fighting compartment with ten strokes of a special pump sucking air through a small test tube. If a pale-green discolouration was present this indicated that carbon monoxide was present but not at a dangerous level. The fighting compartment was then ventilated and the source identified. If the colour was reddish brown merging to a blue-green, the tank was to be evacuated immediately, and ventilated, because choking, difficulty in breathing and suffocation could set in within a few minutes. During the winter of 1943/44, three sets [of testing apparatus] were provided for each unit – none were provided the following winter.

Winterschild

For every vehicle a *Winterschild* (winter noticeboard) was provided on which measures carried out in relation to winter were to be entered exactly. It was attached to the left, beside the driver's seat.

The Tiger belonging to *s.Pz.Abt. 504* that was captured by the British in Tunisia. Today it is in the Bovington Tank Museum; the air-intake pipe is mounted on the rear of the tank. Of course the former enemy took great interest in this technology. (Bovington Tank Museum)

Later, the air intake was installed on the commander's hatch.

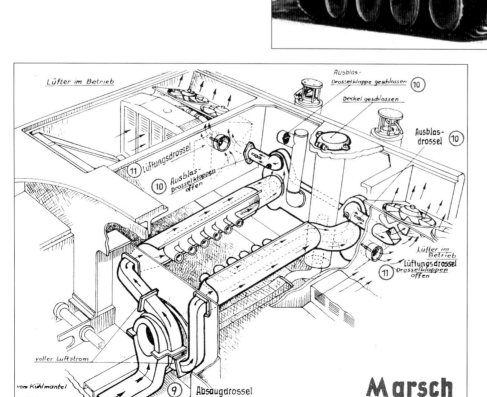

Air ducting from the crew area to the engine compartment and the radiators when travelling on land; notice the capped air-intake pipe (*Deckel geschlossen*). (*Tigerfibel* page23)

Submerged Driving

(from Obering. Arnoldt, supplements by Fletcher, Spielberger and articles in HtVBl 1944)

Development and Testing

Just as the construction of the Tiger was underway, the *Heereswaffenamt* ordered its 'submergibility' to a depth of 4.5 metres, presumably in view of the greater weight of the vehicle and the problems associated with this regarding crossing bridges with limited carrying capacity. Reconfiguring the tank from land to underwater driving was to have been possible in a short time; 50-60 minutes at most. This was referred to as *Unterwasser – Kampfwagenfähigkeit (UK)* (submerged combat vehicle capability).

The ground-breaking work carried out at the Henschel Company's testing facility at Haustenbeck near Paderborn (see Chapter 2) continued almost without interruption until 1945 to the benefit of later developments by the *Bundeswehr*.

Technical preconditions

The *UK* conditions were broadly fulfilled by the following provisions:

1. A three-part air intake that was disassembled for travelling on land and carried on the rear part of the engine compartment in a closed holder on which it was erected. This solution proved unsatisfactory for many reasons and soon after the first underwater runs the first modification was made in which the fresh air supply was taken in through a telescopic pipe on the commander's hatch.
2. Placing the two radiators and their four cooling fans in side compartments beside the engine compartment. When travelling underwater the radiator compartments were flooded as well as the radiators and the cooling fans switched off.
3. An inflatable hose that acted as the turret seal and weapon seals. Blocking the turret and weapons was necessary. However, during the tank's development, changes made it possible to traverse the turret underwater if required.
4. A non-return valve on the exhaust pipe that prevented water entering if the engine came to a stop.
5. Bilge pumps in the fighting compartment so that water entering at unsealed points could be forced out.
6. An air supply for the engine that was taken through the fighting compartment; watertight seals on the engine compartment.
7. Switching of the fuel tank ventilation into the fighting compartment.
8. Adjusting track tension manually before and after underwater driving.

9. Cooling of the transmission in the fighting compartment by the appropriate distribution of incoming fresh air.
10. The provision of flood valves in the floor of the vehicle in the event that an emergency escape under water was necessary.
11. Hatch locks that enabled escape under water without hindrance.
12. Special levers and other features for operating underwater covers and valves from within the fighting compartment for ease of use before and after driving underwater.
13. Special solution for the management of the air flow essential for cooling the exhaust manifold in the engine compartment.
14. Sealing the air intake above the driver / radio area and the air extraction unit in the turret.
15. Turning off the automatic fire extinguisher.

The essential provisions necessary for underwater driving were partly built into the first 495 Tigers. As from November 1943, after the construction of the 625th vehicle (of a total of 1,346) and following a notification in the *Heerestechnische Verordnungsblatt*, important air ducting and throttle valves were no longer fitted. The Tiger II was originally also supposed to be capable of underwater driving but this was only ever implemented in full in prototypes. The telescopic air intake opening on the rear was also finally dropped in September 1944 after the production of the 225th vehicle (of total of 489) when it was covered with a splinter-proof cap.

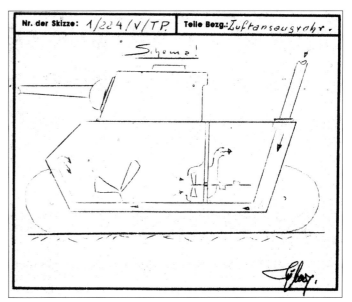

Initially, the fresh air supply was delivered via a duct that ran through the engine compartment and the crew area and through the cool air fan (referred to here as the bulkhead fan for clarity) before returning to the engine. From this it is apparent that, among other things, exhaust gases could not be kept out of the crew area.

Procedures carried out before submerged driving

The devices and levers described here were not identical in every production series model and refer mainly to the Haustenbeck *UK* Tiger. Most of the levers and devices were provided with warning lights that were intended to help prevent inappropriate operation.

Should an order for underwater driving be issued, the crew, as described in Arnoldt's study, had to carry out the following procedures:

a)   Open the cover on the intake manifold opening on the rear engine deck.

Pull out the five intake pipes of graduated diameter, each of which is about 1.35 metres long.

Screw the individual pieces together on the ground using the stepped rubber ring seals stored on the upper part by means of a clip. Tighten each of the ring nuts until contact is made with the metal stop.

Lay the assembled air intake pipe in the direction of travel on top of the tank with the widest part pointing towards the rear.

Stand the intake pipe vertically and insert it into the manifold opening and attaching the three lengths of cable to the eyelets at the front left, front right and rear centre on the rear wall of the tank.

Tension the three cables in the tensioning sockets using the folding crank lever until they are equally tight.

The whole operation takes two men between 10 and 12 minutes if the individual elements are always kept clean and rust free.

b)   Mount the exhaust muffler reed valve cover during which the two pivot pins are removed and allowed to hang free on chains (time required is around 2-3 minutes for one man).

Put in the two tensioning springs that are secured inside the eyelets in each cover. Time required for this work is around 2 minutes for one man.

c)   Turn off the 4 cooling fan connections to the radiators with the selector lever on the bulkhead in the fighting compartment.

d)   Set the float gauges in both overflow chambers to '*UK*' (underwater driving) with the levers on the left and right of the bulkhead. At the same time, a warning light for underwater driving is switched on so that when exiting from the water the cooling fans can only be switched on if the float gauges in both overflow chambers have switched off the two warning lights on the dashboard. If the fans are switched on too early and the water in the overflow chambers has not yet been drained (possibly due to a blocked drain hole), this could damage the radiator and cooling fans.

e)   Close the fairing above the engine compartment using the lever on the bulkhead.

f)   Switch the two valves using the lever on the rear wall to short circuit the air cooling the exhaust manifold which, when travelling on land, leads the cooling air through the air intake above the driver, the fighting compartment, the partition-wall fan, over the two exhaust manifolds in the two radiator compartments located to the left and right.

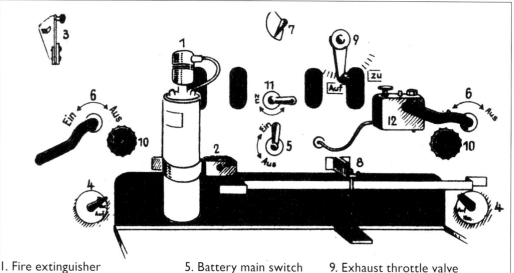

1. Fire extinguisher	5. Battery main switch	9. Exhaust throttle valve
2. Fire extinguisher clamp	6. Radiator fan switch	10. Air outlet throttle valve
3. Floor vent	7. Fuel tank ventilation	11. Air slide gate
4. Fuel switch	8. Suction throttle valve	12. Starter fuel container

The lever on the engine compartment bulkhead which, in preparation for underwater travel, had to be operated – as shown on page 20 of the *Tigerfibel* (with annotations by the author below).

When driving underwater the cooing air for the two exhaust manifolds can no longer be allowed to enter the radiator compartments as these would be flooded. Change-over valves operated by a lever are installed on the fighting compartment bulkhead just before the entrance points of the cooling air to the radiator compartments. These divert the cooling air into the engine compartment where it is taken for use during combustion.

During subsequent travel on land the two red levers on the bulkhead are again changed over so that the cooling air is again drawn to the exhaust manifolds in the radiator compartment before it is blown to the outside.

g)   Closing the forward air-intake fairing located above the driver is performed by means of a lever (sketch on the right).

h)   Turn on the bilge pumps using the lever above the dashboard next to the driver's seat.

i)   Flashing warning lights indicate if one of the bilge pumps has stopped working when travelling underwater because of a blockage in the suction outlets caused by dirt. This is remedied by repeatedly pulling the bilge pump cleaning lever as this displaces the accumulation of dirt at the suction outlets.

j)   Close the flood valves on the floor of the hull while paying attention to the warning lights. After cleaning the hull floor with a hose the flood valves are often not closed so that any remaining cleaning water can run out.

k)   Close the propellant-gas extractor fan above the deck of the hull at the start of underwater travel. The twist grip is located on the ceiling in the fighting compartment.

l)   Activate the turret seal by switching the pressure valve located on the bulkhead to 'UK' [for underwater travel]. A warning lamp accompanied by a bleeping sound indicates that the pressure is below 1.5 bar. Switch to the pressure reserve tank and turn the primary pressure tank to 'load.' If the pressure reaches 8 bar its air supply switches off automatically.

m)   Put the rubber hood on the cannon muzzle using the inflatable cover and Dunlop tyre valve.
Working time = less than 1 minute for one man.
Remove the rubber cover for subsequent driving on land after depressing the valve head.

n)   Mount the cannon mantlet cover (sketch right) for underwater driving using two fitting levers and two men in about 5-8 minutes – this depends on the

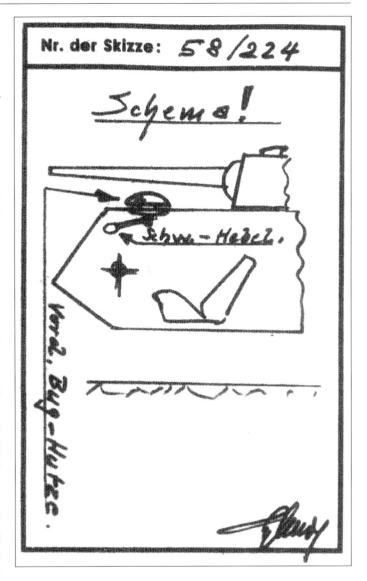

ambient temperature because the rubber cover is more difficult to stretch when stiff.

Fitting the six screws on the collar of the seal takes two men – one working inside the fighting compartment and one on the outside – four minutes work.

Deep threads for sealing and rapid installation.

The muzzle cover, MG mantlet seal and cannon mantlet seal are securely stored in the fighting compartment.

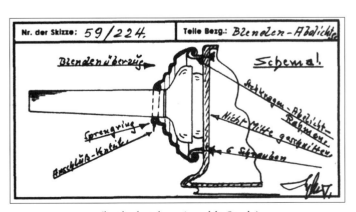

(both sketches: Arnoldt-Study)

o)   Attach the MG-mantlet seal in around 2-3 minutes – one man.

p)   Turn on the two float modules – the switches are located on the dashboard. Two indicator devices now show the degree of water leakage in the engine compartment and fighting compartment separately.
It is possible to turn on the bilge pumps either manually or automatically.

q)   Switch over the fuel venting valves to ventilation to the inside by turning the rotating handle on the bulkhead.

r)   Use the lever located beside the dashboard to increase the engine idle speed. This lever simultaneously switches on the lighting in the crew and engine compartments.

s)   Turn on the switch located on the dashboard that activates the instrument for detecting dangerous levels of carbon monoxide in the fighting compartment.

t)   Turn off the automatic fire extinguisher by means of the lever. This setting of the lever on the bulkhead also was connected to a warning lamp. (…)

v)   Using a switch on the dashboard, turn on the light that illuminates the compass during underwater driving.

w)   Secure the two towing cables on the bow and rear deck in preparation for underwater driving.
The bow, like the rear cable, is a short one of around 2 metres in length and used as an intermediate cable. Both cables are secured to the towing eyes on the hull and clamped in holders on top. Working time = one man around 5-6 minutes altogether.
If a vehicle is bogged down underwater in mud or soft ground, the towing eyes used for recovery on land cannot be reached and this creates considerable difficulty for the diver – the intermediate cables are a way out of this difficulty.

These specified activities suggest that even after the installation of the additional equipment developed in Haustenbeck, a substantial additional training effort that gave an in-depth understanding of the equipment was necessary in order to be able drive a platoon of Tigers through a waterway in relative safety.

On the basis of surviving documents in which the shortage of equipment is described, it appears unlikely that a standard production series Tiger could successfully and safely travel underwater when in action.

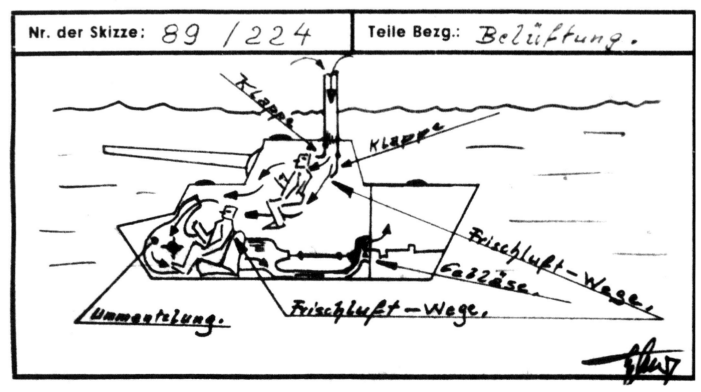

The final development of the fresh air intake (Belüftung) – through the commander's hatch, the crew area, transmission casing, bulkhead fan and into the engine compartment. (Arnoldt-Study)

4 Deployment

In this chapter the tasks of the trained crew (individually and collectively) – and how each crew member, autonomously or on command, went about the activities for which he had practised and trained (as mentioned in Chapter 3) – are explained.

The Tasks of the Commander

In today's parlance the commander had to be a master of 'multi-tasking' (this is described comprehensively in Chapter 5, 'Tactics'). His main tasks in the Tiger armoured fighting vehicle were essentially not different from those in other types of tank. These involved responsibilities under all 'modes of operation' for the maintenance of the technical operational readiness of the tank and, of course, when in combat.

It is however worth emphasising that he had to allow for particular technical performance constraints with regard to tactical effectiveness. In combat, many wrong decisions were made by failing to take into account, or else misjudging, the weight of the vehicle. All too often the commander trusted in the protection of the tank's armour and set off rather carelessly. Frontally the Tiger was very well protected for the conditions prevailing at that time but this was certainly not the case regarding the tank's side and rear. Accordingly, the enemy issued combat advice leaflets highlighting the Tiger's vulnerabilities. On the other hand, the sheer weight of the vehicle was a problem in heavy, marshy terrain and when crossing obstacles of all sorts. Besides the necessary caution required for trouble-free driving on dubious terrain, it was particularly important for the commander to ensure that the driver drove in a style that was sympathetic to the vehicle. For example, if at all possible, sharp turns were avoided – particularly when travelling slowly – in order to prevent damage to the sensitive final drive. This was a painfully common cause of failure, particularly in the heavier Tiger II. Furthermore, water obstacles could only be crossed after having been first reconnoitred.

On 18 April 1943 the field report of *s.Pz.Abt. 503* summarized important requirements of the commanders:

> For gunners, loaders and commanders intensive training should be undertaken in:
> - range estimation,
> - aiming practice,
>
> responding quickly but precisely to targets (no palaver), lightening quick recognition of transient targets and latching on to them so the tank battle is not, except in isolated cases, conducted at short range. Targets are mostly only recognised by their muzzle flashes. The same applies to combat of tank versus tank.
>
> The promotion of tactical understanding, particularly for commanders, is urgently required. He has to be in the situation of being able to assess the position of the enemy in the field. The enemy's infantry must be sought out. (…)
>
> The ability to assess the terrain is a prerequisite for the selection of drivers and commanders of 60 ton vehicles.
>
> Map reading and the assessment of the terrain by reference to maps is still very poor amongst non-commissioned officers and this applies to young officers too. More still has to be done and for drivers of 60 ton vehicles this is of crucial importance.'

Other important tasks of the commander were recognising and assessing technical faults and dealing with unpredictable requirements for the additional care and maintenance of their vehicles. Such measures might become necessary in extreme combat or environmental conditions, or when excessive stress was put on materiel, for example after a long march during redeployment.

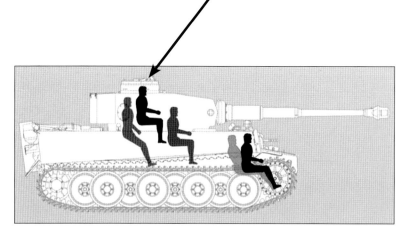

The commander – at the highest point in the tank – did not have his own optical equipment. His battlefield observations were made with the naked eye or using binoculars.

The range of a (stationary or slow-moving) target was therefore determined using the sighting device (here range 1,100 m) with the point of the main sighting triangle aimed at the centre of the target. (Harada)

The standard aiming point was basically the centre of the target because the aiming point of properly adjusted tank optics coincided with the point of impact of the gun.

It was important for the gunner to follow the path of the projectile using his optics and the tracer in the base of the shell. If the projectile missed its target because it was too high or too far to the side, he measured the exact extent of the observed deviation and moved the sighting point of the target reticules for the next shot accordingly by elevating the gun and/or traversing the turret.

Tasks of the Gunner

The core tasks of the gunner are the careful observation of the target area, the rapid recognition and identification of targets and their engagement while observing the firing regulations.

Applying the firing regulations

A distinction was made between *Einschießen* (shooting at a designated target with allowance made for its range) and *Wirkungsschießen* (firing to achieve tactical effect). With the shooting principles established during *Einschießen* (ranging in on a specific target) the gunner moves on to *Wirkungsschießen*.

Because of the elongated trajectory of a shell, *Einschießen* can be omitted for targets at ranges of less than 1,200 m and *Wirkungsschießen* can start immediately.

During *Einschießen* using armour piercing shells (*Panzergranaten/ Pz.Gr.*), their tracer trails and points of impact (range and lateral deviation in relation to the target) have to be correlated.

When firing high-explosive fragmentation shells (*Sprenggranaten*) it is the initial smoke cloud that the gunner has to latch on to.

Einschießen begins with lateral and range setting such that the trajectory leads close to the target.

To begin with, it is necessary to place the shot in the exact direction of the target. Deviations to the side caused for example by a cross wind or – for targets at greater distances – by the spin of the projectile, are allowed for at the same time as any necessary adjustment to the range by setting the aiming point to the opposite side of the corresponding observation. If the lateral deviance of the shot is significant, the target is sighted using the reticule or intermediate *Strich* (division) above which the impact was observed.

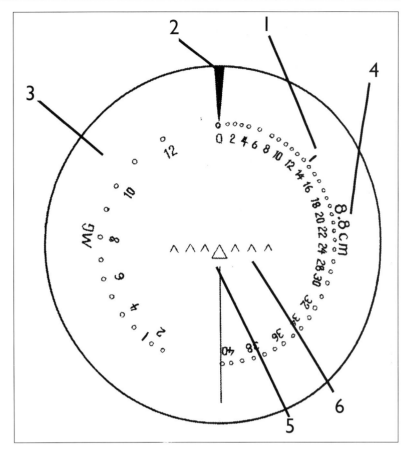

The reticule disc (*Strichplatte*) in the right objective eyechannel of the *TZF 9b* showing the rotatable range bezel (1), the range indicator (2), the distance scale for the MG and *Pz.Gr.* on the left (3) and for the on the right (4) for the *Sprenggranaten*, the central aiming point (5), and next to it, on the right, the auxiliary aiming points (6).

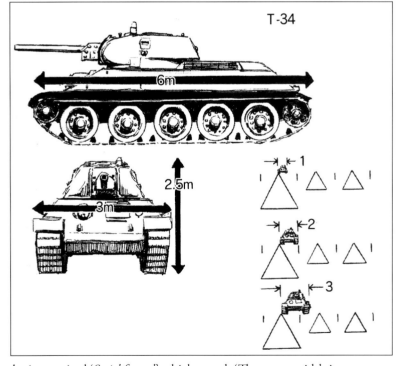

The distance to the target had to be determined using the improvised '*Strichformel*' which stated: 'The target width in metres times a thousand divided by the number of *Strich* (reticule divisions) gives the distance in metres.' To this end the known target widths and lengths were utilized, such as those of the T-34. Therefore, if an approaching T-34 covered 3 *Strich* then it was 1,000 m away; if it covered 2 *Strich* then it was 1,500 m away and so on. Experienced gunners were able to carry out this calculation, without hesitation, in a matter of seconds. Up to a distance of around 1,200 m, and because of the relatively straight trajectory of the *Pz.Gr.*, targets were hit even if there were small miscalculations of the range.

If the trajectory of the shot – as in this example – takes it just above the target, the gunner aims the cannon lower by the same amount (as shown in the picture below) and the following shot strikes the centre of the target.

This so-called 'point-of-aim' technique enabled a quicker correction to the shot than changing the setting on optical sights. However, at greater distances the prospect of hitting the target was reduced because of the curvature of the flight path of the projectile.

In this second example, the flight path of the shot takes it just past the right of the target. The gunner corrects for this by aiming the same amount in the opposite direction and hits the target with the second shot.

Einschießen to establish the range of the target is carried out by *Gabelbildung* if observation to the front or rear of the target is possible and by *Heranschießen* if observation to the rear of the target is not possible because of the terrain or ground cover.

During *Gabelbildung*, two distances are established within which the target in all probability lies. After the position of the first observable shot is made, the range is increased or decreased accordingly. The '*Gabel*' (fork) is created when at a certain distance a shot falls short (-) and another falls long (+). The first correction has to be big enough to allow the 'fork' to be created by the second shot. This is executed in steps of 800, 400, 200, 100 and 50 m.

When firing *Panzergranaten*, the range is increased or decreased in steps of not less than 200 m when firing at targets between 1,200 and 2,000 m and at least 400 m when the range is greater than 2,000 m.

When firing *Sprenggranaten* the steps are increased or decreased by 200 m for distances less than 1,200 m; by 400 m if the range is more than 1,200 m and by 800 m if the distance to the target is greater than 3,000 m.

The steps are carried out towards the centre of the 'fork.'

When firing *Panzergranaten* up to the range of 2,000 m the 'fork' is reduced by 100 m; over 2,000 m (and for *Sprenggranaten* at any range) by 50 m. At ranges greater than 3,000 m the 50 m 'fork' is not used.

Due to range dispersion when using *Sprenggranaten* at distances greater than 3,000 m, it is appropriate to verify the boundaries of the 100 m 'fork' by using a second shot when firing at small targets.

If observation of the target is not possible because of the terrain or ground cover, or if it is necessary to fire over our own troops in the vicinity of the target, then *Einschießen* begins with a greater than estimated or measured range: in such a case shooting begins with small steps moving towards the target from the rear.

If observation to the rear of the target is not possible because of the terrain or ground cover then *Heranschießen* is carried out frontally, providing this does not place our own troops in danger.

If during *Einschießen* at a distance a direct hit, a strike close to the target or if the 100 m 'fork' is verified (this applies only to *Sprenggranaten*) by a long and a short shot, then the *Einschießen* is terminated.

Wirkungsschießen begins at the most favourable distance and direction determined by *Einschießen*, the centre of the 'fork' or the distance at which a direct hit, a strike close to the target or indications of a hit are achieved.

During the course of *Wirkungsschießen* the aiming point and minor improvements in the range of the shot are required. Aiming point adjustments should not exceed the height of the target.

If the target is to be destroyed by *Wirkungsschießen*, rapid fire should follow.

The quantity of ammunition required is determined by the type of target.

Versus live targets without protection from above, *Sprenggranaten* with delayed action impact fuses are used if ricochet is anticipated (*Abprallerwirkung*). Hard ground, flat terrain and grass cover favour ricochets providing the striking angle is no greater than 360 *Strich* (20°). Using ricochet shooting, sufficient effect can be achieved with few rounds. *Einschießen* with *Sprenggranaten* using delayed action impact fuses to *Wirkungsschießen* using ricochets is discontinued once the favourable shooting distance has been determined to within 50 m.

Against armoured fighting vehicles at distances of less than 1,200 m, *Einschießen* is not applicable and *Wirkungsschießen* begins immediately. It starts at around 200 m greater than the estimated or measured range (using the sighting device).

If as a consequence of a large error in the estimation of the range the first shot is too long (+) the reticule range is reduced by 200 m.

If the first shot falls short for the same reason ('allowing the target to disappear'), the aiming point is adjusted. If the aiming point adjustments do not lead to an immediate hit there has been a major error in the estimation of the range (the target is more than 1,200 metres away) and shooting continues using a 400 m 'fork.'

Targeting certain weak points on armoured fighting vehicles might require adjustments to the aiming point.

For large targets (for example large trucks) and for 'flat' targets (such as a massed infantry attack), *Einschießen* using *Sprenggranaten* at distances of under 1,200 m is not applicable unless there is a reference point for the range.

Wirkungsschießen begins against approaching or receding armoured fighting vehicles: for approaching armoured fighting vehicles at under 1,200 m to 2,000 m firing is within the narrow limits of the 'fork'; avoid breaking off fire too early when firing at armoured fighting vehicles withdrawing within the wide limits of the 'fork'; firing ceases when moving armoured fighting vehicles are at more than 2,000 m.

Principle of firing ricochets.

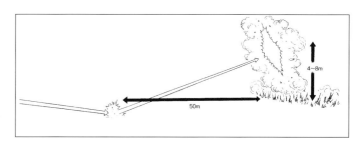

When ranging in on a target (*Eingabeln*), the distance scale on the sighting device was rotated. According to the observed explosion plume – either in front of or behind the target – this was done in large steps (when firing at distant targets) or in small steps (when firing at closer targets) until an impact on the target was observed.

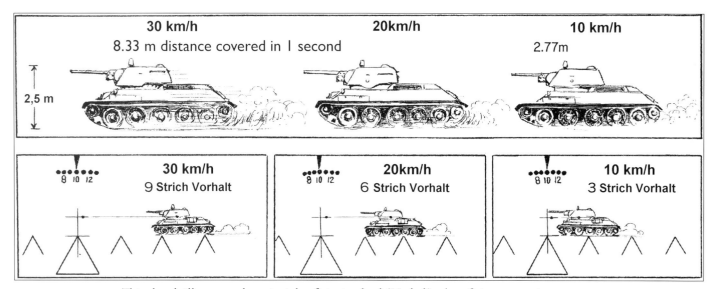

This sketch illustrates the principle of aiming lead (*Vorhalt*) when firing at moving targets.

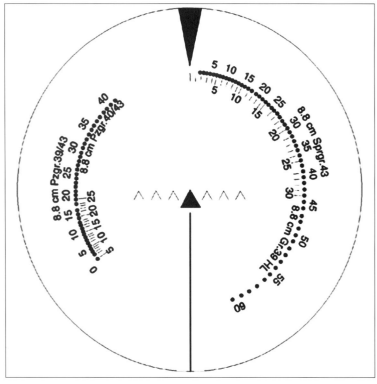

Setting the range on the *TZF 9d* of a Tiger II was rather more complex. The distance scale for the *Sprenggranate 43* with a maximum setting of 60 (approx. 6,000 m) was certainly optimistic because tracer left on the shells only burned for 6 seconds which meant that for ranges of above 4.9 km only the impact could be observed.

When shooting at a transverse or obliquely moving target the auxiliary aiming points are to be used for setting the lead. The gap between the aiming points amounts to 4 *Strich*. One Strich covers a distance of 1 m at a range of 1,000 m.

'Lead' applied for transverse movement at 2,000 m:

	Lead in *Strich* at target vehicle speed		
Munition	10 km/h	20 km/h	30 km/h
PzGr	3	6	9
SprGr	4	8	12

The amount of 'lead' for targets moving obliquely amounts to:
- for a course at 30° half
- for a course at 60° the full value of the transverse rate of movement.

The gunner conducts the firefight either on the order of the commander but otherwise essentially independently. As soon as a target is identified he reports this (for example by exclaiming 'tank'), aims at it and, if necessary, adjusts the range on the sighting device then warns the crew (by shouting *'Achtung'*) before firing. During this time the loader releases the safety catch and the commander assesses whether or not his intervention is necessary (for example if it is too soon to open fire).

If several targets are identified, the gunner fires for as long as it takes to destroy them or the commander orders a change of target or a cease fire.

This procedure has the advantage that it is executed significantly faster than a commander-led firefight.

Furthermore, to establish the state of combat readiness, a round of cannon munition is pre-loaded (cannon in safety mode) and a range determined by the commander is set on the sighting device. All other weapons, turret and anti-aircraft MGs, are likewise loaded.

Thanks to its high muzzle velocity and the reduced wind resistance, the flight path of the *Panzergranate* was relatively little affected so that deviations from the real target distance did not necessarily mean that a shot would miss. A hit high or low down on the target would still have an effect.

Experienced gunners were however still in the situation of being able to safely apply the firing regulations to achieve a high number of direct hits. An effective tactical measure to improve the probability of a first-shot direct hit was to use the so called *'Kampfvisier.'* Depending on the terrain through which a thrust was to be conducted, an aiming range, usually in the region of 800 to 1,000 m, was set on the optics. The first shot was then delivered without further determination of the range of a target. If an experienced gunner reckoned that the target was a little closer than the distance set on the optics, he aimed low; if the target was deemed to be further away he aimed high. An experienced gunner could also estimate the speed of a moving target and instinctively (or on orders from the commander) select the correct 'lead' with considerable accuracy.

The commander and gunner were also supposed to have been sufficiently trained with respect to external ballistic influences and the effect of changed internal ballistic parameters. The lumbering, slow flying *Sprenggranaten* were particularly sensitive to side winds that had a serious impact on their accuracy at larger distances; the same applied to heavy rain that slowed the shot more quickly. Heat haze and also the light at dusk also led to an underestimation of distance; high radiant heat or a barrel that had become hot during firing increased the muzzle velocity and caused overshooting; shooting uphill meant aiming low, and so on.

If the tank stood in a position for an extended period of time, or the gunner knew the assignment that had been ordered (for example in defence), he complied a so-called *'Entfernungsspinne'*, a sketch in which, with the aid of a map, he marked the exact distances to prominent points at which enemy targets might appear and learned these by heart. He also recorded the direction of these landmarks with the help of the turret direction indicator dial. This had the great advantage that even if visibility in these directions was restricted, targets could still be engaged in combat.

During a firefight, and despite the ventilation system, thick smoke filled the fighting compartment between loading procedures.

At the moment of firing a conspicuous flash was seen at the muzzle. Particularly at night, a gunner looking through the optics could easily be dazzled by this. The tank also immediately betrayed its position as it fired.

Another external ballistic feature was the smoke at the tank's muzzle. In the absence of a side wind this could obscure the crew's vision for some time. (Drawings Harada)

A direct hit often had a significant effect on the target that was easily seen – such as the flash of the exploding shell or the detonation of the fuel and munitions.

The Tasks of the Loader

> In the tank, the loader endures the greatest physical stress. After the ammunition stored at his side has been fired he has to fetch the rounds stored in boxes elsewhere in the vehicle. To do this the turret has to be rotated to the 3 or 6 o'clock position, a procedure that has to be trained for and practised because otherwise a delay in the tanks participation in combat arises and this allows the best targets to slip away.
>
> Nine loaders and a radio operator lost consciousness because of over-exertion and carbon monoxide gas. For loaders at least, additional, refreshing meals are required.
> (Extract from a report by *s.Pz.Abt. 506* on 30 September 1943)

It was the loader who did the hard labour during firefights led by the commander and executed by the gunner. The shooting successes of the commander and gunner were recognised and were the centre of heroic tales told in the evenings but the essential contribution of the loader – just as it is today – was less valued, particularly by those who were not well acquainted with the situation. If one examines the inner workings in a tank during a firefight more closely this becomes clear. Especially during combat against a numerically superior enemy (the usual situation), the objective of the commander and gunner was to destroy as many targets as possible in the shortest possible time in order to reduce the probability of themselves becoming a target. However, rapid fire is possible only if the loader performs his task efficiently. To this end, he had the next round ready in his hands so that he could reload immediately after a shot was fired and the spent cartridge ejected. If a different type of round was ordered he had to react quickly by returning the 'old' round to its storage rack and removing the type that had been requested. He had to be alert at all times to ensure that – if the spent-cartridge sack was full – used cartridges scattered on the floor did not get between the rotating turret basket and the hull as this could lead to drastic damage and endanger the combat readiness of the tank.

In principal, because of the shortage of raw materials, he returned empty cartridges to the vacant spaces in the storage racks for re-use. However, in practice they were often disposed of through the open hatch because the spaces that had become vacant on the storage racks had already been immediately re-filled with rounds from more difficult-to-reach racks. This so-called '*Umbunkern*' was undertaken by the loader under his own responsibility during each pause in shooting.

When a firefight was in progress he also kept an eye on the adjustable stop on the recoil gauge. This was located on the inner left side of the deflector and consisted of fixed rails and a moveable slide that showed the extent of the recoil of the breech and cannon. If during sustained firing the slide indicated '*Feuer-pause*' (stop firing), the loader reported this immediately to the commander who could then order an immediate suspension of firing to prevent serious damage to the recoil mechanism, recoil brakes and the cannon's bearings. Excessive recoil was certainly not necessarily due to a technical fault; with every shot the brake fluid in the recoil brakes became hotter and their braking action less effective.

It was simply down to the experience of the crews to judge when firing could be resumed although this also depended on the internal and external temperatures.

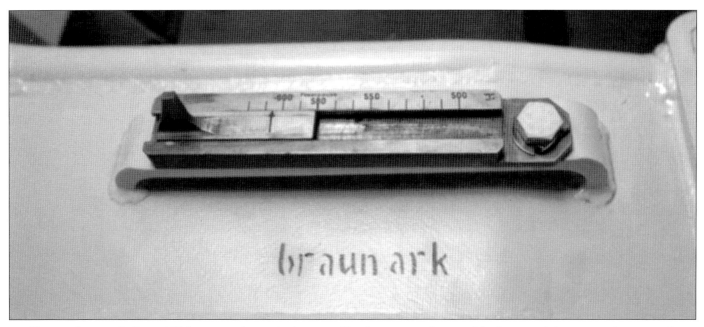

The recoil gauge indicated if the cannon's travel when recoiling became too long as this threatened damage to the weapon's mounting and the recoil brakes in particular. A warning mark (*Feuerpause*) showed when the travel of the recoil reached 580 mm. The embossed '*braunark*' indicated that the fluid in the recoil brakes was to be replenished with a mixture of '*Bremsflüssigkeit, braun*' (brown brake fluid) and '*arktisch*' (arctic) brake fluid.

During these activities he also ensured that the turret MG was in proper working order, installed new ammunition belts and dealt with any problems. Such problems arose rather frequently, for example as a consequence of wrongly loaded ammunition belts. After 200 rounds of rapid fire, the hot MG barrel had to be changed – which in the middle of a firefight was obviously a hectic activity or was simply impossible. This led to the cartridges jamming and could only be resolved by dismantling the MG.

The MG was loaded in preparation for combat readiness. The belts were also changed during ceasefire even if they were not completely empty in order to save valuable time during combat.

The belt sacks were not necessarily hung up for loading the MG or for the disposal of empty cartridges, that is to say a new belt could be put into them or empty cartridges could be removed manually after opening the cover on the belt sack depending on how much time was available for such activities. The crews also took to lengthening the belts (to more than 150 rounds) so that they had more ammunition in the weapon. The ammunition belts were delivered ready to use or were loaded manually by means of a machine in the possession of each company. The latter was in any case only necessary with partly used belts. The belts were loaded in the ratio of 1 in 3 tracer to non-tracer rounds but this was later changed to 1 in 5. The gunners could therefore see the dispersal cone of their fire on or near the target and make corrections without any delay.

At the beginning of a firefight using the cannon or the MG, the loader switched on the extractor fan on the roof of the turret so that the gases from the propellant were sucked to the outside. This 120 watt fan, with an extraction rate of just 12 m³ /minute, was not very powerful and after firing several rounds in rapid succession, or after long periods of shooting with the MG, there was often a thick smoke spreading throughout the fighting compartment. Consequently, and contrary to regulations, the loader's hatch was often opened.

The loader had a seat but, because he could perform his loading duties only when standing, it was raised and folded to the right when not required.

Another duty undertaken by the loader was opening the emergency exit hatch situated to his rear and at an angle (see below) when required. This was locked by metal latch plate clamped in position with two tommy screws. After loosening the two screws the latch slid down and the emergency exit hatch could then be opened. In fact, this hatch was seldom used except, for example, when the tank was under constant fire from the front. Bailing out through the crew's respective hatches was substantially faster and took place first and foremost after a fatal, direct hit.

Tasks of the Tank Driver

For operating a "Tiger" a good driver, who as well as being technically capable as a driver must also have a good general technical training and be able to hold his nerve at critical moments, is crucial.
(*Major* Lueder, commanding officer *s. Ps.Abt. 501* on 3 May 1943)

When training young drivers the emphasis on knowledge of the interactions of technical devices and on instruction in maintenance of the vehicle takes second place to practical driving. It is only when he masters the operations of steering and gear-changing that he can drive properly.
(*Hauptmann* Wallroth, company commander *13./ Pz.Rgt. Großdeutschland* on 27 March 1943)

The driver had to drive the vehicle in accordance with the direct instructions during a firefight or the objectives set by the commander during a march because the Tiger I didn't have a high seat that enabled the driver to see through his hatch while driving. His restricted field of vision had to be supplemented by information given by the crew. In open terrain, it was appropriate to use the inbuilt *Kurskreisel* (gyroscopic direction indicator, see picture below right). Its direction setting and therefore the default target was specified at unit level.

In addition, the driver, as a member of the fighting unit, had to report his observations without being asked for them. He had to react to the automatic fire-extinguisher system warning. He bore the brunt of preparing for emergency operations or the recovery of the vehicle.

He was responsible for driving in a manner appropriate to the characteristics of the Tiger as a technically demanding and exceptionally heavy tracked vehicle, as taught during training. His driving style also had an impact on the well-being of the crew in that he avoided hard bumps in the terrain and abrupt movements of the vehicle as far as was foreseeable and possible. Despite its effective suspension system, the Tiger was nevertheless a place where bumps could result in minor but painful bruises and other injuries. It was not (and still is not) unusual for the crew members of a tank to be seriously, or even fatally, injured as the result of an unfortunate roll-over.

It was the driver's duty during missions to calmly and objectively keep the commander informed of the condition of the vehicle; to use every pause in deployment or marching for making checks; not to allow maintenance requirements to develop through neglect or to flippantly ignore repair needs.

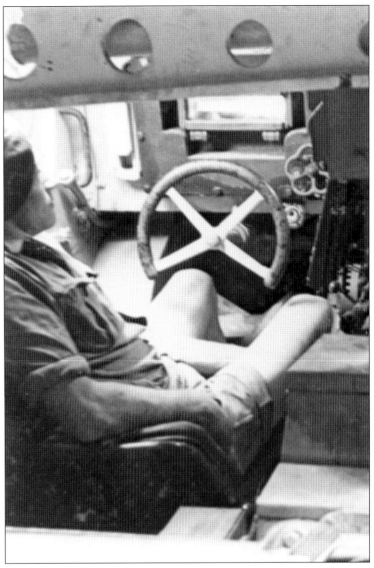

The driver's seat was ergonomically well thought-out and this facilitated fatigue-free driving over long periods of time.

Motto: Der Tiger ist, wenn man's bedenkt, ein Wagen, der sich prima lenkt.

Sorglosen, aber mit Werkstand

26 *Umdrehungen in einer Minute im ³/₄-Takt* macht der feine Mann beim Wiener Walzer. Dann schmilzt die Musik in Deinem Ohr und vermählt sich mit dem Gleichmaß der Bewegung. Langsamer ist langweilig, drehst Du aber zu rasch, dann wirst Du schwindlig und Deine Partnerin geht vor Hitze aus dem Leim.

2600 *Umdrehungen in der Minute im 4-Takt* liebt der Tiger. Dann leistet er für seinen Sprit am meisten. Dein Taktgefühl, Dein Ohr und Dein Drehzahlmesser sagen Dir, wann Du Deine Partnerin auf die richtigen Touren gebracht hast.

Jage sie niemals über 3000 U/min, sonst wird ihr zu heiß. Das Wasser kocht, das Öl hört auf zu schmieren, die Lager, Kolben und Ventile brennen fest — aus . . .

Darum fahre mit dem Kopf, nicht mit dem Hintern!

beobachte ständig Drehzahl **1**	Waserwärme **2** und Öldruck **3** (Bild Seite 40)
suche die beste Bahn,	aber halte die Richtung,
schleiche Dich an,	aber komme vom Fleck,
beobachte,	aber lies das Schaltbrett,
funke,	aber hör auf Motor und Getriebe!

Beim Marsch	Kanone auf 6 Uhr drehen und zurren.
Häuser und Mauern	fahre lieber nicht um. Die Mauertrümmer machen sich in der Wochenschau besser aus als auf Deinem Heck. Durch den Lüfter wird der ganze Schutt angesaugt, der Kühler wird eingedeckt und kühlt nicht mehr. Der Motor wird heiß und fällt aus.

The *Tigerfibel* concisely and clearly summarized important information for the tank driver which he applied with due care and attention. [In these pages the *fibel* advises the driver how to tackle obstacles (e.g. marshes, rivers, bridges, snow, ice, woods, ditches and mines) and on the actions to take in specific circumstances when driving.]

Plane, Blätter, Schutt, Gepäck	dürfen das Luftgitter nicht verstopfen und die Kanone beim Schwenken nicht stören.
Morast, Sumpf	dunkle Stellen, hohes Gras meiden. Lieber weite Umwege machen. Boden zu Fuß erkunden. Nimm einen Mann huckepack und stell Dich auf ein Bein. Wenn der Boden trägt, trägt er auch den Panzer. Zügig durchfahren, nicht lenken, nicht schalten. Geht es nicht weiter, halt und sofort zurück. Nicht festmahlen. Ein anderer Tiger zieht Dich heraus. Seil verankern, Haken in die Gleiskette, selbst herausziehen!
Knüppeldamm	Er muß 3,5 m breit, und alle Knüppel 15 cm dick sein, sonst brechen sie durch oder reißen sich los.
Flüsse	Harter Grund, feste Ufer sind nötig. Wo andere Panzer waten, kommt der Tiger auch durch. Motor abstellen und U-Fahrt vorbereiten: Bodenventil zu, Lenz-Pumpe einschalten.
Brücken	Zu Fuß erkunden, Furten vorziehen. Vor Brücke halten, Tiger so einrichten, daß sie ohne Lenken überschritten werden kann, kleinen Gang wählen, nicht schalten, nicht halten, verkürztes Schrittempo fahren, erst Gas geben, wenn Du 5 m drüberweg bist.
Graben und Trichter	Gerade anfahren, nasse Stellen meiden.
Wald	Tiger wirft Bäume bis 80 cm Durchmesser mit der Bugkante um. Nicht auffahren. Bei zu schmaler Schneise Zick-Zackfahren, eine Seite fährt frei.
Minen	Spurfahren, auf Spur zurückstoßen, nicht lenken, wenn möglich räumen.
Schnee	Trockener Neuschnee bis 70 cm ist unbedenklich. Papp und Harsch, Bruchharsch nur bis zur Bodenfreiheit — 50 cm.
Eis	Kettenglied vor die Kette werfen, Schwungfahren, nicht lenken, Kanten senkrecht anfahren. Eine Kette im Graben oder an Rändern entlangschwindeln. Äste und Streuen hat wenig Zweck.

Kurven:	9	Vor der Kurve runterschalten. Nach Gefühl bis zum großen oder kleinen Bogen anziehen.
		Mit jedem Gang kannst Du 1 großen und 1 kleinen Bogen fahren.
		Je kleiner die Kurve, desto kleiner muß der Gang sein. Wenn es nicht ausgeht — Handbremse — Schalten.
Wenden auf der Stelle:		Auf 1. — 3. Gang runterschalten Kupplung treten rechts oder links anziehen großen Knopf am Wechselgetriebe drücken.
Halten:		Auf 4. — 1. Gang runterschalten Handbremse Kupplung treten Richtungshebel auf 0 Kupplung loslassen.
Rückwärtsfahren: 4 Gänge		Kupplung treten Richtungshebel nach hinten Wähler vor Gangraste Wähler einrücken Gas geben Kupplung langsam loslassen.
Schießbefehl:		Kupplung treten Handbremse anziehen
„*Stellung*".		Wähler auf 2. Gang einrücken
„*Frrrühstück*":		rrrechts anziehen oder
„*Miittag*"; (siehe „Mahlzeiten"); (siehe „Schätzen");		liiinks anziehen Beobachten — Entfernung schätzen — melden — beobachten
Notschalten:		Richtungshebel auf 0 mit dem Schlüssel einen Gang einlegen Kupplung treten, Richtungshebel vor Gas geben Kupplung loslassen

It is important to note that in these excerpts from the *Tigerfibel* the information regarding the maximum engine speed of 2,600 revolutions per minute and 3,000 revolutions per minute originate from before the end of 1943, that is to say before the Tiger and Panther engines had been limited to an engine speed of 2,500 revolutions per minute because of frequent engine failures.

In the page of the *Tigerfibel* shown opposite there is a section entitled '*Wenden auf der Stelle*' (turning on the spot). The '*großen Knopf am Wechselgetriebe*' (large button on the gear selector) mentioned in this section, which was supposed to be pressed when turning the Tiger I on the spot, refers to the activation of the clutch brake. This blocked the transmission mechanism and ensured that even if there was a different rolling resistance on the tracks a precise turn-on-the-spot could be performed.

If necessary, a tank can knock down a substantial tree but travelling through forested land is still problematic because the hull can bottom-out and this can immobilise the tank. Considerable damage can also be caused by trees falling on the tank. (Hoffmann)

Despite its engine power there were limits to the mobility of the Tiger. (Wunderlich)

Driving through houses is tactically self-defeating. The tank can get stuck, fall into the cellar and suffer serious damage to its external storage racks, glass surfaces and hatches. Fittings can be sheared off and dust and debris can block the cooling system ducting which in turn can lead to the engine overheating. (Hoffmann)

There were also restrictions imposed to driving across muddy terrain. This picture shows tank '301' of *s.Pz. Abt. 501* stuck fast on muddy land on 12 December 1943. (BA 672-7630-36)

With the help of *'Kletterbäume'* ('climbing' trees) tied together in front of the tracks – this photograph of a tank belonging to *s.Pz. Abt. 505* in October 1943 with the tree trunk tied to side of the hull – it was sometimes possible free a tank that had become stuck. (Jacob)

An effective means of overcoming a swampy section of land was to construct a 'corduroy road' made of tree trunks as shown in this picture (taken on 12 March 1944) of tanks belonging to *s.Pz.Abt. 501.*

A tank can easily get stuck in fine sand too; abrupt steering movements should be avoided in such circumstances!

Sloping ground has to be approached at 90° rather than at an oblique angle – as shown in this picture of tank '323' belonging to *s.Pz.Abt. 503* (taken in June 1943).

Waterways were supposed to be reconnoitred as a matter of course before driving through them as shown in this picture taken on 15 January 1943 by a tank belonging to *s.Pz. Abt. 501*… (Dullin)

…otherwise things can go wrong – as this picture (taken in July 1943) of tank '212' of *s.Pz. Abt. 502* 'in' the River Moika demonstrates. (Herrmann)

It is imperative to find out the load-bearing capacity of bridges otherwise there may be unpleasant surprize such as the one that befell this tank belonging to *s.Pz.Abt. 508*.

This engineer bridge over the Stry was unable to stand the weight of a tank belonging to *s.Pz.Abt.506* as it attempted a crossing on 25 July 1944.

Built up areas had their own surprizes at the ready, such as this cesspit which brought an abrupt end to *Oberleutnant* Wriedt's desire to move his tank belonging to *s.Pz.Abt. 504* on 16 September 1944.

The '212' has been caught out again as it took the wrong line on sloping ground – at an angle rather than head on. (Lohmann)

Here a tank belonging to *s.Pz.Abt. 501* is crossing a engineer-built wooden bridge with the utmost caution on 21 March 1944. (BA 279-905-12)

Driving on bridges was described in a field report produced by *s.Pz.Abt. 503* on 18 April 1944:

Bridges that were passable in winter are generally not passable during the spring and summer. If they are sufficiently wide, 24-ton *Kriegsbrücken* (military bridges), built as low as possible and using strong wood, are usually passable if the following points are noted:
a) stop at least 5 m in front of the bridge,
b) align the vehicles so that no steering movements are necessary while crossing,
c) choose a low gear and cross the bridge at a slow pace without accelerating; do not change gear on the bridge,
d) only accelerate when the whole of the vehicle is across and the rear is 5 m past the end of the bridge. If acceleration takes place sooner a steeply sloping embankment will collapse.

Activities during rest periods (D 656/23, page 47)

Checking the running gear
1. Track tension, security bolts, track links
2. Nuts on bogie and drive sprockets
3. Rubber tyres if applicable

Checking the engine
1. Investigation of the cause of irregularities that occur such as noises, exhaust smoke and so on.
2. Cleaning air filters, in dusty conditions every 50 km or sooner.

In the event that the fire warning light is illuminated (according to 656/21+, pages 93-94)
1. Bring the engine to idle speed, turn off only if the vehicle has to be left behind.
2. Allow the idling engine to clear any gases from fires and fire extinguishers that might penetrate the fighting compartment.

3. If a fire is noticed before the automatic extinguishers are activated remove the sealed safety clamp on the extinguisher holder and press down the button for a short time. If the electrical system has failed press the button very firmly with the palm of the hand for around 10 seconds.
4. After extinguishing the fire investigate and resolve its cause.

Turning off the engine and work carried out after deployment
1. If the engine is hot, allow it to idle for a few minutes to cool down before switching off.
2. Remove the ignition key.
3. Set the fuel control lever to 'closed' every time the engine is switched off.
4. Turn off the main battery switch.
5. Top up the fuel.
6. Check out the Tiger, examine for damage. Report any damage to a superior rank, repairs undertaken by the driver in collaboration with the *I-Dienst* (repair and maintenance service).

Here the crew of tank '15' of *2./s.Pz.Abt. 506* are checking the running gear while en route to Jezierzany on 14 April 1944. Experienced drivers were able to identify loose components by the sound of a hammer blow.

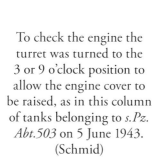

To check the engine the turret was turned to the 3 or 9 o'clock position to allow the engine cover to be raised, as in this column of tanks belonging to *s.Pz. Abt.503* on 5 June 1943. (Schmid)

When negotiating narrow roads the commander and radio operator gave assistance to the driver. This picture shows a tank belonging to *s.Pz.Abt. 501* on 25 November 1942. (BA 49-8-30)

Ditches and trenches are also driven through in a straight line as shown in this picture from 18 January 1943 of a tank also belonging to *s.Pz.Abt. 501.* (Dullin)

A major problem with tank marches is always the formation of immense, highly visible dust clouds. This column of *s.Pz.Abt. 503* is minimising this effect by driving to the side of a dusty track (picture taken on 5 June 1943).

Special measures when operating in winter (according to D 659/51, pages 36ff). Checks undertaken during a march

Operating temperature and oil pressure

- Allow the engine to warm up for at least 5 minutes from idling speed increase to 1,800 then to 2,000 revolutions per minute. Keep the coolant temperature controller closed until the temperature of the coolant reaches 80°C. At this point open it only so far as to keep the temperature constant.
- Because of the viscosity of the oil there is a delay on the oil pressure gauge that is harmless for up to 5 minutes. If the gauge continues to register no oil pressure after 10 minutes, turn off the engine and identify the cause. On the other hand, the oil pressure falls substantially in a warm engine because of dilution with fuel until it evaporates. For this reason it is important to keep a close watch on the oil pressure gauge.
- If the vehicle is cold, drive smaller distances in a particular gear in order to soften the lubricant in the drive and running gear.

Driving in slippery conditions

All abrupt changes of speed and direction cause tanks to slip or skid on a icy roadways.

- Never start or brake abruptly, steer with care, especially when using the brakes as emergency steering.
- Drive slowly and change down gears in good time when approaching climbs, downward slopes and curves.
- Avoid stopping on inclines.
- With the accompanying crews lay stones, wooden wedges or spare track links, or spread sand, to prevent the tank from sliding backwards.
- Overtake with caution because holes and ditches can be hidden by snow.
- Leave a large gap between vehicles when driving.
- Watch out for the formation of black ice when crossing sunny or shady areas.

Overcoming snow drifts

- Crews should investigate suspicious sites and snow drifts.
- Accelerate through snowdrifts in a slight curve.
- Accept detours because they often lead more quickly to the target.
- If the tracks 'grind,' reverse along the same ruts and then take a new route. If that is not possible lay a corduroy carpet, bushes, planks or track links in front of or under the tracks and shovel away the snow.
- Install the ice cleats (*Mittelstollen*) in the tracks.

Driving with ice cleats installed

When there is black ice and snow, special ice cleats can be attached to the tracks to prevent slippage sideways but they cannot stop the tracks slipping on inclines. The ice cleats are worn away after 30-40 km and become ineffective. Changing them during a march is difficult because the track link on which the ice cleat is to be replaced must first be thawed using a blowtorch *(s.Pz.Kp 502* field report about driving in winter 14 April 1943).

The ice cleats were supposed to have been installed on every 5th to 7th track link. For the winter of 1943/44 an issue of 120 *Mittelstollen* per vehicle was planned and in the winter of 1944/45, for each Tiger II, 50 *Mittelstollen* and 100 '*Steckstollen.*'(*HtVBl* 1943, pages 120 and *Sonderbeiblatt zur 18. Ausgabe des HtVBl 1944*, page 4).

Because of the high risk of stress and the threat of damage to the running gear and shock absorbers, speed was limited to 15 km/hr when travelling on made-up road surfaces.

Later, the tracks for the Tiger I and II were provided with 4 or 5 moulded, obliquely oriented, ribs ('*Gleitschutzpickeln* '/anti-slip pimples) on the gripper bar of the chain links but these also wore out on hard surfaces.

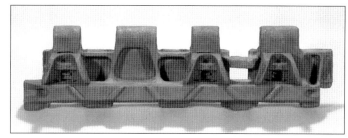

Tiger I track link with latched-in *Mittelstollen*. In the picture (bottom right) the spring-loaded locking latch can be seen (arrowed). Whether or not the ice cleats were actually made available in sufficient numbers, and were properly used, appears questionable. (Photos: Dr. Peter Schwarzmann)

Driving across ice

- Before driving across hollows cut holes, measure the thickness and the quality of the ice. Only clear ice is reliable.
- Weight capacity: 50 cm ice up to 45 tons, 60 cm ice up to 60 tons, 70 cm ice up to 75 tons. This means that the Tiger I requires an ice-thickness of almost 60 cm if it is not to break through.
- Drive slowly, do not stop, turn or overtake.

- The distance between vehicles depends on the strength of the ice such that one centimetre in the thickness of ice is equivalent to a gap of one metre between vehicles.

Preparations for starting after completion of driving

During periods of severe frost, the implementation of the directives for the dilution of the lubrication oil (described in detail in Chapter 3) and keeping the vehicle warm and under cover was the basis for its successful commissioning for the next deployment.

Winter weather is especially tricky because snow drifts at the side of the roads are not easily seen, as this vehicle belonging to *s.Pz. Abt. 502* discovered in January 1944.

But normal roads too can be so slippery that a tank can drop off to the side, such as here on the 15 January 1944 with a tank belonging to *s.Pz. Abt. 501* (Zorn)

Radio Operator's Tasks

The Tiger-specific tasks of the radio operator are straightforward. Routinely, he operated his on-board communi-cation equipment – with its four variants of switch positions – that was to be found to the left of his radio equipment. The selection of the connections available sounds more difficult than in practice. Basically it was not envisaged that the gunner, loader and driver would initiate radio conversations. This was solely the task of the commander or the radio operator on his behalf. If the commander was absent – for example because he was attending a briefing or orders were being issued – the gunner, who was now responsible for the tank, was connected as the commander. The most common practice was for the top switch to be set to 'Bord' (intercom) and the one below to the left, to 'Funk und Bord' (radio and intercom), so that the commander could monitor Receiver 1 – the most important connection for him – and listen to, or instantly speak with, his immediate superiors (platoon or company commanders).

In contrast, it was important that the commanders in the command tanks listened in to both radio networks. It was only when simultaneous conversations came in that the radio operator either took over one of the two networks or the leader kept the callers waiting and took over the second network. The radio operator then concerned himself with the other network. If the leader was tied up, the radio operator answered for the commander, kept the remote station waiting or reported the contents of messages to him later. If necessary the leader renewed the connection himself at a later time. 'Intercom system B' was installed in the command vehicles.

> It enables on-board communication between the commander, intelligence officer (also acting as the gunner), radio operator 1, radio operator 2 and the driver. It is possible for the commander and the intelligence officer to operate switches on radio set 1 or set 2 to switch on the radio equipment of radio operator 1 or radio operator 2 and so operate the radios independently. To further mutual understanding, an illuminated signalling device is installed on the on-board intercom system housing.
>
> (D 9023/1 clause 10)

This too sounds more complicated than it was in reality. Here it must be clearly stated that every tactical leader – irrespective of their level – decided which configuration suited him best. This sometimes also depended on the tactical situation and how important it was that more than one radio network should be monitored by the leader.

The variations mentioned above demonstrate the flexibility of the system although it must be stressed once more that it was favoured by the fact that a 'full-time' radio operator was on board.

On the march – radio silence – the radio operator takes a break ...

The command tanks had an additional so-called 'star' antenna; as seen in this picture of the command tank belonging to *s.Pz.Abt. 507.*

The radio operator's main focus of activity was the equipment installed to his left. This picture shows the early version of the on-board intercom system with just a single transfer switch.

In the *Tigerfibel* on page 49 (see below), there is an overview of the electrical connections of the radio system.

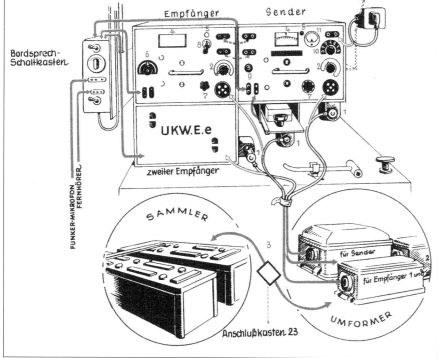

Page 48 of the *Tigerfibel* (see below) provides the radio operator with instructions on how to use the equipment (receiver, transmitter and how to transmit or receive Morse code).

The radio antenna rods were particularly sensitive and easily broken.

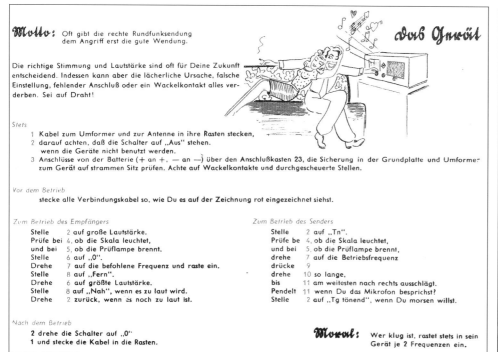

Motto: Oft gibt die rechte Rundfunksendung dem Angriff erst die gute Wendung.

Die richtige Stimmung und Lautstärke sind oft für Deine Zukunft entscheidend. Indessen kann aber die lächerliche Ursache, falsche Einstellung, fehlender Anschluß oder ein Wackelkontakt alles verderben. Sei auf Draht!

Stets
1 Kabel zum Umformer und zur Antenne in ihre Rasten stecken,
2 darauf achten, daß die Schalter auf „Aus" stehen.
 wenn die Geräte nicht benutzt werden.
3 Anschlüsse von der Batterie (+ an +, — an —) über den Anschlußkasten 23, die Sicherung in der Grundplatte und Umformer zum Gerät auf strammen Sitz prüfen. Achte auf Wackelkontakte und durchgescheuerte Stellen.

Vor dem Betrieb
 stecke alle Verbindungskabel so, wie Du es auf der Zeichnung rot eingezeichnet siehst.

Zum Betrieb des Empfängers
Stelle	2 auf große Lautstärke.
Prüfe bei	4, ob die Skala leuchtet,
und bei	5, ob die Prüflampe brennt.
Stelle	6 auf „0".
Drehe	7 auf die befohlene Frequenz und raste ein.
Stelle	8 auf „Fern".
Drehe	6 auf größte Lautstärke.
Stelle	8 auf „Nah", wenn es zu laut wird.
Drehe	2 zurück, wenn es noch zu laut ist.

Zum Betrieb des Senders
Stelle	2 auf „Tn".
Prüfe be	4, ob die Skala leuchtet,
und bei	5, ob die Prüflampe brennt,
drehe	7 auf die Betriebsfrequenz
drücke	9
drehe	10 so lange,
bis	11 am weitesten nach rechts ausschlägt.
Pendelt	11 wenn Du das Mikrofon besprichst?
Stelle	2 auf „Tg tönend", wenn Du morsen willst.

Nach dem Betrieb
 2 drehe die Schalter auf „0"
 1 und stecke die Kabel in die Rasten.

Moral: Wer klug ist, rastet stets in sein Gerät je 2 Frequenzen ein.

Crew Based Tasks

Rearming

While the evaluation of fuel requirements was based on either the distance to be travelled (while marching) or on 'intensity factors' that yielded empirical results, the planning and organizational effort required for the provision of ammunition was in comparison much greater because the amount of ammunition fired varied according to the intensity of combat or the number and type of targets. Basically, the battalions stated their requirements for consumable materials, such as oil and grease, and replacements for damaged components in in their daily reports. The distribution of these, particularly ammunition, had to be undertaken at unit or sub-unit level.

Generally speaking, *Verteilerpunkte* (distribution points) were established either at a logistics centres by the trucks delivering the ammunition or by 'dumping' the required amount. Then, according to their needs, individual crews collected the cartridges and ammunition belts – and other munitions – they required. In the event that their requirements could not be sufficiently fulfilled, the commanders of the units or sub-units decided the amount of ammunition to be distributed to each tank.

The command tanks of the company or battalion commanders always received rather less ammunition because their combat load was in any case less due to the installation of additional communications equipment (Tiger I: 66 8.8 cm rounds and 22 MG ammunition belts). In the Tiger II the two storage racks (each for 11 rounds) in the rear of the turret were usually not used because a direct hit taken in that area during combat had a devastating effect.

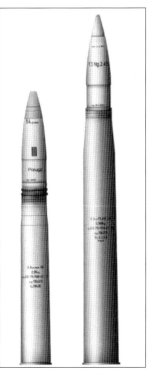

The rounds for the Tiger II cannon (here shown for comparison to the right of a Tiger I shell) were bigger and heavier with a corresponding impact on the tank's carrying capacity and handling.

The picture below shows a distribution point of *s.Pz.Abt. 503* on 23 April 1943; the crews are busy carrying out 'follow up ' work.

To be able to supply the forward positions, *s.Pz.Abt. 505* deployed reasonably well-protected converted former *Pz.Kpfw. IIIs*. This picture shows one of them supplying ammunition. (BA 278-0889-14)

Fuel was usually supplied in 20 litre containers. Sometimes these had to be lugged over considerable distances by the crew if the supply truck could not be driven alongside the tank, as in this picture taken on 5 June 1943 at *s.Pz. Abt. 503*. (Schmid)

In this picture tank '243' belonging to *s.Pz.Abt.503* is being refuelled from a 200 litre barrel with the help of a hand pump and hose in the spring of 1943.

Refuelling

Refuelling with petrol was not necessarily a difficult job but it was physically demanding. Usually – and to the dismay of the crews – fuel was supplied in 20-litre canisters. Only rarely could the supply truck drive up to the tank. In most cases they were dropped off away from roads in the countryside or woods. To this end, the trucks supplying fuel drove on passable routes from one drop-off point to the next (identified if possible by marker or a waiting messenger) and dumped the necessary, or allocated, amount of canisters before moving on to the next drop-off point until their tour was complete. On their return journey they recovered empty containers and stored them on the truck. In the meantime, the crew members developed *'lange Arme'* (long arms) carrying the canisters to their vehicles where the commander or the driver refuelled the tank.

The supply of fuel was clearly much easier if the supply truck could come directly alongside the tank with 200-litre barrels and the fuel pumped directly into the tank using a hose. If this was not practicable the barrel had to be rolled cross-country to the tank and manhandled onto its rear deck. Then a hand pump or the old method of *'Schlauch in denMund'* (hose in the mouth) [i.e. initiating a siphon by sucking the fuel into the hose by mouth] was used to refuel the tank.

For the sake of completeness, it also has to be stated that these measures were predominantly carried out under the cover of darkness!

Because the supply of fuel was difficult to organize on long marches, the tank units largely resorted to carrying one or two barrels on the tanks themselves, as is seen in this picture (taken during January 1944) of a column of tanks of *s.Pz.Abt. 503*. This enabled the regular supply through normal channels to be bridged while underway, or until they reached a new combat zone. (Müller-Nobiling)

It was a good deal more convenient if the fuel truck could stand alongside the tank and its crew to help with pumping, as is shown in this photograph – taken on 23 July 1943 – of a tank belonging to s.*Pz.Abt. 503*.

It suited the tank crew best of all if the fuel truck was equipped with an electric pump, such as is shown in this photograph taken on 12 April 1943 of another tank belonging to s.*Pz.Abt. 503*. (Wolff)

Resupply was a very unpleasant matter during extremely cold conditions as this picture of a tank belonging to s.*Pz. Abt. 503* in February 1944 shows; in the foreground is a 2-ton Maultier, a vehicle that was very agile in the snow.

Fuel was delivered in tanker wagons by rail and then transferred by the supply forces of larger military units (for example divisions or army corps) to barrels, canisters or other tanker vehicles before being taken to central distribution points to be collected by the supply detachments of the smaller units (pick-up, not delivery principle).

Refilling the canisters – an obligatory task that was both mind-numbing and important.
Below: The supply of sufficient drinking water to the troops was also a vitally important task (the canisters had a large white cross on them).

The 200-litre drums could also be filled or emptied with the help of a hand-cranked pump.

If one tank towed another (here the lead tank of *1./s.Pz.Abt 507.*), the cables were crossed to enable better manoeuvrability when negotiating curves. According to regulation D656/4, provision was made for the crossing point of the cables to be fixed by a shackle so that the cable not under tension did not sag.

This picture shows a tank belonging to *11./Pz.Rgt.'GD'* being towed with the cables attached in parallel, in other words wrongly.

Towing a tank on its bogie wheels was very cumbersome. The rolling resistance was high and this damaged the rubber tyres. In such circumstances the regulations allowed for a plank to be attached to the damaged side so that the tank could be pulled as if on a sled. This was however not a practical proposition.

Recovery and towing

The reasons for these activities were varied. In the course of active service this happened to every crew more or less frequently either because of technical problems, damage sustained during combat (for example by mines) or if the tank had become bogged down in the terrain, broken through ice or had even overturned.

If the vehicle was simply in an awkward situation, no extensive technical preparations by the crew were required because the vehicle simply had to be made mobile again.

The measures undertaken for towing over long distances were rather different; in this case a whole range of operational steps were performed to ensure that towing did not lead to serious consequential technical damage to the vehicle. These, and the work carried out on the running gear and tracks, are described in Chapter 3. The latter work was sometimes extensive and carried out if, as a result of damage caused by mines and projectiles, the vehicle first of all had to be made towable.

The Tiger was too much for a single Famo; here two of these indispensable towing vehicles are pulling together in double capstan mode.

The *Bergepanther*, powered by the same engine as the Tiger, was considerably more effective. The two shown here (an early and to its right the later version) belong to *s.Pz.Abt. 301 Fkl.*

Getting heavy tracked
vehicles stuck was not 'fate'
or unavoidable....

...but often the result of carelessness and erroneous assessment of the terrain!

The drivers and commanders of these two tanks belonging to *s.Pz.Abt. 504* were insufficiently attentive during a transit in darkness on 14 September 1944

The result of driver error on the bridge across the Lugo near Santerno on 13 April 1945. The picture shows a tank belonging to *s.Pz.Abt. 504.*

An error by a driver of *s.Pz. Abt. 505* on a narrow road running across a steep slope (5 December 1943).

The following series of pictures taken by *PK* (*Propaganda Kompanie*) correspondent Schmid, illustrate a tank recovery mission undertaken by *s.Pz. Abt. 503* on 4 October 1943.

In an attempt to cross the bed of a stream beside an unsuitable bridge, tank '332' was stuck and unable to free itself under its own power.

Fortunately the water depth was low and none flowed into the hull through the open driver's hatch. Nevertheless the tank is stuck fast up to the top of its tracks. Because the tracks were still turning, the driver was ordered to stop to prevent the tank digging itself deeper.

Help approaches in the form of tank '321', the driver of which must pay close attention to avoid becoming stuck himself. He drives up to the rear of the stricken vehicle whose crew is already preparing the towing cables.

It is always advisable to clear the churned-up mud to the side (right) in order to reduce the resistance to movement. Neither is it much fun exposing the towing eyes before attaching the rescue cables (see above).

The first cable is attached. In this situation this isn't sufficient because it could stretch or even rip under the strain.

The '301' is called over. Its towing cable is attached to the '321.' The two tanks form a 'towing train.'

Standing beside the driver of the first tank, and with the driver of the second tank in sight, the platoon leader has the tanks start their engines and slowly take up the slack on the towing cables. The engine of the stricken tank is started.

On command, the two towing vehicles start to pull. As soon as the driver of the bogged-down vehicle notices the tug, he accelerates to assist the freeing of his vehicle.

A view of the rescued tank; the crew check out the hull and running gear for damage. It is evident that the tank's hull had been sitting in the morass. This made freeing it under its own power an impossible task.

When tanks broke through bridges – this picture shows a vehicle belonging to *s.Pz. Abt. 502* on 23 November 1943 in the vicinity of Putoschka – rescue efforts could take days. On the left of the picture an obliquely oriented approach for the rescue vehicles has already been excavated. (Lohmann)

This vehicle had overturned and lay upside down. In most cases, when a tank was restored to the upright position, the turret separated from the hull causing damaged to the slewing ring, control rods and connecting pipes that required great efforts to repair. (Lohmann)

If something like this happened during an evasive manoeuver – in this case during an attempted crossing of a bridge near Brachelen by a tank belonging to *s.Pz.Abt. 301Fkl* on 24 December 1944 – rescue was no longer conceivable.

If a tank got stuck diagonally in mud or gravel – this picture shows tank '114' of *s.Pz.Abt. 507* on 20 April 1944 – the tracks usually ran off the tank.

They then had to be excavated and opened. Luckily the whole platoon helped with this.

When the track was opened it was laid out in front of the tank so that it could be pulled onto it by another vehicle.

Picture number 7 from regulation document D656/4 shows the attachment of a so-called '*Kletterbaum*' (climbing tree) in front of the two track lanes. Often, a bogged-down vehicle could be freed from muddy ground under its own power by this means. Later, special brackets were delivered for attaching the wires; it was no longer necessary to laboriously run around the towing cables and the fixings were better.

This diagram from the previously mentioned document shows how complex rescue missions were at times.
Because it was not unusual for the towing cables to snap, it was forbidden to enter the danger zone.

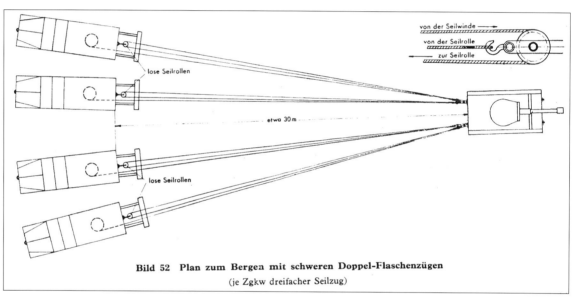

Bild 52 Plan zum Bergen mit schweren Doppel-Flaschenzügen
(je Zgkw dreifacher Seilzug)

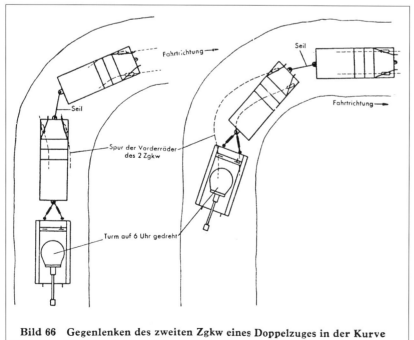

Bild 66 Gegenlenken des zweiten Zgkw eines Doppelzuges in der Kurve

Diagram 52 shows the arrangement for undertaking recovery using heavy duty winding tackle (each towing vehicle with a triple cable arrangement).

Driving in a towing column required a degree of skill. The driver of the second towing vehicle had to sweep further outwards on curves than the lead vehicle. It was for this reason that usually only one cable linked the two Famos.

Diagram 66 shows the path taken by the second towing truck on bends.

Major earthworks had to be performed in order to let the '132' of *s.Pz.Abt. 510* to get through! (Gilbert)

The '114' commanded by *Unteroffizier* Alfred Rubbel of *s.Pz. Abt. 503* is being towed away by only two instead of the prescribed three Famos during *Unternehmen 'Zitadelle'*.

Towing with the help of the 18-ton half-track was generally carried out using a towing bar. This facilitated steering movements. It is noteworthy too that on this vehicle belonging to *s.Pz.Abt. 507* – the picture was taken during December 1944 – the anti-aircraft MG is ready for use.

After the transport track had been laid out at the rear of this tank of the *III./ Pz.Rgt. 'GD,'* it is pulled into position by the tank's own power. (Photograph taken at the end of July 1944)

A scene captured on 10 November 1942 at *s.Pz. Abt. 501*; the outer bogie wheels have been removed (see bottom right of picture) but are waiting to be loaded. A crane heaves the combat tracks onto a rail truck. (Zorn)

It was most convenient if at the station the rail trucks could run up to so-called *Kopframpen* (roll-on-roll-off ramps) so that the tanks could drive off on a level surface. This picture shows the delivery of a new tank for the *'501'* in August 1942 in Fallingbostel; the crates contain the vehicle's tool kit (Zorn)

Loading for Rail Transport

To protect the tanks' mechanisms and to save fuel, the units took every possible opportunity to relocate by rail. Depending on the urgency of the situation this might even be for stretches of only 20 km. A striking feature of the Tiger series as far as loading onto rail transport was concerned was that, because of their excessive width, not only their side-mounted mud aprons but also the protruding combat tracks had to be removed and narrower transport tracks put in their place. The transport tracks were supposed to have been shipped with the tanks on board the six-axel flatbed rail trucks but had to be cleaned and maintained by the crews currently using them. For the first version of the running gear, the outer bogie wheels also had to be removed. The procedure for this is described in the section relating to work on the running gear in Chapter 3.

For express shipments, or if no traffic coming from the opposite direction was expected, the change of tracks was omitted.

Loading and unloading the tanks without a secure roll-on-roll-off ramp, or even a side ramp, presented a special challenge under field conditions. There was in fact a suitable design of ramp available that was also intermittently used on active service. In emergencies, loading with the aid of auxiliary devices, or sometimes even embankments, easily led to the tank overturning and to damage to the rail truck.

The process of loading onto rail trucks can most clearly be illustrated with the aid of photographs. There was ample time to take photographs because some of the crew had nothing to do during the actual loading.

With the transport tracks fitted, the tank protruded only a small amount at the sides. Loading damaged tanks (see below) was a challenge. These had to be pulled onto the rail trucks by towing vehicles.

Loading sideways was a successful technique as this picture taken on 8 October 1943 at *s.Pz.Abt. 502* illustrates.

1942 A r t	Fabrikat und Type	Verlade-Klasse	Eigen-gewicht	Reifengrösse *gew.*	Lade	Fahrbe-reich km
Pzkw.	III (Sd. Kfz.268)Bef.wg.	23 t				
	III (Sd. Kfz.141)	23 t				100
	VI H(Sd. Kfz.182)	SSYMS-Wagen				100
K r ä d e r	le. Krad			3,25–19		300
	m. Krad					
	s. Krad			120–16		250
	s. Krad m. Beiwg. ·		*4,.*	120–16		250
Pkw.	le. Pkw.	II				300
	Tr.Luftschutz-Kw.(Kfz.4)	II	*1610*		*1,3*	350
	le.gl.Pkw.(Kfz. 1)	II	*615*	525–16		400
	ChN Schwimmwg.Pkw.(Kfz.1/20	II				
	kl.Inst.Wg.(Kfz.2/40)	II	*11.*	550–16	*600*	320
	m.gl.Pkw.(Kfz.15)	II	*105.*	190–18		400
	Kr.Kw.(kfz.31)	II		700–20		400
	Flakmannsch.Kw.(Kfz.81)	II	*1700*	210–18		350
Lkw.	le. Lkw.	I b				
	le.gl. Lkw.	I b		32–6DB		
	m.gl.Lkw.(3t A Typ)	I b	*3,6*	190–20	*0,6*	300
	m.Lkw. (3t S Typ)	I b		190–20	*2,5*	300
	s.gl.Lkw.(4 1/2t A Typ)	I	*5,3*	270–20	*10,0*	300
	s.Lkw. (4 1/2t S Typ)	I	*5,2*	270–20		300
	Nachr.Werkst.Kw.Kfz.42)	I	*5,5*			300
	Sammler Kw.(Kfz.42)	I	*6,0*		*0,*	300
	Drehkran-Kw,3t(Kfz.100)	I				300
	Drehkran.Kw.6t(Sd.Kfz.9/1)	I				
Kom.	m. Kom.	I a		32–6		300
Zgkw.	le.Zgkw.1t(Sd.Kfz.10)	II				
	s.Zgkw.18t(Sd.Kfz.9) (Leergewicht 15,8 t)	I mindes Lg.825m	*15,8*	12,75–20		260
	m.Kr.Pz.Wg.(Sd.Kfz.251/8)	II				300
Anhänger	s.Masch.Stz.A(Sd.Anh.24)	III		7,25–20		
	Anh.f.sa.ger.d.(Sd." 23)	IV				
	Masch.Satz.f.Schweiss.					
	Tiefladeanh.10t(Sd.Kfz.115)					
	Tiefladeanh.60t(Sd.Kfz.121)20t			*13.50–20*		
	Sd.Anh.1 achs.(Sd.Anh.51)	IV		6,00–20		
	Portalkran 16t lg.15,4m	S				

Kraftstoffverbrauch 100 km Str.		S o l l						I s t				
		Stab	St.Kp.	1.Kp.	2Kp.	W.Kp.		Stab	St.Kp.	1.Kp.	2.Kp.	W.Kp.
	1		1									
300	25		5	10	10							
600	20		2	9	9							
4												
	17	2	14			1						
10	6			3	3							
	14	1	9	2	2							
17	1	1										
17	1				1	1						
8	34	1	12	6	6	9						
	1		1									
13	3		1	1	1							
25	8	3	2	1	1	1						
35	1		1									
35	9		9									
	1	1										
	1					1						
D 25	9		3	2	2	2						
D 25												
D 35	76		30	7	7	32						
D 35												
D35	1					1						
	1					1						
D 35	5			1	1							
120	3					3						
D 30	2					2						
40	6		2	2	2							
120	10					10						
50	1		1									
	2					2						
	1					1						
	2					2						
	2					2						
	3					3						
	6		6									

This interesting, original document from 1942 is an overview of the vehicles available to the commander of Staff Company '501' and includes their carrying capacity and weight categories. The actual inventory numbers are written in pencil and are difficult to read. The table also lists the fuel consumption.

Often the troops had to 'throw up' makeshift ramps before loading could take place as in this photograph taken in April 1944 at *s.Pz. Abt.502*. (BA 726-225-27)

Unloading to the side was exceptionally difficult in the absence of ramps as is shown in this photograph, taken on 23 September 1942, of a tank belonging to *1./s.Pz.Abt. 502*.

After 1943 a demountable roll-on-roll-off ramp was made available. This could be pulled back by the tank after unloading and then dismantled.

These two pictures show vehicles at the *Tigerlehrgänge* in Paderborn as training for using the demountable ramps takes place. It was important that the tank approached the ramp in an exactly straight line and then drove slowly upwards without making steering movements.

Then came the exciting moment when the tank tipped onto the rail truck! This picture shows a demonstration by a tank of *s.Pz.Abt. 501* in November 1943 in the eastern theatre of war.

This tank belonging to the '*502*' is carefully crossing over a gap between rail trucks as it moves towards its 'own' place on the train – difficult if on a curve. (BA 726-225-36)

The marshal standing to the side of the rail truck points to the mark at its mid-point so that the vehicle is driven as closely as possible halfway over it.

The tank was then prevented from rolling off by batons (above) or – better – by wooden wedges (left) that had been prepared earlier.

Finally, securing cables were attached to all four towing eyes and pulled tight. This picture shows a tank belonging to *s.Pz.Abt. 503* on 11 April 1943.

The cables were tensioned crossing each other in order to secure the tank against lateral movements of the rail truck. The emblem of the *'503'* on the front right of the hull casing has been censored by *PK* photographer Baumann. Note the searchlight on the top left of the turret. (Baumann)

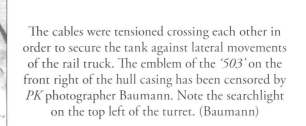

The cannon lashings were attached, the hatches closed and protective covers put over the muzzle of the cannon and the bow MG. This picture shows a vehicle belonging to the *'503'* in December 1942 after being loaded in Göpfritz.

Incorrect mounting of the forward restraint beam by the *1./s.Pz.Abt. 502* in September 1942; also, the cables have not been crossed over.

The railway loading official sometimes used a loading gauge or rod as in this picture taken at the *'508'* in September 1944.

The SSyms rail trucks had wooden planks that allowed the wooden wedges or beams to be fixed to them with large nails. Adjustable restraint rails improved lateral stability. The picture shows the arrival of a new tank for the *'501'* in August 1942 in Fallingbostel.

Personnel were seldom transported in passenger coaches; usually cattle wagons were used for this purpose – as in this picture of the *13./SS-Pz.Rgt. 1 'LAH'*.

The combat tracks were stored under the tank during transit as is shown with this tank belonging to *s.Pz.Abt.510* (notice the wooden support rack for the barrel).... (Gilbert) ...or disassembled for transport on a separate rail truck, as is shown in the picture to the right, (taken in the station in Krakow in March 1943) with new '*503*' tanks.. (Rubbel)

It was standing orders that between every rail truck loaded with a Tiger, another truck was added to better distribute the braking load. In this picture – taken on 5 May 1944 in Orleans – the rule is being obeyed by *s.Pz.Abt.504* but it was also very frequently negated.

Der Generalinspekteur der   Geheim   H.Qu. OKH, den 28. 9. 1943
Panzertruppen
Gr. Org Ia   Nr.4861/43 g.

Bezug: Gen St d H /Chef Transpw.
       Az.43 f 18.02 E 6/Verk.Abt.(V.2)   - 6. Okt. 1943
       Nr.3824/43 geh. v.22.9.43.   17.00

Betr.: Verladeketten f.Pz.Kpfw.Tiger.

       nachr.:   An

                     Heeresgruppe   Nord

1.) Der Pz.Kw " Tiger " wird bis zu einer bestimmten Ferti-
    gungszahl mit Gefechts-und mit Verladeketten ausgestattet.
    Beide Kettenarten sind Ausrüstungsstücke der Panzerkampf-
    wagen.

2.) Hieran ändert nichts die in der D 659/2a -"Merkblatt zum
    Verladen von Gleiskettenfahrzeugen auf der Eisenbahn"-
    befohlene Regelung, wonach nach Ausladung des Pz.Kw.
    " Tiger " die Verladeketten auf dem SSyms-Wagen unterzu-
    bringen sind und als Bestand des SSyms-Wagen zu gelten
    haben.

3.) Die Wartung der Verladeketten ist somit Sache der Panzer-
    truppe (Tigerabteilungen), nicht der Eisenbahndienst-
    stellen. Nach Ausladung im Einsatzgebiet, ist es daher
    Pflicht der Truppe , die Verladeketten verwendungsbereit
    - d.h. gesäubert, ordnungsgemäß zusammengesetzt und voll-
    ständig (96 Kettenglieder) - auf dem SSyms-Wagen zu
    verladen.

4.) Die Kommandeure der Tigerabteilungen bezw. Kp.-Chefs der
    Tiger-Kp., deren Panzer-Kampfwagen auf der Eisenbahn trans-
    portiert werden oder denen Pz.Kpfwg. "Tiger" zugeführt
    werden, haben sich von den Transportführern verantwortlich
    melden zu lassen, daß die Bestimmungen der D 659/2a und
    vorstehender Befehl genauestens durchgeführt sind.

5.) Bei der Truppe noch vorhandene 520 mm breite Verladeketten
    sind umgehend dem für den Einsatzbereich zuständigen Gen.
    d. Transportw. über die BvTO der Armeen zur Verfügung zu
    stellen.

                                Der Chef des Stabes.

The original intention was that the tank units would transport both types of track with them – and encounter corresponding transport problems! After many complaints from the troops, this requirement was finally changed on 23 September 1943 after which the transport tracks remained on the rail trucks.

Often enough the crew had to 'make themselves comfortable' behind their tank during transit as this picture of members of the *III./Pz.Rgt. 'GD'* demonstrates. (BA 732-0133-34)

The ideal situation was when all the tracked and wheeled vehicles could be accommodated on the same transport train – as in this picture of the *Sd.Kfz. 251*s of *s.SS-Pz.Abt. 103*.

The issue of meals from the kitchen was a highlight during stops (bottom left). The anti-aircraft weapons were kept ready for action; in this picture – taken on 25 June 1944 – by soldiers belonging to *s.Pz.Abt. 505*.

Towards the end of the war transport took place under danger from the air, hence the extensive camouflage of this train carrying *s.Pz.Abt. 508* in September 1944 as it travels to Forlimpopoli. Consequently, *Flak-Vierlinge* (four-barrelled anti-aircraft guns) are in position as the unloading proceeds.

After unloading the process of changing the tracks gets underway…again. There is a lack of space but this tank belonging to *s.Pz.Abt. 505* finds a suitable spot in Kortrijksesteenweg in Beverloo, on 26 April 1943, to pull on its combat tracks that have been secured to the front with cables. (Webers)

This crew from the '*LAH*' (*Leibstandarte Adolf Hitler*), after receiving a new tank in Italy, is removing the bolts on the running gear and side-apron brackets so that the bogie wheels and chain skirting can then be mounted. (Wendt)

Long transits in harsh winter conditions were problematic. It sometimes took greater efforts to make the tank mobile again (see the section relating to operations in winter). Notice also the letters 'SNCF' (French National Railway) at the bottom right of the picture.

Steering errors on the rail trucks could end badly, as in this picture taken on 12 August 1944 of a train transporting the *3./s. Pz.Abt. 503.* (von Rosen).

During stops (below) all fastenings were checked.

Otherwise (bottom left) the crews had little to do, as in this picture of members of the *'502'* taken on 3 July 1944.

Narrow waterways were usually crossed using ferry boats. The picture above shows a tank belonging to the '504' crossing the Straits of Messina on 17 August 1943. An impressive picture… not really…just excellent work by model makers in this case!

Another possibility (fufilled by engineer units) was linking pontoon boats as in this photograph of a tank belonging to the '506' as it is ferried across the River Dnjepr close to Saporoschje on 15 January 1943. The ferry was pushed by a barge with an outboard engine (to the left in the picture); paddles were used to help steering movements. On the river bank, a rescue detachment stands at the ready with a boat.

If the river bank on the landing side was too steep, a pier was constructed from pontoons so that the tanks could drive up the river bank without difficulty.

Transport Across Water

To complement the previous section this topic will now be considered briefly.

Crossing major waterways with a Tiger unit required substantial technical and planning effort. Actual sea transport was only ever carried out when relocating the *501* and *502* units to Tunisia. The transport of the *2./s. Pz.Abt. 504* to and from Sicily (during April 1943 and on 17 August 1943 respectively) had been less of an effort.

In the west as well as in the east, the problem was mainly crossing large rivers that were simply too wide for pioneer units to build bridges across. The deployment of suitable ships and ferry boats then came into consideration. The smaller transport tracks – just as with rail transport – had to be carried on barges.

River crossings were made more difficult because they were mostly carried out under the cover of darkness. However, special provisions or training of the crews for this seldom to took place.

Transport by ship required great effort. This picture – taken on 20 November 1942 in Reggio – shows *s.Pz.Abt. 501* as it prepares to board. The unit's embarkation was favoured by the port's existing infrastructure. Nevertheless, – and under the strict scrutiny of the navy loading master – great precision was required when boarding. The tanks retain their combat tracks but the crews had to remove the side aprons. (pictures: Zorn)

When boarding it had to be borne in mind that the ship would settle deeper in the water because of the weight and that the tank was not permitted to drive too quickly. Once on board, the tank had to park exactly in the mid-line of the ship before it was secured with wedges to prevent it sliding in heavy seas. (pictures: Zorn)

Lighter vehicles could be loaded into the ship's hold by crane without any problems. (Weber)

The navy artillery lighters were fairly suitable as tank ferries, as in this photograph of a training exercise by *s.Pz.Abt. 505* on 3 April 1943 on the River Schelde.

If there were no quays were available, aids to gaining the shore had to be constructed.

Loading wheeled vehicles onto barges was much simpler.

In the absence of the enemy the crossing can now be enjoyed. Notice the anti-tank gun (*Pak*) with ground spurs as it stands by to engage targets at sea.

Tanks had to be loaded backwards onto small navy lighters so that they would be able drive out forwards when they reached their destination. This picture – taken on 18 December 1942 – shows tank '142' of *s.Pz.Abt. 501*.

This picture shows a tank belonging to *s.Pz.Abt.504* on 9 March 1943 in Trapani. The tight gap is easily seen; great care had to be taken not to damage the lighter!

The tracks had to be changed before and after loading; the effort required for this has already been described.

5 Tactics

General

Throughout the ages a great many books have been written in which military tactics are described. The number of books that have failed to address this issue is almost as great. The thematic spectrum covers (autobiographical) accounts of operations and battles written by military leaders and descriptions of personal experiences by individual combatants. In these works we generally find precious little about tactics in the strict sense of the term. A battle is a series military encounters each of which might – or might not – proceed according to tactical principles. The description of individual acts should not be committed to paper in terms of tactically correct (or incorrect) conduct because luck and bravery can lead to success even though this is achieved through tactically erroneous acts.

From this it follows that tactics are played out at a particular (lower) level of command and that there are tactical rules of conduct that can be learned and which are therefore the subject of (intensive) military training. This applies particularly to exact descriptions of easily applicable knowledge for fulfilling actual orders…the 'how to.' Many military regulations fall somewhat short in this respect; all too often they merely list 'the what' of what is to be done. With regard to the *Wehrmacht*, this deficit was bridged during the course of the war by numerous information sheets (*Merkblätter*) issued through official channels but also by the units themselves. The information presented in monthly reports was helpful as were the combat and field reports prepared by individual unit leaders. However, the correct conclusions were not always drawn from these.

Many authors made do with filling pages with quotes of regulations without analysing specific tactical principles; 'official' reports were copied without considering that they had been 'sweetened up' and often without deriving any fundamental information from them. Strictly speaking, sketchy presentations of 'formations and movements' (wedge formations, cordons, double rows etc.) are not descriptions of 'tactics' in the real sense of the word but are merely methodical aids for clarifying the principles of proper conduct to leaders undergoing training (troop dispersal, mutual observation, security and observation zones, allocation of areas and such like).

The (still inexperienced) leaders therefore more or less gain only theoretical knowledge the use of which must then be illustrated by practical training. This is done in several stages by: familiarization with the terrain (without large equipment), using sand boxes (and nowadays by combat simulation), by actual combat training with positional referencing and through 'enemy' roll play within the (sub-) unit.

During this, the (technical) performance of their own and the enemy's weapons, the extent of a threat and their ability to respond to it in a tactically appropriate manner, exert great influence.

In summary, it can be said that a commander in chief, within the context of his operational command, can issue orders to his unit leaders at a subordinate level without himself being acquainted with the tactical details. These subordinate leaders were obliged to have mastery of the tactical details because they were required for the fulfilment of missions on the local scale ('*im Kleinen*'). And furthermore: in combined arms combat, that is to say at the level of reinforced formations – battalions, detachments or regiments and later *Kampfgruppen* (battle groups) – it is necessary that all leaders from company level upwards know the deployment principles of the supporting branches in order to be able to assess the extent to which they might contribute to the successful execution of a mission while bearing in mind their strengths and limitations.

The aim of this chapter is to make clear the special tactical parameters that arose with the deployment of the Tiger battle tank. The technical knowledge of the tactically correct deployment of armoured forces in a Panzer III unit was, in principle, no different from one that was equipped with Tiger tanks. I [the author] explain the principles of German tank tactics in my book *Panzertaktik* which covers the period from 1935 to the present and these need not be repeated at this point. *Merkblatt 47a/29, Ausbildung und Einsatz der schweren Panzerkompanie Tiger* (training and deployment of Tiger heavy tank companies), explicitly and clearly highlights:

'19. For the leadership of a heavy tank company, the principles of leadership for a medium tank company are in general valid.'

In this chapter, the particular experience and knowledge gained in relation to the deployment of Tiger units, or better said *Kampfgruppen*, are illustrated, as are the specific technical and logistical requirements that are inextricably interwoven with the deployment of a technically sophisticated weapons system.

In this section, images do the talking by providing detailed explanations through visual examples. Where appropriate, informative passages from surviving (combat) reports submitted by Tiger units and *Merkblätter* are quoted.

Most of the kilometres covered by German tank units were by land marches whether in spring – as in this picture of a column of the '*507*' taken 15 April 1944 (above) – or in snow and ice. The picture to the right shows a tank belonging to the '*502*' at Putoschka on 19 January 1944.

Spring 1944: the range of these tanks of the '*506*' is extended by the 200-litre barrels they carry.

General Combat Tasks

These tasks are indispensable for the conduct of successful operations and the self-protection of the units.

Marches

Planning and implementing marches was a particularly challenging task for the Tiger units. Because the Tiger battle tank was subject to significantly greater wear because of its weight, special measures and regulations were required.

Merkblatt 47a/30 (which describes the 'deployment of Tiger heavy tank units) goes into this in some detail:

1. As a weapon intended for deployment at the focal point of combat the Tiger units are mostly incorporated at the front of march formations.
2. March routes are to be selected by the leadership with great care.
3. Detailed scouting is the responsibility of unit commanders. Reconnaissance and preparation of bridges, fords and narrow sections on the route are of particular importance. The detailed study of maps and the evaluation of existing photographs is required, as is the timely insertion of the scouting and engineer platoon.
4. For march-technical reasons, Tiger units are not to be coupled with other tank units on long marches.
5. To cross bridges of unknown carrying capacity it is preferable to use light tanks with their immediate combat supplies before Tigers.
6. Average speed on marches: by day: 10–15 km per hour by night: 7–10 km per hour.
7. Frequent technical halts are essential. Technical halts are to be ordered after the first 5 km and thereafter every 10–15 km.
8. Roads with a large camber and hard cobble stones are to be avoided.

The following requirements were repeated in the company *Merkblatt* – probably because of their extreme importance – along with two additional items of advice:

21. Tiger companies are not to march as part of motorized and tank units over long distances, particularly in unknown terrain. Bridges and narrow passes might pose obstacles for the Tiger that would jeopardise the fluidity of the march of the whole unit.

22. On night marches – especially on dark nights – it is appropriate for one of the crew members to sit on the outer front corner of the tank's track cover so that he can instruct the driver through his open hatch.

The latter of these pieces of advice is particularly noteworthy because it was unusual to give such detail about the training of the crews in regulations for the tank commanders.

Relatively rigid regulations such as these reflect the bitter experience gained during the early deployment of the Tiger and demonstrate that these vehicles were brought into service before the provision of time and resources for intensive testing that could have yielded this knowledge at an early stage.

In this respect, it is important for the reader to realize that the ordered speed of a march is not the same as the driving speed of individual tanks. As a result of curves, inclines, the negotiation of narrow points in the route and such like, individual vehicles frequently have to reduce their speed and so fall behind temporarily until they are able to speed up. Their speed therefore increases in phases thereby producing a sort of 'concertina-like effect' within the column with the result that the vehicles bringing up the rear often have to drive faster than the ordered marching speed.

Of course in practice, it was occasionally necessary to travel faster than usual to reach a hotspot. Also, in combat it was often necessary to cross areas without cover as quickly as possible in order to expose the tanks for the shortest possible time to enemy observation and fire.

Over-stressing the engines for extended periods of time – regardless of wear and tear – inevitably caused overheating and the disproportionate use of lubricating oil and fuel. This was particularly evident during periods of high temperatures on the Eastern Front and in Tunisia and Italy.

Common reasons for driving at moderate speeds were the avoidance of too much noise (for example at night) and the formation of conspicuous dust clouds. In addition, the notable impact [of marches] on care and maintenance and logistics are explained in the following sections of this work.

The consideration in advance of how water obstacles and emplacements would be crossed or driven through; the use of existing bridges (or ones built by the engineers) and the means of crossing (such as ferries) was of particular importance (see 'Cooperation with the Engineers').

It was inappropriate to permit Tiger columns to march alongside wheeled vehicles. These were generally separated – as in this picture of vehicles belonging to *s.Pz.Abt. 506* – to allow steady driving speeds to be ordered.

The use of radios was forbidden during marches to prevent passing information to enemy reconnaissance. Messages (with the exception of hand signals) were therefore passed on with the help of runners – as in this photo taken on 11 August 1943 – or by means of motorcycle dispatch riders – as shown (below) in this picture taken on 5 June 1943 during a march by *s.Pz.Abt. 503*.

The standard gap between vehicles was 50 m as shown above by a column of the *'502'* in February 1944 (BA 458-79-5). During snowstorms the vehicles travelled closer together so as not to lose contact with each other (picture to the right) as in this column belonging to the *'501'* on 15 March 1944. In dusty conditions, bigger gaps were left so as not to bump into the vehicle in front. The picture below shows a tank belonging to the *'502'* during September 1943.

When there was a danger of an air attack the radio operator – sitting on the tank's hull – was often used as an air observer, as in this picture (taken on 18 March 1943 as the *'504'* marched towards Sfax). (BA 787-510-5a)

The picture below shows the 'solution' of the *'501'* on 24 November 1942. (BA 418-1841-13)

When there was imminent danger of enemy contact (the picture below shows the *'501'* on 22 March 1944) an advance platoon was deployed about half an hour in advance which, if it ran into the enemy resistance either broke it or took up position and warned the column's leader by radio.

It was best to avoid clumping together during hold ups (the picture above shows the *'501'* on 12 March 1944) – or tailgating when at a halt as in this picture (left) of *s.Pz. Abt. 424* in August 1944.

Winding roads and ones through defiles were a problem, particularly when it was dark. This picture shows *2./s. SSPz. Abt. 101* on 8 June 1944. (Scheck)

The gap between vehicles was maintained during halts basically for reasons of dispersal, as in this picture of a column of the *'501'* on the way to Jedeida on 25 November 1942 (BA 557-1018-11a), – unless there was the possibility of suitable cover as seen in the picture to the right (taken on 23 November 1942 after leaving Bizerta) which also shows a vehicle belonging to the *'501.'*

Stops had to be made such that other columns could pass. This picture shows a column of the *'502'* in February 1944. (BA 458-78-35)

Two pictures of the march of *s.Pz.Abt. 503* towards Bogoduchow on 12 April 1943 are shown here. Halts were an opportunity to examine the suspension or take on supplies (below). Notice the makeshift trailer on the Tiger of the commandgroup.

During longer halts (below) the drive components were checked – in this case of a tank (with an open engine cover) belonging to *s.Pz.Abt. 503* on 5 June 1943. Platoon leader *Leutnant* Weinert reports possible damage. (Fotos: Rubbel)

Further scenes from the march of the *'503'* on 12 April 1943: here an advance detachment of *3. Kompanie* (with its car at the side of the road) having encountered a bridge with insufficient carrying capacity are taking a detour reconnoitred by marshalling personnel. Matters are much simpler in such instances if routes for 'heavy loads and tracked vehicles' are already signposted.

The tank man is always wary – even on bridges that have been approved for use. Never drive across with two tanks at the same time!

Scepticism was often enough well
founded as these pictures of an
engineer bridging point for the
Pz.Gren.Div. 'Großdeutschland'
show before (right)…

… and after a crossing (below)

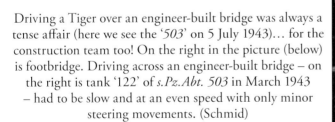

Driving a Tiger over an engineer-built bridge was always a
tense affair (here we see the '503' on 5 July 1943)… for the
construction team too! On the right in the picture (below)
is footbridge. Driving across an engineer-built bridge – on
the right is tank '122' of s.Pz.Abt. 503 in March 1943
– had to be slow and at an even speed with only minor
steering movements. (Schmid)

Only one tank at a time is permitted to cross a water obstacle (like this one belonging to the *'501'* on 12 January 1943). The picture below shows Tigers of the *'506'* crossing the Strypa on 7 April 1944 – wrongly. This would make vehicle recovery difficult in the event of a breakdown.

When travelling in the water itself, an even pressure is applied to the accelerator so that the vehicle does not falter; this would risk getting bogged down. (Zeller)

It so happened that the exit point lay upstream; the picture shows a tank of the *'503'* in June 1943.

A route marshal receives the column at the destination (the picture above shows tanks of the '502') to make sure they don't take a wrong turning. The guide can also ride on the lead tank – the picture on the left shows a tank of the '508' – to pilot the commander directly to his destination. At the destination – for tanks of the '501' on 12 March 1944 (below) this was a village – the aim was to perform a rapid inspection and clear the roadway.

Before undertaking marches or missions, scout detachments should be deployed. Here, *Oberleutnant* Scherf of the *'503'* briefs *Oberfähnrich* Rondorf and *Hauptfeldwebel* Burgis with the appropriate orders. (Wunderlich)

The choice of position and approach routes in attack and in defence also require thorough evaluation. Here, on 22 January 1943, *Major* Lueder briefs the leader of the subordinated grenadiers and *Leutnant* von Bredow (holding a wood-bound combat map). (Lueder)

The key to success is constant observation of the battlefield by the leader; this picture shows a commander of the *4./SS- Pz.Rgt. 1.* (BA 93-82-20)

Reconnaissance and Scouting

Tactical reconnaissance – by the units in combat themselves – and operational reconnaissance (for example, aerial reconnaissance) are essential prerequisites for all tank units whether they are operating within the framework of a battlegroup or within their own unit.

Because reconnaissance measures often require long-range movements and should largely go unnoticed by the enemy, this, in principal, suggests that they should be undertaken by specially trained and appropriately equipped troops. This was classically the task of armoured reconnaissance units with their wheeled armoured fighting vehicles and light battle tanks – the so-called '*Spähaufklärung*' units (rapidly mobile scouting patrols). In addition there were *Pionieraufklärung* (engineer reconnaissance) units that reconnoitred barriers and obstacles such as, for example, waterways.

The combat units had their own reconnaissance platoons for these tasks (see 'Organizational structure'). Because the Tiger heavy combat tanks could be heard over a considerable distance they were unsuitable for such missions and this was consistently stated in the above mentioned *Merkblatt*:

> It is forbidden to assign Tiger tanks missions that can be carried out by light tanks or assault guns and, likewise, they are not to be entrusted with safeguarding or reconnaissance tasks.

This basically coherent ban sometimes had far-reaching consequences. Firstly, attacks without sufficient reconnaissance were ordered. Secondly, inexperienced Tiger leaders took the point of view that their own reconnaissance measures were not called for. This carelessness – and the overestimation of their weapons system – frequently led to missions failing to make an impact (for example against deeply staggered defensive installations) or to the occurrence of drastic, but avoidable, losses.

This ban in no way affected reconnaissance measures carried out at the lowest levels – that is to say battlefield observation by everyone – nor the so-called '*Gefechtsaufklärung*' (combat reconnaissance). The regulation of the latter was the responsibility of the tank company and its purposes were to prevent being surprized by the enemy; to enable movements to be carried out in suitable terrain and to direct its own thrust at the correct point.

On marches in uncertain situations, the deployment of vanguards and lead platoons came into consideration; detachments acted in the manner of reconnaissance scouts and monitored the flanks in order to detect enemy attacks in good time. Unlike long-range reconnaissance which penetrated to a depth of 20 km or more, *Gefechtsaufklärung* was carried out within the immediate few kilometres.

It was the Tiger units' responsibility to 'scout' their own routes. This involved finding expedient stopping places in the assembly areas, or covered positions, as well as (march) routes.

A catchy description for the requirements for reconnaissance can be found in a report by *s.Pz.Abt. 503* on the 12 April 1943:

1. Scouting inbound routes and the terrain is necessary. Take advantage of every rest, every halt, to push on with reconnoitring. Create a '*Straßen-bildkarte*' (maps on which every scouted road with bridges and crossings and so on are marked to make available a picture of all passable and impassable roads). Scouting should not only be carried out on the roads and terrain leading to the enemy but to all the sides too. Reconnoitre anew after each change in the weather, particularly in winter.
2. If scouting groups do not have personnel with sufficient technical knowledge, assign to them an engineer.
2. Always pass on the results of scouting missions to the headquarters ordering the deployment of Tigers.

On the basis of information gleaned by scouting missions, give not only the objective but also the exact route of march for individual Tigers driving to the front or rear (sketches with the route, road junctions and the names of settlements). [This avoids] getting stuck, large detours, higher fuel consumption and [the need for] lengthy search missions. Mark danger points on the sketches (bridges, fords).

Since the use of the Tiger for reconnaissance purposes was somewhat inappropriate, the units had an armoured reconnaissance platoon. This picture shows *Oberfeldwebel* Fischer of *s.Pz.Abt. 502* with his vehicles in September 1943 as they prepare to depart.

Results were transmitted by radio or personally as shown in this picture (taken on 6 April 1944) – also of the *'502'* – during its deployment in the *'Ostsack'* [a bridgehead on the east bank of the River Narva]

Here a tank commander of the *'503'* searches a shot-up enemy tank for documents, maps and such like. Such items were sometimes very useful for German reconnaissance.

The light platoons of earlier units were clearly more suited for reconnaissance missions. In this picture taken on 18 January 1943 we see Panzer IIIs of *s.Pz.Abt. 501* at Djebel.

Tiger tanks were also used for reconnaissance patrol tasks over short distances to maintain contact with the enemy, as in this photo of two vehicles belonging to *s.Pz.Abt. 501* taken on 22 March 1943. (BA 278-884-22)

During large-scale operations such as '*Zitadelle*' (this picture, taken in July 1943, shows a tank belonging to the '*503*') it was very important to undertake reconnaissance of the flanks to prevent being surprised by the enemy. (Lochmann)

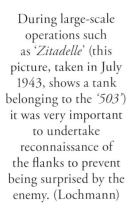

Everyone had to keep a look out, even truck crews. This picture from early August 1944 shows a member of the '*503*' in in Mailly-le-Camp. (Wunderlich)

Keeping a lookout in areas under threat was also part of the security measures to prevent being caught unawares by the enemy. This picture, taken in January 1945, shows a tank belonging to *s.Pz. Abt. 509.*

Single tanks or even whole platoons were deployed as '*Feldposten*' (sentries), like this one belonging to the '*508.*' It's not a bad area from which to make observations but its camouflage was poor and it was neutralized by an attack from the air.

The general and in the end constant danger – especially for the fighting units – required heightened security. Without the need for explicit orders the soldier stays alert and observes his immediate surroundings, especially when the situation is uncertain. Here an *Alarmposten* (sentry) keeps watch at the head of a column of the '*503*.' In the picture below an air-observer – also with the '*503*' – is on duty on 15 July 1943.

Security Measures

Securing his own vehicle or the area in which a platoon or a company stop – be this during rest periods or while on a march – is a vital survival task carried out by all commanders without orders, in other words on their own responsibility. Security is generally coordinated at company level to ensure that there are no security gaps and to conserve forces. The latter aspect was particularly important for two reasons; to offer the majority of soldiers the opportunity for some rest and recreation and to carry out important logistical measures of any sort without disturbance from the enemy. The previously mentioned ban in no way affected such measures since Tiger leaders were supposed to refrain from leaving Tiger groups in exposed positions over long periods of time while they served as security for entrenched soldiers or suchlike.

Security was achieved through the use of observation or sentries (mostly on foot), aircraft scouts, and also by using individual tanks (mostly in half platoons) as '*Feldposten.*' Careful observation on the battlefield (for example before driving into unfamiliar areas of the terrain) also indirectly served as security. In addition, reconnaissance detachments or patrols deployed with specific objectives consolidated the Tiger units' own security measures.

Furthermore, troop units in the assembly and rest areas provided so-called *Alarmstellungen* (alarm positions) on the perimeter for basically all the fighting vehicles so that they could respond quickly to a direct threat, that is to say without the necessity for the issuance of intricate orders.

A *Nachhut (*rearguard) following a distance behind a march column also provided security for their own troop units.

Other essential aspects of security are the camouflage of vehicles (and the tracks they create) and the avoidance of noise.

Special measures for security included the use of natural cover, earth mounds and the excavation of trenches and foxholes.

In the spring of 1943, the crews of s.Pz.Abt.502 reach an assembly area. The advance scouting for suitable stopping places with sufficient space between the vehicles is important in case of attack from the air.

Stopping places were generally approached by reversing as shown in this picture of tank '332' belonging to s.Pz.Abt.503. This was supposed to avoid tearing any telephone cables that had been laid!

Immediately after parking this crew – also belonging to the '503' – removes the track marks that are easily recognizable from the air. (BA 22-2935-19A)

Stands of high scrub are also suitable for providing cover; in this instance for *s.Pz.Abt. 503* on 1 August 1943.

In open terrain extensive camouflage measures are required for protection against aerial reconnaissance. This picture, taken on 13 January 1943, shows *s.Pz.Abt.501* as it prepares for *Unternehmen 'Eilbote.'* (Hartmann)

It is preferable if the supply vehicles can pass close to the tanks; as here in August 1943 at *s.Pz.Abt. 502.*

Finding cover in settlements is a problem; in this case for *1./s. Pz.Abt.502* in Siewerskaja at the beginning of June 1943. Manoeuvring is carried out in confined spaces prevent damage to the infrastructure.

Tanks stand out when parked between houses and are visible from miles around – as in this picture (again of a tank belonging to the *'502'*) taken in Bologubowka in July 1943.

Covering the tank with foliage doesn't really help much. This crew finds a better solution to the problem with the help of a converted barn.

Forested areas don't always offer sufficient cover from above as can be seen in this picture, taken in May 1943, of tanks belonging to *s.Pz.Abt. 502* in the vicinity of Ploermel. (Hugmann)

It was therefore expedient to use camouflage nets to complete the concealment of the tanks; in this case at *s.Pz.Abt. 501* on 13 January 1943 (Hartmann)

This can be dispensed with if the foliage is dense; as in this picture of tank '113' of *s.Pz. Abt. 424.*

At the perimeter of the assembly area so-called *Alarmstellungen* were set up for the tanks if there was an imminent threat, such as here at the '502' on 16 July 1943. The crews had previously made themselves comfortable by digging out a tank ditch (see right). The tank was driven backwards over this at night to provide good cover against air attack for the crew as they slept.

The area is secured by sentries and patrols. The picture shows a guard's tent at *s.Pz.Abt. 501* on 25 November 1942. (Zorn)

Necessity is the mother of invention! Using a wire rope hoist the crew of tank '211' of the '501' have mounted two captured Maxim MGs on the rear of their tank as protection against close-combat troops.

The reflection of strong sunshine can betray a tank's position. This picture shows a tank belonging to s.Pz.Abt. 501 on 15 January 1943 (Dullin)

The white camouflage of this tank belonging to '502' has washed off exposing it to observation (February 1943).

Tank '231' of s.Pz.Abt. 505 releases a smoke canister to obscure it from sight from the front at the beginning of 1944. This can make sense if there is heavy enemy fire. It does however restrict the view of the crew.

The preparation phase before the attack is critical. If possible, the assembly before the attack was supposed to take place in open terrain as in this picture of tanks belonging to *s.Pz.Abt. 503* in July1943. (von Rosen)

Tanks of *s.Pz. Abt. 502* use a depression in the landscape to link up with accompanying infantry on 23 November 1943.

Depressions and slopes in the landscape also served as preparation areas – such as in this picture of tanks of *s.Pz. Abt.505* in August 1943.

Types of combat

Tiger units worked most effectively in combat when attacking in spirited (counter)thrusts – preferably by surprise – from the flanks and with all available forces at their disposal. The battalion *Merkblatt* makes this abundantly clear:

> The Tiger battalion is therefore a powerful focal point weapon in the hands of the troop commanders. Its strength lies in cohesive, ruthlessly led attacks. Dispersal reduces its impact. Thorough preparation for their deployment at a decisive point guarantees a high degree of success.

The strongly fluctuating deployment strength of the heavy tank units ultimately forced the combat-ready vehicles simply to combine with an armoured group that was led by an experienced officer. The occasions on which full-strength battalions were deployed were in the end restricted to large-scale operations with lengthy periods of notice that made it possible to establish more or less 100% combat preparedness. *Unternehmen 'Zitadelle'* in 1943 is a striking example – which also exposed the technical and tactical limits of the Tiger armoured fighting vehicle. The frontal assault against extremely well-defended enemy positions and the questionable advance into heavily mined zones set the limits on the Tiger's tactical superiority.

Storms of fire from *Panzerbüchsen* (anti-tank rifles) and mines with an explosive charge of less than 5 kg usually did little harm to the Tiger but nevertheless caused damage that could gravely affect its combat capabilities. Even although a *Panzerbüchse* fired from close range could not penetrate the Tiger, the enemy riflemen were still in the position of being able to destroy the tank's optics or damage its running gear. In addition, mines and hidden explosive devices that failed to destroy the tracks could however still damage the swinging arms, torsion bars or bogie wheels severely enough to inhibit the tank's mobility or even bring it to a standstill.

Nor was the Russian 7.62 cm medium calibre anti-tank gun capable of penetrating the Tiger's frontal armour from close range but the gun crews were trained to aim at the Tiger's suspension, optical aiming devices, the driver's viewing slit and the commander's cupola, the earlier version of which was not infrequently sheared off with deadly consequences for the commander who sat behind it.

The Tiger's armour protection, which was for its time exceptional, all too often led the crews to attack enemy positions carelessly and to lose sight of the caution required in 'normal' tanks and fail to make proper use of the terrain or to take mutual observation seriously.

Even if the consequential damage usually did not result in total breakdown, it nevertheless led to many technical failures such that the number of combat-ready vehicles available sank significantly. However, attention must be drawn to the fact the performance of the *Instandsetzungdienste* (repair and maintenance services) remained consistently high (see below). In addition to the forgoing, the requirement for replacement parts, ammunition and fuel was also high for Tiger units of which more will be said later.

Consequently, a successful attack by Tigers could only be executed following careful reconnaissance, in suitable terrain and in combination with effective combat and operational support.

If the Tigers attacked in conjunction with other armoured forces they proved themselves highly assertive at the main thrust of the attack. Lightly armoured forces on the other hand showed their effectiveness during combat reconnaissance and in their surveillance of the flanks.

If an attack took place in terrain suitable for armour, the Tiger was subject to the same limitations as any other type of tank such as restricted mobility in certain types of terrain (for example in heavy, swampy ground); the carrying capacity of bridges and when crossing bodies of water.

Cooperation with infantry or (*Panzer*) *grenadiers* was mandatory in urban and wooded areas.

As mentioned in the book *Panzer Tactics* in the manual document H.Dv. 470/7 *'Die mittlere Panzerkompanie'* ('The Medium Tank Company'), which also applied to the Tiger armoured fighting vehicle, no other types of combat besides attack are mentioned. In a very short section of H.Dv. 470/7 *'Panzerregiment und Panzerabteilung'* entitled *'Verteidigung'* ('Defence') the necessity of going over to an immediate counterattack is merely mentioned after stopping an enemy advance.

This sounds simple and trivial but is ultimately the reason behind the superior use of armour at the lower tactical levels by the Germans. Even though they were often at a great numerical disadvantage and therefore in a desperate situation, these offensive actions tipped the scales and, in contrast to waiting and undertaking hesitant actions, were the key to success.

The operational effectiveness of the Tiger with regard to its sighting device and its turret weapons favoured this tactic (see Chapter 3, 'Operating the Tiger'). The probability of the first shot by the 8.8 cm cannon achieving a direct hit was, for that time, very high. At a range of around 1,000 m, experienced gunners scored a hit with almost every shot and at a target range of 2,000 m the success rate lay at around 50%.

Although other operational methods are not explicitly mentioned in the regulations, this should not detract from the fact that, in the second half of the war, the Tiger was predominantly deployed in defensive situations and often in stationary positions, particularly when supporting infantry divisions or when providing moral support for the *Stellungstruppe* (entrenched troops). Tigers were also overused in the role of a 'fire brigade' within large military groups and wore themselves out with marches lasting hours as they tackled one hotspot after the other on the front line. This all too often resulted in the practice of deploying the expensive vehicles in small groups, or even singly, which greatly reduced their combat effectiveness.

Tank platoons were of particular importance even when the company or combined arms units were the main pillars of an attack. This was emphasised many times in *Merkblatt* 47a/30:

6.   The armoured fighting vehicle VI executes combat missions in platoon subunits and in exceptional instances in half platoons or individually for safeguarding security and the provisioning of its own units.

    Loss of a platoon leader or half-platoon leader, severance of connection with a platoon or half-platoon leader, the rapidly changing course of combat as well as confusing terrain often demand the autonomous operation of individual armoured vehicles.

And furthermore:

15.   The platoon forms the combat entity within a company. Deployment or subordination to a medium tank company or Panzer grenadier [company] are the exception.

    They could be required for reinforcing a medium company in special missions (advance tasks), for the reinforcement of Panzer grenadiers when crossing rivers and combat against reinforced positions.

16.   The platoon carries out the attack with constant, rapidly alternating firing and movement. The half-platoon and individual tanks oversee and support each other's action. Short stops for firing and a rapid advance to the next firing position are necessary. Long jumps forward are to be made, never less than 200 m. The driving direction and the firing positions are to be changed frequently while exploiting the terrain.

To exploit a success by decisive pursuit or during the breakthrough it can be expedient for all platoons to move simultaneously in order not to offer the enemy's weapons a good target by pausing.

The *Kompanie-Merkblatt* also highlighted that:

32.   The defence of the flanks requires particular attention.

The *Abteilungsmerkblatt* also went into the use of the Tiger in wooded areas and villages:

> Considering the Tiger's large blind spot and the extent to which its cannon protrudes, it is not to be deployed in house to house fighting in townships. This also applies to combat in wooded areas.

Clearly, the *Kompanie* and *Abteilung* commanders of Tiger units had been provided with a supporting written document which they could use to point out to troop leaders incorrect – and therefore contrary to regulations – deployment of their tanks. However, all too often practical experience and necessity due to scarce resources forced deviations from the norm.

If assembly in open terrain was unavoidable, the tank commanders maintained a gap between vehicles to avoid clustering such as in this picture of *s.Pz.Abt. 503* near Rostov in January 1943. (Wunderlich)

By the time the advance was underway the vehicles had already adopted their dispersed attack formation, as shown in this picture of *s.Pz.Abt. 505* at the Ohrdruf exercise area at the end of August 1944. (Krönke)

The stand-off between over-watching tanks and those further to the front – the picture shows vehicles of the '503' in July 1943 – was about half of the combat range, that is to say about 200 to 400 m depending on the line of sight.(Wunderlich)

In the training guidelines of *OKH/Ausb.Abt.(II)* of 5 May 1944 we find additional, and particularly important, advice for conduct in attack:

- During an **attack** of our own **in terrain with restricted visibility**, or in urban combat, *Panzergrenadiere* or **scouting detachments should lead on foot** in order to identify enemy tanks early and secure a suitable attack direction or firing position in good time. **Advance by leapfrogging**, with cannons always ready to fire; the commanders should not be frightened to have the next position reconnoitred on foot.

- If the **attack** is across open terrain **against enemy tanks that are in hidden positions** (in woods or at the edge of townships) **lure them to fire** by a feint attack or disengage in a certain direction so that the bulk of the attack can take place from a direction that is unexpected and surprizing to the enemy.

- **If an enemy tank front is suddenly encountered evade** their fire **immediately** and renew the tank-attack at a **different position**.

Experience in recent fighting has again shown how important it is to **immediately blow up enemy tanks that have been knocked out or immobilized** in order to make it impossible for the enemy to recover and repair them later. **Therefore:** reiterate this to the troops and train them in the rapid execution of the permanent destruction and blowing up of enemy tanks.

Furthermore: never allow our own tanks to fall into enemy hands without first destroying them or to be abandoned out of hand because they have sustained minimal damage.

The recovery or destruction of tanks that have been incapacitated is the duty of all troops!

Withdrawl of armoured fighting vehicles on reaching attack objectives.

During attacks supported by armoured fighting vehicles these must not be left in a forward position on reaching the attack objectives but be pulled back so that they are ready to counterattack.

The timing of the withdrawal depends on the preparedness of the defending troops in territory that has been won.

Armoured fighting vehicles should in general remain forward and give **fire support** for infantry until they have organized their **defence**; that is to say until they are sufficiently dug in and the tank and artillery defences have been prepared.

Although these instructions were entirely correct they were in reality frequently violated. In terrain with restricted lines of sight, and trusting in the Tiger's level of protection, attacks were carried out without advance scouting detachments; without withdrawing when encountering strong enemy positions and tanks remained in attack objectives

that had been won. The latter was often at the urgent request of the German infantry who were otherwise unable to hold the positons they had won by themselves.

The order to promptly destroy abandoned enemy tanks was completely unrealistic. This advice came to pass because the Soviet recovery service had proved to be very effective and towed away vehicles that all too often took part in combat again just a short time later. The Tiger crews 'only' had their own *'Acht-acht'* [a soldier's term for the 8.8 cm tank cannon] to destroy enemy tanks but indiscriminately firing more shots at wrecks made no sense. With the best will in the world it was only in exceptional cases that enemy tanks were 'checked' and retrospectively blown up because the tank companies did not have their own explosives.

The findings stipulated in the *Merkblättern* are also notable for another reason; they repeat verbatim the wording in the 'special' *Merkblättern* about the command and deployment of Tiger companies or battalions (see the section 'Leadership' that follows later).

The problem was all too often that the infantry units in most cases did not have – or had not read – the tank data sheets because their leaders simply took the view that they bore the brunt of the combat and the tanks just had to be sent for. This only changed with the introduction of the *Panzergrenadiere* who were also a mechanized fighting force. The command authorities had no option but to create additional information opportunities in order to pass on these important findings.

Forces following to the rear remained in march formation in order to be readily available.

On reaching the attack objective the tanks were supposed to remain in position only as long as it took for the infantry to prepare their defences such as in this picture of a tank belonging to the '502' taken on 6 April 1944.

If the attack objective is in open terrain, the tank platoons choose positions such that every direction could be covered so that the forces following are able to link up with them. The picture shows the '503' in summer 1943.

If strong enemy forces are met head on, their fire is answered immediately while other forces combine to deploy against the enemy's flank. This picture also shows the '503.'(Wunderlich)

Pictures taken during an exercise showing *s.Pz.Abt. 503* with the *7. Pz.Div.* on 5 June 1943. At the beginning of the attack, suppressing fire is laid down on enemy positions that have been identified. (Photos: Lochmann)

The tanks approach as close as possible to the continuing friendly artillery fire to exploit its effect.

The forces in staggered formation further to the rear don't pause but follow at a distance so that they will be immediately available, especially for assaults against the enemy's flanks.

The (lateral) separation should be 100 m and greater so that the defender has to make large changes in the traverse of his weapons when aiming.

Red identification flags were placed on the turrets of the tanks in the furthest forward positions – as on this one belonging to the '505' during Operation 'Zitadelle' – as visible signs that enabled the German pilots to find their bearings.

Dispersal was also important because then the enemy's artillery strikes were only moderately successful. The commander of tank '233' of s.Pz.Abt. 503 should have got his head under cover in good time.

Even more important than crossing open sections (as rapidly as possible) was avoiding danger from the flanks. Here, tanks of the '503' are driving far enough away from possible enemy emplacements on their left flank.

The same cannot be said of these tanks belonging to the '505'! Great danger threatens from the hill on their left. (Wehmeyer)

In such cases it is appropriate for some of the tanks to have their turrets pointing in the direction of the threat; in the event of sudden fire from the flank it would be too late to do this. The photograph shows tank '323' of *s.SS- Pz.Abt. 101* in mid-May 1944 during an exercise in Amiens. (BA299-1805.12)

The driver's skill is crucially important (the picture shows tank belonging to the '505'). He exploits the terrain as he drives according to his position in the platoon, or to direction points, and when his tank comes under enemy fire swings the heavily armoured bow towards it if at all possible.

It is appropriate to keep away from chains of hills or stand exposed in the open as shown above by a vehicle belonging to the '503.' or below by tank '132' of *s.Pz.Abt. 501* on 15 January 1943.

When advancing at speed, as in this picture of the '505' during *Unternehmen Zitadelle*, it is a matter of fighting down targets quickly to maintain the forward momentum. (Laux)

Firing takes place during short stops in the combat area, as ordered, before immediately falling back into formation again. The picture shows tank '211' of the '505.' (BA 278-872-9)

An attack force has already been spotted (the picture again shows the '503' during exercises with the *7. Pz.Div.*) but in such circumstances the formation of dense clouds of dust is useful because this helps to obscure the enemy's vision. (Lochmann)

Tank attacks in heavily wooded areas are a problem, such as here, on 6 April 1944 during an operation by *s.Pz.Abt. 502* in the '*Ostsack*.' The tanks can come under fire from weapons of every kind and from any direction. In the picture below an abandoned *Pak* (anti-tank gun) can be seen in its emplacement; at short range these were easily capable of inflicting damage on Tigers.

The same applies to movements through corn fields as shown in this picture of a group belonging to the '*510*' in summer 1944. Enemy close-combat fighters could easily be hiding and ready to attack the tank from the rear. In such a situation one's own accompanying infantry are very important!

After emerging from a forest (this is also a picture from the '*Ostsack*' period) the tanks are not supposed to drive carelessly into open ground but – while remaining at the edge of the forest – make observations of the terrain.

At the edge of hills only proceed far enough to enable the commander to see over them, as shown in this picture of tank '123' belonging to *s.Pz. Abt. 505* during an attack in November 1943. (Wehmeyer)

If the enemy counter-attacks, drive the tanks to a '*Feuerfront*' (firing line) as shown in this picture of the '*503*' taken near Tschugujew in June1943. (Lochmann)

Danger also lurks when approaching settlements because many possible cover positions are available to the enemy. This picture shows the *'503'* at the beginning of July 1943. (Schmid)

It is even more dangerous breaking out of built up areas, as in this picture of the *'503'* taken on 5 July 1943 in Michailowka. (Schmid)

As darkness sets in the tanks are well lit by the fires and are even easier to engage. This picture shows the attack on Tagino by *s.Pz.Abt. 505* on 17 July 1943.

The creation of so-called *Panzerdeckungslöcher* (tank concealment ditches) – such as this one being demonstrated by *s.Pz. Abt. 503* on 27 June 1943 – restricts the tank to a specific position upon which enemy fire can be concentrated. (Lochmann)

Defensive positions in open terrain are always problematic – particularly if the enemy enjoys air superiority. This picture shows a Panzer III belonging to *s. Pz.Abt.501* on13 January 1943. (Hartmann)

Taking up positions at the edge of a wooded area has the disadvantage of restricting the lines of sight and offering less opportunity for manoeuvring into a new position. This picture shows tanks of the '502' in spring 1943.

It was problematic if – by virtue of an order from an ignorant commander – Tigers were deployed in static positions or in a line in '*Verteidigung*' (defence) operations mode, perhaps with mandatory orders not to move from the spot.

It was substantially more effective, even in defence, for the tanks to be ready to move in order to throw back a frontally massed enemy in a counterattack or – better – to outflank him in a comprehensive manoeuvre that inflicted severe losses. In his *Gedanken über den Einsatz der Pz.Gren.Div. 'GD' in der Abwehr- und Panzer-Schlacht bei Targul Frumos 2.-5. Mai 1944, Generaloberst* Hasso von Manteuffel wrote:

> The dispersal of armoured forces had to be avoided under all circumstances in favour of maintaining the strength of the armoured core. Tanks should not content themselves with throwing back the enemy's attacking armour from good firing positions but annihilate them, there where they see them or assume [their presence]! For this reason they themselves must attack again and again (...). Only use as much of the tank force for defence as is required to master the situation. Tank combat must be conducted from depth; at all times one must have at one's command a reserve of tanks, particularly ones of large calibre (Panzer V and VI).

The long range of the Tiger's weapon allowed a wide choice of position. In other words, only a part of the armoured forces block frontally. Most of the positions selected – diagonally to the rear or also elevated – make a very flexible defence possible; one that allowed for opening fire at a time that surprizes the enemy and has a synchronised impact on the depth of their attack formation. This hits an enemy attack hard because – with rapid fire – heavy losses are inflicted on them and this slows the momentum of any attack. There are many descriptions proving that even a few Tigers could, at a local level, often drive out the enemy through their sheer presence.

If there was no enemy in front of their own positions, or if the enemy was forced to break off an attack, it was in principal not advisable for all tanks to remain in their positions because this made reconnoitring simpler. While a few vehicles continued to secure and observe, most of them pulled back to so-called *gedeckte Aufstellungen* (concealed emplacements) with, if possible, good camouflage (for example wooded areas) from which, in the event of an alarm, they were able to leave quickly and drive to their forward positions. If necessary the routes to these positions were marked. In the positions themselves, the crews determined the distance to marked points as accurately as possible in order to be able to fire on enemy targets detected there using exact settings on their sighting optics. This was usually carried out with the aid of '*Entfernungsspinnen*' [literally 'distance spiders'] – sketches indicating important landmarks and the distance to each drawn in perspective on a sheet of paper.

When waiting in position the tank has only a slight advantage – its first shot will betray its position and camouflage will be of little help.

It's more suitable to hold the tank in readiness in reconnoitred positions such as this tank belonging to *s.Pz. Abt. (Fkl) 301* near Steinstraß on 28 February 1945.

Waiting in readiness in nearby assembly areas (this scene shows *s.Pz.Abt. 508*) tanks can be quickly and effectively deployed in a counterattack to stabilize a defence. (Heimberger)

Townships are also suitable exit points for counterattacks. This picture shows a Tiger belonging to *s.SS-Pz.Abt. 502* on the outskirts of Storkow on 25 April 1945.

It is vital that defensive positions in woodland are secured by infantry such as in this picture showing *s.Pz. Abt. 502* on 6 April 1944.

Though nonsensical from a tactical viewpoint, Tigers were often deployed individually to give moral support to badly struggling entrenched troops. Here, tank '324' of *s.Pz.Abt. 502* fulfils this task in August 1943.

This picture shows a tank belonging to the '504' in a partly concealed position – at least part of the hull and the running gear are protected from enemy fire. After opening fire it must quickly move into another position.

Because tanks in delaying combat are always only in position for a short time, elaborate camouflage was not needed as we can see in this picture of tank '114' of *s.Pz.Abt. 507* taken in October 1944.

Hidden positions in which the tank is difficult to spot are very suitable; this is a tank belonging to *s.Pz.Abt. 503* in May 1943.(Rubbel)

Having immediately available withdrawal routes to the rear is extremely important to prevent being outflanked by the enemy as this picture showing a vehicle belonging to the *'502'* close to a house in spring 1943 illustrates. (BA 276-702-28)

The combat method towards the end of the war changed entirely to *Hinhaltender Kampf* (delaying action) but this was not explicitly mentioned in the regulations.

Rapid relocation marches over great distances and widespread withdrawal movements were certainly not among the strengths of the Tiger units. The reasons for this were the technical vulnerability of the vehicles and their comparatively restricted range (see section on 'Marches'). These marches presented the supply units with ultimately insurmountable challenges and were also the reason for the majority of losses of Tigers due to technical overloading and the abandonment of vehicles because of a lack of fuel supplies.

In delaying actions themselves, the attacking enemy was allowed to advance on alternating positions to slow his advance and, if possible, wear him down by inflicting heavy losses. This meant knowingly giving up territory.

But this also offered the opportunity to smash the bunched enemy forces with unexpected counterattacks – preferably in their open flanks – or to force them to withdraw.

A number of German troop leaders skilfully applied this so-called '*Schlagen aus der Nachhand*' strategy to overcome or stabilize critical situations.

However, the vast majority of tanks were lost in this tactical form of engagement and were surrendered to the advancing enemy because of a shortage of fuel or technical damage. In such cases there was a clear command to render the vehicle useless. To this end all tanks had on hand at first three, and then later two, so-called *Zerstörpatronen* (destruction cartridges) in the form of thermite rods. One was intended for use on the breech of the cannon and the other for the engine compartment (see illustration that follows).

To avoid unwelcome accidents during withdrawal operations, the extensive reconnaissance of possible withdrawal routes is even more important than finding suitable emplacements, particularly at night and twilight – as this picture of a tank belonging to *3./s. Pz.Abt. 508* near La Fortunata on 14 September 1944 demonstrates.

The withdrawal of friendly forces deployed farther ahead is surveilled by tanks in suitable positions to prevent the enemy from launching an assault on them. Here we see tanks of *s.Pz. Abt. 506* performing this task on 4 February 1944.

Too hasty withdrawal movements through difficult terrain, especially in winter, run the risk of getting bogged down like this tank belonging to the '*502*' in January 1944. Recovery of the vehicle in such circumstances was generally no longer possible.

Zerstörpatronen (Thermite rods)

a   Container for Z 85 cartridge with its airtight spring-secured cap in front
b   Zerstörpatrone Z 85 with retaining tab (on top) for gun tube
c   Container for Zerstörpatrone Z 72 (retaining clips open)
d   Sprengpatrone Z 120 for the engine compartment
e   Sprengpatrone Z 34 (earlier version for the gun tube)
f   Exerzierpatrone Z 34 made from wood
g   Accessories: detonator, reserve detonator, copper contact plate

This picture shows a tank belonging to *s.SS-Pz.Abt. 503* in Pariser Straße, Berlin, after the fighting in April 1945. A *Zerstörpatrone* inserted into the front part of the barrel has rendered it unusable. Contrary to orders, according to which the *Zerstörpatrone* was to be ignited in the breech of the cannon, this was how they were usually used. After a simple change of barrel, the tank would have been ready to fire again.

The tank leader at every level – this picture, taken east of Rostov in January 1943, shows *Hauptmann* Lang of *s.Pz.Abt. 503* – required special characteristics to be successful: boldness but also a special flair for getting through critical situations.

The company commander is a key figure – this picture shows *Oberleutnant* Scherf of the *'503'* in conversation with his platoon leaders on 1 January 1943. His character and abilities shape the unit and play a decisive role in its success or failure!

The tank man (now and then) might also dismount from his vehicle. In this picture, taken in July 1943, *Abteilungsführer Major* Burmester of *s.Pz.Abt. 503* surveys the terrain with his chiefs and platoon leaders.
(Photos: Rubbel)

Command and Control

There is continual disagreement between fighting branches of the armed services as to whether it is more difficult to command combat conducted by dismounted infantry or engagements carried out by (rapidly moving) armoured forces. The infantry leader's task is indisputably complex and demanding when it comes to overpowering enemy positions and fortifications during an attack; it is also a hard struggle in every sense when defending. Countless conversations with commanders of all types of weapons (and at all levels) – as well as the personal experience of the author – have confirmed that quite different temperaments and mental attitudes can, and must, exist between them and that ultimately they are not comparable. In addition, it was often stressed in these conversations that the one would not have wished to have 'switched' roles with the other.

Significant differences are, among other things, the distances that must be conceived of and the consequential rate of change in the military situation.

However – and this also applies to the deployment of armour – in combat neither hesitation nor carelessness should be a guiding principle for the leadership. In contrast to the cover-seeking grenadier, the tank is mercilessly exposed and its armour does not make it invulnerable to all threats. This was all too often a painful experience for Tiger commanders at all levels. The act of commanding tanks must at all times be geared towards the dominance of one's own units and refocusing on the need to react more quickly than the enemy.

This was facilitated by – if at all possible – the thorough training of the leaders and an efficient means of command. An experienced tank commander had no problem stepping from a Panzer III or IV into a Tiger. On the contrary, he could take advantage of the superior fighting capability of the system with regard to protection and firepower. An inexperienced commander who thought of his vehicle as a rolling bunker and wanted only to accumulate 'kills' often made incorrect leadership decisions and jeopardised the operational success of everyone. In principle therefore, there was no difference between a 'normal' tank commander and the commander of a Tiger.

These weapon-specific features were expressed primarily in the course of a firefight. Here they resulted in tactical-technical possibilities such as were found in no other battle tank in the Second World War.

In the *Merkblatt* issued for the heavy tank battalions, it was assumed that the main task was to annihilate enemy tanks:

> When combating enemy tanks, swift action and firm leadership are the prerequisites for success. By constantly changing the method of attack the enemy can be confused and deceived time and time again.

The following combat methods have essentially proven themselves:

a) Enemy tanks are tied up by fire from the light tank units. This enables the Tiger units to go around them to attack from the flanks or from the rear while the remainder of the tanks give constant support to their attack through frontal fire.

b) The Tigers achieve supremacy over the enemy tanks by a rapidly executed frontal or flanking attack while supported by the fire of the remaining tanks.

This sub-section of the *Merkblatt* is by itself not very informative because it seems very formulaic and describes just one (of many possible) examples. In reality, combat against tanks is clearly much more sophisticated.

The remarks in the *Kompanie-Merkblatt* (a data sheet issued at company level) are more communicative:

34. The heavy tank company's most important task is combating enemy tanks. This takes precedence over any other task.

35. Independent and swift action by the company leader and firm leadership by issuing clear orders are the basis of success. Immediate attack is usually the best solution.

36. Constantly changing attack methods confuses and deceives the enemy.

These include:

a) Opening fire suddenly from suitable positions (reverse slopes or perimeter positions) at an effective distance and from an unexpected direction.

b) When enemy tanks counterattack, form a firing line; deploy part of the force to provide flanking fire. Allow the tanks to come forward and in doing so turn off the engines in order to hear them better. Destroy the enemy in a follow-on thrust.

c) Encirclement or bypassing in difficult terrain.

d) Deployment against the flanks and rear while exploiting the position of the sun, the wind direction and groundcover.

e) When unexpectedly running into a strong defensive line, especially one with tank obstacles, cease fire immediately and start a new attack at an unexpected location. Use smoke wisely.

f) If attacking in terrain with restricted lines of sight or settlements, send scouts or *Panzergrenadiere* in advance in order to detect enemy tanks early and gain suitable attack directions or firing positions while proceeding under cover of reciprocal fire.

g) When fighting across open terrain against enemy tanks that have been set up in concealed positions, lure them to fire using feint attacks or withdraw in a particular direction then attack in force from an unexpected direction.

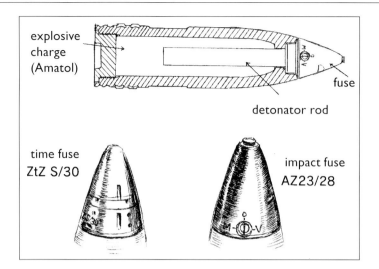

explosive
charge
(Amatol)

fuse

detonator rod

time fuse
ZtZ S/30

impact fuse
AZ23/28

Sketches showing the two common
fuse types screwed into the front of
the *Sprenggeschoss* (high explosive
rounds). The percussion fuse could
be set to '*ohne*' (without) or '*mit*'
(with) time delay.

Photo of the AZ23 without the sensor
cap on top.

View of the detonator from below into
the detonator's bore for insertion of
percussion cap in live ammunition.

With the aid of a fuse key the length of
the time delay is set before the shell is
loaded.

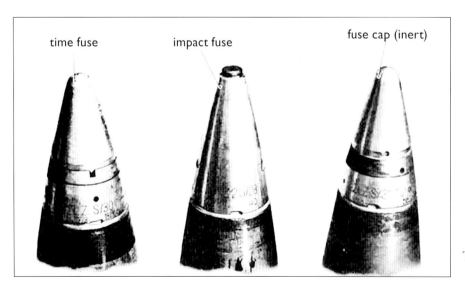

time fuse

impact fuse

fuse cap (inert)

The types of fuses
(screwed on).

h) When hostile tanks withdraw pursue and annihilate them immediately.

37. Enemy thanks that have been knocked out or immobilised by fire are to be blown up during rear-guard fighting.

It is apparent from the style and content of this document that these principles could only have been committed to paper by an experienced commander. It would be difficult to formulate the nature of the deployment of tanks more accurately or clearly.

The same statements can be found in today's tank regulations but with a stronger emphasis on the rapid strikes to which contemporary vehicles with their fully stabilized weapons and optics – unlike those of earlier tanks – are very well suited.

Regarding combat with the Tiger itself, the *Kompanie-Merkblatt* has this to say:

7. With its 8.8 cm tank cannon the Panzerkampfwagen VI engages:

   with the *Panzergranate*: armoured targets and embrasures,
   with the *Sprenggranate*: nests of resistance, *Pak* and gun emplacements, mass targets (columns and reserves).
   The long range of the 8.8 cm gun makes it possible to bring targets under fire to good effect over long distances.

8. The add-on high-angle gunsight makes it possible to engage targets at ranges of up to 9,000 m. However, against enemy artillery and massed targets and with good observation more rewarding use of the weapon is only possible at up to 5,000 m if the armoured fighting vehicle cannot approach the target more closely because of obstacles in the terrain or if transient targets are involved.

9. The 8.8 cm cannon is fired when stationary. The armoured fighting vehicle is brought into position frontally against enemy fire (angle of impact and armour protection!). When firing ceases, concealed and reverse-slope positions are to be occupied.

10. The high-speed trajectory of the 8.8 cm shell makes it necessary to use it with special attention to the safety of our own forces when firing over their heads.

11. The *Panzerkampfwagen VI* engages unarmoured targets at close quarters with its turret and bow machine guns. Massed targets at ranges up to 800 m can also be successfully engaged with the machine guns.

Some explanation is appropriate here. The long shooting distances referred to above require some critical assessment. The low muzzle velocity of the high explosive fragmentation shell (*Sprenggranate*) of 800 m/s meant that its flight trajectory was very curved so that the likelihood of a direct hit decreased greatly as the range of the target increased; it was also very sensitive to side winds. This accounts for the barely 10% probability of hitting a target at a range of more than 3,000 m with the *Sprenggranate*. In reality, reasonable target engagement looks somewhat different. The *Sprenggranate* for the Tiger I usually came with the AZ 23/28 percussion detonator. For the engagement of

bunkers and targets behind cover, the *ZtZ S/30* time-delay detonator could be screwed on instead. The time delay could then be set to between 2 and 35 seconds using a special key for turning the time-delay selector on the detonator (see pictures above), or this could be set to 'O.V.' (*ohne Verzögerung*/ no delay). Usually the *Sprenggranate* intended for use as a flak shell was delivered with the time-delay detonator already fitted. With a fragmentation projection of 20 m in width and 10 m in depth it was particularly effective against surface targets.

The main ammunition used against enemy tanks was the *Panzergranate 39* which had a muzzle velocity of 773 m/s. This was a slightly lower initial velocity than that of the *Sprenggranate* but its considerably lower mass (7.65 kg in comparison to the 10.2 kg of the *Sprenggranate*) meant that its deceleration was less. The *Panzergranate 40* with its tungsten-steel tip and a muzzle velocity of 930m/s was clearly more effective but shortages of raw materials prevented its production from late autumn 1943. In any case, the number of completed shells (8,000 in 1942 and 8,900 in 1943) was small in comparison to the *Panzergranate 39* at 21,200 and 324,000 respectively. The *Hohlladungsvariante* (HEAT/hollow charge variant) of the *Panzergranate 39* was also produced only in small numbers. It had an acceptable 90 mm penetration capability, independent of the range of the target, but because of its low muzzle velocity of only 600 m/s, it was too inaccurate at distances over 500 m. In *'Erfahrungen im Panzerkampf'* (Experiences in Tank Battles) produced by the *Oberkommando der H.Gr. Süd - Abt. Ia* (Supreme Command of Army Group South, Division 1a) on 3 April 1943 the following was said of this type of ammunition:

> In contrast, because of its wide dispersal characteristics, the HL-B-Granate is to be used up to 500 m at the most. If a hit is scored at some point by the HL-B-Granate at great expenditure of ammunition then its effect is good. However, the troops have no trust in the HL-B-Granate. An increased supply of the *Panzer-Kopfgranaten* is what is wished for.

Concerning the gun performance a report issued by the *(13.) Tiger-Kompanie* of *Panzer-Regiment Großdeutschland* on 27 March 1943 says:

> With the Kw.K. a direct hit at distances between 600 and 1,000 m is almost always achieved with the first shot. At such distances a frontal shot on a T-34 with a *Panzergranate* achieved an absolutely resounding effect. The shell pierced the frontal armour and even destroyed the engine at the rear. In only a very few cases did a frontal shot on a T-34 cause it to catch fire. Shots from a similar distance to the side or rear part of the hull, or from behind to the rear deck of the enemy fighting vehicle, resulted in an explosion of the fuel tank in 80% of cases. In reasonably favourable weather conditions, resounding success against the T-34 can be achieved at ranges of 1,500 m and more with economic use of ammunition.

Captured enemy vehicles were always thoroughly investigated. This also included ballistic tests. This picture shows a mobility comparison trial between German vehicles and the American M3 on open ground in Hillersleben.

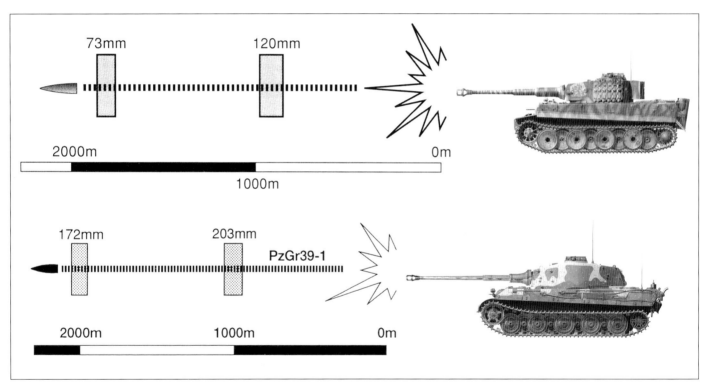

The penetration performance of longer gun tube of the Tiger II was significantly higher than the Tiger I's weapon. The shell's much larger propellant charge was clearly a contributing factor.

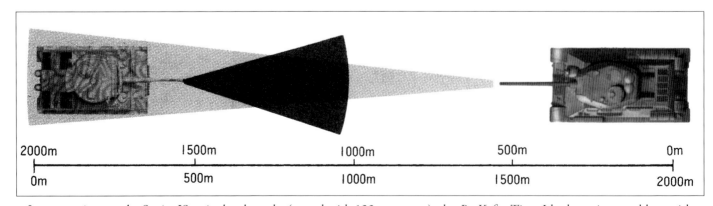

In comparison to the Soviet JS series battle tanks (armed with 122 mm guns), the *Pz.Kpfw.* Tiger I had a serious problem with respect to the range of its cannon and could easily come under fire earlier and from a greater distance.

The Kw.K. 43 L/71 cannon of the *Pz.Kpfw.* Tiger II was significantly more powerful. This was a result of the higher internal pressure inside the longer barrel (6.28 m against the 4.928 m of the Tiger I) and the ammunition's much larger propellant charge (the *PzGr39/43* was1.1253 m long in comparison to 0.873 m in the Tiger I). The weight of the round was also much greater (22.8kg for the *PzGr 39/43* in comparison to the 14.5 kg of the *PzGr 39/36* used by the Tiger I). The speed of the shell in flight was correspondingly faster. The *PzGr 39/43* had a muzzle velocity of 1,000 m/s whereas that of the *PzGr 40/43* was 1,130 m/s with an approximately 65% greater penetration performance at all ranges with a nearly identical weight of shell.

The previously mentioned shortage of raw materials was also the reason why no sub-calibre kinetic energy penetration shells were introduced although these had already been developed. The German armour-piercing shells did indeed have a hardened sub-calibre core but it had a ballistic calibre-sized cap that remained firmly attached to the projectile's core. In a true sub-calibre round, the sabot [a device to keep an sub-calibre projectile centralized in the barrel of an artillery piece] detaches itself when it leaves the weapon's barrel so that only the narrower penetrator continues in flight. According to the physical 'mass times the square of the velocity' principle, the higher the velocity of the projectile when it strikes the target the better is the penetration. With the same propellant charge, a heavier and larger kinetic energy penetration shell experiences less acceleration than a narrower one. To maximise the force on a target, a high penetration shell weight can be achieved by adopting the longest possible design of projectile. Furthermore, full-calibre heavy projectiles experience considerably more deceleration due to wind resistance than narrower ones of similar weight. Modern arrow-like penetration shells are up to 70 cm long and are accelerated to about 1,700 m/s and have a penetration capability equivalent to 800 mm of steel at a target range of 2,000 m. At that range the Tiger II gun using the *Panzergranate 40/43* could penetrate just 152 mm and the Tiger I a mere 84 mm using the *Panzergranate 39*. The mere weight of a shell therefore tells us little about its ballistic performance. Additionally, 'thick' and slower moving shells were more easily deflected from sloped armour plating.

With the right tactics, the Tiger I was capable of asserting itself against a partially superior enemy. In the fifteenth issue (September 1944) of the monthly '*Nachrichtenblatt der Panzertruppen*' (News Sheet for the Armour Branch), there appeared an assessment of an engagement involving several Tiger Is against several JS-IIs which stated:

> (…) the firing rate of the 'Josef Stalin' was comparatively slow.

The company commander learned the following lessons from his company's combat against the 'Josef Stalin':

1. As soon as the 'Tiger' makes an appearance most of the 'Josef Stalins' turn away and attempt to withdraw from the firefight.
2. In many cases the 'Josef Stalin' only engages in a fire fight at greater distances (over 2,000 m) and then only when it is in a perimeter position.
3. The enemy crews are prone to bailing out immediately at the first shelling.
4. The Soviets make great efforts to prevent the 'Josef Stalin' in particular from falling into our hands and make every attempt to tow it away or blow it up.
5. The 'Josef Stalin' can be taken out even though a frontally penetrating shot is not so readily achieved at long range (another 'Tiger' *Abteilung* in the east reported that the 'Josef Stalin' could only be penetrated frontally from a distance of under 500 m).
6. An attempt should be made to engage the 'Josef Stalin' from the flank or rear and to destroy it with concentrated fire.
7. In addition, engagement in a firefight against the 'Josef Stalin' is not permitted if under platoon strength. Deployment of a single Tiger leads to its loss.
8. After achieving the first hit on a 'Josef Stalin' blinding it by bombardment with *Sprenggranaten* has proven to be expedient.

Statement of the *Generalinspekteur der Panzertruppen*:

1. These experiences are in accord with other 'Tiger' units and are correct.
2. Regarding point 4; it would be desirable if all our 'Tiger' crews made the same effort as the enemy. 'Never let an intact "Tiger" fall into enemy hands.' Every crew must fulfil this policy with exemplary commitment.
3. Regarding points 6 and 7:
   With current deployment of the [enemy's] 12.2 cm tank cannon and 5.7 cm *Pak* in the east and the 9.2 cm *Pak-Flak* in the west and south-west, the 'Tiger,' on grounds of its characteristics, can no longer disregard the combat principles that pertain to other types of tank.
   Just like any other single vehicle, this includes driving to the top of a rise in order to 'to see the lie of the land.' On one such occasion recently, three Tigers took direct hits from a 12.2 cm that killed all but two of the crew.
   The principle of tank tactics – that tanks should only crest a hill quickly and together (in leapfrogging movements) and under protective fire, or otherwise make a detour – was not unknown to this tank unit. The idea of the 'thick skin', of the 'invulnerability' and the 'safety' of the Tiger crews that has become established in other units – and in part amongst the tank troops too – must finally be refuted and stamped out. For this reason, reference to the observance of the general engagement regulations for combat of tank against tank is especially important for Tiger units.

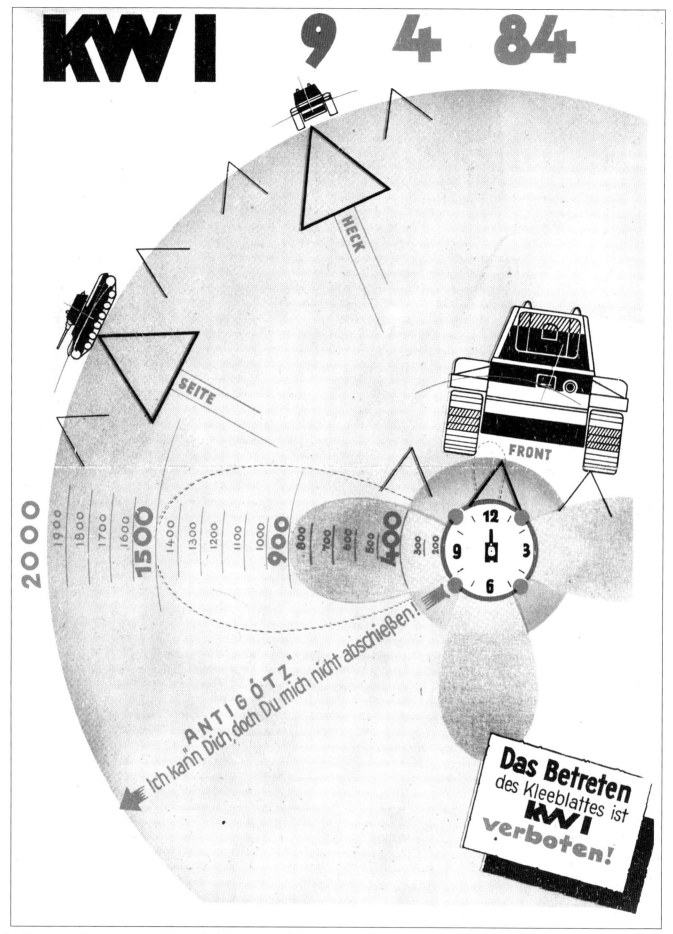

The German tank crews received so-called 'Antigötz'-Tafeln – tables that referred to the types of tanks used by the enemy. The one referring to the Soviet KV-1 is shown above in its original dimensions. On it, the ranges (in grey typeface) are shown at which the Tiger could take out the enemy tank from the front, side or rear. The shaded colour shows the areas of the Tiger that could be penetrated by the KV-1's shells within the ranges indicated. In the bottom right corner is the warning 'the KV-1 is forbidden from entering the clover leaf.' (D656/27)

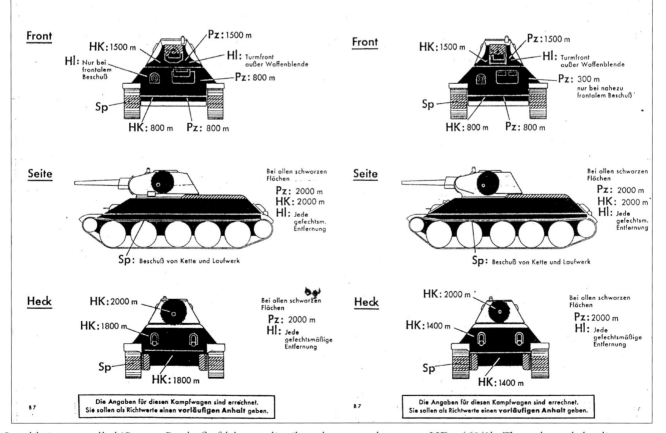

In addition, so-called '*Panzer-Beschußtafeln*' were distributed as a supplement to HDv 469/3b. These showed the distances at which the different locations on the enemy tanks could be penetrated by the KwK 36 cannon and the type of ammunition that should be used.

Grundsätze für das Schießverfahren gegen schwer zu bekämpfende Panzerfahrzeuge

1. **Kaltblütigkeit** bewahren: Ausreichende Entfernung zum Ausmachen „schwacher Stellen" und zur Erzielung vernichtender Wirkung anstreben!

2. Feindpanzer möglichst aus **verdeckter Stellung** und aus **unerwarteter Richtung** bekämpfen! Im offenen Gelände auf Feindpanzer „über Ecke" des eigenen Panzerkampfwagens schießen (größter eigener Panzerschutz!).

3. Trotz sorgfältig **gezieltem Einzelschuß hohe Feuergeschwindigkeit!**

4. Aufmerksame **Beobachtung der Geschoßwirkung!** Nicht jeder Treffer wirkt sofort vernichtend.

5. **Günstigen Aufschlagwinkel anstreben!** Größte Wirkung, wenn Bug oder Seitenfront voll erkennbar, schlechteste bei Schrägfahrt (45"). Auf runde oder gewölbte Türme grundsätzlich Turmmitte anhalten!

6. Die richtige **Munitionsart** wählen! Angaben dieser Panzer-Beschußtafel beachten. **Hartkerngranaten (HK)** nur verwenden bis höchstens **2000 m** Entfernung und nur dann, wenn mit **normalen Panzergranaten (Pz)** bzw. **HI-Granaten (HI)** Wirkung nicht zu erzielen ist.
   Sprenggranaten (Sp) – Zünderstellung „o V" - können erzielen
   behindernde bzw. zerstörende Wirkung beim Beschuß von Waffen und Blenden, Sehschlitzen, Optik und Gleisketten,
   vernichtende Wirkung bei günstigen Treffern auf die Motorentlüftung am Heck (Inbrandschießen),
   vernichtende Wirkung bei Treffern auf die Turmfront dicht oberhalb des Turmdrehkranzes oder unter den überragenden Teil des Turmhecks der Pz Kpfw **T 34 A und B** durch Abheben und Verschieben des Turmes, ebenso bei Treffern auf die Turmfront des **MK II** unterhalb der KwK. Diese Turmtreffer sind jedoch selten.

7. In dieser Panzer-Beschußtafel bedeuten:

Munition:	Wirkung:
Pz = 8,8 cm Pzgr Patr 39 KwK 36	■ = Vernichtende Wirkung
HI = 8,8 cm Gr Patr 39 HI KwK 36	▨ = Behindernde bzw.
HK = 8,8 cm Pzgr Patr 40 KwK 36	zerstörende Wirkung
Sp = eingeführte Sprgr Patr	□ = Keine Wirkung

Die mit Erfolg zu beschießenden „schwachen Stellen" der Panzerkampfwagen sind durch **Bezugsstriche** mit dem **Kurzzeichen** der entsprechenden Munitionsart verbunden.
Meterzahlen bei den Kurzzeichen für die Munitionsart geben die **obere Grenze der Entfernung** an, bis zu der mit Sicherheit mit einem Panzerdurchschlag zu rechnen ist. Bei **HI-Granaten** wurden keine Entfernungsangaben gemacht, da diese Geschosse alle angegebenen schwarzen Flächen **bis 2000 m Entfernung** durchschlagen können. Jedoch wird die **gefechtsmäßige Entfernung** (Treffreichweite) je nach Größe der Zielfläche und den vorliegenden Verhältnissen (Feindeinwirkung, Sicht usw.) vielfach geringer sein. **Einzelheiten** über Munitionswirkung usw. siehe im Textteil dieser Vorschrift (H. Dv. 469/3 b).

B 7

The manual H.Dv. 469/3b *'Panzerabwehr aller Waffen'* also describes the principles for engagement of difficult-to-combat enemy tanks. For the Tiger I crews, these – and ten *Beschußtafeln* for various enemy tanks – were added as an attachment to the *Tigerfibel*. Part of this document, which begins with the advice to stay calm, is shown in its original dimensions to the left.

In every official source quoted here, the concern that the Tiger crews might use the terrain too carelessly is raised. This picture – taken on 5 December 1943 – shows a tank belonging to *s.Pz.Abt. 502* in an exposed position on top of a hill making it visible to everyone for miles around. (Lohmann)

4. With reference to point 7, it must be said that the line of thought is quite correct but on the other hand 3 'Tigers' cannot flee from 5 'Josef Stalins' simply because they are not allowed to engage in a fire-fight when present in less than platoon strength. In the present situation there are cases in which whole platoons are not always available. In combat between tanks, the number of tanks is much less decisive than superior leadership in combat. No changes are made regarding the loss of a 'single tank.'

5. In connection with this, it should be noted that tanks of the 'Josef Stalin' series can be destroyed not only by 'Tigers' but also by Panzer IVs, 'Panthers' and assault guns from the flanks or from the rear.

To maintain secrecy, no dates or troop units were named in the news sheet but it referred to an engagement on 22 July 1944 in the vicinity of Leikumi. On that day a total of six Tiger Is belonging to *1./s.Pz.Abt.502* annihilated, amongst others, seventeen JS-IIs. The company commander mentioned in relation to this was *Oberleutnant* Baumann. The unit that was reprimanded because of its three losses to 12.2 cm cannons only four days later north-west of Dünaburg while carelessly positioned on a hilltop was ironically enough also *s.Pz.Abt. 502*. The opinion of the Inspector General [of the armoured troops] is in many respects interesting and revealing. It is both a reminder and a 'dressing down.' It also expressed the concern that the 'Josef Stalin' was a dangerous opponent that discouraged the Tiger crews. The evaluations made by the *Waffenprüfamt* (the department responsible for testing weapons) as the result of intensive ballistics tests on captured enemy tanks in Hillersleben – which were issued on 23 June 1944 – were transcribed exactly by officers at the *Chef des Generalstabs des Heeres* (Chief of General Staff of the Army) on 29 June 1944 but these were not distributed to the Tiger units.

These, amongst other things, stated:

It can be said that, with respect to weapons and armour (…) c) the Tiger with the KwK 36 cannon is superior to the 'T 34 – 85' but is inferior to the 'Josef Stalin 122.' (…) e) the Tiger II is far superior to the 'T 34 – 85' and to the 'Josef Stalin 122.

The emphatic statement that the same rules of engagement applied to the Tiger as well as all the other types of tank, are accurate and were repeatedly supported by painful experience (see the section on 'Propaganda'). It should however be noted that in 1942 and 1943, propaganda, particularly that of the press, repeatedly praised the 'invulnerability' of the Tiger. Viewed in this light, reality can be seen to have overtaken such rhetoric.

The crews' experiences of, and comments about, the deployment of smoke shells and the mortar tubes for *S-Minen* (anti-infantry mines) subsequently installed on the rear of the Tiger were somewhat mixed. The latter of these was supposed to render close-quarter infantry harmless but they failed to prove themselves in action. They were removed in autumn 1943 and replaced with close-combat weapons. The smoke grenade dischargers on the sides of the turret proved just as impracticable. Firstly, they were not projected far enough forwards and, according to the crews, they obscured their own vision. Secondly, they could be displaced by shots from hand weapons with the same undesirable effect.

Nevertheless, they were popular in places where the enemy deployed swarms of dive bombers – such as in Italy on the Western Front and, from 1944, with increasing intensity in the east. Here they proved themselves extraordinarily effective when ignited manually and simply thrown onto the engine cover or close by the tank. If the turret was then rotated into an atypical position with the cannon raised or pointing downwards while the tank remained motionless, the effect created was deceptively similar to that of a direct hit by the enemy. The completely incorrect and exaggerated reports by British and American pilots amply prove the success of this strategy.

The instruction to position the tank 'frontally to the enemy' is essential. This ensures that the front of the tank's hull points towards the target with the most protective part of its armour.

Of course, if surprize threats appear from the flanks in an attack not all of the tanks can simply come to a halt and turn in a new direction. In such cases it proved successful if some of them turned their turrets in the direction of a potential threat so that they could return fire instantly; otherwise the aiming movements of the Tiger took far too long despite being powered by the engine.

Command at the lower levels is roughly divided into tactical (unit level and downwards) and operational command (combat by combined arms formations). Here we see Major Lueder of *s.Pz.Abt. 501* issuing orders to the leaders of subordinated forces on 22 January 1943. (Lueder)

At company level it proved useful to issue orders to all the commanders at the same time. This avoided mistakes that might arise when messages are passed on from one person to another. The company leader's intent will come to knowledge to everyone as in this picture taken at *s.Pz.Abt. 502* in January 1944.

In large-scale operations undertaken in conjunction with other units, the commanders' vehicles also link up to form a command group – as in this scene showing *Panzerregiment Bäke* in January 1944. (Boike)

The tanks' radio communications had a restricted range and only one or two circuits could be operated at the same time. This problem was solved by cooperation with radio stations installed in armoured personnel carriers (*Funkstellen-SPW*). This picture shows a scene at *s.Pz.Abt. 501* on 15 January 1943. (Dullin)

Motor-cycle messengers are an indispensable tool of the leadership. In this scene we see them gathered at the command tank of *3./s.Pz.Abt. 503*. (Wunderlich)

The battalion commander – here we see *Hauptmann* Dr. König of the '509' – determines which vehicles will accompany him. The leader of the accompanying grenadiers has stopped his armoured personnel carrier next to the command tank and maintains close contact. (König)

Leading from the front in an unprotected wheeled vehicle with conspicuous command panels was only possible in peaceful situations such as in this picture of *3./s. Pz.Abt. 503* (taken in June 1943 near Kharkov). (Wunderlich)

Keeping a constant track of one's orientation in the terrain is vitally important – here we see *Hauptmann* Scherf of the '*503*' in March 1944 studying his map.(Wunderlich)

In action, leading was mostly accomplished by hand signals and shouts; the picture shows a column of the '*502*' on 25 November 1943.

Finally in this section, further remarks regarding the means of command (*Führungsmittel*) follow.

As is well known, the better their radio communications equipment, the greater was the degree of responsiveness of an armoured group. Accordingly each *PzKpfw*. Tiger E or B was equipped with the UHF radio set 5 and Fu 2 UHF radio set (receiver only) as well as the *Bordsprechanlage 20* (intercom). This allowed two circuits to be operated in parallel. If several companies attacked within the framework of a battalion there were discrete command radio networks within each company. With the Fu 2, the platoon leader could direct the tanks in his platoon and also listen into the company command network. Instead of the Fu 2, the company commander had an Fu 8 transceiver (Fu 7 in the Tiger II) and communicated with the battalion commander. If all the tanks were deployed together (which increasingly became the usual case) the tanks were led by a single command network. Connection with the battalion commander or a command post was maintained using the receiver.

Using the transceivers, the command tank of the battalion command group kept in contact with the company commanders or subordinated detachments; the second transceiver was used to contact the commanding officer and, where applicable, the battalion radio station. The commanding officer kept contact with his subordinate leaders using a battalion command network and with his superior officers (via the radio station at the division or corps level). However, though he could hear (circumstances permitting) the latter of these, he was unable to contact them – possibly because of the limited range of his 20 W (and later 30 W) transmitter. In this case the higher-command radio traffic went via the battalion command post which, by means of an extendable stationary mast, could achieve a significantly greater range of up to 25 km. Depending on the terrain, the range of the Fu 5 amounted to at least 3 to 6 km; with the Fu 8 the range was at least 10 km whilst moving and almost double that when stationary. The radio operator also received training in *Tastfunk* (Morse code) as this almost doubled the transmitter's range.

The responsiveness of the radio installations was also greatly favoured by the fact that the Tiger had a radio operator as the fifth member of its crew. One has to bear in mind that the analogue radio apparatus at that time required constant monitoring and frequent manual adjustment. This became necessary after a certain time depending on the humidity of the environment, the location of the participants in the radio network and other factors. If another crew member had been entrusted with this a subsidiary task – as it was in the tanks of other nations – this would certainly have created serious communications problems. The presence of a radio operator had another – and even greater-advantage in that it relieved the strain on the tank commander whose attention was of course concentrated

on his tactical leadership. In the meantime the radio operator could listen into the 'connection to the top' and inform the tank commander if he had been called or had received important orders and information. The battalion commander had an assistant in the form of an ordnance officer or an adjutant in a second vehicle who could maintain separate connections (usually to the radio station in the command post that transmitted important situational information, for example from neighbours).

Based on operational experience (in very fluctuating operational conditions) all Tigers delivered after the middle of 1944 were wired and fitted with mountings so that the tank units could, with very little effort, convert every vehicle into a command tank.

At an early stage the newly formed Tiger units also requested armoured personnel carriers to act as (forward) command posts. The background to this was not that the unit commanders wished to lead the combat from them – they did that of course from their tanks or '*Gruppe Führer*' – but that armoured command-and-communications vehicles *(FüFu-Fahrzeuge)* would have been very suitable to form a (forward) mobile command post or work as a relay station for the headquarters of larger military units to which they were subordinated.

The *Ia Ausb. Beim Gen.Insp.Pz.Trn* (the first training officer at the General Inspectorate of the Armoured Troops) rejected this request on 8 July 1943 on the following grounds:

The provision of two additional armoured vehicles for the communication platoons of the armoured units (Tiger) is considered to be neither appropriate nor necessary.

Reasons:
1. The physical separation of the medium wave radios from the leaders of the armoured units by installing them on special armoured vehicles would be a step backwards in the organization of the motorized and armoured units of the signals service whose successfully strived for goal was, and must be, to create the closest possible links between the commanders and the means of communication. It is only the pre-existing physical limitations that have in places forced the installation of radio apparatus essential for the commanders in several armoured command vehicles which however, when deployed, can remain nearby.
2. The proposed installation of radio apparatus on a heavy armoured personnel carrier, which for tactical reasons cannot follow the unit headquarters during a tank attack, would mean that the APC would soon lag behind so that: either the radio link sideways/to the rear is broken because the radio messages can reach the signals detachments but not the tactical commanders, or the radio link is made unnecessarily more complex and extended because, by way of example, recordings of messages on medium wave would then have to be transmitted to the tactical commander on shortwave.

Passing on orders in the form of writing – as shown in this picture of a platoon leader from the '502' in February 1943 – was rather unusual at company level. Usually notices and entries on a map were sufficient (BA95-97-33)

The leader of the logistics forces also fulfilled a permanent leadership function. In this picture from 1 July 1943, we see *Feldwebel* Großmann, the *I-Gruppe* (repair and maintenance) leader for *3./s.Pz.Abt. 503*. The use of identification signs (behind him on the right of the picture) made it easier to find the repair and maintenance detachments.(Großmann)

An explanation about coded radio messages on different communication channels and by Morse code that is both awkward and devoid of meaning follows with the advice (!) that anyhow communications with the commander could be delivered without being encoded. In addition, the provision of a second small communications detachment (that would provide cover in areas without radio traffic) was rejected without reasonable grounds. This is a good example of justified claims made by fighting troops being treated with irrelevance by a bureaucracy far from the front line. Here too, forceful arguments were made on both sides. These had nothing to do with the spatial connection or separation of vehicles, or the means of radio communication, but were much more about the development of flexibility in the scope their application in a variety of situations. The outcome was that Tiger units improvised and often 'siphoned off' one or two armoured personnel carriers from the reconnaissance platoons for use in the above mentioned purposes.

The reason for this threadbare rejection might of course be that it was simply not possible to provide the heavy tank units with additional armoured personnel carriers. However, additional field telephones were at least provided…

The fact that the logistics units did not have long-range communications equipment was also problematic. A summary of an evaluation of operational reports by *Panzerlehrgänge* Paderborn on 28 May 1943 stated:

> By keeping in constant contact with the commander of the Tiger units, the leader of the supply troops must always be in the position of being able to precisely fulfil wishes regarding supplies. If personal contact is not possible (during combat) then the logistics train is to be equipped with a radio post.

These two photos of the radio posts belonging to *Panzerregiment 'GD'* taken at the beginning of 1943 show several types of radio equipment of various wavebands (capable of bridging long distances) being operated signals troops assigned to this duty. At the bottom of the picture (above) the signals officer with overall responsibility can be seen. The antennae with splayed rods (right) can be raised to a height of up to 3 m to increase its range in the ultra-high frequency (UHF) wave band. (Photos: Lempe)

The grenadiers are the troops with which tanks operate most closely. In this picture we see a battle group belonging to *s.Pz.Abt. 506* at the beginning of 1944. Travelling on the tank is however only advisable during the approach to the area of operations!

Close cooperation with the dismounted troops, as shown in this picture of the *'502'* taken on 25 January 1944, slowed the movement of the tanks to a considerable extent and reduced their striking power. (BA 457-58-28)

In more open terrain a separate approach is better (here we see tanks belonging to the *'507'*) – their objective is the same but their partial missions are different. (Grimm)

Collaboration with Other Weapons

For the Tiger force commander, collaboration with other branches for combat support was no different from that of the 'normal' tank man with the significant exception that he collaborated with the engineers.

This special circumstance merits some consideration. The significantly greater weight of the Tiger armoured fighting vehicle in comparison to the existing Panzer III and IV presented some great challenges for the tactical leader and for the support provided by the engineers. This was particularly so if critical sections of the terrain were to be crossed and water obstacles or ditches had to be overcome. The Tiger units' own engineers were there to remove only small obstacles or to render scattered mines harmless. On the other hand, the engineers belonging to the larger units to which the Tigers were usually assigned were often, due to the lack of equipment, not in the position of being able to provide effective support.

Two eloquent examples from reports by *s.Pz.Abt.505* and *s.Pz.Abt. 503*, show how extensive minefields could exert an negative influence on German operational command.

On 7 July 1943, *Major* Sauvant of *s.Pz.Abt.505* reported:

During an attack on 7 July 1943, four vehicles ran onto mines in front of the Russian barbed wire. There was only a marked alley through it. The boundaries to the side, which should have indicated its lateral extent, were missing. Because of this it was not clear to the vehicles, as they advanced on a wide front, that there was a minefield. The unit had not been previously informed that a minefield had been laid there. The *Abteilung* commander, who was on the same hill as the leading vehicle, only realized himself that there was a danger from mines when two of our men waved vigorously. The company commander, who was travelling beside me, understood the signs immediately and ordered a halt just as four vehicles ran onto the mines. In spite of this the four vehicles were still capable of moving and they followed the company at a great distance. As the attack continued two vehicles from the same platoon again ran onto mines on an unmarked minefield between the two wooded areas south of Werch

Tagino through which our own infantry and also a few assault guns had already passed. The remaining two tanks in the platoon stopped and realized then that the running gear of their vehicles had been damaged in the first incident which prevented them from continuing to follow. (...) In a further attack to the south-west, towards the high ground north-west of Step through open terrain, the doctor's tank and another Panzer VI, and later during the withdrawal yet another Panzer VI, ran into arbitrarily positioned blocking positions. (...)

On 6 July the *Abteilung* conducted an attack from Step in an easterly direction into the flank of an enemy attack that was supported by tanks. In the ensuing tank battle in the vicinity of the southern edge of Step-223, six ran into mines:

Stab:	2 Tigers, 1 infantry ecort tank
1. Komp.:	5 Tigers
2. Komp.:	5 Tigers
(...)	

Out of action:

By shelling:	2 Panzer VI total losses
	2 Panzer VI running gear damage
	2 Panzer VI running gear and radiator damage
By mines:	16 Panzer VI running gear damage

Transmission damage: 3 Panzer VI'

Of the 31 tanks in the *Abteilung* (*3. Kompanie* was still in transit), more than half were knocked out by mines. The main reason for this was insufficient reconnaissance from the air and by engineers. It was only by salvaging parts from badly damaged tanks and working round the clock for two days that the *Werkstatt* managed to get 14 tanks serviceable again. It also so happened that there were insufficient spare parts for the running gear components at the *Abteilung*.

A similar tale of woe about a battle on 5 July 1943 from Graf Kageneck, the commmnder of *s.Pz.Abt.503*, follows:

The *III. Panzerkorps* reports the loss of 13 Tigers in a Kompanie that mustered 14 Tigers on the morning of 5 July. Nine Tigers were knocked out by mines. The repair of each would occupy about two or three days.

The close support of dismounted forces is of crucial importance when fighting in towns and villages. This picture shows Tigers of the '*503*' as they approach Michailowka on 5 July 1943. (Schmid)

Cooperation with the *Panzergrenadiere*, who only dismounted from their vehicles when it was necessary, was always effective – otherwise they remained on their APCs so that they could be readily available. A battle group belonging to the '*502*' is shown here. The picture was taken on 19 April 1944.

When an obstacle is overcome the infantry must form a bridgehead. This scene shows infantry belonging to *s.Pz.Abt. 501* under tank supervision from the other side of the riverbank on 15 January 1943. (Photos, also on next page: Dullin)

The reasons for the unusually high loses were as follows:

1. From the outset there was not a single map available for use in which the minefields laid in front of the bridgehead by the German units were shown. Two completely different maps were available but neither of them reflected the reality. That is why two Tigers drove onto mines immediately after setting off. Another two Tigers suffered mine-damage as the attack continued over an area that was shown as mine-free on the terrain maps.

2. Clearing the mines was carried out very superficially and another three Tigers were knocked out of action by mines in lanes that had been marked as clear.

3. An eighth Tiger drove onto enemy mines immediately in front of a hostile position although it was briefed by engineers that had been inserted in advance. The ninth Tiger drove onto mines as it attempted to take up a position because of a reported enemy tank attack on the left flank.

Deviating from the original plan, according to which the Tigers attack simultaneously with the *Panzergrenadiere* and immediately behind the mine-clearing engineer detachments, the Tigers were deployed in front of the engineers and grenadiers. On the evening of 5 July, five Tigers were 50 to 80 metres ahead of the infantry detachments.

Eight Tigers were knocked out as the result of carelessness or incorrect tactical deployment over two or three days. It is for this reason that, during this time interval, they were not available for their true purpose of engaging enemy armour and heavy weapons.

The relationship between the [Tiger] *Abteilung* and the *III. Panzerkorps* was not exactly harmonious. The commander of *Abteilung 503* had already explicitly criticized the splitting of the *Abteilung* into companies for allocation to the corps' three attacking armoured divisions. Then, on 21 July 1943, in a pretentiously worded reference to cooperation with a Tiger unit, the *Oberkommandierende General der Panzertruppe* (commander in chief of the armoured corps) Breith, who was widely considered to be rather obstinate, alluded to just about everything that his [Graf Kageneck's] units had themselves done wrongly. Graf Kageneck was of course quite correct on this point. After weeks of preparatory planning by the attacking forces it was competent to demand that enemy blocking positions had been carefully cleared.

To overcome small clefts in the terrain, such as brooks or swampy areas, the time-consuming construction of corduroy roads and fascines, or backfilling, was possible given an appropriate period of notice. Major obstacles or waterways required machines or bridge-building equipment that could only be supplied by specialist engineer units. Before Tigers were deployed in such terrain, it was therefore imperative to plan ahead carefully and proactively. The same applied to transit across major waterways with respect to the timely deployment of ferries or means of sea transport (see Chapter 4).

Light APCs followed at a distance if at all possible, as is shown in this picture of the '*501*' taken on 18 November 1942.

Because there was no advice in the *Merkblatt* relating to the correct 'deployment of a heavy tank battalion', the *OKH/Ausb.Abt. (II)* (Supreme Command of the Army/Department II/Training) issued additional information sheets to fill this gap:

Cooperation with the infantry:
The following facts have to be borne in mind when **'Tigers' are deployed in cooperation with the infantry:**
The 'Tiger', in view of its highly effective weapon and strong armour, is to be deployed chiefly against enemy armoured fighting vehicles and anti-tank weapons and only in exceptional cases against infantry targets. Its strength lies in a weapon that can successfully fight down enemy tanks and other targets at distances of 2,000 metres.

'Tigers' are heavy vehicles that exert high pressure on the ground. This necessitates proactive and thorough reconnaissance of the terrain. The inadequately reconnoitred deployment of 'Tiger's does not usually result in success but in the avoidable loss of expensive materiel.

The 'Tiger' cannot remain hidden from enemy reconnaissance. From experience, the Russian engages every single 'Tiger' with concentrated fire from every weapon.

The 'Tiger' conducts its firefight with its cannon from a stationary firing position which depends on the terrain and should be hidden. Because of the long range of its gun, it is irrelevant if its firing position lies 100m farther forward or to the rear.

From this it arises that for cooperation with the infantry:
The 'Tigers' support the infantry by combating enemy tanks and anti-tank weapons with extensive direct fire.

This means that a 'Tiger' strives to conduct combat at distances of over 1,000 m.

Ground reconnaissance must extend to ascertaining if rivers, bridges or swampy areas are navigable. A rule of thumb that applies to swampy land is: the ground can bear the weight of a 'Tiger' if one soldier can take a second one piggy back and stand on one leg without sinking in!

The assault infantry must stay far enough away such that they do not suffer any losses from concentrated defensive fire directed at the 'Tigers.'

The 'Tiger' must have freedom of movement so that it can select 'firing stops' appropriate to the terrain and [combat] situation. They are not to be tied to the infantry.

For as long as the 'Tiger' is stationary and firing the grenadiers must work their way forwards under its protective fire. When the 'Tiger' makes a 'leap' forward, the grenadiers support it with all of their weapons. The 'Tiger' is not invulnerable to mines. Usually only minor damage arises but under enemy fire this is difficult to repair. Because of its great weight, an immobilized 'Tiger' is difficult to recover.

If an attack with 'Tigers' runs into an enemy minefield and a detour is not possible, the engineers must be deployed to clear the way. The 'Tigers' take over the task of providing covering fire with their weapons.

Because the commander's cupola is installed on the left side of the turret, his view to the right is restricted. This creates a blindspot on this side which exposes the vehicle to the risk of close combat. Every Bolshevik that destroys a 'Tiger' in close combat is mentioned in a Russian Army report!

It is wrong to deploy 'Tigers' singly. As protection against enemy close-combat troops it fights in close contact with the infantry.

The suggestions and objections of expert 'Tiger' commanders are to be given careful consideration.

This gives the reader a vivid impression of the effort to which the *OKH* went to pass on the German infantry's painfully negative experiences during their day-to-day cooperation with tanks in general and the 'Tiger' units in particular. The above account includes tactical advice as well as banalities and even petty rules.

It must be stressed once more that, in 1943/44, the (foot) infantry were hopelessly outdated as far as their organization and equipment were concerned. It was ultimately unfair to constantly accuse the tanks of incorrect deployment. The infantry were always overjoyed when Tigers were on hand but the possibilities of cooperation were, in the final analysis, limited.

Pictures reminiscent of the trench warfare and attacks by combat vehicles in 1917-18 but taken on 23 November 1943 on the Eastern Front: the accompanying tank (belonging to the '*502*') is forced to match the foot soldiers' slow speed of advance.

Another scene from the same attack – one that should be avoided if at all possible. When the infantry bunches up behind a tank they too become the target of every enemy weapon.

On 25 February 1944, a single tank belonging to the '*502*' stands amidst the infantry positions in no-man's land 'rejoicing' in its role as a stationary target.

In the phase when the enemy in the attack objective was under suppressing fire, cooperation with the artillery was important in order to carry out a timely bombardment. Here a crew belonging to the '*503*' is watching the deployment of a rocket battery in January 1943. (Wunderlich)

Tank groups conduct rapid, large-scale movements which means that the artillery's *VB* (*vorgeschobene Beobachter/forward* observers) also had to be capable of moving independently. (BA 667-7130-33)

During large-scale attacks the Germans found it advantageous to embed their self-propelled armoured howitzers far to the front in order to make optimal use of their long range as shown in this picture of *Gruppe 'Bäke'* in January 1944. (Boike)

The deployment of immediately subordinated combat aircraft (for example Stukas) was mostly planned at a higher command levels. Before their approach, the attack troops moved into line in order to immediately exploit the effect they had on the on the enemy positions.

When working in close cooperation, the battle group was accompanied by forward air-controllers mounted on armoured personnel carriers. These had long-range communications equipment at their disposal. (Etzold)

The German reconnaissance aircraft (for example, Fieseler Storch) could pass on their findings either by air-drop or personally, such as in this picture taken at the beginning of March 1943 at *13./Pz.Rgt. 'GD.'*

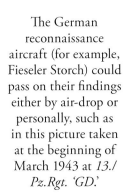

Because of a shortage of aircraft – the enemy had these in abundance – the German anti-aircraft defence assets were of critical importance. For example in this picture, taken in Italy during August 1944, we see members of *s.Pz.Abt. 504* keeping a lookout. (Hirlinger)

The 2 cm *Vierlinge* could be also be deployed when dismounted, as shown in this photograph, taken in June 1943 at the '*503*.' This made them much easier to camouflage. (von Rosen)

During marches or attacks – this picture shows the '*505*' in May 1944 – the accompanying Flak-equipped carriers performed securing duties. These could offer immediate fire and were also greatly feared when deployed in ground combat. (Etzold)

The 2 cm *Vierling* – mounted on a Panzer IV chassis and delivered in dribs and drabs during the last year of the war – was more effective in terms of the level of protection it offered and its mobility; this picture shows a vehicle belonging to the '*503*' in Budapest on 14 October 1944. (von Rosen)

A not to be underestimated factor was relations with the population and civilian agencies. This could be rather hostile, as for this column of the '*503*' in June 1943 in Kharkov.

...or rather friendly; as in this march through Budapest (also by the tanks of the '*503*'). (von Rosen)

One of the great dangers for the otherwise well-protected Tiger were mines with an explosive charge of 5 kg or more. Tank '122' of the '501' was caught out by one on 28 February 1943. Marks left by incoming fire clearly show that it was the target of weapons of all sorts after it was immobilized.

Often, it was better to remain still and wait for the engineers to do the clearing-up work. Explosive devices and other obstacles that could not be cleared were removed by being blown up.

In February 1944, s.Pz.Abt. 508 sought its own solution to master the danger posed by mines – the picture shows (in the middle distance) a knobbly roller that was used for this purpose. (Schlamm)

After their deployment in Nettuno, the '*508*' also converted a Tiger for laying explosive charges that were intended to detonate mines that had been detected. This model was later erroneously referred to as a '*Bergetiger*' (recoveryTiger).

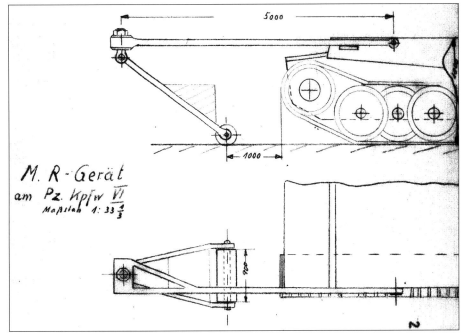

M. R - Gerät
am Pz. Kpfw VI
Maßstab 1: 33 ⅓

These practices were later taken up by official authorities and a mine-clearing device for mounting at the front of tanks was 'developed.' The diagram to the left shows a contemporary diagram of the device.

In fact the side-mounting brackets for this mine-clearing device were then occasionally welded onto Panthers and Tigers. The picture, taken at the Wezep training area, shows a vehicle belonging to *Funklenkabteilung 301* (a radio-controlled vehicle unit) that had been taken over from *s.SSPz.Abt. 103.* and modified in such a way.

Before the Tiger units were equipped with the engineer variant of the APC, the mine-clearing equipment had to be transported by truck which meant that it also had to be moved manually over considerable distances. Until then, the '505' made do by modifying a few 'old' Panzer IIIs as engineer tanks. Here we see two of them on 14 October 1943.

In this picture, the '503' demonstrates that ditches can be significant obstacles. Engineers have to bevel the entry and exit points. (v. Rosen)

Equipping with radio-controlled explosive charge carriers, as in this picture of *3./s.Pz.Abt. 508*, put tank units in the position of being able to breach obstacles themselves. (Herwig)

Another 'core business' of the engineers is building bridges and crossings, here for the *s.Pz.Abt. 503* on the Donets River on the 5 July 1943. (Schmid) The Tiger crews are already waiting impatiently...

...before they drive over the completed engineer-built bridge made from prefabricated parts or timber...one at a time, otherwise a rescue attempt might be required before they can carry out their mission! (Schmid)

Swampy places, or unnavigable fords, too, are strengthened with earth and construction materials for a tank belonging to *s.Pz.Abt. 505* in August 1943.

During attacks on strongly reinforced positions, tanks are hit by a variety of weapons. This picture, taken on 29 February 1944, shows a tank from the '508' near Cisterna. The driver was lucky that a serious hit to his observation port only tore off the upper part of the shutter. (Ebinger)

Tigers with the old drum-shaped cupolas had them sheared off every now and then by large calibre hits, as shown in this picture of *Feldwebel* Weller's tank of the '502', with a deadly outcome for him. The picture datesfrom 1 September 1943.

This sort of fatal effect inflicted by weapons – this vehicle belonged to the '503' – made any thought of refurbishment distinctly far-fetched. This tank was a typical total loss. (Pertuss)

The Effect of Enemy Weapons

To properly assess the combat value of the *Pz.Kpfw.* Tiger, it is appropriate to include a section that details and clarifies how the protection of this tank should be evaluated with respect to the main causes of failure.

Assessing the respective causes of failure (see tables in Volumes I and II of *Tigers in Combat*) might create the impression that the *Pz.Kpfw.* Tiger was comparatively susceptible to damage and not particularly robust but the assessment of mission reports puts this impression into perspective. Time and time again, reference is made to the tank's great ability to take hits, in part from large-calibre weapons, and still fight on.

A report issued on 27 March 1943 by *13./Pz.Rgt. 'Großdeutschland'* notes that:

> Apart from certain initial problems, the Panzer VI has proven its value. It can now be said that its reliability is superior to that of the Panzer III and IV; by ensuring that regular, careful inspections and maintenance are carried out, that is to say one technical service day for each three days of deployment, it will – as it does now – give outstanding service.

There were many reasons for the failures. It should be clearly stated that a penetrating hit to the armour was by no means always the cause of the crew's need to abort a mission. There were other, more common, causes for failure; the destruction of (part) of the running gear and damage to important operational components in the tank's interior among them. Seen from this viewpoint, the Tiger offered its crew a high degree of physical protection and comparatively good 'life insurance.' In comparison to light and medium weight tanks there were significantly fewer losses of personnel.

Because of the Tiger's generally well-known ability to withstand ballistic impacts, the primary objective of the enemy was to utilize combat tactics that – apart from the tank's actual destruction – offered the most promising results:

- Opening fire only when (depending on the calibre of the weapon) there was a good prospect of effect.
- Inflicting damage that would limit the vision and effectiveness of the crew.
- Immobilizing the tank.

The first of these categories has of course applied throughout the ages. Even in the Stone Age or in ancient times, a defender was aware of whether he had a good or poor prospect of disabling his target. The effectiveness of a weapon has always depended on several factors. With regard to the protection offered by the Tiger's armour, the prospect of an enemy achieving success – after the impact of the projectile – depended on the calibre of their weapon and the distance to the target (see sketches that follow). Consequently, diagram-based instructions were issued that made the prospects of success at various distances and aiming points clear to their own crews. The German tank and tank-destroyer crews were issued with similar documents known as '*Panzer-Beschußtafeln*.'

Furthermore, visually descriptive, informative diagrams were distributed which made it clear in which areas the [German] crews were better protected or in which they themselves were at risk of being eliminated (see pictures). But of course the Tiger commanders often did not have the choice of keeping out of danger by maintaining the necessary distance from the target. For the defender of a position – at least in the initial stage of a battle – such a choice was possible because he could decide the most suitable time to open fire. However, for an attacker knowingly entering into contact with the enemy, this advice was not at all helpful.

In summary, it can be said – in purely quantitative terms – that most of the enemy (anti) tank cannons were not capable of penetrating the Tiger at tactically useful distances.

The following exceptions have to be mentioned: on the Soviet side – weapons with calibres of 85 mm (with limitations), 100 mm and 122 mm; on the British side – the 17 pounder (76.2 mm); and the US Army's 76 mm (with sub-calibre ammunition) and 90mm cannons.

The statement regarding quantity must of course be put into perspective. Even though the enemy's tank defences could not be extensively equipped with weapons of these higher calibres, the sheer number available to them was always much greater than the number of Tigers and/or Panthers on the German side.

The hostile combatants' main objective was therefore to use suitable tactics to reduce the fighting power of the Tiger or to bring it to a standstill.

Weapons of smaller calibre were also used against certain points on the Tiger in the full knowledge that would not have a decisive effect on their target. Apart from the running gear, the Tiger's targeting and observation devices were shot at in order to destroy the glass surfaces or to create a splinter effect in the interior of the tank. In the most 'favourable' scenarios, the ammunition or fuel lines or fuel tanks were hit causing fire or an explosion inside the tank, or members of the crew were wounded. Finally, a near miss by heavy calibre shell could knock the optics out of adjustment, jam the turret or (in the early models of the Tiger I) shear off the barrel-shaped commander's cupola.

The effect of enemy weapons (photos on previous page)
1   Cannon out of alignment (*501*)
2   Elevation blocked (*501*)
3   Hull casing torn off (*503*)
4   Main sight damaged (*503*)
5   Bow MG destroyed (*503*)
6   Driver killed (*503*)
7   Turret crew killed (*506*)
8   Radio operator killed (*506*)
9   Engine destroyed (*508*)

Unit number in brackets

The running gear was a prominent target for every type of weapon and for mines of all sizes. The running gear was not particularly vulnerable to small and medium calibre weapons but here too the quantitative effect came into play. Though holes in a bogie wheel were perhaps harmless, wheels or swinging arms that were blown off often blocked the tracks causing them to run off the wheels or snap.

The ***Gefechtsberichte*** (combat reports) eloquently describe this.

Report of *s.Pz.Abt. 506* on 30 September 1943:

Classification of losses for the Tiger to enemy fire and other damage during the first seven days and nights of deployment from 20 to 26 September 1944:

1. 6 Tigers lost to direct hits and burning. The armour was penetrated cleanly. The calibre of the shots are unknown. The tanks were completely burned out, blown up and in territory held by the enemy. The tanks were hit from a range of around 1,000 m. They appear to have been hit either by anti-tank guns, Russian assault guns or artillery.
2. 1 Tiger was knocked out by a T-34 at a range of 200 m. Two clean penetrations in the side of the hull. Hull warped, gears, radio and electrical installations damaged, crew wounded. The tank was recovered but cannot be repaired in Russia.
3. 4 drivers', 4 radio operators', 1 loader's and 2 commanders' hatch covers blown off. Internal equipment was damaged and the crews wounded by splinters.
4. 8 cannons and 4 gun gimbals were damaged by shell-fire, 3 of the cannons seriously.
5. 3 final drives broken by hits to the hull armour. The hull's protruding side-wall acted as a projectile trap preventing its deflection. A 1 cm crack was created that allowed the oil to run out. One tank cannot be repaired in Russia.
6. 3 instances of the armoured protection of the driver's viewing slit and 6 of the driver's glass blocks shot-up or otherwise damaged.
7. One armour protection for the exhaust destroyed.
8. 15 hatch-cover latches broken by projectiles.
9. The running gear on 21 tanks was also badly damaged by projectiles, this included 6 drive sprockets and two guide wheels.
10. 6 radiators damaged by splinters from hits on the turret.
11. 14 engines rendered inoperative by water leakage from radiator (due to enemy fire), water hammering and oil contamination of the combustion chamber.
12. 3 air intakes and 2 ventilator fans were destroyed.
13. 16 towing cables and 9 track installation cables were shot to pieces.
14. All dry filters, external rear-mounted toolboxes and turret carrying bags shot to pieces. (…)
15. On-board intercom systems failed on 17 Tigers due to vibrations from shell impact.

Descriptions such as these demonstrate the massive extent to which the tanks came under fire and the diversity of the damage they suffered.

A report by the commander of *III./Pz.Rgt. 'Großdeutschland,' Major* Gomille, on 31 August 1943, specifically describes the effect of the Soviet 12.2 cm calibre cannon (first introduced on the ISU-122 self-propelled gun):

15 August 1943, (…) While driving through the two defiles, the *Abteilung* received furious fire from numerous, well-camouflaged anti-tank guns and several T-34 assault guns from the right flank of the settlement Grun. It was only after a long combat that this enemy was fought down. During this fighting, *Hauptmann* von Villebois, the commander of *10. Kompanie*, was badly wounded. (Eight hits by 12.2 cm shells from a T-34 assault gun were taken, amongst them six hits to the turret and one penetrating shot to the hull. Of the six hits to the turret, three of them only caused small bulges while two resulted in splinters twice the size of the palm of a hand flying off into the combat area. These hits also rendered the electrical firing mechanism unusable and several protective glass blocks were destroyed or blown from their mounting brackets. At the point of penetration the hull was peeled back to about 50cm from the welding seam and very badly contorted which meant that repair in the unit workshop was not possible.)

♦ Немецкий «тигр» шёл прямо на огневую позицию пушки гвардии младшего сержанта Бутенко. Немецкие танкисты не замечали отлично замаскированной на прямой наводке нашей пушки. Наводчик орудия гвардии красноармеец Карпов не спускал с прицела вражеского танка. «Тигр» подошёл совсем близко. Орудие открыло огонь. Завязался короткий бой. «Тигр» запылал.

Артиллеристы! Бесстрашно подпускайте танки возможно ближе, бейте их прямой наводкой! Жгите немецкие «тигры»!

♦ Сапёр гвардии старшина Трубицын обнаружил ночную стоянку немецких танков. На дороге, где должны были проходить танки, он заложил мины. Утром на расставленных старшиной Трубицыным минах подорвались три немецких танка.

Было это 6 января. А через несколько дней, 9 января, герой-сапёр повторил свой подвиг. На минах, расставленных им в тылу у врага, взорвались ещё 2 немецких танка.

Сапёры! Действуйте и вы, как гвардеец Трубицын! Выслеживайте танки врага, взрывайте их своими минами!

Гвардеец!

Бей немецкие танки всеми средствами — снарядом, гранатой, миной, зажигательной бутылкой, огнём бронебойки!

Смелый и умелый сильнее танка!

Г—170011. Издание красноармейской газеты «Красное Знамя». Зак. №12

СМЕРТЬ НЕМЕЦКИМ ОККУПАНТАМ!

БЕЙ ТАНКИ!

Как поразить немецкий танк Т-VI («тигр»).

Бей по бензобаку   *Бей по пушке*

Против танка Т-VI следует применять все противотанковые средства: огонь пушек, противотанковых ружей, крупнокалиберных пулемётов, а также противотанковые гранаты, мины и зажигательные бутылки.

Массовым огнём из всех видов оружия по смотровым щелям можно ослепить экипаж танка, а огнём из пушек и противотанкового ружья по подбашенным щелям заклинить башню. Огнём из орудия любого калибра и противотанкового ружья можно повредить командирскую башенку или сорвать её силой удара снаряда. В случае срыва командирской башенки необходимо забросать танк гранатами или зажигательными бутылками, уничтожить экипаж и поджечь танк. Особенно ответственными деталями танка являются его ведущие (передние), ведомые (задние) колёса и гусеница. В то же время это и самые уязвимые места танка. Колёса и гусеница представляют хорошую цель для ведения прицельного артогня из орудия любого

Just like the German *Panzerjäger*, the Soviet soldiers received combat instructions indicating the weak points of the *Pz.Kpfw*. Tiger I: this document was issued after the first encounters with *1./s.Pz.Abt. 502* that took place near Mga in spring 1943.

калибра. При попадании снаряда колеса и гусеница разрушаются, и танк выходит из строя.

Уязвимым местом являются и опорные колёса танка. Они легко разрушаются при попадании снаряда и противотанковой гранаты. С правой и левой стороны танка в области ведомого (заднего) колеса и двух задних опорных колёс размещены бензобаки. Между ними, в середине танка — двигатель. Броня бортовых листов, прикрывающих бензобак, пробивается снарядом 76-миллиметровой пушки. Поэтому следует сосредотачивать прицельный огонь артиллерии по бензобакам.

Огневые средства необходимо располагать так, чтобы удар наносился танкам меньше по лобовой его части, а больше по кормовой, так как там и броня тоньше, и больше уязвимых мест, и цель шире.

Днище танка имеет броню в 28 мм, что даёт возможность широко использовать против танка мины. От взрыва мины днище коробится, а гусеницы и опорные колёса разрушаются. Кроме минирования участков местности, необходимо применять передвигающиеся мины (мины с привязанными двумя верёвками, при помощи которых бойцы из своих щелей и окопов подтягивают мины под гусеницы в момент прохождения танка).

Если танк по какой-либо причине остановился, не следует оставлять его без внимания до тех пор, пока он не будет окончательно подорван или сожжён. Остановка может произойти из-за небольшой

УСЛОВНЫЕ ОБОЗНАЧЕНИЯ

Стреляй из пушек всех калибров и из противотанкового ружья.

Стреляй из пушек всех калибров.

Забрасывай бутылками с горючей жидкостью.

Бей противотанковой гранатой.

неисправности, и экипаж, устранив её или оставаясь в танке (если он подбит), будет продолжать вести огонь по нашей пехоте и истребителям танков. Во всех случаях надо стараться забросать танк гранатами или зажигательными бутылками, а экипаж истребить.

Советский воин, смело иди против вражеского танка! Он не устоит перед тобой. Старайся подпустить фашистский танк или подойти к нему как можно ближе и ты попадёшь в мёртвое пространство, выгодное для единоборства.

Круши броню врага, как наши герои!

♦ Артиллеристы противотанкисты гвардии майора Бородай за первые 3 часа боя сожгли 7 немецких танков. Выдающийся подвиг совершил наводчик 57 мм пушки, парторг батареи тов. Бочаров. Вражеский снаряд вывел из строя расчёт, тяжело был ранен и Бочаров. Обливаясь кровью, герой-парторг один продолжал вести огонь из своего орудия. Громил врага в упор, наверняка. Он сжёг два немецких танка.

Действуй и ты, воин, так же смело и стойко, как парторг-гвардеец Бочаров!

♦ На перекрёстке, где сходились три дороги, находился разрушенный дом. За его передней стеной и выбрал себе позицию для нападения на танк гвардии старший сержант Азизов. «Тигр» подходил всё ближе к перекрёстку. Вот танк сделал поворот и очутился бортом к Азизову. Резкий взмах руки, и под «тигр» полетела противотанковая граната, за ней — вторая. С разбитыми гусеницами «тигр» замер на месте.

Выбирай позицию, как старший сержант Азизов: у перекрёстка дорог, за стеной дома, в канаве, под мостиком, чтобы танк поражать внезапно, наверняка.

♦ Гвардии рядовой Олифер бесстрашно подполз к немецкому танку и метнул в него связку ручных гранат. Танк был уничтожен. Связку сделал так: пять ручных гранат, заряженных и поставленных на предохранительный взвод, крепко связал бичевкой, проводом, проволокой: четыре гранаты рукоятками в одну сторону, а пятую — в противоположную. Возьми связку за рукоятку пятой гранаты и брось её в танк. Эта граната рвётся первой и взрывает всю связку. Можно сделать связку из трёх гранат.

Воины-гвардейцы! Уничтожайте танки врага связками гранат, как уничтожает их гвардии рядовой Олифер!

The thickness of the armour of the Tiger I and the Tiger II in mm shows that frontal protection was given the highest priority. The sloping surfaces on the Tiger II (the angle is given after the slash) increased the depth of armour that had to be penetrated.

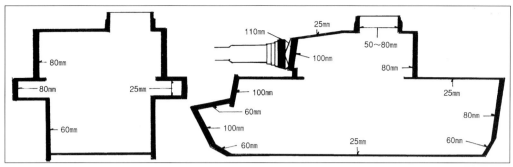

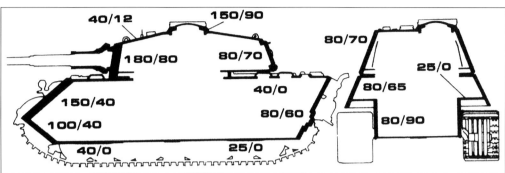

The headlines on the previous page sound very martial:

'Guard soldier!'

Bold and skilful, stronger than a tank!

STRIKE THE TANK!

How to slay the German Panzer T-VI ('Tiger'). Smash the enemy's armour (you too) just like our heroes (of the Soviet Union)!

Another piece of Soviet combat advice captured at the end of 1943.

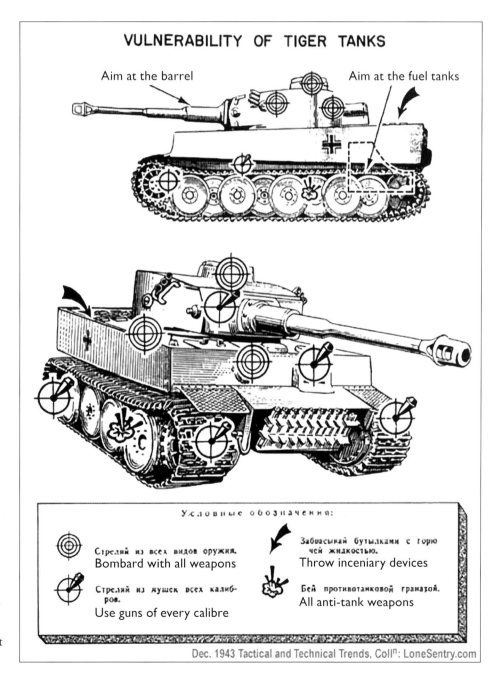

Geschütz	Munition	Durchschlag auf Entfernung von m:		
		v. vorn	v.d.Seite	v. hinten
45 mm Kan.Mod.37	Unterkaliber[+]	--	200 m	200 m
45 mm Kan.Mod.42	Unterkaliber	--	500 m	500 m
57 mm Kan.	Unterkaliber	500 m		
	Pz.Spr.Gr.[++]	--	600 m	600 m
76 mm Flak	Unterkaliber	700 m		
	Pz.Spr.Gr.	--	500 m	500 m
76 mm Kan.	Unterkaliber	100 m	700 m	700 m
86 mm Flak	Pz.Spr.Gr.	--	1000 m	1000 m
122 mm Kan.	Pz.Spr.Gr.	1000 m	1500 m	1500 m
152 mm Kan./Haub.	Pz.Spr.Gr.	500 m	1000 m	1000 m

[+] russische Bezeichnung für Hartkern-Granate

[++] russische Bezeichnung für Panzergranate.

The effect of enemy weapons on the Tiger was analysed after the initial combat experiences. The *Panzeroffizier* responsible for this at the *Chef des Generalstabs des Heeres* (Chief of General Staff of the Army) issued a secret document on 12 September 1943 that contained a table, shown on the left, about the effect of Soviet anti-tank guns.

Marks typical of mass firing on the Tiger from all sides with weapons of all calibres.

The anti-tank crews – just like those of the *Wehrmacht* – reveived combat instructions appropriate for the calibre of the weapons being used. This picture refers to the use of the 4.5 cm *Pak* against the Tiger I. The shaded areas on the tank indicate the areas that should be targeted. The Soviets also continued to develop their munitions; the table (below) is taken from a report about the use of sub-calibre shells by the T-34. This was issued on 25 July 1943 by *Fremde Heere Ost* (German intelligence service).

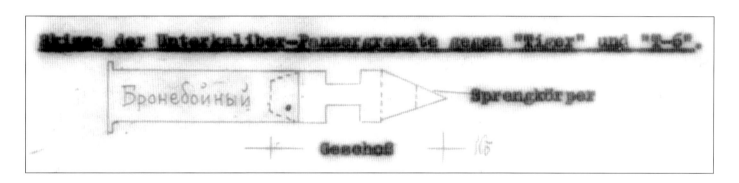

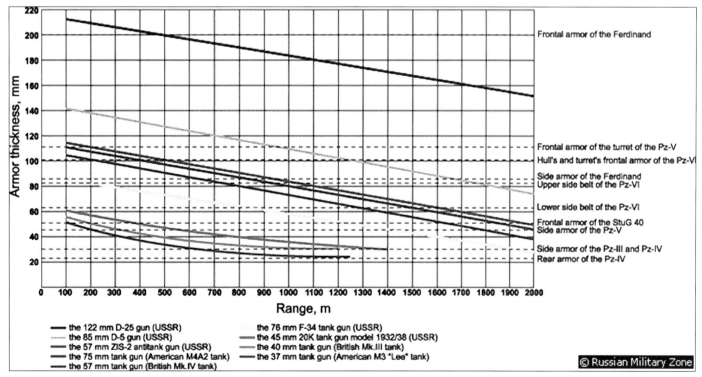

This graph shows the durability of German tanks against selected Soviet and other tank cannons in relation to their firing distances. The second line from the top, which refers to the 122 mm cannon, makes it clear that this weapon also posed a great danger for the Tiger I.

'Minor' causes but major effect! Concentrated fire at particular points on the Tiger could lead to damage that caused loss of mobility. Hammering the roadwheels with fire from anti-tank rifles could cause the rubber bands to become detached and rip off pieces of the wheels causing a loss in track tension that could result in the track running off the drive sprocket. (Photos: Pertuss)

The roadwheels could be ripped off or destroyed by shots from mid-calibre anti-tank guns with consequential track jamming.

Roadwheel hubs that had been shot away leaked oil or grease making them run hot with subsequent seizing.

The following detailed account by *s.Pz.Abt. 502* covering the the period 22 June to 21 August 1944 is particularly telling. A somewhat abbreviated version is reproduced here; the chassis numbers of the vehicles are shown inside brackets.

III. *Panzerkampfwagen* total losses, not salvaged, destroyed and surrendered to the enemy:

1. On 24 June 1944 (…) put out of action by artillery and assault gun hits to the turret. (…) recovery was impossible due to heavy artillery, *Pak* and tank fire and because the main battle line was pulled back. The vehicle was destroyed by our own fire. Damage: could not be properly established. (…) (250232).

2. As in1.
Damage: drive wheel, track and several bogie wheels destroyed by direct hit by artillery fire. (…) (250774).

3. Immobilized on 26 June 1944 (…) by direct hit from artillery fire (rear and right hand side running gear). Recovery no longer possible because of heavy artillery, *Pak* and tankfire.
Damage: rear, radiator and engine badly damaged. Vehicle set on fire by 5 *HL-Granaten*. (250 706)

4. Destroyed by 2 hits from 12.2 cm heavy anti-tank gun on 26 July 1944. Hit to the left side of the hull between the running gear and the upper part of the hull armour plating
Damage: the ammunition was hit. Tank totally burnt out. (250 242)

5. As in 4. (250 782)

6. On 26 July 1944 (…) hit by 15.2 cm assault gun.
Damage: driver's viewing slit penetrated and base of gun mantlet and turret roof hit. Tank burnt out. (250 259)

7. On 24 July (…) a hits from 15.2 cm assault gun to the right side drive sprocket and right side of the turret at the level of the loader.
Damage: turret penetrated. 2 crew dead. Vehicle burnt out and left in enemy hands. (250 462)

8. On 6 August 1944 (…) several hits by 12.2 cm and 7.62 cm *Pak* and tanks to the left side of the turret and hull.
Damage: various penetrating shots. Vehicle burnt out and later exploded. (250 780)

9. On 9 August 1944 (…) 2 severe hits by 8.5 cm shells to the engine compartment.
Damage: Penetrating hit to the left side of the hull at the height of the engine. Tank totally burnt out and in enemy hands. (250 196)

10. On 11 August 1944 (…) 3 severe hits by 8.8 cm *Pak* of German origin (*Pak* 43L71).
Damage: vehicle totally burnt out and in enemy hands. (250 806)

11. On 13 August 1944 (…) hit from *Pak* of German origin in the hull between the running gear and the upper part of the hull on the left at the height of the gunner's vision slit. 3 men dead. Vehicle totally burnt out, initially recovered but later surrendered to the enemy. (250806)

IV. *Panzerkampfwagen* VIs recovered from the battlefield and refurbished:

1. On 24– 26 June 1944 (…) rendered immobile by artillery fire to the left side drive wheel. Further direct hits to the roof of turret.
Damage: final drive on left side blown off together with drive wheel. Turret roof dented in two places (approximately 80 cm in front of the commander's cupola). Gun mantlet damaged by splinters. Turret fittings torn off. Balancing spring linkage rod damaged. Cannon could not be elevated. (250222)

2. On 24–26 June 1944 (…) 15.2 cm shell hit from assault gun to the gun-mantlet pipe. Artillery hits to the driver's hatch cover. Vehicle caught fire for a short time, precise cause unknown.
Damage: Barrel of tank's cannon damaged by fragments. Recoil travel limited. Radio and electrical equipment destroyed. (250 246)

3. On 26 June 1944 (…) Direct hit to the right side of turret at the height of commander's cupola. According to a member of the crew this was by our own fire.
Damage: Turret edge distorted. Dent measures 212 mm long, 135 mm wide and 60 mm deep. Bearing block for gun elevation mechanism destroyed, console bent. Weld-seam ripped about 100 mm from turret roof. Weld-seams for head and side seams torn off. (250 702)

4. On 26 June 1944 (…) an artillery ricochet hit on turret about 15 cm below the left upper turret angle at the height of the commander's cupola. 15.2 cm assault gun hit to hull to the front and left of the driver's hatch cover. On-board weapons attack by Russian fighter plane.
Damage: External damage to armour plate at turret about 350 mm in length and 240 mm in width. Deepest penetration at impact site 23 mm. The track link holding bracket was torn away at this point. 2 m tear to upper turret welding seam. Burst welding seam on the commander's cupola. Welding seam on gunner's viewing slit burst. Emergency exit hatch damaged, MG hits and artillery splinters in the 'steel rucksack' behind the turret. (250234)

5. On 27 June 1944 (…) rendered immobile by hits from artillery and 12 cm mortar fire on the engine cover.
Damage: engine compartment cover deformed. 950 mm long tear. Engine cover badly damaged. Radiator cover torn off. Coolant supply nozzle damaged. Running gear on both sides and muzzle recoil brake on cannon damaged by splinters. (250 748)

An interesting detail regarding repairs can be seen on this vehicle belonging to the '*501*' – entry holes on the side of the hull are plugged with metal stoppers. Picture taken14 February 1943. (Preßmar)

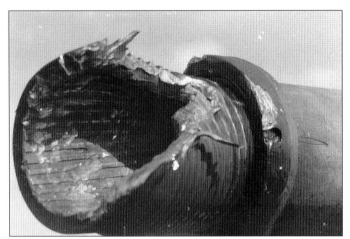

This doesn't look too serious…however the gun barrel needs replacing; a task that takes a considerable amount of time.

Parts that had been broken off could sometimes be welded together again, such as in this picture of a turret from a tank belonging to the '*503*' taken immediately after *Operation Zitadelle.* (Küpper)

This was by no means possible if the damage was structural or the armour plates were ruptured. This picture shows a Tiger of the '*506*' after a substantial direct hit by a 15.2 cm shell on 13 August 1943.

6. (…) hit to the gun mantlet by a *Pak* 7.62 cm. Another hit by a *Pak* 7.62 cm on the gunner's vision slit. Glancing hit by *Pak* 7.62 cm on front of hull. Direct hit by *Pak* on running gear.
Damage: welding seam on bottom right of turret front wall split. Loss of material from the gun mantlet. Turret suspension mechanism damaged by fragments. Mounting block for the turret traverse mechanism affected. Driver's prism shot to pieces. Welding seam in the vicinity of left final drive torn open for 300 mm. Handwheel for closing the driver's vision slit cover broken off. Tracks torn off. Fuel tank punctured and fuel lost. Oil cooler damaged. The Tiger drove on for around 800 m before having to be towed. (250 780)

7. (…) damage caused by a 7.62 cm hard-core shell on the right below the corner of the gun mantlet. Hit by *Pak* of same calibre on the barrel sleeve at the left side of the gun mantlet.
Damage: loss of material on right side of gun mantlet. Damage to the barrel sleeve such that the barrel remains in the rearward position after firing. Gun cradle jammed. Hard-core shell strike on left part of gun mantlet almost penetrated but remained stuck in it. (250 269)

8. (…) 7.62 cm *Pak* hit on the recoil brake and muzzle of cannon.
Damage: barrel unusable because of deformation of muzzle. Shell in barrel destroyed by explosives. (250 781)

9. On 1 August 1944 by driving onto 3 German land mines that had been captured by the Russians. Damage: hull deformed in the middle. 111 cm longitudinal crack, 162 cm transverse crack. Turret turning platform displaced upwards and warped by explosion. Turret traversing mechanism damaged. Track and running gear on left side severely deformed. Various swinging arms bent out of shape. (250 778)

10. Direct hits by artillery shells on the left running gear and base of barrel on gun mantlet. Commander's cupola hit by *Pak* 4.7 cm. 5 direct hits by *Pak* on hull. Gun mantlet badly shot up by 2 cm cannon. Damage: running gear on left side badly damaged. Electrical installations out of action. Firing continued using the emergency firing system. Glass vision block shot to pieces by anti-tank rifle. Participation in combat was not impaired by *Pak* and anti-tank rifles hits. (250 463)

11. Hit by 7.62 cm *Pak* on the left of driver's vision-slit visor, hit by *Pak* on left edge of gun mantlet, hit by *Pak* on track links on left side of turret, hit by 7.62 cm *Pak* on front armour in the vicinity of radio operator (21 mm penetration depth).
Damage: loss of material on driver's visor and gun mantlet mountings. Antennae base broken off. Radio out of action as a result of impact shocks. MG mounting seized. Brackets for track links torn off – three on top and two below. Jammed hatch cover on the commander's cupola. Bracket for MG-belt sacks torn off. (250 778)

12. (…) Two 7.62 cm *Pak* hits below the gun mantlet. *Pak* hits on left side of hull, upper part of the *Panzerkasten*

at the height of the engine. Damage: turret jammed, turret screws torn out. Traversing mechanism jammed. Loader wounded. Radiator cover and upper hull edge damaged at the height of the engine (glancing impact). (250 798)

13. On 5 August 1944 (…) driving onto 4 German land mines captured by Russians. Damage: transmission and engine badly damaged. Running gear on both sides damaged. Both batteries defective. Radio equipment out of action. Both front shock absorbers damaged. Traversing gear and turret locking mechanism defective. (250 263)

14. (…) 7.62 cm *Pak* hit to the gun mantlet. Glancing impact by *Pak* 7.62 cm on commander's cupola on turret. Damage: gun sleeve and mantlet almost penetrated. Swivel arm on the commander's cupola cover shot away. One vision prism cover shot away. Light fittings and Bosch sockets torn off. (250 771)

15. On 6 August 1944 (…) hit by 8.5 cm tank shell on right side of turret. Armour piercing round hit at an angle of around 60 and 70 degrees penetrating to a depth of approximately 80 mm. *Pak* hit to the running gear on left side. Tank nevertheless still able to proceed under its own power. Damage: external damage but no major harm. (250 770)

16. On 8 August 1944 (…) a direct hit by A German 8.8 cm *Pak* 43 (captured by the Russians). Distance 800–900 m. Penetrating shot to the right side of the hull at the height of the engine.
Damage: projectile detonated inside the vehicle causing partial explosion of the ammunition. Tank partially burned. 3 dead, 2 badly injured. Turret platform, linkages and both MGs defective. Ammunition brackets and some internal equipment badly damaged. (250 773)

17. On 13 August 1944 (…) direct by artillery shell on radio operator's hatch.
Damage: wide rip the along the radio operator's hatch. Transmission damaged by fragments. Radio equipment, turret MG, radio operator's MG all destroyed by splinters. Driver's viewing prism and fittings damaged. Traversing mechanism jammed. Radio operator killed instantly. (250 771)

18. (…) 8.5 cm tank shell hit on barrel sleeve left side. Impact by projectile of same calibre on gun mantlet on right side. Damage: loss of material on barrel sleeve and gun mantlet (see photos below). Otherwise no damage. (250 781)

19. 3 direct hits by 7.62 cm *Pak* on front wall to the right of driver's viewing slit visor. 2 *Pak* hits on front of turret. Damage: multiple tears to welding seams on upper part of hull casing. Cannon displaced on cradle. Gun sleeve damaged. Handwheel for closing driver's viewing slit broken off. Consequential damage to gun mounting on mantlet. Loading and safety switches damaged. Securing screws on gun-mounting broken off. Brackets for optical equipment loosened. Radio operator's MG damaged. Welding seam on MG ball-mounting torn open. Radio equipment and lighting out of commission. (250 495)

Tigers – such as tank '231' of the '503' – came under fire from swarms of anti-tank weapons. This picture shows the tank at the Henschel factory in Kassel after it had been delivered for repair. Fortunately, no shots penetrated the fighting compartment. Notwithstanding this, the tank was sent to Paderborn where the turret was used for training. (See Chapter 2)

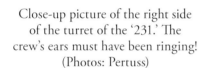

Close-up picture of the right side of the turret of the '231.' The crew's ears must have been ringing! (Photos: Pertuss)

Leutnant Vermehren's Tiger – belonging to the '501' – came under such fire on 27 February 1943. It can only be hoped that the crew managed to bail out. (Hartmann)

20. (…) 8.5 cm *Pak* hit on left side of turret at the height of the commander's cupola. Damage: 4 track links torn off. Turret slewing ring sprung out of position. Turret jammed. Screws for traversing mechanism sheared. (250 804)

21. (…) 8.5 cm *Pak* hit to barrel. Hit by same calibre projectile to left side running gear. Damage: penetrating shot to right side of barrel. The cannon's barrel is unusable. Roadwheels on running gear partially destroyed. (250 663)

The enormous workload of the tank mechanics hardly bears thinking about. Several vehicles had been hit on more than one occasion. Most of the damage by enemy fire that failed to reduce a tank's fitness for combat is not listed here.

However, depressing descriptions such as these should not detract from the otherwise good protection against projectiles offered by the *Pz.Kpfw.* Tiger. One can imagine how much more effect hits such as these had on the Panzer III and IV.

This hit on the barrel of the cannon might look harmless but was nevertheless extremely dangerous; firing it again was not advisable. Otherwise the same thing could happen to the crew as happened to the '117' of the '502' in August 1944.

Severe hits to the slewing ring – like this one on tank '302' of *s.Pz.Abt. 502* – often jammed the turret.

Sometimes a so-called *Steckschüsse* like the one shown in this picture could have a devastating effect because it 'sprayed' metal shards or threw objects around in the interior of the tank causing injury to the crew.

The objective of the enemy was always to ignite the fuel in the rear of the tank or the ammunition stored in the hull. This often brought about a severe detonation such as the one that wrecked tank 'S34' of *13./SS-Pz.Rgt. 1.* There remained very little time – if any at all – for the crew to bail out.

It is remarkable that the *Abteilungen* themselves were able to remedy a great deal of the damage caused by enemy fire; details of this are given in a report made by *s.Pz.Abt. 506* on 15 January 1944:

8. Welding:
Major welding work on 41 tanks (...) was carried out between 20 September and 31 December.
In 5 cases the guard bar on the final drive had to be welded on; this damage was ascribed to shell fire.
In 4 cases ventilation air intake nozzles in the fighting compartment had to be welded on; in one of these cases the ventilation flap had to be made from scratch.
It would be advantageous to set the ventilation nozzles deeper so that they cannot be torn off by high explosive shells and this would avoid the hand grip being blown off. The latter has caused injury to the crew.
28 shot holes were fixed by welding on steel plates.
1 penetrating shot to the turret (120 mm) and 1 to the radiator compartment repaired by welding in custom-made steel plugs.
2 cracks in welding seams (300 to 400 mm) on bow burned out and newly welded by means of carbon electrodes and grinding.
For this welding work 35 kg of 'Böhler FOX A 7, FOX EV 65 and FOX UMZ' nickel electrodes were used.
Minor welding work is not specified here.

This report was evaluated by the *Inspekteur der Panzertruppe or the Generalinspekteur der Panzertruppen*. Regular meetings took place with those technical personnel responsible at the individual office levels as well as with industry representatives.

The reader is already aware of the fact that the Tiger I and II were subject to numerous technical and structural changes during the course of its planning and development and that these were carried out mostly in response to concrete suggestions for improvements or deficits noticed by the troops. These changes concerned not only the tank's steadfastness under enemy fire but also increasing the durability of those components subject to wear and tear. Here too numerous changes were either incorporated into production series in question or modified components and parts were supplied to, and fitted by, the units themselves.

The following is an example of a field report by *s.Pz.Abt. 506* dated 15 January 1944:

Shortcomings in the crew compartment:
It would be more appropriate to install the auxiliary generator in the command vehicle on the gunner's side because most of the shells have to be stored on the loader's

side. The hinges on the loader's hatch must be protected. They have been repeatedly shot off causing wounds to the loader.

In the older optics, the objective lenses lack a wiper. The gunner can hardly reach them with his hand.

There is still sufficient space to install racks for shells next to the radio operator. This vacant space is completely unused.

The cartridge sack has to be deeper so that it is able to accept more cartridges. The loader often does not have time to empty the sack after every sixth shot. This would also enable more spent cartridges to be returned.

The MG 34/40 is prone to jamming. Because the loader is mostly busy at the cannon and so has little time to clear stoppages, the MG is unfortunately often completely unused. The installation of the MG 42 into the tank should be considered. The greater expenditure of ammunition is already sustainable.

A heating system for the crew compartment is absolutely necessary *(after April 1943 it was dropped because of the danger of fire in the engine)*. Most of the winter clothing that was delivered cannot be fully used because it restricts movement.

When under fire, the repeated failure of the on-board radio is uncomfortably conspicuous. Light signals that could be used as an additional means of allowing the commander to communicate with the driver would be appropriate.

After a travelling for a long time, the turret traverse lock becomes loose so that the slightest tilt of the vehicle makes the turret swing about. This allows damage to occur when the cannon strikes houses or trees and so on. Crush injuries to crew members have already occurred in fighting compartments as a result of this.

Hits of this sort often occurred on the old style of cupola; in this picture *Oberleutnant* Scherf of the '503' takes a close look at the damage. (Lochmann)

A capable medical service was crucially important. In rest areas or in villages, 'normal' medical stations could be established such as this one set up by personnel of the '508.' (Hirlinger)

The tanks themselves often had to take wounded personnel to the first aid stations – as in this picture of the '505' taken on 27 December 1943.

Evacuating the wounded took a turn for the better with the arrival of the Sd.Kfz. 251 (*Sonderkraftfahrzeug 251*). This picture from spring 1943 shows a makeshift or 're-assigned' APC belonging to *s.Pz.Abt. 501*.

The field aid stations took care of the transport of severely wounded and brought them to field hospitals.

Logistics (Including Medical Service)

General

Their bravery, high level of training, superior combat power and the – at least during the first half of the war – ability to effectively confront combined arms forces in combat contributed to the great success of the German armoured units in the Second World War – but so too did the superior skills of the German logistics branch. It consisted of the maintenance, supply and medical services.

The somewhat inadequate equipment provided for – and value placed upon – the medical services (***Sanitätsdienst***) of the German heavy armour units have already been referred to in Chapter 1. It must be clearly stated that the lower levels of medical care in the *Wehrmacht* (level 1 –first aid within crews and detachments and level 2 – stabilizing and passing the patient to the next stage of medical care) were, in comparison to other armies and to the conditions prevailing today, rather badly organized. But this in no way detracts from the commitment and competence of the personnel involved – a fact repeatedly verified by the consistently positive descriptions of former soldiers.

The adequate provisioning (***Versorgung***) of the Tigers, with particular regard to fuel and ammunition, was the key to local success but the lack of this was all too often the cause of substantial losses. The sheer number (and size) of the 8.8 cm shells required and the Tiger's high fuel consumption regularly overextended the supply services. The tactical striking distance of a fully armed Tiger was comparative large but the same cannot be said of its driving range, particularly in heavy ground. It was therefore imperative to constantly refuel the Tiger for tactical reasons in preparation for periods of intensive combat during which – while under threat by the enemy – this was not possible. At times it was necessary for individual vehicles to pull back for refuelling. This reduced number of cannons facing the enemy with serious consequences for the fighting strength of the Tigers as a group.

The sometimes questionable, poor cooperation with the logistics forces at higher levels was problematic. Basically, the subordination of a heavy tank battalion to a larger military unit was coupled with a duty to provide it with supplies. However, in reality this not infrequently led to friction because the new commander with overall responsibility treated his own units preferentially or because the sudden, and significantly higher, volume of necessary supplies was simply not available. There were often times during which Tiger battalions remained idle in their positions because of a lack of fuel and so were not available to assist the hard-pressed German troops.

Nevertheless, it must be stressed that the accomplishments of the supply services were well regarded – in marches and during periods of combat they worked around the clock. A few examples coming from reports clearly describe the challenges.

Report by *s.Pz.Abt. 503* on 10 October 1943:

> Spare part requirements for Tigers during the period 1 August to 21 September 1943: almost 276 tonnes, supply units covered 14,000 km in the last nine months; fuel supply units transported 1.5 million litres of petrol and 250,000 litres of diesel fuel in the same time interval (equivalent to 88 tankers).
>
> From 5 July–30 September 1943 the following spare parts were installed by *s.Pz.Abt. 503*: 813 bogie wheels, 32 drive sprockets, 32 roadwheels, 980 track-link bolts, 4 complete tracks (6 tonnes) as well as 260 individual track links, 32 gearboxes and 28 engines. Added to this were numerous replacement parts for repairs, including that of engines, that were not returned (another 10).
>
> In total, 97 instances of severe running gear damage (19 of these by mines) were repaired, as well as 35 cases of severe turret and 19 of severe hull damage. 10 unserviceable tank cannons had to be replaced together with 12 commanders' cupolas.

Interestingly, the report mentions the 'normal' waiting period for the supply of spares – an average of six weeks – as being too long and that these usually had to be picked up from a from an intermediate storage facility that was too far away. This meant that a state of readiness could only be established at the beginning of operations by priority deliveries sent directly from the central depot in Burg.

These shortcomings forced the troops themselves to stockpile as much as possible, which of course had disadvantages for the whole supply chain. In mid-1943, the *Ia* training officer of the General Inspectorate of the Armoured Troops ordered the delivery of one registered spares package for every ten new vehicles as basic equipment. However, this did not take place in practice.

A field report by *s.Pz.Abt. 503*, issued 25 November 1944, shows just how decisively the lack of spares could affect operational readiness:

> On 31 October the unit rolled into a new position within the framework of the *LVII. Pz.-Korps* in the vicinity of Kecskemet in order to intercept the Russian spearhead on Budapest. In difficult, and in places swampy, terrain that was most unsuitable for tanks, defects began to show up suddenly, particularly in the drive sprockets, tracks, track tensioners, and ventilation fans. Within a few days and for the want of spare parts – requested but not delivered in good time – this led to technical failures in most of the battalion.

Lack of supplies – especially of fuel – led to far more losses than occurred in battle, particularly towards the end of the war. Technical failures of every kind accrued in addition to the diminishing ability to rescue abandoned vehicles and pass them on [for repair] in good time.

The few tanks that were still combat worthy were shunted from one division to another and given tasks that were inappropriate, impractical and unsustainable.

The task of the '*Kutscher*' ('coachman') was tough with few breaks such as the one illustrated in this picture from 23 November 1942 at the '*502*.' Notice the 'range extender') on the roof of the cab. (Toell)

Supplies arrived by various means of transport as can be seen in this picture taken in September 1943 in the assembly area assigned to *s.Pz.Abt. 502*. (BA 461-212-6)

Bottlenecks, such as the one shown here, could crop up even in the middle of a battle and had to be cleared by any means available. This picture of vehicles belonging to the '*502*' was taken on 6 April 1944.

Field kitchens such as this one belonging to the '*501*' (photographed in the vicinity of Bialystok on 10 December 1943) were generally to be found towards the rear of the supply detachments. The food had to be collected by the *Versorgungsunteroffizier* (NCO in charge of supplies) or the '*Spieß*' and transported forwards. The preference was to set up alongside settlements as shown in this picture (below) – taken near Pleskau in April 1943 – of a kitchen and water trailer belonging to the '*503*.'

The arrival of the *Kompaniefeldwebel* (company sergeant) with food, personal items and post was always welcomed. This picture, taken in May 1943, shows members of the '*502*' at Chateau forest Bois du Loup.

Tank crews, then and nowadays too, strive to be self-sufficient. Here we see the crew of tank '211' of the '*503*' stockpiling loaves of bread.

Usually the Tigers were taken to the repair stations with the aid of Sd.Kfz.10 Famos (prime movers). Details of this are explained in Chapter 4. (BA 461-214-3)

The transport units at corps or army level were equipped with trailers that made moving heavy loads over long distances by road much easier but these were available only in small numbers. The picture shows a vehicle belonging to the '504' on a former British trailer.

Damaged equipment was often transported by rail; here we see an already loaded vehicle from the '503' at the station in Koriszinse on 29 September 1943.

Recovery and Evacuation to the Rear

From the very beginning, Tiger units were not well equipped for this task. The technical limitations and the disproportionate effort required to recover Tigers have already been described in sufficient detail in the Chapter 4.

A solution to this serious deficiency was requested from the time when Tigers were first deployed as, for example, in a report made by *2./s. Pz.Abt. 502* dated 29 January 1943:

> II. The 18-t *Zgkw*, [18 ton half-track vehicle] is much too light; even using 3 or 4 of them it is almost impossible to tow away 1 *PzKpfwg*. VI in heavy ground. On sloping ground the *PzKpfwg*. pushes the *Zgkw*. away. Greater braking power is required. Trials have shown that on steep ground, 3 *Zgkw*. are required at the front and 2 behind to act as brakes in order to take the *PzKpfwg*. over steep ground under reasonable control. It is recommended that each unit receives 2 Tiger chassis (vehicles that have been withdrawn from use) as a means of towing.
>
> III. Towing away a Tiger with 4 or 5 *Zgkw*. on the route of advance hinders the traffic for the whole length of a column. Marching within a column is difficult. Starting and stopping suddenly within a column is almost impossible. Towing at night over long march routes is impossible because the carrying capacity of every bridge has to be tested; narrow valleys or other such obstacles are beyond consideration at night.
>
> IV. Towing the Pz. Kpfwg. VI with 4 *Zgkw*. over a stretch of 150 km resulted in damage to the clutch and gears of all 4 of *Zgkw*. The gears of 1 *Zgkw*. were so badly damaged that the whole transmission unit had to be replaced.

Following on from this, a number of specific technical suggestions for the improvement of the recovery equipment were made.

A report by *s.Pz.Abt. 503* on 10 October 1943 states:

> In their first 9 months of deployment, each of the 18 ton trucks covered on average 7,000 km while towing,' (not counting relocation marches).
>
> During the period 22 June to 21 August 1944 – in other words two months – at *s.Pz.Abt. 502* we find the following results: 244 towing events 'during which the towing platoons – on average three 18 ton *Zgkw*. – covered 4,280 km.' Here it was apparent that during predominantly long evasion operations the distances covered lengthened!

The availability of the powerful *Bergepanther* for this critical task changed little from the middle of 1944. Firstly, these expensive vehicles were only available in small numbers (see table, Chapter 1) and secondly, they were derived from the Pz. Kpfw. Panther and were only conditionally suitable for towing the significantly heavier Tiger II. On the other hand, its winch performance was always adequate. Despite a ban to the contrary, it was usually Tigers that towed wrecked vehicles over long distances and in doing so often ruined their own final drives. Transport for the evacuation of broken down vehicles that did not cause them further damage – in the form of low-loader trailers or the like – were as good as non-existent at the rear of the front line. Because essential repairs and major restorations of badly damaged vehicles took place in special repair workshops, these vehicles – if possible –were transported by rail. Having said that, the effort required to manoeuver immobilized vehicles onto a wagon was anything but trivial.

The ongoing inadequacy of provision of suitable recovery apparatus for the larger German units made itself felt during the enemy-enforced withdrawals.

A few examples of this follow.

Technical Report Nr. 6 by *s.Pz.Abt. 501* in Tunisia on 3 May 1943 states (chassis numbers in brackets):

> Annihilation by concentrated *Pak* and artillery fire and shelling by enemy Churchill tanks. The exact nature of the damage cannot be ascertained because the Tiger is inside the enemy's main combat line. The *Pz.Kpfw*. is however completely destroyed. (250031)

This report is pure nonsense. This vehicle (turret Nr. '712') was simply abandoned and fell into American hands during a battle. Later, they took it to Aberdeen where it underwent intensive examination.

> Final drive damaged by shellfire. Attempted recovery prevented by the approach of the opponent. The Pz. Kpfw. was blown up. (250013)
>
> Immobilized by hit from *Pak* to the rear of the engine compartment. Salvage was not possible on account of the situation, detonation carried out. (250024)
>
> Both tracks were damaged when (250017) ran onto mines while making a detour around the immobilized Pz. Kpfw. 250013. Hindered by lack of recovery equipment and the rapid advance of the enemy, it was necessary to blow up the Pz. Kpfw.
>
> 250024 was blown up after its final drive was forced off when the track rolled up on it. Because of an immediate threat by the enemy recovery was no longer possible.

With regard to the sturdiness of the engine the report stated:

> 5 engines operated without significant faults for nearly 3,000 km.

In a field report by *s.Pz.Abt. 503* dated 10 October 1943, an interesting statement is to be found relating to compensating for the technical shortcomings of the over-stretched 18-t-*ZgKw.*:

> In order to supplement the 18-ton towing vehicles that have been worn out by the constantly high demands placed on them during their deployment, the battalion has, so far successfully, used a still-mobile Tiger with an irreparable hull and turret that had become inoperative as a 'Berge-Tiger'.

In particular, the 18-ton towing vehicles – four of which often have to be coupled together for the purpose of towing – show signs of fatigue in the front and rear cross members, to which the trailer couplings are attached, by constantly breaking off. To reinforce the rear beams, the workshop attached, by means of screws and welding, 25 mm-thick boiler plates (railway) that had been cut to the correct shape. To further stabilize the rear cross member, diagonal braces were welded on between the cross member and the longitudinal chassis beams. The front cross members were replaced with reinforced steel 'U' beams. During rigid towing on open ground it is apparent that there is insufficient movement of the trailer coupling. This causes lateral jamming that leads to the repeated breakage of the towbar coupling fork.'

Finally, a better supply of spare parts was called for. The question arises as to whether or not it would have been more effective to plan to use from the outset one or two partly finished Tigers (without turret weapons) per company as a means of towing. The resultant loss of 'guns to the enemy' would certainly have been offset by the increased number of recovered vehicles!

When there is an accumulation of damaged equipment it usual to establish collection points, for example in covered areas, from which the vehicles would be retrieved little by little.

Major repair facilities such as the one at Sanok (see above) operated at army-group level. This saved taking the vehicles back to the manufacturer in Germany. The picture (right) shows Tiger '4' of the '502' outside the Henschel facility in Kassel. Standing to its right is an assembly module used in the construction of tank hulls. (Pertuss)

The timely relocation of repair facilities and the equipment gathered at them also required advance planning. This went badly wrong at the '503' when 21 Tigers fell into enemy hands in one fell swoop near Potasch on 30 March 1943!

Evacuation by train could also go wrong – here we see three Tigers of 'SS 102' loaded onto a train that fell into American hands on 8 September 1944, at Braine.

Captured equipment was always a matter of great interest for the victor. In the foreground of this photograph of an improvised exhibition of captured equipment in Italy we see a Tiger that previously belonged to the '508.'

Who does not know of the many photographs of scenes that document the sometimes chaotic environment in which the repair and maintenance services worked, of the adverse conditions under which they fulfilled their extremely important duty? This picture shows the '*502*' in October 1943. (BA 457-56-15)

12 November 1943, in Orscha with *s.Pz.Abt. 505*. (Boche)

Work in the open air; *s.Pz.Abt. 424* in autumn 1944.

12 December 1942 with *s.Pz.Abt. 501*; a captured Ford is put to good use.

Repair and Maintenance

It is not the main purpose of this book to examine all of the many facets of this topic which of course were very important as far as operational readiness of the Tiger was concerned. This could form the content of another, more extensive, book about the Tiger which of necessity would be heavily focused on technical matters.

From the descriptions given in Chapters 3 and 4, the reader can easily see that these tasks were very complex and could only be successfully fulfilled thanks to the well-trained specialists in the military workshop sections of the *Wehrmacht* as whole and the Tiger units in particular. The general doctrine for their use and their remits applied basically to all armoured units and therefore also to the Tiger formations. The distribution of work within the different armoured units followed the same principles. At the level of the tank crew, the focus was on technical care and service with a small proportion of maintenance work. At the company unit or sub-unit level there was limited self-sufficiency with regard to the maintenance of the vehicle; the focus here was on the identification of defects and providing personnel for supporting the repair and maintenance service at combined-arms unit level, that is to say the crews of damaged vehicles remained with their tanks and worked under their guidance.

However, the heavy armoured battalions had to be more self-sufficient because they were only occasionally subordinated to major military units. There was therefore a series of distinctive features in structure and equipment that differed from those in units of other Panzer regiments. In addition, the anticipated higher maintenance and repair requirements of the Pz. Kpfw. Tiger, was taken into account in the *Truppeneinteilung* (TOE) by the allocation of their own tank workshop company rather than only a platoon. According to *Merkblatt b* of 1942 (which referred to vehicle repair and maintenance services for tank units) these were only intended for tank regiments. The original intention was to split the repair and maintenance services into three levels:

> The company *I-Gruppen* (repair squads) will repair minor defects.
> The staff company *I-Staffel* will deal with medium damage.
> Severe damage will be remedied by *Panzer Werkstatt Kompanie* (tank workshop company).
> (*Gen.Insp. der Panzertruppen – Ia Ausb.* 8 June 1943 '*Einsatzerfahrungen mit den Tigern*')

These regulations clearly had to be applied more flexibly on a day-to-day basis and this included the use of mobile repair teams from the *Werkstattkompanie* ('flying platoons'

as called for by *Major* Lueder's [instructions of] 18 March 1943), especially when a heavy tank battalion had been split prior to deployment. It was important too that the repair services were informed of major damage so that they were better able to structure their response. This was not an easy matter with poor radio equipment. Communication was often maintained using radio sets of damaged tanks.

To establish the different states of readiness, and also in the course of routine maintenance, all crew members carried out a great many checks. However, unlike today, there were no information and warning displays or diagnostic interfaces or such like that could have made these tasks more effective. It was therefore essential that the driver, and if possible the whole crew, had a good basic technical understanding so that they could recognise potential faults at an early stage and so avoid entering critical operating conditions in the first place. Care and maintenance and technical servicing are in the true sense of the terms not '*Instandsetzung*' (repairs) – the collective term for these activities in German is '*Materialerhaltung*' – as these should mostly consist of predefined routine activities necessary for establishing the combat worthiness of the vehicle, a particular state of operational readiness, the fitness of components or whole systems for service, or taking measures made necessary by wear and tear.

Experienced crews were also in the position of being able to carry out automatically such activities that were actually reserved for the repair personnel if these had finally reached the limit of their physical endurance, or the time they had available, because of continual stress. This was aided by the fact that the crew – often in the absence of the commander – remained present when work was being carried out on their tank and so were able to 'look over the shoulder' of experts and also because the tank mechanics and drivers – at least to begin with – had completed factory placements (see above).

Another reason for the overall effectiveness of the repair services was that, because of their specialist knowledge (and also the workshop equipment available to them), they were able to carry out much of the work – such as the processing of materials – themselves. At a certain level of damage it became more effective to turn the vehicles away and transport them to repair factories or even back to the manufacturer. Often there was nothing to be done except to strip out spare parts for other damaged tanks.

Much like today, whole component assemblies were dismantled and exchanged for replacements, or the damaged assemblies were repaired at higher maintenance levels and returned if necessary.

Another aspect that requires special consideration is that of the supply of spare parts. This requirement was, bearing in mind the normal wear and tear and the usual periodic work, already relatively high. With breakdowns resulting from damage and the ensuing additional repair effort required, the demand for spare parts increased significantly and often could not be covered by stockpiling them. Examples from reports provide impressive evidence of this.

> Without taking into account the spare parts still required after the effects of shocks from mine explosions, the following spare parts have become necessary during this mission (lasting from 18–21 January 1943 and involving up to nine Tigers): 27 rubber tyres, 6 tyre pressure rings, 7 double roadwheels, 14 outer roadwheels, 6 inner roadwheels, 64 track links, 59 track bolts, 4 crank arms, 2 torsion bars, 1 shock absorber, 5 rubber buffers, 1 guide wheel, 1final drive…
>
> (Report by *s.Pz.Abt. 501* dated 27 January 1943)

The following is taken from the report by *s. Pz.Abt. 501* dated 3 February 1943:

> Pair of Tigers shelled on 31 January 1943 by artillery; hit to fan cover plate on turret, tank serviceable again after three hours. Hit on the other vehicle on the upper hull plate, shell fragments blocked turret bearing; tank had to break off contact with enemy and could only be made serviceable hours later after lifting the turret.

The performance level of the repair services during combat was impressively high and ultimately crucial for the combat strength of the unit, often more so than the number of shells fired by enemy tanks. This is singled out time and time again in the reports submitted by the battalions. The following statements are given as examples.

Report by *s.Pz.Abt. 502* relating to the battles during summer 1944.

Period 23–30 June 1944: up to 32 Tigers I tanks in the area, combat readiness on average 43.7%; workshop released six repairs.

Period 4–27 July 1944: up to 45 Tigers in area, 41.2% serviceable, workshop released 48 repairs;

Period 28 July–6 August 1944: up to 43 Tigers in area, 31.2% serviceable, workshop released 45 repairs. Report by *s.Pz.Abt. 503* after *Operation Zitadelle* in 1943. Period 1 August–21 September 1943: 38 tanks available at beginning, on 24 August 49 Tigers, just short of 30% serviceable on a daily basis (approximately 12 vehicles), 240 major repairs carried out in reporting area.

An interesting detail is to be found in a document relating to the deployment of tanks in the Italian theatre issued by *s.Pz.Abt. 504* on 3 October 1944:

> The workshop services and part of the workshop for tank repair are to be sent forward to the vicinity of the tanks in action. (location: repair services 3–5 km behind tank positions; fully functional tank repair workshop 10-12 km behind active tank units).

In combat it was found that damaged tanks did not necessarily need repairs that took a long time – often all that was required was quickly available expertise and tools that were not carried on the tank. These vehicles could be available for redeployment on the front line within a short period of time. It is of course important to bear in mind that there was a growing danger that the workshops would come under threat (for example by artillery) and that with the approach of the enemy they had insufficient time to relocate (it took time to dismantle the gantry crane!) However, it soon became apparent that that after a short time, and almost without exception, all tanks required repairs during which they were not available for deployment. The technical field report by *s.Pz.Abt.506* dated 15 January 1944 serves as an example of this:

> Received for repair: 20 September–31 December 75 damaged tanks
> Number of these refurbished : 62 tanks
> Number of these requiring repairs in homeland: 6 tanks

In this period, among other things, 39 engines, 16 gearboxes and 13 steering assemblies were either removed and reinstalled or exchanged. On 60 tanks, severe damage to the running gear was repaired; on 28 tanks track drive components were replaced; on 28 tanks the cooling system was damaged and 14 tanks had damaged brakes repaired. Extensive welding work was carried out on 41 tanks.

As previously mentioned, the standard regulations incorporated advice with repair instructions for technical components that did not fall within the responsibility of the fighting crew members. The servicing schedules also contained advice usually intended for the repair squads or the workshop companies. Nevertheless the crews themselves ultimately benefited greatly from knowledge of this 'foreign' content which was at least perfectly suitable for making important technical interactions clear to them and this, in turn, prevented the incorrect operation of tanks. What concerned the crews in the context of incidental tasks can be summed up by saying that they functioned as a 'extra pairs of hands' for the repair personnel if their tank had suffered a (partial) malfunction; that is to say they were not themselves responsible. In the picture section that follows, a whole series of such examples are provided.

It was always problematic when tank companies – or even individual tanks – were deployed far from their battalion for a long period of time. The 'host' units were only partially in the position of being able to provide technical support because of a lack of spare parts and the inadequate workshop facilities in their own workshops (they had none of the special tool kits for the Tiger, no gantry cranes, and no expertise). Where at all possible, the Tiger battalions therefore put together a so-called *Versorgungspaket* (support team) with an *I-Gruppe* (repair squad) provided for each company, a section from the repair platoon (with an allocation of spare parts) and a truck from the munitions section (with 8.8 cm tank ammunition). Fuel supply and vehicle recovery support was provided by the unit to which the Tigers were subordinated. It has to be stated that the bottom line here was that this was a purely an emergency solution that led to the subordinated Tiger groups not being adequately served and the rest of the unit being gravely weakened.

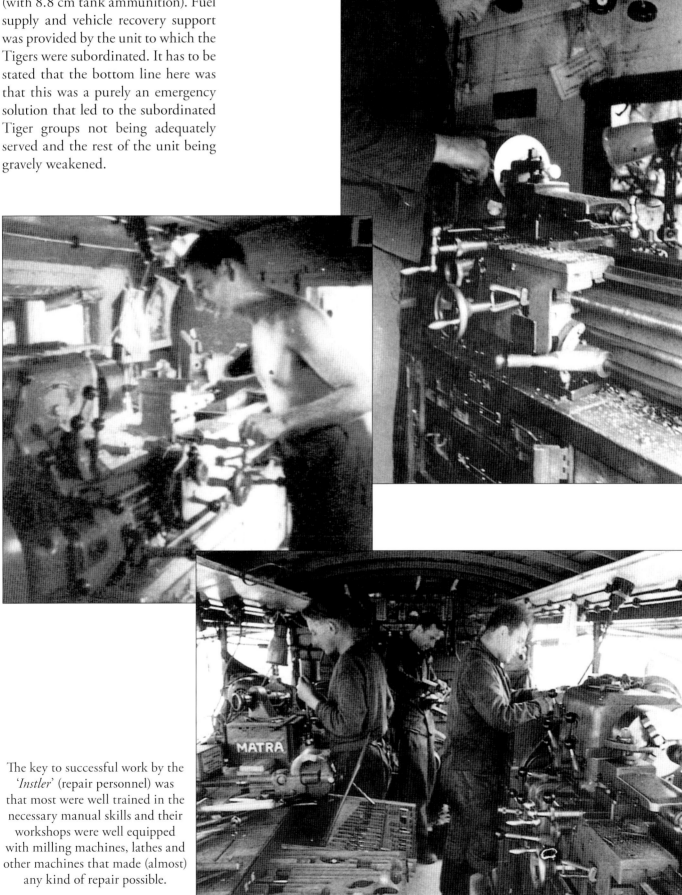

The key to successful work by the *'Instler'* (repair personnel) was that most were well trained in the necessary manual skills and their workshops were well equipped with milling machines, lathes and other machines that made (almost) any kind of repair possible.

Many of the repair services officers – here we see *Oberleutnant* Stiegler, chief of the '505' *Werkstattkompanie* in October 1943 in Orscha with his *Oberwerkmeister* (senior workshop supervisor) – had an engineering degree and were well trained for their tasks. (BA 278-875-16a)

The *Oberwerkmeister* played a large part in the success of the repair staff – here we see *Werkmeister* Späth of the '503' on duty, as he listens to the sounds made by an engine in a sorry state. This picture was taken in Orscha on 16 July 1943.

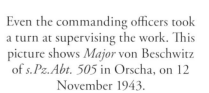

Even the commanding officers took a turn at supervising the work. This picture shows *Major* von Beschwitz of *s.Pz.Abt. 505* in Orscha, on 12 November 1943.

The sergeants and NCOs of the repair services – who were usually qualified craftsmen – instructed the mechanics or, if the task was a complex one, did the work themselves. This picture, also taken in Orscha, shows repair personnel belonging to the '505' at work in October 1943. (BA 278-875-32)

The platoon leader – here we see *Leutnant* Schnitzlein of the '508' – and the leaders of the *I-Gruppen* were involved mostly with the determination of the cause of damage so that this did not have to be done at the repair facility. (Herwig)

The crews remained with their tanks and acted as handymen as in this picture, taken at the '501' on 12 December 1942. In this way the crew developed a better relationship with the technical staff.

1, Kfz.-Art	**Werkstatt-Auftrag-Nr.**		Schadstellen	Instandsetzungsarbeiten	Std.
2. Fabrikat	Werkst.-Einh, den		7. Motor		
3. Typ	Instandsetzungsdurchführung 1)		8. Kupplung		
4. WH-Nr.	a) truppeneigener Werkst. (W. Kp.)		9. Kühlanlage		
5. Fgst.-Nr.	b) n. truppeneigener Werkst. (Park / Heimat-Inst.)		10. Kraftstoffanl.		
6. Einheit			11. Auspuffanlage		

(Unterschrift der entscheidenden Stelle)

Abgabe an Kf.-Park oder Heimatinstandsetzung

Abgang Datum	verladen von Station	— abgeschleppt 1) nach Station	Fahrt-Nr.	Empfänger	fahrbereit ja - nein	schleppfähig ja - nein

fehlende Aggregate: 2)

(Unterschrift des Einheitsführers)

Verbrauchte Ersatzteile

Zu diesem Auftrag gehören	Übergabe nach Instands.	Verwaltungsmäß. Prüfung
Stoffverlangzettel Nr.	Datum	
	Befund	
Werkstatt-Arbeitszettel		
	Übergeben:	
Rechnung Nr.		
	Unterschrift des Werk- bzw. Schirrmeisters) übernommen:	
(Unterschrift des Werkmeisters)	(Unterschrift, Dienstgrad, Dienststelle)	(Unterschrift des Prüfenden)

Anmerkungen :
1) Zutreffendes unterstreichen
2) Abgabequittungen beifügen, wo nicht vorhanden — Ausfallbescheinigung

5a III. I. 45. 100000 Hugo Hsaicke, Berlin

Schadstellen	Instandsetzungsarbeiten	Std.
7. Motor		
8. Kupplung		
9. Kühlanlage		
10. Kraftstoffanl.		
11. Auspuffanlage		
12. Wechselgetriebe		
13. Zusatzgetriebe		
14. Kraftübertragung		
15. Ausgleichsgetriebe		
16. Lenkgetriebe		
17. Aufbau		
18. Rahmen		
19. Bremsanlage		
20. Vorderachse		
21. Hinterachse		
22. Lenkung		
23. Federn		
24. Kettenantrieb		
25. Laufwerk		
26. Kettenspanner-Leitrad		
27. Hilfsrahmen		
28. Gleiskette		
29. Elektr. Anlage		
30. Zentralschmierung		
31. Generator		
32. Verschiedenes		
	Gesamt-Stunden	

Order must prevail – in this case bureaucratic order! A *Werkstatt-Auftrag* (job instruction form) was filled in by the troops – the front and rear of one is shown above. This remained with the vehicle until it left the workshop and was used to record the work and used parts required and as the basis of a request for new parts. The arrival and departure of the vehicle was also documented.

The *Abteilung* had a reserve of basic spare parts which, over the months of the war, was modified in light of the use that was made of them. However, the battalions usually administered their own supplies to circumvent the occurrence of bottlenecks during the long delivery cycles. This scene shows the '*501*' on 12 December 1942.

Heavy loads such as the ventilation inserts shown here at the '503' had to be lifted onto the Tigers in great numbers. The 3-t-Bilstein crane mounted on a 4.5-t-Büssing-NAG 4500A truck fulfilled this task well. (Wunderlich)

The 3-t-Bilstein was always in demand for lifting the engine compartment cover plate and the power plant itself as seen in this picture taken at the '501' on 12 December 1942.

It took two cranes – and a good deal of skill by the operators – to lift this turret of a tank belonging to s.Pz.Abt. 502 in summer 1944.

The 6-ton crane on the Famo 18-ton halftrack was significantly more powerful. This one is atwork at *s.Pz.Abt. 502*.

A deceptive picture; a engineer unit loaned this 10-t-Faun crane to the '*504*' in Fallingbostel in February 1943.

For much of the work in the interior of the Tiger it was necessary to remove the turret, for example when work is being carried out on the turret traversing mechanism drive... (BA 278-874-34)

...or the drive shaft needs to be replaced...

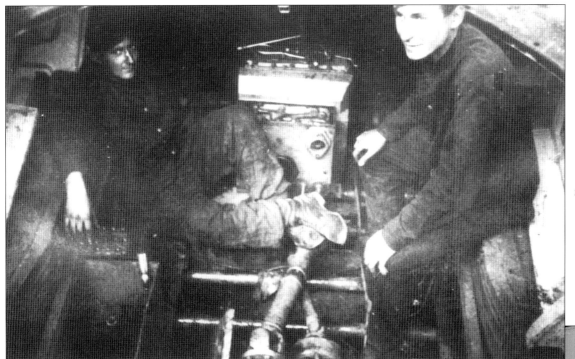

... or when the bearings on the torsion bars are replaced, for example after being damaged by a mine explosion beneath the hull. (Byrden)

The main workhorse for lifting heavy loads was the legendary, and portable, gantry crane – the so-called 'Strabo' (*Straßenbock-Kran*) produced by Firma Fries in Frankfurt. The principle of the factory crane was, so to speak, transferred to the '*Straße*' (road). The picture (left) shows a scene from *s.Pz. Abt. 503* in January 1943.

When danger threatened, and also to make camouflaging the crane easier, it was lowered – as seen in this picture at *s.Pz.Abt. 506* in spring 1944.

Tiger I and Tiger II units Tiger I und Tiger II Einheiten	Strabokran version							K.St.N.	QTY Anzahl	Replacement Ersatz
	1942	1943		1944		1945				
	15t	15t	16t	15t	16t	15t	16t			
s.Pz.Abt.501	x		x		x		x	1187 b	2	4
s.Pz.Abt.502	x	x	x	x	x	x	x	1187 b	2	2
s.Pz.Abt.503 / FHH	x	x	x	x	x		x	1187 b	2	2
s.Pz.Abt.504		x			x		x	1187 b	2	2
s.Pz.Abt.505			x		x		x	1187 b	2	2
s.Pz.Abt.506			x		x		x	1187 b	2	2
s.Pz.Abt.507			x		x		x	1187 b 1.11.44	2	2
s.Pz.Abt.508			x		x			1187 b	2	
s.Pz.Abt.509			x		x		x	1187 b 1.11.44	2	2
s.Pz.Abt.510					x		x	1187 b	2	
13./Pz.Rgt. GD		x						1185 d	1	
III./Pz.Rgt. GD		x	x	x	x		x	1185 d	1	1
s.Pz.Kp. »Hummel«		x			x		x	1185 d	1 + 1	
s.Pz.Kp. »Meyer«										
13./SS-Pz.Rgt.1	x	x	x					1185 d	1	
8./SS-Pz.Rgt.2	x	x	x					1185 d	1	
9./SS-Pz.Rgt.3			x		x			1185 d	1	
s.SS-Pz.Abt.101 (501)			x		x		x	1187 b	2	2*
s.SS-Pz.Abt.102 (502)					x		x	1187 b	2	2*
s.SS-Pz.Abt.103 (503)					x		x	1187 b	2	2*

Volker Ruff's very informative book contains this inventory table for Tiger units.

This series of photographs shows the removal of a turret at *s.Pz.Abt. 503,* in summer 1943, from mounting the hoisting plates on the turret side-spigots and the attachment of cables to the crane hooks, to the adjustment of the crane with a hand crank and the slow lift followed by a swing to the side – with three men keeping the turret in balance – and then setting it down onto two wooden trestles. During the manual, sideways positioning of the turret, great care was taken to avoid striking anything with the turret basket. (Photos: Kipper)

A similar series of photographs taken by the *Propagandakompanie* photographer Wehmeyer at *s.Pz.Abt.505,* on 12 December 1943, shows the sequence of events during the installation of the turret which had been set down on four 200-litre barrels. It is evident that there is now a more expedient method of hoisting turrets, namely the use of adjustable tensioning screws (turnbuckle screws). These can be seen attached to the ring on the crane's lifting hook. By adjusting these, any lop-sidedness in the turret could be levelled – the crew members no longer had to clamber about on it. Manual alignment was only required when the load was lowered. The hull was then driven under the freely suspended turret. The procedure shown here is using the later 16-ton variant of the crane to which a series of improvements had been made. During the slow process of lowering the turret, scrupulous care again had to be taken to avoid the slightest damage to the slewing ring or turret basket.

The *Torbogenkran* (gate-arch crane) used by the Panzer III/IV and assault gun units. This picture shows it being used by the '*508*' to lift a turret – a task that overloaded the crane.

If no replacement components were available, engines or gearboxes had to be laboriously dismantled, as is shown in this picture taken at the '*508*.'

Removing the whole power plant was undertaken with reluctance; here it is sufficient to remove only the cylinder head of a Tiger II. This picture of the '*503*' was taken in Mailly-le-Camp.

The working conditions in a factory were almost heavenly. Here we see a tank belonging to *s.Pz.Abt. 508* at the Arco factory in Rome in February 1944. (Schlumberger)

Support by the repair and maintenance troops subordinated to combined arms units was an everyday occurrence. Damaged equipment could be taken to their facilities or mobile teams could be sent to the battalion *Werkstattkompanie*. (Jung)

Ground that was cut-up and boggy made the deployment of tanks much more difficult, as is shown in this picture of the '*502*' in September 1943. (BA 461-217-13)

Failure to reconnoitre bridges brings tank '321' of the '*503*' to a standstill near Kirsino on 28 August 1943. (Herrmann)

High cornfields could be full of nasty surprizes, even for this column of the '*503*' as it marches towards Wissokopolje on 16 August 1943.

Employment of the Tiger Battalions

There are numerous reports indicating the irrational use, or misuse, of the valuable Tiger units by the combined arms units to which they were subordinated.

Here are a few examples:

It must be achievable, by strict orders issued by command posts, to ensure that Tiger units are never, under any circumstances, deployed in below-company strength (…). The Tiger must be, and remain, a battering ram in attack and a buffer stop in defence. The troops are generally of the view that the Tiger can do anything. It has to be appreciated that a new design has faults and weaknesses that can only be remedied by further development based on experience. For these reasons there is a danger that Tiger units are assigned tasks that can easily be handled by existing normal armoured units. Due to ongoing relocation and therefore greater demand on the running gear and engines without the required time for technical servicing, faults develop such that Tiger units are missing when they are needed. Workshops must be able to work in one place for as long as possible (a railway station is suitable). When changing positions they need to know exactly where they are going. The Tiger units must provisionally remain the last reserve of the troop leader, stand prepared behind the section where the focal point is, and be ready for action in order to act decisively when all other means fail.

(*Hptm.* Lange, CO 2./s.Pz.Abt. 502 on 29 January 1943)

These statements were later copied almost word for word in a paper entitled 'Summary of Reports about the Operational Experiences of the Tiger' issued by the *Panzerlehrgänge* on 28 May 1943. This demonstrates that the reports from the front line were in fact read and evaluated. Further important statements were made in this paper:

Basically, deployment in boggy ground is to be forbidden. Such blocking tasks fall to the assault guns working in close connection with the infantry. This also applies to combat in woodland. Fighting in large towns and villages probably cannot be avoided. Here, the deployment of the Tiger takes place on wide or main streets and in close connection on both sides with storm troops who must take over the protection of the flanks in order to offset the large dead areas of the tank's cannon.

Securing and protective tasks for Tiger units are to not to be accepted.

The qualities of the 8.8 cm cannon often lead to it also being deployed as artillery against determined targets. These cases are in any event to be limited and exceptional because this will cause a bottleneck in the supply and replenishment of ammunition.

Of course some statements were misleading such as, for example, in this operational report by *s.Pz.Abt. 503* on 12 April 1943:

Use (Tigers) only if strong enemy artillery and *Pak* has to be reckoned with. Otherwise it is better to call for lighter units.

In a field report issued by *s.Pz.Abt. 503* on 10 October 1943, there are blatant examples of the incorrect use of Tiger tanks:

In defence the Tiger was mainly used as a bunker in the front line and served repeatedly, surrounded by a very small covering force of our own infantry, for days on end as the backbone of the main combat line. There were times in the battle both at day and at night when the Tigers had to hold, and did hold, the front line without grenadiers. For several nights the tanks then had to be closely secured by dismounted crew members – an unwelcome impairment of the tank crews' combat readiness.

An inevitable consequence of the use as a 'bunker' was that the enemy systematically and with all available weapons – from 7.62 cm *Pak* to 17.2 cm artillery – ranged in on the Tigers and, because he had ammunition in sufficient quantity at his disposal, in time he achieved corresponding successes (4 solitary Tigers were total losses after direct hits by artillery). Withdrawing the Tigers deployed in the front line back to reverse slope positions and the repeated absence of our own infantry would have led to the front line being pulled back and because of the proximity of the Russian infantry – the Russian artillery observers often lay just a hundred and fifty metres away in the corn and sunflower fields – would have had little success.

In this context the use of Tigers as communications vehicles between individual infantry positions in their own main combat line – which often led to breakdowns– should be mentioned. The recovery of one that had broken down in the midst of hostile infantry proved to be extremely difficult and could only be carried out using several Tigers. Sudden breakthroughs by the enemy during withdrawal movements forced the immediate deployment [of Tigers] in terrain that had not been reconnoitred and which was mostly unsuitable for tanks.(…) The deployment of a stand-alone Tiger company was not an exception because the grenadiers were battle weary and sometimes were not present at all. On this account, the performance of the Tiger could often not be fully exploited and territory that had been quickly retaken from the enemy could not be held.

Irrespective of frequently erroneous tactical understanding of the correct deployment of tanks with grenadiers (the situation is seen from the 'grass roots' perspective of the infantry) the report also clearly responds to the increasingly excessive demands placed on the generally courageous fighting of the German infantry towards the end of the war. All too often, the presence of a few Tigers was used to stabilize a sector of the battlefield or help the hard-pressed infantry.

Passages from a report by *s.Pz.Abt. 503* on 25 November 1944 mention their operational experience with the Tiger:

> In these weeks (…) the *Abteilung* has been given no time for technical servicing despite the ongoing urgency for this. This was partly due to the situation but also partly to the lack of understanding of the superior commands that only ever asked two questions: 'How many do you have ready for action?' and 'How many will you have ready in the next few days?' Despite this, until 30 October (since 19 October) there were on average 25–30 tanks (of 47) in action.
>
> As a consequence of a lack of a means of towing, the *Abteilung* was faced with the decision of either blowing up damaged tanks that were in front of the main combat line or recovering them with Tigers that were still deployable. Of course it then became apparent that the vehicles assigned for towing also had technical faults. It was only by the timely and preparatory loading of tanks onto trains at the last moment that the *Abteilung* escaped further losses of armoured fighting vehicles.
>
> In summary it can be said; that the Tiger II has proved itself in every way and is a weapon feared by the enemy; that Tiger formations, when deployed cohesively and in a tactically correct way, always bring resounding success; that the tactical requirements of a Tiger *Abteilung* are not respected by most superior authorities.

These statements were summarized in the *Merkblatt für die Höheren Truppenführer über den Einsatz einer schweren Panzer-Abteilung 'Tiger'*, an information sheet that was distributed to all command levels from division upwards from June 1943.

A. The tactically correct use of a Tiger *Abteilung* depends on the characteristics of the Tiger and the purpose for which it was created. The deployment of this outstanding, special weapon promises success if the following 25 points are observed:
1. Close links between Tiger commanders and the headquarters responsible for issuing orders.
    Rationale:
    Planning in advance is imperative for Tiger formations. All preparations for their deployment (reconnaissance and supply) require more time compared to other weapons.
2. Issue orders to Tiger commanders as early as possible.
    Reason: see 1.
3. As a matter of principle, issue orders to Tiger commanders first.
    Rationale:
    The Tigers bear the brunt of the breakthrough. They are to be incorporated into the first strike at the focal point.
4. Never subordinate a Tiger formation in an attack by an infantry division.
    Rationale:
    In difficult situations the link between the division and *Abteilung* breaks down. The infantry divisions do not have the forces equipped with the means of keeping pace with the Tigers nor are they used to fighting

alongside them. The Tigers' successes usually cannot be exploited by the infantry, the conquered territory therefore cannot be held.
B. Marching
5. Allow the Tigers to march alone.
    Rationale:
    The stress on the automotive parts of Tigers is at its least if they are given the chance to travel quickly without changing gear, braking or restarting. The Tiger also interferes with the march of other formations. Narrows, bridges and fords often hold surprises for Tigers and can cause traffic jams.
6. Bridges less than 24 tons capacity have to be strengthened for Tiger formations.
    Rationale:
    Bridges less than 24 tons can support the Tiger only in suitable conditions. Frost, thick ice and long periods of rainfall reduce their capacity.
7. Do not demand forced marches.
    Rationale:
    Additional wear on engine, gears and running gear is the consequence. The combat worthiness of the Tiger will already have been used up on the road rather than in action. The average speed for a Tiger formation is 10 km/hr by day and 7 km/hr by night.
8. Have them march as little as possible.
    Rationale:
    The weight of the Tiger causes excessive wear during marches.
C. Combat
9. The intention to deploy Tiger formations is to be carefully checked against maps, aerial photographs and reconnaissance results and talked through with the Tiger commanders.
    Rationale:
    The successful deployment of the Tiger formations depends on the extent of careful planning of this kind. The Tiger commander must always be listened to because only he can make a clear-cut assessment of the capabilities of his unit.
10. The Tiger formation must be the weapon the *Truppenführer* [commander of a battle group] uses at the focal point of an attack.
    Rationale:
    The close order deployment of a Tiger unit at the focal point ensures success. Each dispersal puts that in doubt.
11. As a matter of principle, deploy the Tiger unit in conjunction with other weapons.
    Rationale:
    After a breakthrough, it is the Tiger's task to thrust rapidly towards the enemy's artillery and destroy it. All other weapons have to support the completion of its objective. At the same time, the light tanks and assault guns destroy the infantry's heavy weapons and *Pak*. Our own artillery holds down the enemy's artillery and covers the flanks. *Panzergrenadiere* follow mounted on the tanks and take possession of the conquered areas. They provide close-combat protection for the Tiger. Light tanks then exploit this success and expand the tactical breakthrough into an operational breakthrough.

12. Give the Tiger formations sufficient engineers – armoured if possible.
Rationale:
For Tiger units, bridge strengthening, the widening of carriageways, anti-tank ditches and fords as well as the clearing of a great many paths through minefields are often necessary.

D. Provisioning

22. Do not direct the Tiger units to the workshops and repair services of other armoured units.
Rationale:
Other armoured units have neither the necessary expertise nor spares for the Tiger.

23. Inform the Tiger commanders in good time about the anticipated duration of breaks in the fighting and do not order any state of alert during these.
Rationale:
Only knowledge of the time that will be available ensures the proper planning and execution of repair work.

24. After a Tiger *Abteilung* has been deployed for a lengthy period, allow two to three weeks for the restoration of their fighting power.

Rationale:
Otherwise during subsequent deployments the percentage of technical failures will climb increasingly quickly.

25. If possible, assign Tiger workshop companies to accommodation with solid ground in the vicinity of a rail station.
Rationale:
The erection of the heavy cranes that are a prerequisite for every kind of workshop activity is only possible on a solid base.
The replenishment of special spare parts, particularly ones that are very heavy, requires the workshop to be situated near a station.

It is pointless to highlight the extent to which these measures were violated. In many cases – by referring to the *Merkblatt* – the commanding officers of the *Abteilungen* could often turn down absurd assignments. However, outspoken and courageous leaders such as these were also removed by narrow-minded commanders of *Kampfgruppen* (battle groups)!

Breaking through settlements was supposed to be carried out only in exceptional cases. This photograph, taken on 5 July 1943, shows a tank belonging to *2./s.Pz.Abt. 503* in Kisseljewo. (Schmid)

Tiger überrollt sowjetische Artilleriestellung

Zeichnung von Feldwebel Edwin Grazioli

Fragen um den Tiger

Der deutsche Panzerkampfwagen vom Typ „Tiger" verdankt seinen schnell erworbenen Ruhm der Tatsache, daß Engländer, Amerikaner und Sowjets ihm nichts Gleichwertiges entgegenzusetzen haben. So steht er überall im Mittelpunkt des Interesses, so kreisen Fragen und Vermutungen um ihn, denn wer möchte nicht gern wissen, was es mit diesem Giganten der deutschen Rüstung auf sich hat. Dasselbe gilt auch für den Nebelwerfer, jene von Geheimnissen umwitterte Waffe, der die deutschen Grenadiere den Namen „Brüllende Kuh" gegeben haben. In Wort und Bild ist darum auf diesen beiden Seiten das Wissenswerte über beide Waffen übersichtlich zusammengestellt.

Aus welchen Front-Erfahrungen wurde der Tiger gebaut?

Antwort: Die Erfahrungen in den bisherigen zahllosen Panzerschlachten auf allen Kriegsschauplätzen haben gezeigt, daß die Abwehrwaffen des Gegners so stark verbessert wurden, daß kleinere und leichte Panzer von ihnen, vor allem von der Pak, außer Gefecht gesetzt werden konnten. Es mußte also ein Panzer geschaffen werden, dem unsere Feinde nichts Gleichwertiges entgegensetzen konnten. Dieser Panzer ist der „Tiger".

Wie groß sind die Ausmaße des Tigers und wieviel wiegt er?

Antwort: Der „Tiger" ist mit Rohr weit über sieben Meter lang und über drei Meter breit und wiegt rund 60 Tonnen. Trotz dieser gewaltigen Ausmaße wirkt der Panzer in jedem Gelände, ganz gleich ob es gebirgig oder eben ist, schnittig und elegant.

Leichter zu lenken als ein PKW.?

Antwort: Abweichend von allen bisherigen Typen hat er ein neues Lenksystem. Er ist leichter zu lenken als ein Personenkraftwagen. Genau wie dieser besitzt er ein Steuerrad, das der Fahrer leicht mit zwei Fingern lenken kann. Darum treten auch keine Ermüdungserscheinungen beim Fahrer auf, zumal die Durchlüftung im Panzer sehr gut ist.

Wie weit kann der Turm gedreht werden?

Antwort: Der Turm des „Tigers" ist so aufmontiert, daß er schnellstens nach allen Seiten hin gedreht werden kann. Es gibt daran keine Grad- oder Stricheinteilung. Die ... ur.gen erfolgen also nicht um 180 Grad, nicht nach links oder rechts, sondern die Kommandos sind nach Uhrzeiten festgelegt. Nach drei Uhr — das bedeutet eine Schwenkung um 90 Grad, nach sechs Uhr eine um 180 Grad, nach neun Uhr gleich 270 Grad und nach zwölf Uhr bedeutet die Schwenkung also eine ganze Drehung um 360 Grad. Die Drehungen werden dabei im Sinne des Uhrzeigers ausgeführt.

Inwieweit ist der Tiger angreifbar und was hält die Panzerung aus?

Antwort: Die Kämpfe im Osten haben gelehrt, daß der „Tiger" sehr schwer anzugreifen ist. Weder Geschosse der sowjetischen Panzerbüchsen noch Pak noch Artilleriegeschosse durchschlugen die Panzerung, sondern verletzten ihn nur.

Welche Erfolge hatten die zuerst im Osten eingesetzten Tiger?

Antwort: Bei ihrem ersten Einsatz südlich des Ladogasees im Osten schossen vier „Tiger"-Panzer im Zeitraum von zwei Stunden 25 sowjetische Panzer ab. Kleinere Feindpanzer flogen schon beim ersten Treffer in die Luft. An einem darauffolgenden Tage wurden etwa 50 sowjetische Panzer einschließlich des T 34 abgeschossen und an einem noch späteren Tage insgesamt 128 sowjetische Panzer der verschiedenen Typen.

Können Minen dem Tiger und seinen Ketten schaden?

Antwort: Gegen Beschädigungen durch Minen bieten die über 70 cm breiten und starken Ketten und auch die Wanne eine gewisse Sicherheit. Die Ketten sind deshalb so breit, weil das Gewicht des Panzers sehr hoch ist. Sie sind sehr stabil gebaut. Schäden können von der Panzerbesatzung selbst wieder beseitigt werden, da jeder Panzer Ersatzketten mit sich führt.

Kann man den Tiger im Nahkampf vernichten?

Antwort: Da der „Tiger" stets in Begleitschutz fährt, ist er von vornherein gegen Nahkampfmittel gefeit. Die hohe Bauart des „Tigers" macht es unmöglich, einen anderen Weg auf den Panzer hinauf zu nehmen als über die Ketten. Beim Fahren ist es unmöglich, auf ihn hinaufzuklettern.

Wie hoch ist die Marschgeschwindigkeit des Tigers?

Antwort: Die Durchschnittsgeschwindigkeit des „Tigers" beträgt 40 Kilometer. Auf guten Straßen kann er sie selbstverständlich erhöhen, während sie sich im sandigen und bergigen Gelände verringert. Seine Steigungsfähigkeit ist groß und selbst steile Abhänge nimmt er ohne größere Schwierigkeiten. Ein Meter dicke Bäume entwurzelt er ohne Schwierigkeiten.

Wie hat sich der Tiger in den bisherigen Kämpfen bewährt?

Antwort: Mit dem „Tiger" besitzt das deutsche Heer eine Waffe, die allen bisherigen feindlichen Panzerwaffen überlegen ist. Das bewiesen auch die Erfolge, die die „Tiger"-Panzer in den Schlachten in Sowjetrußland errangen. Weder der sowjetische T 34 noch der amerikanische „Sherman" noch der „Grant" oder „Lee" sind ihm gewachsen. Deutsche Panzerbesatzungen werden laufend auf den „Tiger" umgeschult.

Propaganda

Unlike almost any other ground-based weapon system, the Tiger lent itself to being used as the subject of propagandistic publications and announcements which, on the one hand, bolstered the will to prevail amongst the German population and soldiers and, on the other hand, intimidated the enemy.

Furthermore, sensational (*Wochenschau*) newsreel films focussed on the Tiger's superior performance parameters. These cleverly attempted to create an aura of invincibility and superiority over enemy tanks with the intention of spreading dread and terror in the mind of the enemy. This campaign was also taken up by the regional and major newspapers in the Reich at the beginning of 1943. Examples of these are incorporated into the picture section that follows.

This propaganda readily achieved its desired effect and even today there persists a fascination with this weapon system. However, this propaganda also had an unfortunate side effect – it awakened exaggerated expectations (that were not always borne out in reality) amongst the crews that culminated in reckless conduct in combat.

In fact it was actually forbidden for crews to take pictures of the Tiger – even of the interior – for private purposes. This was in principle the task of the photographers of the *Propaganda-Kompanien* (propaganda companies/*PK*). However, in practice this ban on taking photographs was not monitored – there are thousands (in total much more than 10,000) of private photos of the Tiger and other tanks. Amongst these are many snapshots showing crew members on, in front of, or beside 'their' Tiger during stops, in rest periods, while marching or during transport by rail. There are also many pictures of repair or maintenance activities. For understandable reasons there were far fewer photographs taken during actual deployment. There are also very few colour photographs because monochrome was still the prevailing standard. More and more 'colour' photographs are turning up but these have merely been coloured by

hand. For understandable reasons there are fewer photographs from the last year of the war – who would wish to 'rejoice' in the breakdown or (self) destruction of their own vehicle?

Early official photographs were retouched to blot out identification symbols and turret numbers for reasons of secrecy. The identification symbols on combat vehicles was actually prescribed and standardized from 1942, as was the position of turret numbers and such like. However, in a great number of cases there were departures from these rules; sometimes with considerable artistic extravagance. This to some extent makes it much easier to assign the snaps to particular troop units or even to specific points in time. Details of this can be found in Volume I and II of the 'Tigers in Combat' book series. In the picture section that follows, a few additions or corrections are mentioned.

The poster on the previous page (*Fragen um den Tiger*/questions about the Tiger) clearly expresses the intention behind its publication at the start of 1943. It was widely distributed and reprinted in many newspapers. Many artistic variations were also printed, such as the one shown on the right which is taken from a page in the May 1943 edition of the 'Motor Schau' ('Motor Show') magazine.

In the spring of 1943, a film was made at Senne that shows a Tiger in action as it crashes through a house and a wooded area. These images might have impressed the uninitiated but must have raised the hackles of soldiers and the technically competent viewers amongst the audience.

Individual images were printed in many newspapers in the following weeks together with sensational comments. The image on the right demonstrates the print quality attainable in daily newspapers at that time. (Atlantic-Boesig)

These stills from 'Waldurchfahrt' are, from the view of soldiers, rather more than just questionable. From April 1944 such pictures were used in many contemporary publications. The comment at the bottom of the picture on the right reads 'The Tiger, the most modern combat vehicle in the world.'

The propaganda show took place on 27 March 1943 in the northern part of the evacuated settlement of Haustenbeck with the area having been painstakingly examined and the driver briefed the previous day.

In the first phase, the tank drove through the dried-up Knochenbach valley and its wooded slopes. To round off the demonstration the tank performed several lively to and fro passes.

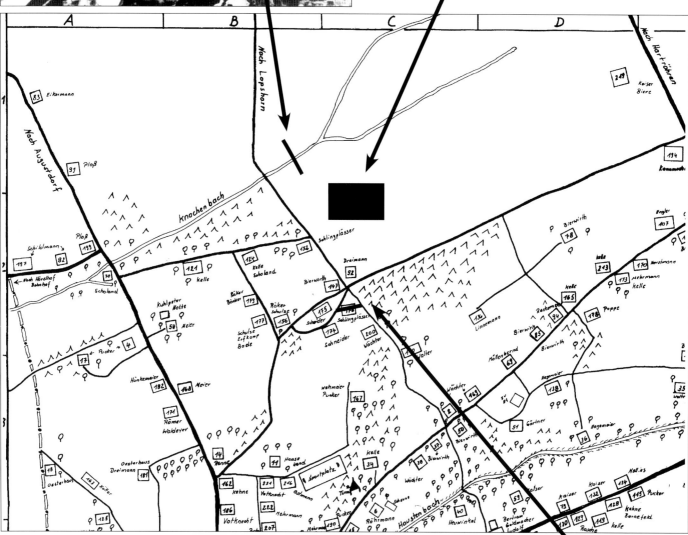

Finally the tank drove through the right part of house Nr. 196 – referred to as the '*Schlingpässer Haus*' after the previous owner. This must have been the final stage of the show because after this the tank was no longer serviceable and had to be thoroughly cleaned – out of sight of the press. The sketch was drawn by the Sennelager chronicler, Walter Göbel.

Der „Tiger" stößt durch ein Haus

Deutschlands neuester Panzerwagen, der modernste der Welt — Es gibt kein Hindernis

Links: Der neue deutsche Panzer „Tiger" bei einer Einsatzübung: Die „Tiger"-Besatzung brauchte hier nicht einmal ihre Kanone, sie erledigte die „feindliche Stellung" durch Ueberwalzen. Rechts: Der „Tiger" an der Front: Getarnt und dem Gelände angepaßt, wartet er auf den Befehl zum Einsatz. Auch diese rollende Festung ist eine Spitzenleistung deutscher Waffentechnik

Scherl-Bilderdienst u. PK-Aufn. Kriegsberichter Zellmer (Wehrbilderdienst)

Es hat sich viel geändert, seit im ersten Weltkrieg bei Cambrai Panzerwagen an der Front eingesetzt wurden. Diese damals als „fahrbare Festungen" bezeichneten Geräte hatten zwar eine Höchstgeschwindigkeit von 15 Kilometer in der Stunde, wurden jedoch nur selten mit höherer Geschwindigkeit als drei bis acht Kilometer in der Stunde benutzt. Der Aktionsradius schwankte zwischen 30 und 50 Kilometer. Wenn man damit die „Tiger" vergleicht . . .

Mit der Wiedererstarkung der deutschen Wehrkraft wurde auch der Ruf nach neuen Panzerwagen laut. Man forderte kleine, schnelle Wagen mit großer Wendigkeit, die auch im Verband operieren konnten. So entstand unter sorgfältiger Ausschöpfung aller vorliegenden Erfahrungen und Kenntnisse in dreijähriger Entwicklungsarbeit der deutsche 5½-Tonnen-Panzerwagen, der von einem 60-PS-Motor getrieben wurde. Schrittweise wurde der Wagen auf 6, auf 9 Tonnen usw. vergrößert, so daß bei Kriegsbeginn Panzerwagen zur Verfügung standen, die allen Feindkonstruktionen ebenbürtig und überlegen waren.

Eine gewisse Ueberraschung bedeutete im Osten das Auftreten der bolschewistischen Panzer T 34 sowie KW 1 und KW 2, denen die vorhandenen deutschen Wagen in Panzerung und Waffen nicht mehr gewachsen waren. Trotzdem konnte auch hier durch geschickten Einsatz und überlegene Taktik der Kampf erfolgreich aufgenommen werden, da in der Geschwindigkeit lediglich der T 34 mehr leistete, dafür jedoch eine erheblich geringere Wendigkeit aufwies. In nur kurzer Entwicklungszeit gelang es deutschen Ingenieuren nun unter planmäßigem Einsatz durch Reichsminister Speer, einen neuen Panzerwagen zu entwickeln, der allen Konstruktionen überlegen ist, die es sonst heute noch an anderer Stelle gibt.

„Tiger" wird dieser neue deutsche Panzerwagen von den Soldaten genannt. Und wie ein „Tiger" schaut er aus, wenn er mit seinen wuchtigen Ketten durch den Wald bricht und dabei selbst Bäume von fast einem Meter Durchmesser wegknickt. Seine überlegene Größe tritt besonders überzeugend in Erscheinung, sobald man den „Tiger" neben den russischen Panzerwagentypen oder neben seinen älteren deutschen Brüdern sieht. Die Panzerung aus dickem Stahl, der eine hohe Widerstandsfähigkeit erhielt, ist so gut, daß ein Leutnant, der im „Tiger" die ersten Angriffe an der Ostfront mitgemacht hat, scherzhaft die Formulierung prägte, daß man sich darin „Wie in einer Lebensversicherung" vorkäme. Diese Auffassung wird zweifellos noch durch die ausgezeichnete Bewaffnung des Panzerwagens unterstrichen. Der leicht drehbare Turm ist mit einem großkalibrigen Langrohrgeschütz versehen, wie es bisher in noch keinem Panzerwagen eingebaut wurde. Durch besondere Maßnahmen gelang es, auftretende Rückstoßkräfte und Rohrschwankungen unschädlich zu machen, ohne die Zielgenauigkeit ungünstig zu beeinflussen. Wie von Panzermännern berichtet wird, konnte der „Tiger" sowohl im Osten als auch in Afrika Feindkräfte mit ausgezeichneter Feuerwirkung auf größere Ent-

fernung bekämpfen, wofür panzerbrechende Granaten zur Verfügung stehen. Außer mit der Kanone ist der Panzerwagen noch mit Maschinengewehren und Maschinenpistolen bestückt.

Im Einvernehmen mit Reichsminister Speer gab die Presseabteilung der Reichsregierung kürzlich Gelegenheit, die Leistungen des „Tiger" kennenzulernen. Und diese waren selbst für erfahrene Frontkämpfer mehr als überraschend. Trotz seines außerordentlich hohen Gewichtes von über 50 Tonnen zeichnet sich diese neue für die deutsche Front geschaffene Waffe

durch große Schnelligkeit und Wendigkeit aus. Selbst hohe Steilhänge überwindet er ab- und aufwärts ohne Schwierigkeiten. Von der Wucht des Kampfwagens kann man sich vielleicht eine kleine Vorstellung machen, wenn man erfährt, daß er bei der Vorführung einen Eichbaum von fast 1 Meter Durchmesser schon beim ersten Stoß umlegte und ein zweistöckiges Haus in glattem Schwung durchfuhr und dabei völlig zum Einsturz brachte! Für den „Tiger" gibt es keine Hindernisse. Dieser neueste deutsche Panzer ist eine

Spitzenleistung, die deutscher Ingenieurgeist und deutsche Arbeitskraft sowie die Kampferfahrungen unserer Panzermänner schufen. Seine Stärke liegt in seiner technischen Ueberlegenheit und nicht in bedingungslosem Masseneinsatz nach sowjetischem oder amerikanischem Muster. Seine Entwicklungsstufe sichert auch weiterhin den überragenden Vorsprung der deutschen Technik auf dem Rüstungssektor. Der „Tiger" wird überall dort bereitstehen, wo die Kampflage seinen Einsatz zur Sicherung von Front und Heimat erfordert. Heinrich Kluth

After a period of delay, a campaign was started in the printed media at the beginning of 1943 to introduce the new 'overpowering' fighting vehicle to a wider readership. This was after the disaster of Stalingrad and was urgently needed to restore the morale of the population. From film sequences, weekly newsreels (*Wochenschauen*) for cinemas were also produced with a caption specifying their location as the *Ostfront*.

'Normal' photographs (below) taken at this demonstration were also made available to the press.

Sonnabend, 17. April 1943

Anzeiger

Reichshauptstadt   61. Jahrgang

Modernster Panzer der Welt im Einsatz

Fahrbare Festung „Tiger" vor Leningrad bewährt

An verschiedenen Fronten ist seit einiger Zeit diese neue Panzertype eingesetzt. Starke Panzerung und großkalibrige Kanonen mit einer alles durchschlagenden Feuerkraft zeichnen den „Tiger" aus

The moral-boosting brochure *Wehrmacht im Kampf* presented this photograph of the Tiger immediately after it had driven through the house that had collapsed around it. The vehicle is completely covered with debris and rubble. Even if the engine does not cut out because of a lack of air, the air filter is so full of dirt that engine temperature will rise to a critical level. Damage to brackets and optical devices, the base of the antenna and hinges on the hatches and so forth is unavoidable.

The first significant deployment of Tigers eastwards of Leningrad was too hasty and somewhat less than successful but was nevertheless described in glowing terms in the press (such as here in the 17 April 1943 edition of the *Berliner Anzeiger*.) Descriptions such as 'mobile fortress' are reminiscent of the mode of thinking applied to tank warfare during the First World War.

„Tiger" verbreiten Schrecken
Bewährung bei Charkow und am Donez

In den Kämpfen um Charkow und am Donez verbreiteten die neuen deutschen „T i g e r"= Panzer bei den Bolschewisten panischen Schrek= ken, sowohl durch die Wucht ihrer äußeren Form als auch durch die starke Wirkung ihrer jede Panzerung durchschlagenden Granaten. Der Feind hat dieser gefährlichen deutschen Waffe nichts Gleichwertiges entgegenzusetzen. Wenn die gigantischen Ungetüme angriffen, wichen die bol= schewistischen Panzer, selbst die T 34, zurück.

Der „Tiger" hat sich bereits in der Schlacht zur Rückgewinnung von Charkow bewährt. Am dritten Tage des Kampfes brachen fünf Panzer eines Verbandes der Waffen=SS in die brennenden Häuserschluchten der Stadt ein. Sie wurden geführt von einem der mächtigen neuen „Tiger"=Panzer. Dieser stieß weit in den Feind hinein, zerschlug mit seinen Granaten feindliche Widerstandsnester und überrollte einige Barrikaden, bis er vor einer sowjetischen Lang= rohrkanone stand, die vom Feind als beste pan= zerbrechende Waffe gerühmt wird. Die Bolsche= wisten eröffneten auf kurze Entfernung das Feuer. Schuß auf Schuß traf die Panzerung, doch jede Granate prallte funkensprühend ab. Der „Tiger" rollte unbeirrt weiter auf das Geschütz zu. Als der Panzer auf 20 Meter herangekommen war, öffnete der Kommandant die Luke, winkte den vor Entsetzen gelähmten Bolschewisten zu und zer= malmte dann, von neuem mit aufheulenden Mo= toren anfahrend, das feindliche Geschütz.

Am Donez griffen Panzergrenadiere seiner= zeit die Bolschewisten in ihrem letzten Stütz= punkt diesseits des Flusses an. Ihnen voraus durchfuhren zwei „Tiger" die weite Senke zwischen der deutschen und der feindlichen Stellung, überquerten einen Bach und krochen am jenseitigen Hang hinauf. Zwar wurden sie von bolschewistischen Schlachtfliegern entdeckt, deren Bombenabwürfe aber keinerlei Wirkung hatten. Wie aus dem Boden gewachsen erschienen die Kolosse plötzlich vor der Stellung der Sowjets, die vergeblich versuchten, einen Widerstand zu organisieren. Unaufhaltsam rollten unsere Panzer weiter und walzten die feindlichen Pak=Stellun= gen in Grund und Boden. Mehrere Sowjetpan= zerkampfwagen versuchten die Lage zu retten. Sie wurden jedoch durch die „Tiger", bevor sie in Aktion treten konnten, unter Feuer genommen. Schon der erste Schuß durchschlug die Stirnseite des vordersten Panzers, und die Explosion riß ihn auseinander. Die übrigen Feindpanzer drehten darauf schleunigst ab.

The recapture of Kharkov early in 1943 was of course highlighted in the press – as was the role of the Tiger armoured fighting vehicle. The headline reads 'Tigers spread Terror.'

The accomplishments of the supply companies and the technical performance of weaponry and power units were also presented, as in this picture from issue 15 of the magazine *Signal* in 1943.

The Tiger was in the forefront of propaganda in the media in spring 1943 ('frightening the enemy').

The Tiger armoured fighting vehicle was a highly sought after subject for the photographers of the propaganda companies.

A whole series of pictures appeared starting in spring 1943. The picture above, for example, shows a tank belonging to *s.Pz.Abt. 502* in January 1944 while the one on the left shows another tank of the same *Abteilung* on 25 July 1944.

This is one of the first realistic snaps of a Tiger. It shows a vehicle of the '*501*' during a march from Bizerta to Djedeida on 24 November 1942. This picture was published for the first time in several newspapers in February 1943 but without a date – and without the anxious-looking grenadier to the left of the rolling monster. (Wörner)

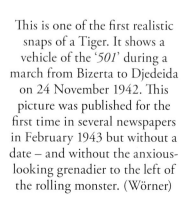

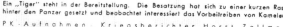

Ein „Tiger" steht in der Bereitstellung. Die Besatzung hat sich zu einer kurzen Ras
hinter den Panzer gesetzt und beobachtet interessiert das Vorbeitreiben von Kamelen

P K - A u f n a h m e n :   K r i e g s b e r i c h t e r   H o r s t   Z e l l m e

Eine deutsche Panzergruppe hält. Schwerste Panzer vom Typ „Tiger" fahren an ihr
vorbei nach vorn, um schwere feindliche Panzerstreitkräfte zu zerschlagen.
Links. Soeben ist dieser „Tiger" aus seiner getarnten Bereitstellung hervor-
gebrochen und wird in Kürze die feindliche Verteidigung überrennen. — Unten:
Staunend beobachten Soldaten den Vormarsch dieser schwersten deutschen Panzer
(Siehe auch Seite 9)

The arrival of Tigers in Bizerta at the end of 1942 (and later in Tunis) attracted an audience. The appearance of such photos in newspapers other than those in Germany could of course hardly be prevented. Nevertheless these photographs were only released in the Reich after retouching with the tank's muzzle brake 'removed.'

These pictures show two examples of 'castrated' Tigers that were printed in 1943 in edition 14 of the *Illustrierten Beobachter* (Illustrated Observer). (Hilkenbach)

(Photographs on the following pages by Schulz)

The deployment of Tigers in North Africa was the first to be treated in detail by the press as in this (see previous page) April 1943 edition of the magazine *Wehrmacht*. (All photos by Zellmer)

When everything was 'all over' in Africa, another article appeared in the May edition that made a comparatively objective comparison with the American M4 Sherman tank. The article begins by describing the Sherman as having 'agile tracks' and a 'snarling' engine and goes on to compare it with its 'mighty opponent, the Tiger.'

Der amerikanische Panzer »Sherman«

PK. Durch die Straßen von Tunis rollt der amerikanische Sherman-Tank — lebendig, mit beweglichen Gleisketten und knurrendem Motor, mit Beutemunition in den Rohren und jenem deutschen Spähtrupp, der ihn an dem nebelgrauen Morgen des 22. Februar auf den Hügeln von Speitla erbeutete, als Besatzung. Die Fahrt ging von den Hügeln herunter durch das Meer der Olivenhaine in Richtung auf Sfax. Die tunesischen Kolonisten sahen staunend zu, die Araber lugten vorsichtig aus ihren weißen Dörfern. Die Fahrt ging an altrömischen Ruinen vorbei und quer durch die ausgetrocknete Dürre toter Jahrhunderte und hat so schließlich Tunis erreicht. Es sind ungefähr 350 Kilometer. Das hat viereinhalb Tage gedauert, was im ganzen der Marschleistung dieses Stahlkolosses kein schlechtes Zeugnis ausstellt. Er wird von einem Flugzeug-Sternmotor von 400 PS getrieben, erreicht eine mittlere Geschwindigkeit von 40 Kilometer und hat fünf Mann Besatzung. Die Ausmaße — 6,15 Meter Länge, 2,65 Meter Breite, 2,71 Meter Höhe — geben seinem Erscheinen einen gedrungenen Eindruck. Das Ding wiegt etwa 31 t, es wurde im Hafen verladen, während unter dem makellosen Himmel Afrikas die deutschen Jäger kreisten und kein feindlicher Bomber den Einbruch in diese tödliche Zone wagte. Jetzt ist nach manchen Etappen auf einem Versuchsfeld in der Nähe Berlins dieser Star der amerikanischen Rüstung in die Hände der Waffenexperten gelangt, die ihn in offenen Gefechten nochmals auf Kampfkraft und Widerstandshärte untersuchen. Schon die Voruntersuchung auf tunesischem Boden ergab, daß dieses rollende Bergwerk aus Stahl an sich keine schlechte Schöpfung ist. Ein deutsches Panzerregiment hat es erbeutet.

Eine Wanderung durch das Trümmerfeld der amerikanischen Panzer an der Chaussee nach Speitla vorbei bis an den Paß von Kasserine zeigt, daß diese Schwergewichte der amerikanischen Rüstung ebenso sterben können wie andere Tanks auch: durch einen Schuß in die Gleisketten, durch einen anderen, der das Benzindepot aufflammen ließ, durch jenen blanken Schuß, der frontal kam, und zwar den Stahlgußmantel nicht zerlegte, aber doch in seiner weiter ebbenden Erschütterung die Besatzung betäubte oder den Kommandanten, den Richtschützen oder den Funker erledigte. Einige Tanks, deren technischer Organismus nicht völlig zerstört worden ist, lassen erkennen, daß die Besatzung trotz des Schutzmantels so angeschlagen wurde oder einem psychischen Schreck unterlag, daß sie ausgestiegen ist. Die Form des Stahlmantels zeigt eine wulstige Modellierung. Von der drehbaren Haube herunter ist das Metall so kurvig gebogen und geknetet, als hätten menschliche Hände es hier nur mit

Ton und nicht mit dem härtesten Erz zu tun gehabt. Der Koloß rollt auf Gleisketten voran, deren Glieder mit Gummiwulsten besetzt sind; dadurch hat er einen gleichsam weichen und ganz gewiß auch geräuschloseren Gang, als ihn sonst Panzer haben. Der Vorteil im offenen Gelände ist klar. Die verstörten USA-Offiziere, die von den deutschen Grenadieren mit vorgehaltener Pistole vom Schlachtfeld geholt worden sind, erkannten aber bald, daß sie ihre stählerne Kohorte eng, ja zu eng zusammengehalten hatten und in einem Talgrund dann aufgerieben wurden. Der Amerikaner war in diesem Falle einem falschen Begriff des Igels zum Opfer gefallen. Der Untergang des amerikanischen Panzerregiments ist mit einem Bruchteil der deutschen Angriffskraft erkauft worden. Aber, so muß man hinzufügen, mit einem unendlich Vielfachen von dem, was Erfahrung, Kühnheit und Kriegskunst den deutschen Kommandeuren im Laufe von vier Kriegsjahren beigegeben haben, Kommandeuren, Richtschützen und Panzerfahrern. Die mörderische 7,5-Zentimeter-Kanone oder das Flakgeschütz unserer Panzer sind auch nicht am ersten Tag des Krieges erfunden worden. Daher die vorfühlenden, gleichsam tastenden Treffer, die in aufsteigender Folge bis zum letzten Fangschuß gegeben werden; daher auch die unsichtbare Zusammenarbeit zwischen dem Fahrer, der geduckt hinter dem Gleiskettenwerk hockt, und dem Kommandanten, der seine stählerne Rüstung durch das Auf und Ab der Bodennischen und Höcker, der Kaktusschatten und Olivenbäume wie zwischen Tiefen und Untiefen einer gefährlichen See anfahren läßt, ja, in der Tat seinen Panzer nicht ungleich einem U-Boot-Mann an das feindliche Opfer heranbringt. Dieses

Heranbringen, Ausweichen und Umkreisen haben auch die Amerikaner versucht. Wir haben sie an einem der folgenden Tage gesehen, wie sie hinter der Kimme eines Hügels als schleichende Karawane davonzogen und nur die Geschützrohre und die Spitze ihres Turmes wie ein fernes Periskop herüberäugten, wir haben erlebt, wie die starre Gefechtshaltung am Tage der ersten Begegnung bald durch eine größere Elastizität bei unserem Gegner abgelöst wurde. Die anderen Typen sind leichter umgelegt worden, die General Grants, die Stuarts und General Lees, die vielen MTWs, die Mannschaftstransportwagen der US-Army, die mitsamt ihrer Munition als gellendes und prasselndes Raketenfeuerwerk noch durch Dämmerung und Nacht verbrannten.

Aber auch Shermans waren unter den Opfern. Am ersten Tag war der Unterschied zwischen der deutschen dynamischen Gefechtsführung gegenüber der amerikanischen starren etwa der, wie er zwischen den schwärmenden Tirailleurs der napoleonischen Ära und den viereckigen Menschenkadern des vorausgehenden Jahrhunderts bestand. Aber schon für die folgenden Gefechte trifft der Vergleich nicht mehr zu. Der Amerikaner hat die Rechnung zunächst nur mit dem Material gemacht. Man darf und muß es wohl zugeben: mit einem Material, das als Masse mit wulstigen

...und sein großer Gegner »Tiger«

Formen, dicken Querschnitten der Armierung, hochbeladener Munition und imponierend durch seine Vielzahl — wenn es uns imponieren sollte — uns entgegengeworfen wurde.

Die Panzerung am Turm hat die beträchtliche Stärke von 85 Millimeter, um an den übrigen Stellen an der Wanne und den Abdeckungsplatten am Heck zwischen 45, 55 und 65 Millimeter zu schwanken. Die Kanone selbst hat das Kaliber 7,5 Zentimeter. Interessant ist ein 12,7-Millimeter-MG als Fliegerabwehrwaffe, freischwebend neben dem Turm montiert. Ein MG befindet sich am Bug. Die Reservemunition ist beträchtlich: 100 Schuß 7,5, 8000 Schuß MG (!) und 300 Flak-MG. Die Schußgeschwindigkeit der Kanone liegt bei der Fahrt auf ungefähr 10, im Stand bei 12 in der Minute. MG und Kanone dürfen nicht gekoppelt oder überhaupt nicht zusammen schießen.

Der Krieg Amerikas ist mit großer Intensität am Konstruktionstisch geführt worden. Was indes fehlt, ist die Mannschaft, die ein solches Material virtuos und, wenn es sein muß, mit kaltem Blute bedient, und es fehlt der Stratege, der alles haben müßte, Mannschaften und Material, das nun wirklich in die Stromlinienform des Schlachtfeldes gebracht worden ist, und eine souveräne taktische Erfahrung.

Kriegsberichter Eberhard Schulz.

Mit der Fertigstellung des ersten deutschen Panzerkampfwagens vom Typ „Tiger" ist ein Panzer geschaffen worden, dem Engländer, Amerikaner und die Sowjets nichts Gleichwertiges entgegenzustellen haben. Die deutschen Panzer haben schon im bisherigen Kriegsverlauf auf allen Kriegsschauplätzen bewundernswerte Leistungen vollbracht. Die Erfahrungen in den Panzerschlachten haben gezeigt, daß man mehr von dem Einsatz kleinster und leichter Panzer abkommt, weil die Abwehrwaffen so stark vervollkommnet wurden, daß Panzer von ihnen, vor allem von der Pak, immer leichter außer Gefecht gesetzt werden können. Die markantesten sowjetischen Panzerkampfwagen vom Typ „KW 1", „KW 2" und „T 34" machten, traten sie in Massen auf, den deutschen Truppen gewisse Schwierigkeiten. Der deutschen Front mußte also eine Waffe geschmiedet werden, die leichter mit den feindlichen Panzerkampfwagen fertig wurde als die ihr bisher zur Verfügung stehenden. Die Ausführung eines solchen Planes ist schwierig, wenn man bedenkt, daß der Bau eines neuen Panzertyps vom ersten Federstrich auf dem Reißbrett an bis zum fertigen Panzerkampfwagen im Frieden rund drei Jahre dauerte. Alle erworbenen Erfahrungen wurden also von den deutschen Ingenieuren unter Leitung des Heereswaffenamtes beim Bau des neuen Kampfwagens vom Typ „Tiger" berücksichtigt. Die neue Waffe mußte so konstruiert werden, daß sie imstande war, jeden feindlichen Widerstand zu brechen, und es mußte schnellste Fertigstellung gewährleistet sein, sollte er der kämpfenden Front zur Verfügung gestellt werden.

Es ist der deutschen Rüstungsindustrie gelungen, den „Tiger" jetzt bei der kriegsmäßigen Umstellung der deutschen Rüstungsindustrie in überraschend kurzer Zeit zu entwickeln und fertigzustellen. Trotz seiner Größe wirkt der „Tiger" beinahe schnittig in seiner äußeren Form. Er ist über 7 Meter lang, über 3 Meter breit, hat u. a. als Bewaffnung eine Langrohrkanone. Der Aktionsradius liegt im Bereich von 100 Kilometern und mehr. Der Turm ist in kürzester Frist nach allen Seiten hin drehbar.

Abweichend von allen bisherigen Typen hat dieser neueste deutsche „Mammutpanzer" ein

neues Lenksystem erhalten. Er ist leichter zu fahren als ein Pkw. Genau wie dieser besitzt er ein Steuerrad, das der Fahrer mit zwei Fingern lenken kann. Trotz seines Gewichts treten Ermüdungserscheinungen beim Fahrer nicht auf. Der „Tiger" besitzt einen Benzinmotor. Auf die Verwendung des Dieselmotors ist verzichtet worden, da er

schwerer als der Benzinmotor ist. An Munition kann der „Tiger" bedeutend mehr mitnehmen als alle bisher bekannten Typen. Das gleiche gilt für den Treibstoff. 600 Liter, also drei Fässer Benzin, kann er ohne Raumschwierigkeiten stets mit sich führen. Das Innere des Panzers ist geräumig, seine Schwere gewährleistet ein völlig ruhiges und sicheres Schießen. Für die Besatzung bedeutet der „Tiger", wenn man im Kriege überhaupt davon sprechen kann, eine höchste Sicherheit. Er wird vorwiegend nicht als selbständige Kampfeinheit eingesetzt, sondern ist stets von anderen Panzern und Grenadierverbänden begleitet, die ihm Flankenschutz gewähren.

Zum ersten Male wurde eine „Tiger"-Abteilung Mitte Januar 1943 südlich des Ladoga-Sees eingesetzt. In dem kurzen Zeitraum von zwei Stunden schossen vier „Tiger" fünfundzwanzig sowjetische Panzer ab. Die kleineren sowjetischen Panzer flogen schon bei dem ersten Schuß in die Luft. In einem Nachtkampf wurden zehn kleinere sowjetische Panzer einfach gerammt. Bei Puschkin wurden auf größte Entfernung an einem einzigen Tage rund fünfzig sowjetische Panzer einschließlich des „T 34" abgeschossen. An einem späteren Tage wurden insgesamt 128 sowjetische Panzer vom Typ „KW 1", „KW 2" und „T 34" vernichtet. Diese großen Abwehrerfolge an einer Front, gegen die die Sowjets mit geballter Kraft anrannten, sind in erster Linie den „Tigern" zuzuschreiben. Wo die Sowjets in der Folge merkten, daß, wie sie sie nannten, die „deutsche Geheimwaffe" angewendet wurde, stellten sie sofort ihre Angriffe ein.

Diese Kämpfe südlich des Ladoga-Sees und auch die in Tunis, wo „Tiger" eingesetzt sind, sowie an anderen Fronten, haben gelehrt, daß der „Tiger" schier unangreifbar ist. Keine Waffe hat ihm bisher etwas anhaben können. Weder die Geschosse der sowjetischen Panzerbüchsen noch die der Pak, selbst die der 10,5-cm-Artillerie durchschlugen die Panzerung des „Tigers". Gegen Beschädigungen durch Minen bieten Ketten und Wanne eine gewisse Sicherheit. Bei ihren bisherigen Einsätzen haben die Besatzungen der „Tiger"-Panzer weder Verluste an Verwundeten noch an Toten gehabt.

Neben seiner Tätigkeit als Panzerzerstörer kann der „Tiger" auch als Rammbock benutzt werden. Feindliche Widerstandsnester in Häusern z. B. kann er vernichten, indem er einfach durch diese „hindurchmarschiert". Einen Meter dicke Bäume legte er einfach um.

Mit dem „Tiger" besitzt das deutsche Heer eine Waffe, die allen bisherigen feindlichen Panzerwaffen überlegen ist. Dadurch, daß die Panzerbesatzungen laufend auf den neuen Typ umgeschult werden, wird der Front eine Verstärkung geschaffen, die sich während der Abwehrkämpfe bereits ausgewirkt hat und in der Zukunft immer stärker auswirken wird.

Heinz Dieselmann.

The next press review was based on photographs taken on 14 May 1943 by the *Propagandakompanie* reporter Schröter when he was with *1./s.Pz.Abt. 502* in the vicinity of Tos(s)no. In these photos the smoke grenade canisters were partially removed by retouching before the pictures were made available for release.

Several of the photographs in this series are well known. They were used in several publications and also as front cover pictures.

Another photo from this series shows that the number '2' on the turret of the tank has been retouched to protect secrecy.

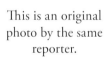

This is an original photo by the same reporter.

Photos that had less audience appeal were not put to further use.

A visit by a Turkish military delegation – to whom the '*503*' showed the Tiger's capabilities in demonstrations and a field exercise that took place on 27 June 1943 – was exploited only for internal propaganda. Standing next to the scissor binoculars on the left is the leader of the Turkish delegation, General Toydemir, with the commander of the *7. Pz.Div. Generalmajor* von Funck (who was in charge of the demonstration), and at the binoculars on the right, *Generalfeldmarschall* von Manstein.

The next time the Tiger was used for propaganda purposes was before and during *Operation Zitadelle,* in summer 1943. This press photo, taken by war reporter Ollig, shows the '*503*' as it relocates on 3 July 1943. Again, the turret numbers have been retouched.

Another, similarly 'dealt with' press photo of the '*505*', has a flag on the turet as an identification aid for German pilots.

Feldwebel Müller of the *3./s.Pz.Abt. 503* together with a member of the '*300*' on the eve of the offensive as they listen to a longwave broadcast of a speech by Hitler on a Wehrmachtsempfänger WR1P. (Rubbel)

Numerous photos of the battle itself were taken by the propaganda companies, this example showing *s.Pz.Abt.505* on 22 July 1943 appeared in the *Illustrierte Berliner Zeitung*. It has been retouched in an amusing way…three steel helmets have been added to the luggage box on the turret in order to obscure the turret number ('121'). This would have meant that this tank had a six-man crew! (Laux)

As a result of the ferocity of the fighting another opportunity arises to emphasise the Tiger's ability to absorb 'punishment.'

In Ruhe werden die Treffer der schweren Abwehrwaffe des Feindes betrachtet, die dem „Tiger" nicht viel anhaben konnten

PK-Aufn.: Kriegsber. Wolff-Altvater (PBZ.), Kriegsber. Bauer-Altvater (Atl.)

Munition für den „Tiger". Diese Panzer haben bei dem Gegenangriff im Raum von Bjelgorod erneut ihre gewaltige Überlegenheit bewiesen

Aufn.: ∬-PK. — Büschel (Wien-Bild)

Incorrect rearming of a tank belonging to *13./SS-Pz.Rgt. 1.*

Das Lazarett der Tigerpanzer

Unweit der Hauptkampflinie hat sich die Reparaturwerkstatt der Tigerpanzer eingerichtet.
Ein kräftiger Kran dient dazu, den Turm vom Wagen zu heben

PK-Aufn. Lohse   61260   Presse-Hoffmann

From the middle of 1943, the Hoffmann Press Service published high-quality postcards with Tiger motifs that were coveted as collector items both during and after the war. (Here a '503' vehicle)

It stood to reason that the comic strips that appeared in the *Tigerfibel* would also be used in postcards.

Begegnung auf der Vormarschstraße
Eine Tigerpanzer-Kolonne überholt einen Troßwagen der Infanterie im Raum von Bjelgorod

PK-Aufn. Lohse
Presse-Hoffmann

Mit Tiger und Infanterie gegen den Feind
Am Tigerpanzer vorbei geht die Schützenreihe in die vorbereitete Ausgangsstellung

PK-Aufn. Lohse
61332
Presse-Hoffmann

Two public relations cards showing tanks belonging to *2./s.Pz.Abt. 503* on 31 July 1943.

"TIGER-CHIRURGIE"

In der gewaltigen Mühle der Materialschlachten des Ostens werden an Mensch und Waffen gigantische Anforderungen gestellt. Der deutsche Soldat und sein Gerät bestehen Tag und Nacht alle Zerreißproben. Ohne Wunden jedoch geht es in diesem Kampf nicht ab. Selbst unsere „Tiger"-Panzer sind gegen gelegentliche Kratzer nicht gefeit. Für die verwundeten Kolosse stehen aber erfahrene Panzer-Chirurgen bereit, die sie in kürzester Zeit wieder einsatzbereit machen.

Der Feldwebel der Instandsetzungsstaffel hat soeben durch Funk die Nachricht erhalten, daß ein „Tiger" mit Kettenschaden den Kampfplatz verlassen hat. Sofort begibt er sich mit dem nötigen Handwerkzeug nach vorne

Der beschädigte Panzer hat sich, gegen Feind-Fliegersicht geschützt, etwas vom Kampfplatz abgesetzt, um die Ankunft des Instandsetzungstrupps abzuwarten, der die leichte Beschädigung schnellstens repariert

Mit Hilfe eines Kranwagens wird das beschädigte Treibrad gegen ein neues ausgetauscht

Rechts: Währenddessen hat ein anderer Teil des „Sanitätspersonals" die Kette abgenommen und ein schadhaftes Glied in Eile ausgewechselt

Der Treffer eines feindlichen Sturmgeschützes hat trotz des großen Kalibers an der Stirnseite nur eine flache Einbuchtung hinterlassen

PK - Aufnahmen Kriegsberichter Wolf-Altwater (H. H.)

Wehrmacht magazine in July 1943 with 'Tiger Surgery'.

The Tiger was in the forefront of propaganda in the media in spring 1943 ('frightening the enemy').

This poster is taken from a page in the May 1943 edition of the *'Motor Schau'* ('Motor Show') magazine.

This American soldiers' magazine from January 1944 shows a Tiger that had already been 'tamed' in Tunisia in April 1943. It had once belonged to *1./s.Pz.Abt. 504*.

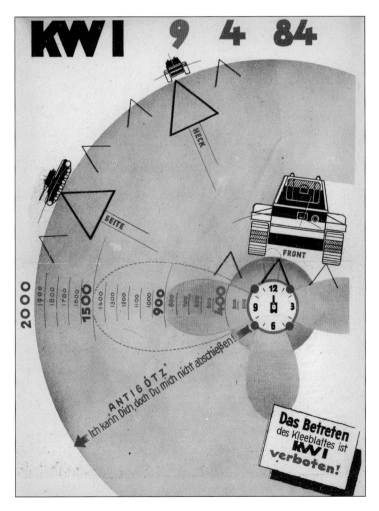

The German tank crews received so-called *'Antigötz'-Tafeln* – tables that referred to the types of tanks used by the enemy. The one referring to the soviet KV-1 is shown above in its original dimensions. On it, the ranges (in red typeface) are shown at which the Tiger could take out the enemy tank from the front, side or rear. The green colour shows the areas of the Tiger that could be penetrated by the KV-1's shells within the ranges indicated. In the bottom right corner is the warning 'the KV-1 is forbidden from entering the clover leaf.' (D656/27)

Colour images of a tank from '*502*'.

Tigers belonging to the '*507*' in the advance on Tarnopol on 7 June 1944.

Top left and above: photographs in this series are well known, they were used in several publications and also as front cover pictures.

This photo shows that the number '2' on the turret of the tank has been retouched to protect secrecy.

A tank crew and commander of the '508'.

The workshop of the '508' on the Acro factory grounds in Rome.

These American photos shows the 'Tiger grave' of Beja at the beginning of March 1943. (*Life*)

These American photos shows the 'Tiger grave' of Beja at the beginning of March 1943. (*Life*)

These American photos shows the 'Tiger grave' of Beja at the beginning of March 1943. (*Life*)

A left-behind Tiger from the '*508*' cleared from the road.

Tschernyschewo, 19 February 1943 ('*502*').

Oberleutnant Stadler of *13./Pz.Rgt. 'GD'* supervises the rearmament of this tank in June 1943.

This is no Tiger…but it is nevertheless interesting. This B-IV explosives carrier has just placed its load which is now to the front of the vehicle.

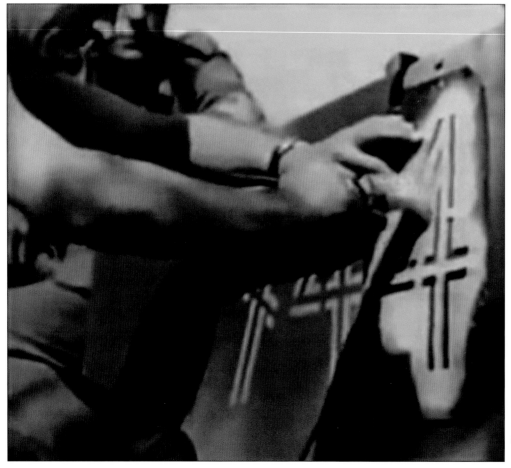

This picture documents the practice of painting turret numbers with the aid of a stencil. Subsequently, the breaks in the stencilled numbers would be filled in by hand.

In August 1943 the performance of industry was highlighted in the magazine *Wehrmacht*.

"TIGER"

der neueste Panzer
der deutschen Wehrmacht

PK-Aufnahmen: Kriegsberichter Schmock (Wb), OT-Kriegsberichter Maier. — Fotos: Ruge, Schuppe (HH 3), Boesig (Atl.)

Oben: Dem besten Soldaten der Welt die besten Waffen der Welt! Der neue 60-Tonnen-Panzerkampfwagen „Tiger", die Spitzenleistung deutscher Waffentechnik, ist eine glänzende Erfüllung dieser Forderung. — Links: Generaloberst Guderian, der Inspekteur der Panzerwaffe, besichtigte an der Ostfront das Panzerregiment „Großdeutschland" in Begleitung seines Kommandeurs Oberst der Res. Graf Strachwitz, dem der Führer die Schwerter zum Eichenlaub des Ritterkreuzes verlieh.

122

Bild rechts: Wo der „Tiger" bisher aufgetreten ist, wurde er zum Schrecken unserer Gegner. Geländeschwierigkeiten und Hindernisse vermag dieser Koloß an Kraft und Schwere mühelos zu überwinden.

Solange es Waffen gibt, hat zwischen denen des Angriffs und denen, die der Abwehr dienen, ein Wettlaufen stattgefunden. Das bekannteste Beispiel für diesen ständigen Kampf liefert die Kriegsmarine mit der Entwicklung der Kaliber der Schiffsgeschütze und der Dicke der Panzerplatten. Schließlich sind beide bei etwa 40 Zentimeter angelangt. Der gleiche oder jedenfalls ein sehr ähnlicher Wettlauf begann mit der Erfindung des Tanks, und zwar zwischen dem Geschützkaliber des Panzerkampfwagens und der panzerbrechenden Waffe, an erster Stelle also der Panzerabwehrkanone. Beide suchten sich an Durchschlagskraft und Reichweite ständig zu übertreffen und haben die Verwendung immer stärkerer Panzerplatten gegen das tödliche Durchbohrtwerden zur zwangsläufigen Folge gehabt.

Auch dieser Wettlauf wird aller Voraussicht nach einmal unentschieden ausgehen; aber das ist nicht das Entscheidende. Es kommt vielmehr nur darauf an, im entscheidenden Augenblick, also zum Beispiel jetzt, entweder den Kampfwagen mit der überlegenen Kanone und Panzerung oder die bessere panzerbrechende Waffe, am besten aber beides gleichzeitig, zu besitzen. Da aber um diese Ziele heute die fähigsten Waffeningenieure aller kriegführenden Länder kämpfen, ist selbst ein nur kleiner Vorsprung schwer zu erringen. Wieviel mehr Anerkennung, ja Bewunderung verdienen deshalb unsere Panzerkonstrukteure, nachdem es ihnen mit dem „Tiger" gelungen ist, zur Zeit mit einem Vorsprung von einer „ganzen Runde" vor den Panzern aller unserer Gegner zu liegen. Wenn man zum erstenmal vor diesem neuesten

*Unten: Das für einen Panzer ungewöhnlich lange und kräftige Geschütz in dem um 360° schwenkbaren Turm ist mit seiner Rasanz und Durchschlagskraft die gefürchtete Waffe des „Tiger".
Rechts: Beim Nehmen eines Hindernisses, wie hier dem Durchbrechen eines Hauses, wird das lange Geschützrohr nach hinten geschwenkt. Hier ist ein „Tiger" gerade im Begriff, ein Haus glatt zu durchfahren.*

In the 1944 edition of the *Wehrmacht* yearbook the Tiger was highly praised but this was done without undue exaggeration.

Erzeugnis deutscher Waffentechnik steht, so macht, neben der Größe des Panzers im ganzen, das ungewöhnlich lange und kräftige Geschützrohr in dem um 360° schwenkbaren Turm wohl den stärksten Eindruck. Ausschlaggebend für die Wahl dieses Geschützes war in erster Linie die Erfahrung, daß bei den ständig zunehmenden Entfernungen im Kampf der Panzer gegen Panzer derjenige unbedingt im Vorteil ist, der als erster durchschlagend trifft. Das durchschlagende, sichere Treffen aber hat, abgesehen vom Kaliber, eine möglichst rasante Flugbahn und diese wiederum eine entsprechende Rohrlänge zur Voraussetzung. Die äußerst rasante Flugbahn dieses „Tiger"-Geschützes ermöglicht das direkte Zielen auf Entfernungen, für die der Gegner sich erst durch Kurz-weit-Schüsse einschießen muß und dadurch kostbarste Zeit verliert. Zu diesem oft allein schon entscheidenden Vorteil aber besitzt der „Tiger", vor allem an der Stirnseite, eine Panzerung, an der selbst auf kurze Entfernungen die Ge-schosse sowohl der gegnerischen Panzer als auch der bisher verwendeten panzerbrechenden Waffen in der Regel wir-kungslos abprallen. Diese Tatsache verleiht der Besatzung ständig das Gefühl unbedingter Überlegenheit und großer Sicherheit und wirkt sich dementsprechend aus.

Das überlegene Geschütz und die bessere Panzerung aber würden allein noch nicht ausreichen, um eine neuzeit-liche Panzerschlacht zu gewinnen oder einen Durchbruch zu erzielen. Abgesehen von der Zahl der jeweils zur Verfügung stehenden Panzerkampfwagen und dem überlegenen tak-tischen Einsatz ist deshalb deren Geschwindigkeit, Wendig-keit und Geländegängigkeit von mitentscheidender Bedeu-tung. Wenn es nun schon keineswegs einfach war, leichte und mittelschwere Panzerkampfwagen so durchzukonstruieren, daß sie schließlich mit jedem Gelände fertig wurden, so war dies für einen Panzerkampfwagen wie den „Tiger" mit seinen rund 60 t Gesamtgewicht eine anfangs unmöglich erschei-nende Aufgabe. Aber auch diese wurde gelöst. Allerdings bedurfte es hierzu außergewöhnlicher Mittel und des Ein-satzes der tüchtigsten Ingenieure und Spezialisten der Fertigung auf den verschiedensten Gebieten.

Nicht weniger als 650 bis 700 PS haben sich als erforder-lich erwiesen, um diesem Stahlkoloß die notwendige Ge-schwindigkeit (bis zu 45 km/st) zu verleihen und ihn in freiem Gelände Steigungen bis zu 40% anstandslos erklimmen zu lassen. Die Kraftquelle, ein flüssigkeitsgekühlter Zwölf-zylinder-V-Motor, liegt im Heck des Panzers. Von dort wird die Antriebskraft durch eine Kardanwelle auf ein Achtgang-getriebe, das vorn zwischen dem Fahrer und dem Funker untergebracht ist, übertragen und von diesem an die Wellen der Zahnkranzräder, die die Ketten antreiben, weitergeleitet.

Um nun so einen 60-Tonnen-Panzer zu schalten und zu steuern, würden auf die Dauer die Kräfte selbst eines Schwerathleten nicht mehr ausreichen. Infolgedessen mußte man von der bisher üblichen, direkt wirkenden Knüppelsteuerung und der normalen Schaltung für das Getriebe abgehen. Man ersann dafür eine Lenkung, die im Prinzip darin besteht, daß der Fahrer, wie bei einem normalen Kraftwagen, nur ein Handrad zu drehen braucht, während die eigentlichen Kräfte, um den Panzer durch Einzelabbremsen und -beschleunigen der Ketten Kurven fahren zu lassen, durch ein ölhydraulisches System aufgebracht werden. Das Handrad dient somit nur zur Steuerung bzw. Auslösung dieser Kräfte. Ähnlich ist es mit der Schaltung. Für diese ist nach einem schon vom Kraftfahrzeug her bekannten System nur ein kleiner Vor-wähler vorgesehen, während der eigentliche Schaltvor-gang sich anschließend automatisch, also ebenfalls an-strengungslos für den Fahrer, vollzieht. Die Munition sowohl für das Geschütz als auch für die Maschinen-gewehre ist ebenso wie der Kraftstoffvorrat für den Motor so reichlich bemessen, daß die bisher längsten Gefechte ohne Verknappungen durchgehalten werden konnten.

Ein Panzerkampfwagen von der Größe und der Kampfkraft des „Tiger" ist, ähnlich wie ein hochwertiges Kriegsschiff, kein Massenerzeugnis. Aber selbst wenn der „Tiger", stets begleitet von Panzern geringerer Größe, an irgendeinem Frontabschnitt in nur wenigen Exem-plaren in das Kampfgeschehen eingreift, dann räumt er auf! Einem Mammut aus Stahl gleich, bricht er, wenn es sein muß, durch jeden Wald, legt Mauern und Häuser um, und schon auf Kilometerentfernung sitzt jeder Schuß. So wurde er mit seinem ersten Erscheinen der Schrecken aller gegnerischen Panzer, die sich, sobald das mächtige

Fortsetzung und Schluss dieses Artikels. Der Umbruch wurde verändert, „tigerfremde" Fotos entfernt.

Wehrmachtberichte

1. März bis 30. April 1944

Das Oberkommando der Wehrmacht gab bekannt:

25. April 1944

Südwestlich Kowel wurde nach mehrtägigen harten Kämpfen unter schwie-rigen Geländeverhältnissen die Masse einer bolschewistischen Kavalleriedivision eingeschlossen und vernichtet. Die Sowjets verloren dabei mehrere tausend Tote und zahlreiche Gefangene. 38 Geschütze sowie zahlreiche andere Waffen wurden erbeutet.

Der Unteroffizier K n i s p e l in einer schweren Panzerabteilung im Osten schoß in der Zeit von Juli 1942 bis März 1944 101 Panzer ab.

Das Schlachtgeschwader Immelmann hat sich unter Führung seines Kommo-dore, Ritterkreuzträgers Oberstleutnant S t e p, an der Ostfront besonders bewährt.

As the article continued towards its end its composition was altered; photos that were 'alien' to the Tiger were removed. Successes were sometimes presented in the form of decorated pages in *Wehrmacht* reports. In this example, *Unteroffizier* Knispel of *s.Pz.Abt. 503* receives special mention without his unit being named.

'Training instructions' were also printed. (see following pages)

ILLUSTRIERTER BEOBACHTER

Sich überrollen lassen

Die Überwindung der Panzerscheu

Er gibt das erste Beispiel.
Ruhig sitzt der Major in seinem Loch, während der Panzer über ihn hinwegrollt. Einige Erdbrocken, die auf ihn fielen, schüttelt er beim Herausklettern lachend ab

In schmalen, tiefen Löchern, die von den Panzern aus kaum zu erkennen sind, hocken die Grenadiere in der Erde und lassen ruhig die Stahlkolosse über sich hinwegrollen. Um den jungen Soldaten den Schreck vor dem Panzer zu nehmen, wird ihnen in frontnahen Übungen das Erlebnis des Überrolltwerdens vertraut gemacht. Mit eiserner Ruhe werden sie dann an der Front den feindlichen Panzer auf sich zukommen und vorüberrollen lassen.

Der Panzer hat das erste Loch überrollt,
und etwas zaghaft warten die Kameraden in den andern Löchern auf das große Erlebnis, das ihnen den Schreck vor der Panzerüberrollung nehmen soll

Rasch sind die Grenadiere in das Schützenloch gesprungen.
Sie lassen sich von dem Ungetüm überrollen, denn sie wollen ihrem Major nicht nachstehen.

ILLUSTRIERTER BEOBACHTER

Jetzt dröhnt der Erdboden, und die Ketten rasseln dicht über dem Kopf.
Erdklumpen, die von den Ketten losgerissen werden, fallen in das Loch. In wenigen Sekunden ist der Spuk vorüber

Hier ist der schmale Graben an einem Ende verbreitert worden,
damit eine eingebaute Filmkamera diese Überrollung für einen Lehrfilm festhalten kann. So wird den jungen Soldaten gezeigt werden, wie es richtig gemacht wird.

GEGENSTOSS
an der
AUTOBAHN

Die letzten Aufnahmen
des Kriegsberichters Lutz Knobloch

Zum viertenmal versuchten die Sowjets in den ersten Dezembertagen mit der gewaltigen Stoßkraft von 32 Schützen-divisionen, unterstützt von 6 bis 8 Panzerbrigaden und Schlacht-fliegern, an der Autobahn Minsk—Smolensk das Tor nach Westen aufzubrechen. Mit ungeahnter Wucht rannten die bolschewistischen Massen gegen die Stellungen weniger deut-scher Divisionen an. Sechs Tage währte die Schlacht mit einer Härte und Erbitterung ohnegleichen. Worte sind zu schwach, um die Leistungen unserer Soldaten zu würdigen, die dieser gewaltigen Übermacht bei Regen und Schnee im verschlamm-ten Gelände heldenmütig standhielten und dem Feind unvor-stellbare Verluste zufügten. An einzelnen Stellen, wo der Druck der Sowjets besonders stark war, gelangen den Bolschewisten örtliche Einbrüche. An diesen Stellen wurde mit größter Erbitte-rung gekämpft. In schneidigen Gegenstößen, oft unter schwierig-

sten Bedingungen, schlugen unsere tapferen Grenadiere zusam-men mit Panzern und Sturmgeschützen die Sowjets immer wie-der zurück. Das Schlachtfeld, von ungezählten Granattrichtern übersät, lag meist unter einer trügerischen Schneedecke verhüllt und forderte von der Infanterie das Höchste an Härte und Aus-dauer, das wütende Abwehrfeuer der zäh sich wehrenden So-wjets das Letzte an Mut und kämpferischer Entschlossenheit. Die starken Herzen der Grenadiere trugen die Entscheidung.

Bei einem dieser Gegenangriffe nahe der Autobahn fand der Kriegsberichter Leutnant Lutz Knobloch, von dem die „Wehr-macht" oft packende Kampfbilder bringen konnte (der Be-richt „Westlich Smolensk" in Nummer 24 vom 17. November sei besonders erwähnt), neben den stürmenden Grena-dieren den Heldentod. Als letztes Vermächtnis barg seine Leica diese Bilder.   Kriegsberichter Ulrich Majewski

February 1944 edition of the *Wehrmacht* magazine.

Newspaper reports came in from all theatres of war with Tigers sometimes playing only a photographic role. This caption for this picture (right), taken on 15 February 1944, refers to the difficulties caused by heavy rain and shows a tank belonging to *s.Pz.Abt.508*.

An der italienischen Front

Die frie
Dur

Der 1000. Erfolg einer Panzer-Abteilung

Normale Späh- und Stosstrupptätigkeit an der lettischen Front

Der Dienstag verlief an der lettischen Front bei normaler Späh- und Stosstrupptätigkeit ohne grössere Kampfhandlungen. Ein Angriff in Regimentsstärke beiderseits der Bahn Riga-Pleskau brachte dem Feind keinen wesentlichen Erfolg.

Artillerie bekämpfte feindliche Fahrzeugbewegungen auf der Insel Moon.

Bei den jüngsten Kämpfen im Gebiet der baltischen Inseln haben sich norddeutsche Landungs-Pionier-Einheiten unter Führung von Generalmajor Henke besonders ausgezeichnet.

Die schwäbisch-ostmärkische schwere Panzer-Abteilung 502 schoss am 26. September unter Führung ihres Kommandeurs, Hauptmann von Förster, den 1000. Feindpanzer seit Beginn ihres Osteinsatzes im Herbst 1942 ab. In der gleichen Zeit verlor die Abteilung nur 25 eigene Panzer.

„Ein Kampf, hinter dem der Fanatismus der ganzen Nation steht, kann nie anders als mit einem Sieg enden!"

Reichsminister Dr. Goebbels.

Frontwerkstatt für „Tiger", in der durch Feindeinwirkung oder Materialschäden ausgefallene Panzer in kürzester Zeit wieder instand gesetzt werden.

Serie 101cb · 5.9.44 · Bild 7 · ⚡PK-Zeichnung: Berner (Seb.) / Pk.-Foto: Kriegsberichter Schlegel-Breg (PBZ.) · Akt. Bilderdienst J. J. Weber, Leipzig · Verantw. Leitung: H. Schluke, Leipzig

In the last year of the war there was a move to openly name the unit designations. For example, in the article shown above, the '*502*' is mentioned.

As the successes dwindled away to nothing, the media content resorted to pathos to stimulate the will to resist.

The same messages (see previous page) were sometimes 'packaged' in a different way. In the centre of this photograph we see *Hauptmann* Leonhardt, commander of *3. Kompanie*.

„Tiger" - Kampfgruppe schoß den 1000. Panzer ab.

DNB. Berlin. 11. 10. 44. Eine „Tiger"-Kampfgruppe, die zwischen Düna u. Rigaer Bucht kämpft, konnte jetzt den 1000. Panzer abschießen. Das geschah im Morgengrauen, als sich sechs sowjetische Panzer in die deutschen Linien heranschoben, um sie mit aufgesessener Infanterie zu durchbrechen. In 1200 Meter Entfernung eröffnete der Führer der deutschen Kampfgruppe, Hauptmann Christoph Leonhardt, das Feuer u. erzielte bereits mit dem ersten Schuß einen Treffer, durch den der vorderste Sowjetpanzer liegen blieb. Auch ein zweiter sowjetischer Kampfwagen, ein moderner T 34, geriet in Brand. Daraufhin drehten die anderen sowjetischen Panzer ab.

Die Helden haben nur noch einen Panzer

Ritterkreuzträger Major Jähde, Kommandeur der Abt. 502, mit seinen Männern

Pillau, 22. April 1945
Noch immer halten sich deutsche Truppen auf der Frischen-Nehrung und im brennenden Pillau. Darunter auch die

Panzerabteilung 502, eine der erfolgreichsten Panzerformationen der deutschen Wehrmacht.

Mehrere ihrer Offiziere wurden mit höchsten Tap-

An die Überreste der deutschen Truppen im Raume von Pillau
Soldaten und Offiziere,

Eines der Sowjet-Flugblätter an die deutschen Soldaten

ferkeitsauszeichnungen dekoriert, der zur Abteilung 502 gehörende Unteroffizier Kramer trägt das Ritterkreuz. Er schoß mit seinem Tiger allein 50 sowjetische Panzer ab.

Die letzten Nachrichten von der Abteilung 502 besagen, daß die Truppe nur noch über einen einzigen Panzer verfügt. Auch den anderen im Raum Pillau stehenden deutschen Soldaten gehen Munition und Lebensmittel aus. Die Russen fordern in Flugblättern zur Kapitulation der Streitkräfte auf.

Ein von der Abteilung 502 erbeuteter Sowjet-T 34

Fast auf den Tag genau vor einem Jahr, am 25. 4. 1944, erhielt Leutnant Hans Bölter (Mitte) das Ritterkreuz. Er war mit wenigen Panzern in die Bereitstellung der 6. sowjetischen Gardepanzerarmee bei Riga gefahren. Inzwischen wurde er zum Hauptmann befördert und erhielt das Eichenlaub. Links: Obergefreiter Lönnecker. Er fährt den letzten Tigerpanzer der Abteilung 502. Rechts: Unteroffizier Kramer. Er schoß über 50 Panzer ab.

Towards the end of the war, nothing could be glossed over. In the press article shown above, the last battles of what remained of the '502', in the area of Pillau (East Prussia), are reported. The editorial staff of this Hamburg newspaper were already at sixes and sevens…the photo of *Major* Jähde (no longer CO) is more than a year old.

Unsere Losung ist:

Kein Soldat der Welt soll besser sein als wir!

30.9.44.

Fhj. Ofw. Gebhardt

Zugf. 2./Pz. Abt. 507

Der Oberbefehlshaber der Heeresgruppe Nord

Generaloberst

Schörner, the commander in chief of *Heeresgruppe Nord*, always came up with something to strengthen morale! The signed document has the heading, 'Our watchword is: no soldiers in the world are better than us!'

Personal achievements, such as those of gunner *Rottenführer* 'Bobby' Warmbrunn, were exploited. Here he is standing under the artfully positioned 'kill' rings on a tank gun barrel before being awarded the Knight's Cross on 16 January 1944. (Kessel)
From time to time, the *Propaganda Kompanie* pictures can trigger a little smile on the face of an insider. A crew would certainly not carry out sweaty work on a track wearing such headwear.

The press agencies, such as *Transocean-Europress*, also received material such as this picture published in its 4 March 1944 edition. The picture shows the repair of major mine-damage to the running gear of a tank belonging to the '508.' (Vack)
Magazines issued by other *Wehrmacht* braches also featured the Tiger. The picture appeared in *Der Adler* on 12 October 1943. (Rheinländer)

The new Tiger II was also put to use in propaganda material. With this in mind, *s.Pz.Abt. 503*, newly equipped with this tank, staged a spectacle for the media in Sennelager on 29 September 1944 that was also featured in the *Wochenschau*. First *Oberleutnant* von Rosen plays the commander reviewing the front…

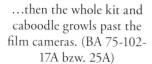

…then the whole kit and caboodle growls past the film cameras. (BA 75-102-17A bzw. 25A)

The support of Germany's last ally, Hungary, was also shown. Here, a tank belonging to the '503' is cheered by passers-by in Budapest on 14 October 1944. (BA 82-90-19-X18)

Nummer 5 1. Februar 1945
Copr. 1945 Deutscher Verlag

Berliner

54. Jahrgang   Preis 20 Pfennig

Illustrierte Zeitung

Im Morgengrauen rollen Panzer durch den Nebel.

Panzer rücken vor!

Während der Nacht sind bolschewistische Kräfte vorgedrungen. Deutschen Panzern gelang es, sich unbemerkt in die Flanke der Angreifer vorzutasten. Ueber sumpfiges Gelände und Wassergräben, immer wieder im Nebel sichernd, mahlen sich die Stahlkolosse ihrem befohlenen Einsatzraum entgegen. Wenn eine schwierige Stelle zu passieren ist, lagern sich die Panzergrenadiere zu kurzer Rast — der steigende Tag wird all ihre Kräfte in Anspruch nehmen!

PK.-Aufnahme: ℋ-Kriegsberichter Grönert (TO.)

Towards the end of the war the information in the media became increasingly vague: no dates and no indication of locations. In this photograph a tank belonging to the *9./SS-Pz.Rgt. 3* is in action with grenadiers of the *II./SS-Pz.Gren.Btl. 'Totenkopf'* near Neszmely, Hungary, on 2 January 1945. Normally, a bogged-down tank would not have been shown in the press. (Grönert)

The Allies too liked to use the Tiger as an object of propaganda. In this picture we see General Eisenhower, the commanding officer of the Supreme Headquarters of the Allied Expeditionary Forces (SHAEF) visiting an upturned Tiger that belonged to the '*503.*' But everything is not quite as it seems; the accompanying report proclaims Bradley's arrival at the *Westwall* in autumn 1944 but the photo was taken during the Normandy battles.

In the *Yank* magazine there is a report about the examination of tank '712' of *s.Pz.Abt. 501* at the American testing facility in Aberdeen USA. This tank was captured in Tunisia.

This American soldiers' magazine from January 1944 shows a Tiger that had already been 'tamed' in Tunisia in April 1943. It had once belonged to *1./s.Pz.Abt. 504.*

At the end of this section, a few rare pictures, such as this group of Tigers belonging to the '*507*' in the advance on Tarnopol on 7 June 1944.

A whole series of colour pictures of Tigers come from Allied sources. This one shows a Tiger belonging to the '*506*' that was captured by the US Army in Gereonsweiler on 15 December 1944 – it now, probably wisely, carries identification symbols that are visible to pilots.

A 'roll out' at Henschel in Kassel in July 1943.

Tank of '501' in Tunisia in early 1943.

Crew members of the '504' in Italy cleaning their tank's gun barrel.

A tank crew of the '506' and a commander of the '508.'

The workshop of the '508' on the Acro factory grounds in Rome.

These American photos shows the 'Tiger grave' of Beja at the beginning of March 1943 (Life)

A vehicle of the '508' cleared from the road.

Tschernyschewo, 19 February 1943 ('502').

Oberleutnant Stadler of *13./Pz.Rgt. 'GD'* supervises the rearmament of this tank in June 1943.

Two particularly scenic pictures (above and on the following page) show *schwere Panzerkompanie 'Meyer'* at rest in the Brenner Pass on 31 July 1943 with the company leader standing next to the turret. (Meyer)

This is no Tiger...but it is nevertheless interesting. This B-IV explosives carrier has just placed its load which is now to the front of the vehicle.

This picture documents the practice of painting turret numbers with the aid of a stencil. Subsequently, the breaks in the stencilled numbers would be filled in by hand.

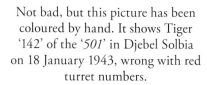

Not bad, but this picture has been coloured by hand. It shows Tiger '142' of the '501' in Djebel Solbia on 18 January 1943, wrong with red turret numbers.

Annex

Amendments to Volumes I and II

Almost twenty years have passed since the publication of the English edition of Volumes I and II of *Tigers in Combat*. During this time I have collected further data and photographs. In addition, many observant readers have supplied amendments and have also brought errors to my attention. This is not surprizing given the vagueness of primary sources, lapses in memory and errors that occurred during the transfer of reports.

On the 23 pages that follow, I would therefore like to make amendments, supported by photographs, regarding the identification symbols on vehicles in the various Tiger units and also make some corrections. There are also some findings regarding reorganizations that took place.

The command tank of *s.Pz.Abt. 501* in Tunisia is seldom shown in photographs. This picture from 25 November 1942 makes it clear that on this vehicle the outlines on the turret numbers were very narrow.

After the first losses, the *1. Kompanie* of the '*501*' was in part renumbered following reorganization. This photograph from Manouba, taken on 18 December 1942, shows Panzer IIIs with the numbers '132' and '115.'
(Hartmann)

This photograph shows the '132' under American 'occupation.' The turret of Tiger '141' which was blown up on 1 March 1943 near Beja can be seen in the background.

An early original photo of Tiger '712' (in the foreground) at the Aberdeen proving ground shows that after the subordination of the remaining tanks to *Panzerregiment 7* the turret numbers were done in black paint with a white outline.

After restablishment on the Eastern Front and the application of white camouflage at the beginning of 1944, the turret numbers were applied, just as before, but in black-paint outline. (Collection belonging to Karl-Heinz Münch)

In spring 1944 nothing initially changed regarding the numbers; the somewhat idiosyncratic *Fleckentarnung* camouflage patterns were simply painted around them.

After its destruction in July 1944, the newly refitted *Abteilung '501'* (later designated *'424'*) was fully equipped with Tiger II tanks. The turret numbers were painted in red with white outlines at the side and towards the front of the turret (as in *3. Kompanie*) or, in other companies, directly under the *Balkenkreuz* in somewhat smaller numerals.

The command group likewise had the numbers exactly under the *Balkenkreuz*. At first the numerals '001', '002' and '003' were used. Because this identified them as command tanks, the numbers '501' and '502' were used later ('002' was captured by the enemy at the beginning of July). In this picture the '502' is shown with its anti-aircraft MG mounted. This tank was lost on 13 August 1944.

With the intake of 18 Tiger I tanks from the *'509'* at the end of September 1944, a brisk renumbering began in the *Abteilung*. Tank '10?' occupies the foreground in this picture. Behind it is a Tiger II with the identification number '113' belonging to *Abteilung '424'*; this was incorrectly identified as belonging to *s.SSPz.Abt. 502* in Volume II.

This picture from May 1943 shows tank '5' of *1./s.Pz.Abt. 502* in Tossno. As yet, this tank has scarcely been documented.

After replenishment, exceptionally large and – as is apparent from this picture of tank '32' taken in July 1943 – too obtrusive white numerals were painted on the turrets.

After a few days these numerals were therefore 'toned down' a bit by the addition of black outlines. The adjacent vehicle is one of just three remaining Panzer III tanks. Apparently they were numbered consecutively from '04' to '06.'

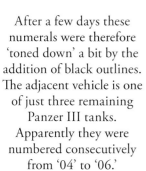

In summer 1943 tank '113' attracted a great deal of attention after the application of its new white identification number (*1. Kompanie* only); after the white camouflage paint was washed off it still showed its history – formerly, it was numbered '3' and thereafter '14.' So far, so good…

…looking from the other side we can see a number '1' (directly below the open turret hatch) to the right of a barely visible '3.' This tanks has therefore been renumbered a total of four times. (BA 457-56-4 and 5)

In this photograph we can see why *3./s.Pz.Abt. 502* also had their (black) turret numbers on the sides of the hull. In June 1943 the company was ordered at short notice to Coetquidan for several 'visitor days' for troops in training. The *Balkenkreuz* (without the white parts) and the tank identification number were hastily applied to the sides of the hull. After deciding the final position should be on the side of the turret towards the front, the numbers on the hull remained where they were. (Koob, in the Karlheinz Münch collection)

Later, some of the crew
were unable to part with
their beloved mammoth
(beside the radio operator's
MG).

There exists little documentation
regarding the identification numbers of
the command tanks; this picture shows
tank 'II' in autumn 1943.

After achieving a significant
excess of stock, all turret
numbers were painted in
the familiar black colour in
March 1944...

...in spring 1944,
and for the first time,
an order to use white
for the identification
numbers was received.

However, this did not please the new commander,
Major Schwaner, who stipulated that the
identification numbers should be in red with a
white border. Tank '318' is shown in the picture.

For quite a while the *2. Kompanie*, which
for a long time fought separately from the
rest of the *Abteilung*, 'danced to a different
tune.' They retained their black numerals
when in action in the '*Ostsack*' as shown in
this picture from 6 April 1944.

As is well known, *s.Pz.Abt. 503* initially used white numbers with a black border that were also painted on the rear turret-box.

Some chroniclers allow themselves to become confused by the different turret numbers used by the *2. Kompanie*. The reason is that this unit was first intended for the '*502*' before being eventually assigned to the '*503*' on 14 January 1943. (Wunderlich)

After arriving at the assembly area for *Operation Zitadelle* the company then dutifully painted on the turret numbers using manufactured '503' type stencils, as did *1. Kompanie*.

The *3./s.Pz.Abt. 503* kept their former white numerals for quite a long time, indignantly 'embellishing' them with black paint.

Two shots of Tiger '300' of *3./s. Pz.Abt. 503* – on the right at the exercise area at Mailly-le-Camp …

…and (left) at the end of September 1944 (newly delivered) at the military exercise area at Senne with its transport tracks already fitted before its departure for Hungary. (Wunderlich)

Some crews belonging to the newly formed *s.Pz.Abt. 505* didn't merely dab on the unit symbol (a knight on a charging steed) onto the front of the hull casing (centre of picture) using a stencil and white paint, they also artistically painted in (some of) the contours using black paint as is shown in this picture of the '233' taken at the end of April 1943 before the march to firing and military exercises at Beverloo. In a similar fashion, the turret numbers were added to the turret boxes as shown (below).

The turret number '05' on this Panzer III is revealing; it shows that this tank was not only subordinated to the company but also that a light tank platoon had been formed.

Tank 'II' of the command group was simply marked with a rhombic symbol.

Attaching additional track links to the side of the turret meant that the numbers were pushed forwards and consisted of simply a white outline; this picture shows the '114' immediately before the launch of *Operation Zitadelle* with the wire mesh typical of the '505' installed on the tank's hull.

Later, *3. Kompanie* developed its own individual style with the addition of large-sized, improvised numerals.

In the wake of the replenishment of the *Abteilung* between the end of 1943 and the beginning of 1944, the '505' adopted a substantial *Ritterdarstellung* (symbol of a knight) on the turret with the tank's number now on the gun mantel tube.

White camouflage was usually applied over the symbol of the knight and the tank number added afterwards in black paint.

The knight on horseback appeared again in spring. Because the numbers painted in black on the barrel were difficult to remove, *3. Kompanie* improvised by initially painting a yellow box on the gun mantel tube. In this picture, taken on 27 May 1944, we also see *General* Decker.

On a tank, newly delivered in May 1944 to Lublin, the figure of the knight was rendered in a simpler fashion towards the front of the turret. The numbers on the gun barrel would have been added later.

The numbering of the Tiger II after the reorganization in Ohrdruf in July/August 1944 is confusing. Looking at the '212' (right), it is easy to understand...

...how this confusion arises. One must understand that the company number (in this case '1') was always painted on the left side of the gun mantel tube – this tank's identification number is therefore '124' and not '241.' (Krönke)

One never tires of looking at this artistic addition of the *Willing-Löwen* (*Major* Willing was the first commander of the *Abteilung*) of *s.Pz.Abt. 506* painted on the rear turret box.

When first painted, the red numbers (*1. Kompanie*) and yellow numbers of *3. Kompanie* were outlined with fine black lines. However this did not continue for very long.

This is a rather rare picture of a Tiger II belonging to the '*506*' that was abandoned beneath the hills of Ruhland in December 1944; the '109' of the *1. Kompanie* to be precise.

This picture of a standard identification number of a tank belonging to *s.Pz.Abt. 507* shows that the white numerals were not always completely surrounded by a black border.

The identification signs were also painted on the turret's rear box, as in this example of the back-up command tank that carries the letter 'C.'

The Tiger II tanks also had differently sized numbers painted on the turret – but not on all vehicles. This photograph shows the '402' after it had been badly shot up on 9 April 1945; presumably this tank belonged to the command group of the *Abteilung*?

At *s.Pz.Abt. 508, 1. Kompanie* was the first to the deviate from the practice of using same-sized numerals. They 'attached' the platoon and tank number in small sized numerals to the company number (a white '1' with outline). This picture was taken at the end of February 1944 during the attack on the Nettuno bridgehead.

After a receiving a reprimand by the *Abteilung*, the 'attachments' were removed but were, somewhat stubbornly, painted in small white numerals on the side of the hull. (Eima – Collection of Karlheinz Münch)

Later, a personal touch was maintained by painting an ostentatiously large numeral on the side of the turret.

Following the shift from the use of white 'Latinised' numerals, *s.Pz.Abt. 509* painted the turret numbers in black (sometimes without a white border).

Later, only a simple black number appeared on the rear of the turret.

This picture shows a typical rendition of an *Abteilung* turret number after being equipped with Tiger II tanks. (Schwalbach)

There were no identification numbers on the vehicles that were acquired directly from the remnants of the '*510*' and '*511*' by the Henschel factory in Kassel.

General Ramcke asks an enlisted soldier belonging to *Tiger-Kompanie 'Meyer'* – recognisable by the *Baltenkreuz* (Baltic Cross) on the front of the tank's hull – for a briefing. (Karlheinz Münch collection)

A rare picture of a Tiger I belonging to *1. Fallschirm-Panzer-Division 1 'Hermann Göring'* that was left behind after the fighting in Teplice. This cobbled-together Panzer battalion had one ('Ist') platoon consisting of three used Tiger I tanks. This one had the turret identification markings 'I05.'

The *13./Pz.Rgt. 'GD'* makes it difficult for anyone interested in tank identification numbers! The company command tanks carried the numbers '1', '3' and '6' and later they also had a vehicle with the number '2' (see above), or – painted over several times – one with the number '7' (see right).

Also at the *III./Pz.Rgt. 'GD'*, the turret identification numbers (here we see tank 'B21') were not only painted in black, as they were in the beginning, but later also in white with a black border.

The turret identification numbering also evolved inconsistently at the heavy tank company of *Pz.Rgt. 'LAH.'* To begin with, they were composed of black lines (see right).

So that these white numbers were not blanked out when white camouflage paint was applied, a rectangular section was simply left unpainted.

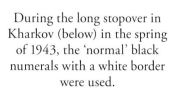

During the long stopover in Kharkov (below) in the spring of 1943, the 'normal' black numerals with a white border were used.

With the launch of the 'S' identification markings, a few crews simply painted the white outline of the numbers and, contrary to orders, did without the additional black contour lines. Even then, they didn't bother to paint in the 'loose ends.'

The 'S51' on the turret box of the tank in the background has been correctly painted although perhaps its position is a little too low.

The 'S05' number on the company command tank was later painted in darker so that it stood out better against the white camouflage.

The '841' of *8./SS-Pz. Rgt. 'Das Reich'* in white camouflage... only the cross and number are left uncovered.

In the interim, the tanks belonging to *s.Kp. 'DR'* painted their old runic symbol on the hull.

Later, this company also adopted the 'S' type identification numbering although only as a white outline. The level of the little company 'mascot' symbol (in white at the left side of the picture) varied from time to time.

This picture shows a tank belonging to the *3./s.SS.Pz.Abt. 101* in the transitional stage with white turret numbers. The unit symbol of the 'LAH' has not been obliterated by the Zimmerit coating and can be seen on the small area left uncovered. (Karlheinz Münch collection)

The same white numbers are painted on the turret box; the unit emblem (a shield with crossed keys) is on the left of the rear hull casing.

This photograph shows the '322' that once belonged to *s.SS-Pz. Abt. 501* at the Aberdeen Proving Ground and confirms the distinctive colour scheme used for the unit's turret numbers.

Here we see *Oberscharführer* Fey's *(s.SS-Pz.Abt. 102)* abandoned '132.' The barrel sports a large number of 'kill' rings, earned largely during the fighting in France on 8 August 1944.

This tank was towed away by the Free French troops and now stands in the museum in Saumur.

Tank '214' in service with the Hungarian forces; black numbers continued to be used for identification markings by vehicles taken over from the '509.'

Tank '142' (reserve command tank) of
1./s.SS-Pz.Abt. 103 with simple white-
border numbers.

Evidence that tanks belonging
to *2./s.SS-Pz.Abt.503*, like *1.
Kompanie*, had large numbers
formed in black outline; the '233' is
shown in this picture.

After the fighting in Berlin had
ended, the command tank ('I') of
s.SS-Pz.Abt. 503 was towed away
by the Russians.

Literature List

Technology and development

Jentz, Thomas » Germany's Tiger Tanks – D.W. to Tiger I
    und V.K. 45.02 to Tiger II
Spielberger, Walter » Panzerkampfwagen Tiger
Fletcher, » Tiger! The Tiger Tank: A British View
Fletcher u.a., » Tiger Tank – Owner's Workshop Manual
Dr. Maus, H. » Panzerkampfwagen VI "Tiger II"
    (Jahresgabe Panzermuseum 1988)

Specific topics and components

Arnoldt, Kurt » Studie über Tauchfähigkeit bei Kampfwagen
    vom 14.2.1964, WTS G 2350/5/137
Burr, Gustav u.a. » Typenhandbuch, Technische Daten aller
    Motoren der MTU und ihrer Vorgängergesellschaften
    von 1909 -1999
Deneke » Tarnanstriche des deutschen Heeres 1914 bis heute
Friedli, Lukas » Repairing the Panzers Volume 2
Göbel, Walter » Haustenbeck
Göbel, W. u.a. » Panzer-Versuchsstation 96 (in Schlänger
    Bote Nr. 94, 96-97)
Grimm, Karl » Senne, Sand und Soldaten (1957)
Jentz, Thomas L. » Panther
Köhler, Frank » Kampfpanzermotoren in Deutschland 1938-
    1990 – ein Überblick anhand ausgewählter Panzertypen,
    BWB
Köhler, Frank » Schalt- und Lenkgetriebe der Kampfpanzer
    in Deutschland, BWB
MTU Friedrichshafen, Typenhandbuch, Technische Daten
    aller Motoren der MTU Friedrichshafen von 1909-1999
Piesczek, Uwe (Hg.) » Truppenübungsplatz Senne
Ruff, Volker » DER STRABOKRAN (2011)
Dr. Schwarzmann, Peter » Panzerketten
Spielberger, Walter J. » Der Panzerkampfwagen Panther und
    seine Abarten
Treue/ Zima » Hochleistungsmotoren, Karl Maybach und
    sein Werk
Vogel, T. » Tiger Tank – E – 181, Ausf. E (Sd Kfz 181),
    Technical Illustrations and Turret Plans, Volume I

Unit and deployment histories

Schneider, Wolfgang » Tiger im Kampf Band I u. II
Kleine, Egon » Tiger. Die Geschichte einer legendären Waffe
    (Schwerpunkt: s.Pz.Abt. 502)
Carius, Otto » Tiger im Schlamm (s.Pz.Abt. 502)
Touratier, Guilhem Batailles » Hors-Sèrie - Tigres a
    Leningrad (1./s./Pz.Abt. 502)
Rubbel, Alfred u.a. » Erinnerungen an die Tigerabteilung
    503
Lodieu, Didier » 45 Tiger en Normandie (s.Pz.Abt. 503)
Szàmvèber, Norbert Nehèpàncèlosok (s.Pz.Abt. 503/FHH)
Peyrani, Federico » I carri armati Tiger in Sicilia (2./s.
    Pz.Abt. 504)
Schneider, Helmut » Chronik (s.Pz.Abt.) 507
Hirlinger, Kurt » Panzer-Abteilung 508 (und s.Pz.Kp.
    Meyer)
Jung, Hans-Joachim » Geschichte des Panzerregiments
    "Großdeutschland"
Wendt, Werner » Geschichte der s.Pz.Komp. LSSAH und
    s.SS-Pz.Abt. 101/501 Partly reprinted in Agte, Patrick –
    Michael Wittmann – although with faulty additions.
Schneider, Wolfgang » Tiger der Division Das Reich (mit
    s.SS-Pz.Abt. 102/502)
Fey, Will » Panzerkampf im Bild (s.SS-Pz.Abt. 102 in
    Auszügen)
Schneider, Wolfgang » Tiger der Division Totenkopf
Mujzer, Peter Hungarian Mobile Forces (Tigers with the
    Hungarian Army).
Jentz, Thomas » Tiger I & II Combat Tactics
Klages, Ron » Trail of the Tigers (Statistiken)
Ritgen, Helmut » Die Schulen der Panzertruppen des Heeres
    (Jahresgabe Panzermuseum 1992)

Modelling and diorama construction

Waldemar, Trojca » Tiger I, Tiger II, Tiger in Color

For reasons of clarity only those publications which
    served as sources or are especially recommended for
    knowledgeable readers are listed above.

Internet:
http://company.varta.com/de/content/konzern/chronik.php
http://de.wikipedia.org/wiki/Bleiakku
http://tiger1.info/EN/AirPrecleaners.html

Reports by Individual Tiger Units

Unit	Date	Period/Topic
500	28.05.1943	
501	16.12.1942	
501	27.01.1943	18.-22.01.43
501	03.02.1943	31.01.-01.02.43
501	18.03.1943	
501	03.05.1943	Technical report
s.Pz.Komp. 502	14.04.1943	Mobility in Winter
2./502	29.01.1943	
502	19.08.1944	24.-30.06.44
502	20.08.1944	04.07.-17.08.44
502		22.06.-21.08.44 (Techn. report)
503	12.04.1943	02.-22.02.43
503	15.03.1943	
503	08.07.1943	
503	10.10.1943	01.08.-21.09.43
503	25.11.1944	
504	03.10.1944	
505	08.07.1943	07./08.07.43
505	KTB	29.01.43–15.12.44
506	30.09.1943	09.-26.09.43
506		20.-29.09.43
506	04.10.1943	
506	15.01.1944	
509		19.-31.12.43
GD	03.04.1943	
GD	27.03.1943	07.-19.03.43
GD	31.08.1943	
GD	01.12.1948	02.-05.05.44

List of Regulations and Manuals

Manuals and official documents:

D124/1 Das Maschinengewehr 34, Teil 1
D214 8.8 cm KwK 36
D420/167 Anleitung für die Munition der 8.8 cm KwK 36
D632/17, Pz-Kühlwasserheizgerät 42 vom 23.11.42
D632/21, Heißluftbläser Gebr. Winkelsträter, Baumuster: HB 50 vom 15.1.43
D635/16a, Kurbelwellen-Benzin-Anlasser (Bauart Bosch) als Aufsteckgerät, Ausführung 1943 vom 20.10.43
D635/5, Kraftfahrzeuge im Winter, Anweisungen für Wartung und Bedienung, Ausgabe 1943 für den Winter 1943/44 vom 7.7.1943
D635/50 Kraftfahrzeuge in Staub, Hitze und Schlamm
D655/1a, Pz Kpfw Panther, Ausführung A und D und Abarten, Gerätbeschreibung und Bedienungsanweisung zum Fahrgestell vom 21.7.44
D655/1b, Pz Kpfw Panther, Ausführung A und D und Abarten, Bilder zur Gerätbeschreibung und Bedienungsanweisung zum Fahrgestell vom 21.7.44
D655/3, Panzerkampfwagen Panther, Werkstatthandbuch zum Maybach-Motor HL 230 P30 – HL210 P30 vom 1.5.44
D655/5, Pz Kpfw Panther, Ausführung A und D, Handbuch für den Panzerfahrer vom 1.11.43
D656/21+, Tiger E, Firmen-Gerätbeschreibung vom März 43
D 656/21 PzKpfw VI, Gerätebeschreibung und Bedienungsanweisung für das Fahrgestell
D 656/21a Panzerkampfwagen Tiger, Ausf. E, Durchsichtbilder des Wechsel- und Lenkgetriebes
D656/22, Panzerkampfwagen Tiger Ausf. E (Sd. Kfz 181) und Panzerbefehlswagen Ausf. E, Gerätbeschreibung und Bedienungsanweisung zum Turm vom 7.9.44
D656/23, Pz Kpfw Tiger Ausführung E, Handbuch für den Panzerfahrer vom 10.5.44
D656/24, Panzerkampfwagen Tiger Ausf. E, Fristenheft vom 15.1.43
D656/25 Beladeplan für Pz Kpfw Tiger Ausf. E
D656/27, Die Tigerfibel vom 1.8.43
D656/30a Pz Kpfw Tiger Ausf. E Instandsetzungsanleitung für Panzerwarte Laufwerk vom 22.3.44
D656/30 b und c, PzKpfw Tiger Ausf. E, Instandsetzungsanleitung für Panzerwarte, Motor und Triebwerk vom 1.3.44
D656/32 Merkblatt zum Durchdrehanlasser in Pz. Kpfw. Panther und Tiger
D656/43, Tiger Ausführung B, Handbuch für den Panzerfahrer vom 1.9.44
D656/44, Pz Kpfw Tiger Ausführung B, Fristenplan vom 1.6.44
D656/60 Panzerkampfwagen Tiger Ausf. E, Begleitheft
D659/1 Kurskreisel für Panzerkampfwagen
D659/2 Verladen auf der Eisenbahn
D659/2a Pz. Kpfw. Tiger und Panther, Verladen auf der Eisenbahn

D659/4 Bergen von Pz. Kpfw.
D659/5, Selbsttätige Feuerlöschanlage für Panzerkampfwagen vom 1.1.45
D659/50 Panzerkampfwagen im Winter
D659/51, Panzerfahrer im Winter vom 1.9.44
D674/180, Sonderwerkzeug für Fahrgestell des PzKpfw Tiger Ausführung E vom 7.4.43
D949/2 Der 10- Wattsender UKWc
D988/2 Der UKW-Empfänger e
D1008/1 Die Funk- und Bordsprechanlage im Pz. Kpfw. VI
D1008/5 Anleitung: Die Funk- und Bordsprechanlage im Pz. Kpfw. VI
D9023/1* Die Funk- und Bordsprechanlage im Pz. Bef. Wg. VI
D9023/5 Anleitung: Die Funk- und Bordsprechanlage im Pz. Bef. Wg. VI
H.Dv. 469 Panzerabwehr aller Truppen
H.Dv. 469/2a Pz. Erkennungsdienst Rußland
H.Dv. 469/2b Pz. Erkennungsdienst England-Amerika
H.Dv. 469/3b Pz. Panzer-Beschußtafel 8,8 cm KwK 36
Merkblatt 47a/27 Schießanleitung und Schulschießübungen für den Tiger vom 7.1.44
Merkblatt 47a/29 Ausbildung und Einsatz der schweren Panzerkompanie Tiger vom 29.5.43
Merkblatt 47a/30 Einsatz der schw. Panzer-Abteilung "Tiger" vom 20.5.43
OKH Zusammendruck der Ausbildungshinweise Nr. 10-23 vom 5.5.44

Erweiterte Instandsetzungsvorschrift zur Gerätebeschreibung und Bedienungsanweisung für Olvargetriebe OG 401216 A, o. D.
Gerätbeschreibung und Bedienungsanweisung für Olvargetriebe OG 401216 B, o. D., ca. August 1944
Gerätbeschreibung und Bedienungsanweisung, Firma Maybach, Maybach Olvargetriebe OG 401216, o. D.
H.Dv. 471 / M.Dv. Nr. 239 / L.Dv. 100, Handbuch für Kraftfahrer, Berlin 1939, Unveränderter Nachdruck 1942
H.M. 1943, Beitrag Nr.181 v. 18.2.1943
H.M. 1943, Beitrag Nr. 322 v. 3.4.1943
Heerestechnisches Verordnungsblatt 1943, Beitrag Nr. 219 vom 6.8.43
Heerestechnisches Verordnungsblatt 1943, Beitrag Nr. 432 vom 1.11.43
Heerestechnisches Verordnungsblatt 1943, Beitrag Nr. 477 vom 27.11.1943
Heerestechnisches Verordnungsblatt 1943, Beitrag Nr.362 vom 25.9.43
Heerestechnisches Verordnungsblatt 1944, Beitrag Nr. 186 vom 8.3.44
Heerestechnisches Verordnungsblatt 1944, Beitrag Nr. 189 vom 11.3.1944
Heerestechnisches Verordnungsblatt 1944, Beitrag Nr. 255 vom 31.3.44
Heerestechnisches Verordnungsblatt 1944, Beitrag Nr. 319 vom 10.5.44
Heerestechnisches Verordnungsblatt 1944, Beitrag Nr. 427 vom 7.6.44

Heerestechnisches Verordnungsblatt 1944, Beitrag Nr. 430
vom 9.6.44

Heerestechnisches Verordnungsblatt 1944, Beitrag Nr. 431
vom 28.6.44

Heerestechnisches Verordnungsblatt 1944, Beitrag Nr. 714
vom 21.9.44

Heerestechnisches Verordnungsblatt 1944, Beitrag Nr. 885
vom 27.11.44

Heerestechnisches Verordnungsblatt 1944, Beiblatt zum..,
Formänderungen Tiger E und Abarten, 22. Ausgabe
vom 29. Oktober 1944

Heerestechnisches Verordnungsblatt 1944, Beiblatt zum..,
Formänderungen Tiger II, 24. Ausgabe vom 18.11.44

Heerestechnisches Verordnungsblatt 1944, Sonderbeiblatt
zur 18. Ausgabe des... vom 22.8.1944

TL 6032, Vorläufige Technische Lieferbedingungen für
Motorenöl der Wehrmacht (So) o. D.

TL 6033, Vorläufige Technische Lieferbedingungen für
Motorenöl der Wehrmacht (Wi), Datum unleserlich

TL 6034, Vorläufige Technische Lieferbedingungen für
Getriebeöl 8E, o. D.

TL 6352, Vorläufige Technische Lieferbedingungen für
bunte Tarnpaste, Ausgabe vom (unleserlich, 15.9.44?)

TL 6355, Vorläufige Technische Lieferbedingungen für
weiße Tarnpaste, 1. April 1944

Leaflets

Paderborn:

1 Allgemeine Angaben über den Pz. Kpfw. Tiger
2 Das Turmzielfernohr (T.Z.F.9c)
3 Munitionsunterbringung im Pz. Kpfw. VI
5 Verwendung und Anbringung des Einheitsgerätes (Fuchs)
6 Tätigkeit zum Inbetriebsetzen des Schwungkraftanlassers
7 Höhenrichtaufsatz
8 Die Bordsprechanlage (mit Skizze)
9 Das Boehringer-Sturm-Ölgetriebe
10 Bedienungsanweisung und Störungen des
Turmschwenk-werkes
11 Beschreibung der Trennwand des Pz. Kpfw. VI (mit Skizze)
12 Die selbsttätige Löschanlage
13 Schaltgetriebe und Auspuffkrümmerkühlung
14 Abschleppen bei Motor-Getriebe-Laufrollenschaden
15 Gliederung einer schweren Panzer Kompanie
16 Erfahrungen im Wintereinsatz im Osten (Ofw. Beyer)
17 Zusammenwirken der Pz. Kpfwg.-Besatzung
18 Waffentechnische Hinweise für die Besatzung
19 Aufbau der zerlegbaren Verladebrücke
20 Das Schießen von Pz. Kpfw. Tiger mit 8.8 cm KwK.
21 Visierbereich der Pz. Kpfw. Kanone für 2 m Zlelhöhe
24 Panzerschießlehre (Unterlagen Putlos)
25 Das Maybach-Olvar-Getriebe und deren Betätigung bei
Notschaltung
26 Die elektrische Abfeuerung
28 Kurze Beschreibung des E. M. o. 9. m.R.
Merkblatt über die Ausbildung am Pz Kpfw. Tiger,
Ausbildung und Einsatz der schweren Panzer-Kompanie

Putlos:

57 Zusammenwirken der Kpfw. Besatzung
58 Panzer-Schießausbildung am Sandkasten
65 Das Schießen mit der 8.8cm KwK
321 – 75 Gerätebeschreibung zur 8.8 cm KwK36
322 Waffentechnische Hinweise
323 Praktische Hinweise
324 Schulschießübungen mit KwK 8.8 cm 36
374 Pz. Schießausbildung Teil A

Training wall charts

UT für *Pz.Kpfw.* Tiger Fahrgestell
UT [Nr]. 656/1 Laufwerk
UT [Nr]. 656/2 – (Motor)
UT [Nr]. 656/3 Wechselgetriebe
UT [Nr]. 656/4 Steuerung
UT [Nr]. 656/5 Lenkgetriebe
UT [Nr]. 656/6 Leitrad mit Kettenspanner
UT [Nr]. 656/7 Krafstofförderung
UT [Nr]. 656/8 Kühlanlage
UT [Nr]. 656/9 Turmschwenkwerk
UT [Nr]. 656/10 Höhenrichtmaschine, Geschütz- und
MG- Lagerung
UT [Nr]. 656/11 Turmschwenkwerk und Panzer-
Führerkuppel 8.8 cm KwK
UT [Nr]. 656/12 Geschützrohr im Schnitt
UT [Nr]. 656/13 Luftvorholer
UT [Nr]. 656/14 Wirkungsweise des Luftvorholers
UT [Nr]. 656/15 Rohrbremse (Wirkungsweise der
Rohrbremse).
UT [Nr]. 656/16 Sicherheitsschalter zur Rohrbremse
UT [Nr]. 656/17a Verschluß, Teile der
Bewegungseinrichtung
UT [Nr]. 656/17b Verschluß, Verschlußkeil
UT [Nr]. 656/18 Gesamtplan der elektrischen Abfeuerung
UT [Nr]. 636/1 Die 8.8 cm KwK 36 Geschütz
UT [Nr]. 636/2 Luftvorholer
UT [Nr]. 636/3 Wirkungsweise des Luftvorholers
UT [Nr]. 636/4 Rohrbremse (Wirkungsweise)
UT [Nr]. 636/5 Hydraulischer Sicherheitsschalter zur
Rohrbremse

Remarks of the *Generalinspekteur der Panzertruppen* (Inspector of Armoured Troops)

vom 27.04.43
vom 08.07.43
September 1944 (Nachrichtenblatt)

Panzeroffizier im Generalstab des Heeres vom 11.04.43 und
vom 12.09.43

OKH Wa Prüf 6 (IIIf) v. 23.10.41 (Lieferbedingungen Fa.
Henschel für *Pz.Kpfw.* VI, Ausf. H 1)